LIFE HAS BECOME MORE JOYOUS, COMRADES

Dear Sandy,

Thank you for being a lovely colleague + friend and for many fun meetings on the way to and from AAASS

Love,

Karen Petrone

Indiana-Michigan Series in Russian and East European Studies
Alexander Rabinowitch and William G. Rosenberg, general editors

Life Has Become More Joyous, Comrades

Celebrations in the Time of Stalin

KAREN PETRONE

INDIANA UNIVERSITY PRESS
Bloomington & Indianapolis

This book is a publication of

Indiana University Press
601 North Morton Street
Bloomington, IN 47404-3797 USA

http://www.indiana.edu/~iupress

Telephone orders   800-842-6796
Fax orders   812-855-7931
Orders by e-mail   iuporder@indiana.edu

The paper used in this publication meets the minimum requirements of American National Standard for Information Sciences—Permanence of Paper for Printed Library Materials, ANSI Z39.48-1984.

Manufactured in the United States of America

Library of Congress Cataloging-in-Publication Data

Petrone, Karen.
Life has become more joyous, comrades : celebrations in the time of Stalin / Karen Petrone.
    p.   cm. — (Indiana-Michigan series in Russian and East European studies)
Includes bibliographical references and index.
    ISBN 0-253-33768-2 (cloth : alk. paper) — ISBN 0-253-21401-7 (pbk. : alk. paper)
1. Holidays—Soviet Union—History. 2. Festivals—Social life and customs—1917–1970.
I. Title.   II. Series.

GT4856.A2 P48 2000
394.26947—dc21

                                                    00-023201
1   2   3   4   5   05   04   03   02   01   00

To the memory of my mother, my father, and Aunt Rosie

CONTENTS

ACKNOWLEDGMENTS

The early stages of this work were funded by the History Department, the Center for Russian and East European Studies, the Rackham Graduate School, the Institute for the Humanities, and the Regents of the University of Michigan. Awards from the International Research and Exchanges Board and the Fulbright-Hays Foundation enabled me to conduct archival research in Russia. The Social Science Research Council supported the writing of the dissertation. The University of Kentucky provided two Summer Research Fellowships that enabled me to return to Russia to conduct additional research and to complete manuscript revisions. A summer stipend from the National Endowment for the Humanities also contributed to the timely completion of this book. This work would not have been possible without the generous support of these many institutions.

At the University of Michigan, I was very fortunate to have the support of two wonderful mentors, Jane Burbank and William Rosenberg. I thank them for their expertise, their concern, and their unwavering support over the past twelve years. I am also indebted to Ron Suny, Valerie Kivelson, Kathleen Canning, and Herbert Eagle for their advice and encouragement. I owe a huge debt of gratitude to my mentor at the University of Kentucky, Daniel Rowland, who has cheerfully and unfailingly guided me through the complexities of balancing teaching, research, and life in general.

Many, many, colleagues have read and commented on drafts of the manuscript or helped with research suggestions. The most steadfast of these include Daniel Rowland, Kenneth Slepyan, Choi Chatterjee, Robert Edelman, Lynn Mally, Kathleen E. Smith, and Richard Stites. I am also grateful to Tom Ewing, Deborah Field, my undergraduate thesis advisor Cathy Frierson, Sheila Fitzpatrick, John McCannon, Jon Mogul, Jeremy Popkin, Dan Ringrose, Cynthia Ruder, Jeanmarie Rouhier-Willoughby, Stephanie Sandler, Tom Schrand, Gretchen Starr-Le Beau, Irina Tarakanova, Jim von Geldern, Barbara Walker, Neia Zorkaia, the many Moscow archivists who assisted me in finding pertinent materials, the participants of the University of Kentucky Social Theory Program Working Papers Series in Fall 1996, the participants of the "Inventing the Soviet Union" Conference at Indiana University in November 1997, and the participants of the "Stalin Period" Conference at the University of California, Riverside, in March of 1998. Thanks as well to Lynn Hiler, the anonymous reviewers at Indiana University Press and *Slavic Review*, and my editors at Indiana University Press, especially Janet Rabinowitch.

I would like to thank the many colleagues who conducted archival research in Moscow in 1991–1992 and 1995 for their expertise, their good humor, and especially for Thanksgiving dinner in 1991. I warmly thank all of my friends and colleagues in the History Department at the University of Kentucky for making Lexington such a nice place to live and work. There are many other dear friends who have helped me in big and small ways over the years, and I would especially like to mention Emilie Greco, Doug and Evelyn Mao, and Dana Rabin. I am grateful to *all* of the members of my extended family (last time I got into trouble for leaving a few cousins out!) for their love and support, and especially to my sister Diana Hartman, my aunt Carmen Maggiore, and my mother-in-law, Mary Efron.

This book has two sisters. As I was in the process of giving birth to this book, I also gave birth to two daughters whose patient and cheerful personalities greatly assisted in the completion of this manuscript—special thanks to Mara and Anya. And, last but not least, to my fellow juggler, the man who helped me keep all the balls in the air, Kenneth Slepyan. Without Ken's deep and abiding commitment to two equal careers and to equal division of parental responsibilities, this work would have been impossible. I thank him with all my heart for being such a terrific colleague, husband, and friend.

LIFE HAS BECOME MORE JOYOUS, COMRADES

1

INTERPRETING SOVIET CELEBRATIONS

In January 1937, as the Soviet government staged the second Moscow show trial uncovering the supposed treason of "the Anti-Soviet Trotskyite Center," Soviet cadres had just finished celebrating the ratification of the new Stalin Constitution and organizing *elki* (New Year's trees) for children. Soviet libraries, clubs, and theaters were about to commemorate the hundredth anniversary of the death of the greatest Russian poet of the nineteenth century, Aleksandr Sergeevich Pushkin. These celebrations were part of the "new outbreak of festivity" that followed the population's sacrifices during the First Five Year Plan, the campaign of terror against the peasantry during the collectivization of agriculture, and the devastating famine that ensued.[1] Celebrations occurred as the purges and political repression of the Soviet elite intensified and most of the Soviet population struggled with poverty and deprivation. A public discourse of celebration expanded to reach more and more Soviet citizens just as the scope of permissible public speech was severely curtailed. One frequent explanation for these paradoxes is that the Soviet state used celebrations to divert attention from the excesses of the regime.[2] To dismiss Soviet celebration discourse as a mere diversion, however, is to lose a valuable opportunity to understand how the Soviet system operated in the 1930s. Whether or not it represented objective truth, celebration discourse shaped social realities even as it was shaped by them. This work is both an analysis of celebration discourse and a social history of celebration, focusing on the interrelationship between Soviet language and social structures and practices in Stalin's Soviet Union.

Speaking Soviet[3]

Before discussing the ideas articulated in the language of Soviet celebrations, it is necessary to understand the role of official language in Soviet society. Because of extremely strict censorship, and because those who spoke publicly against Soviet power could be arrested, exiled, or killed, analysts have tended to view Soviet official language as totalizing. For many years the prevailing view both in the Soviet Union and among European and American scholars was that the Soviet population either fell under a kind of "mass hypnosis," blindly accepting the official version of a happy life in the Soviet Union, or, under conditions of extreme coercion, pretended or forced themselves to believe out of fear.[4]

Other analysts of Soviet ideology have emphasized the importance of the creation of a new Soviet political language in propagating Soviet power throughout the Soviet Union. Through this new political discourse, Soviet officials shaped their own worldviews and formulated the identities that they wanted to project onto others. Peter Kenez has argued in his study of Soviet mass mobilization in the 1920s, *The Birth of the Propaganda State*, that through a "catechism-like method," Party schools "transmitted a way of thinking, which assumed that there was one and only one correct answer to any question."[5] The propagandists trained in these Party schools preached their newfound learning to peasants, who treated the incomprehensible words as "magical incantations, powerful, unchallengeable."[6] Kenez's work points to ways in which adopting the identity of an agent of the state gave individuals power over those who did not do so. Fluency in the new political language set some in the village or the factory apart from and above the others.

Kenez believes that by promulgating its "catechism" throughout the 1920s, the Soviet "propaganda state" increasingly "succeeded in preventing the formulation and articulation of alternative points of view." The Soviet people began to take the Soviet worldview for granted and "the distinction between belief and non-belief and truth and untruth [was] washed away."[7] Kenez argues, to put it another way, that a new Soviet discourse, backed up by physical coercion, allowed Soviet citizens only one public identity: that of loyal believers in the Soviet system. Jochen Hellbeck pushes this argument even further. His analysis of the diary of Stepan Podlubnyi, the son of a *kulak*[8] who endeavored to purify himself of his alien class origins, suggests that Soviet discourses prevented citizens from articulating individual identities "independently of the program promulgated by the Bolshevik State."[9]

Most analysts who see Soviet propaganda as a totalizing force that created a compliant population tend to minimize the contradictions within official discourse. Discourse analysis, on the other hand, points to the fractured nature of all discourses and the multiple meanings and inevitable contradictions within them. While Soviet ideologues created powerful categories with which to describe the world and did their best to forbid the expression of alternative discourses, I argue that they could not control the way that the official discourses they created were used by others or entirely eliminate alternative worldviews. By focusing on the discourse of celebrations as one of a limited number of ways that citizens could articulate ideas in public, this work analyzes the categories and concepts that Soviet and Party leaders used to promote legitimacy and authority and the ways that these ideas could also be employed to express alternative, unofficial, and subversive viewpoints.

During celebrations Soviet cadres presented the fundamental tenets of Soviet state ideology in an extremely concentrated form.[10] For example, during the Pushkin Centennial one Pushkin scholar proclaimed: "Pushkin is in harmony with us because of his faith in the victory of progress, his realism . . . and his striving for the creation of a genuine popular art. This is why Pushkin's celebration has become a mighty holiday of the whole Soviet country."[11] This brief quotation introduces several of the central themes of Soviet public discourse in the 1930s: the ideas that the special enthusiasm of the Soviet people made it their destiny to lead the way to communism, that the great cultural achievements of the old Russian elite now belonged to the entire Soviet people, that Soviet art should be realistic and "genuinely popular," and that Russian culture bound all of the Soviet nationalities together as one mighty country. Celebration discourse, then, provides an excellent field on which to examine official representations that reveal the aims and ideals of the Soviet government.

The ideas that appeared in Soviet celebration discourse, however, were sometimes much less straightforward. One biographical article about Pushkin, published in the journal *Krasnyi arkhiv*, for example, dwelt on the way that the tyrannical government of Nicholas I destroyed Pushkin's personal freedom:

> They made [Pushkin] present his works to the regular censor. He could not leave the city without the permission of the chief of gendarmes. The vigilant glance of the secret police followed him at his every step and penetrated his correspondence. His striving to see the cultured world, the progressive countries, remained an unfulfilled dream. Tsarist turnpikes did not let Pushkin out of the country.[12]

While this passage explicitly refers to the 1830s, it raises issues of censorship, the power of the secret police, lack of privacy, and a ban on travel that had a great deal of resonance in the terror-stricken society of the 1930s. It allows for multiple and contradictory interpretations since it can be read either as a statement of fact about Pushkin's time or as an indictment of Stalinist repression. This passage shows how the dissenting voices of those living under Stalinism can be detected through a close reading of official discourse. The ambiguities and inconsistencies in celebration discourse permit an examination of conflicts and struggles for power within Soviet society.

Cadres, Citizens, and Identities

Hellbeck argues that because of the way in which "Soviet state power instilled an individual with subjecthood"[13] there were few, if any, opportunities to articulate non-Soviet identities. Recent social histories of the 1930s, however, have revealed more complicated responses to Soviet linguistic and physical coercion. New scholarship shows how Soviet workers and peasants put up a great deal of opposition to Soviet attempts to construct them as loyal Soviet citizens. Using recently accessible archival sources, Sheila Fitzpatrick's work on peasants on collective farms, David Hoffmann's analysis of peasant migration to Moscow, Stephen Kotkin's case study of workers in Magnitogorsk, and Sarah Davies's discussion of popular opinion[14] have documented the resistance of peasants and workers to Soviet demands for discipline and the imposition of official Soviet culture. These works have called into question the view of an all-powerful state and a completely intimidated and repressed population. Fitzpatrick, Hoffmann, Kotkin, and Davies have shown that the public identity of "loyal Soviet citizen" was not a fixed category. It was a fluid and rather elastic identity that could be used by workers and peasants to forward their own interests as well as by the state to force compliance with its policies. These authors argue that Soviet people accepted and identified with some of the key ideological claims of the Soviet "welfare state," and learned how to "speak Bolshevik" when it was beneficial to them but also preserved elements of their pre-revolutionary worldviews. Thus hybrid identities were created during celebrations.

In addition to exploring the multifaceted linguistic character of celebrations, this study also analyzes the discourse of celebration to detect the ways in which competing Soviet agencies, institutions, and officials used celebrations to express conflicting opinions, even if they rarely admitted that they were engaging in debate. Recent studies of Stalinism have uncovered a great deal of conflict between authorities in Moscow and lower-level local officials.[15] Those propagating the discourse of celebration in the center and at the regional and local levels did not always speak with one voice. Bureaucratic practice in the Soviet Union also created barriers that the central government's discourse could not penetrate. The government's aims were not always understood, passed along through proper channels, or effectively communicated to the population by local officials. The corruption and ineptitude of Party and government officials produced mistakes, accidents, and moments when official discourse and bureaucratic practice unintentionally revealed the brutal and repressive nature of the Soviet government. While celebrations were supposed to prove that the Soviet Union was a unified and efficiently governed country, they sometimes revealed chaos, inefficiency, and disorder.

The public face of the Soviet Union was profoundly changing in the 1930s and celebrations introduced new Soviet policies to the public. Stalin and the top Soviet elite abandoned the internationalism of the 1920s and instead promoted a patriotic Soviet rhetoric. After the rise of Hitler in 1933, the Soviet Union pursued a Popular Front policy, allying itself with the socialist parties of Europe. Official policies about education, the military, the family, the church, and production all underwent an evolution in the 1930s. Authority was restored to teachers in the schools and officers in the army. Marriage and the family became sacred institutions. The 1936 constitution restored the voting rights of priests. Egalitarian wage scales were replaced by piece rates and the creation of exemplary workers.[16] The vast changes in Soviet public discourses created confusion in places where a new discourse and resulting practices had appeared before old ones had entirely disappeared. Soviet society of the 1930s has been called the "quicksand society" by Moshe Lewin in part because of the great upheavals and migrations of population.[17] In the same way, Soviet public discourses in general, and celebration discourse in particular, can be termed "quicksand discourses" with old and new ideas constantly sinking and reappearing. The unstable definitions of normative Soviet behavior created linguistic and behavioral spaces in which oppositional ideas could form.

In her work on Soviet literature of the post-war era, Vera Dunham described the "big deal" between the Soviet state and the mid-level bureaucrats who were granted privileges in exchange for loyal service. As Sheila Fitzpatrick has shown, this process of elite formation began in the 1930s.[18] The identities that Soviet celebrations created in the 1930s were therefore not simply "Soviet." Celebrations provided opportunities for Soviet citizens to identify their social locations in the newly forming hierarchies and assert their social status in relation to those around them. This book focuses on how they created and sustained social hierarchies, both by enabling citizens to envision their status and by allocating material resources to elite Soviet citizens.[19] During celebrations multiple Soviet identities were formed as individual citizens competed to gain particular types of social status. The form and content of celebration varied significantly depending on the status of their audiences; by looking at these variations we can gain insight into the making of a new Stalinist elite. The tendency toward hierarchy in Soviet life also shaped the social relations depicted in celebrations because festivals modeled ideal hierarchical relations between leaders, heroes, and citizens.

The quality of Soviet cadres profoundly affected the state's ability to convey its ideology and determined the extent to which celebrations became sites for undermining that ideology. In the 1930s the Party's presence in the countryside was weak, and though urban areas tended to be more closely supervised by the Party, its presence did not necessarily guarantee effective control of specific factories, schools, or housing developments. The purges of the Party that took place throughout the 1930s made a difficult situation all the worse. Party cadres and non-Party cultural workers were constantly on the move, either being purged or changing jobs. Under such conditions, the organization of celebration sometimes suffered from chaos and neglect. On the other hand, local bureaucrats did not usually pass up the opportunity to use moneys earmarked for holiday merry-making. Holidays were significant times during which organizational manpower and other resources were expended. Because of the inefficiency of the governing system and the concentration of scarce resources in the organization of celebration, holiday time was distinct from everyday time. During holidays, cadres and citizens interacted under special social, political, and economic circumstances.

When Stalin told Stakhanovites in November 1935 that "life has become better, comrades; life has become more joyous, and when you are living joyously, work turns out well," he promised these special workers a better standard of living in exchange for their hard work.[20] He also officially endorsed the idea that participating in festivities was appropriate behavior for model Soviet citizens. The asceticism of the 1920s and the political radicalism of the First Five Year Plan that had allowed few opportunities for pleasure were replaced by officially sanctioned entertainment and gaiety. Soviet citizens were now not only supposed to understand the superiority of Soviet life with their minds, they were also supposed to feel it with their emotions. Katerina Clark has argued that the plots of socialist realist novels revolve around a spontaneous hero who gains Bolshevik consciousness and is synthesized into the New Soviet Man.[21] In the celebration culture of the mid-1930s, cadres invited Soviet citizens to be spontaneous so that they would form emotional attachments to the Soviet state and thereby gain consciousness. Celebrations show how Soviet officials tried to create legitimacy through emotional appeals and mobilize citizens through apolitical gaiety.

While cadres influenced the ways in which the discourse of celebration operated, the discourse of celebrations also shaped the work of cadres. One of the most important aspects of socialist realism in the 1930s was its projection of the future onto the present as it celebrated the yet-to-be-achieved successes of the Soviet state. By the mid-1930s, Soviet discourse increasingly proclaimed that victory had been won and the glorious future had already arrived.[22] As a result, it became more and more difficult for cadres to address the problems they faced in the present using official language. The discourse of Soviet celebration thus constrained the actions of cadres who were charged with communicating the advantages of Soviet life. Focusing on the interactions of cadres and citizens reveals the extent to which celebrations were able to achieve the goals set by the top Party and government leaders in Moscow.

In conditions of upheaval and chaos, Soviet celebrations in the 1930s played a significant role in the dissemination of political ideas. Because of time pressures and the scarcity of "politically literate" cadres, political education campaigns focused primarily on Party members.[23] The goal of raising the political level of the rest of the population was neglected in the 1930s. The main vehicles for teaching the population what it meant to be "Soviet" in the 1930s were the political activities surrounding celebrations.

The 1937 diary of collective farmer Ignat Danilovich Frolov illustrates the power of Soviet holidays. Still using the pre-revolutionary Orthodox calendar, Frolov made daily observations about the weather and farming that demonstrate that he was hardly influenced by official discourses. The farmer documented the penetration of Soviet administration into his life with observations that "they" exchanged passports or checked on the collective farm's "war readiness," but there is only one reference to his own participation in Soviet life outside of production. The farmer wrote on the anniversary of the October Revolution, October 25, 1937: "Today I was at the demonstration in Kolomna and we celebrated at Sanya's and Gegorushka's."[24] The commemoration of the October Revolution holiday was the only time in the entire year that the collective farmer took part in the ideological and cultural world of the Soviet state.

The work of Party cadres at the local level was also often organized around holiday celebrations. While the model propagandist was supposed to work year-round to educate the population in the language of the Soviet state, weaker cadres, if they mobilized their constituencies at all, did so in bursts around holidays. In 1936, a Party inspector complained about the work of the club of the Tractor Formation collective farm in Stalingrad Territory:

> The work of the club is limited to the organization of songs and dances for youth and putting on plays during revolutionary holidays. For example on March 8, 1936 [International Women's Day] . . . the youth gathered at 10:00, sang revolutionary songs, danced to a harmonica and string orchestra, . . then scattered and returned home. What should the club do on the 9th of March? Neither the collective farmers nor the director of the club had anything to say about that.[25]

The failure of political education in the 1930s thus made public celebrations a crucial tool in articulating Soviet power since they might be the only time that any kind of Soviet ideological message reached a substantial part of the population.

Discourse and Power

Although the word "discourse" is generally used to describe utterances appearing in speech or in print, my definition of celebration discourse is much broader. By celebration discourse I mean all communications about celebration that appear not only in voice or print but also in visual images and musical compositions. This study of celebrations includes both the discursive and social practices involved in the communication of messages of celebration. The bureaucratic and cultural practices associated with the organization of celebrations profoundly affected the ways that the discourse of celebration was transmitted and received. The celebratory practices of the population also played a role in determining the success or failure of an official holiday message and in shaping possible responses to Soviet ideology.

The notion that a study of a particular discourse can reveal the operation of power in a society is, of course, inspired by the work of Michel Foucault.[26] Foucault's attention to the construction of categories through which some ideas are included in a discourse while others are excluded is fundamental to this project. My approach is different from Foucault's however, in that pinpointing the actions of specific human agents is as important to this project as the examination of the more general practices associated with the transmission and reception of ideology. While I do believe that the subjectivities and identities of the human agents I examine are created through discourses, I see individual actors shaping discourse even as it shapes them.[27] Celebration discourses and practices offer opportunities for individuals to question or support the dictates of the state. I focus on the diffuse celebration practices through which citizens and agents of the state exercised power over others, but, unlike Foucault, who minimized the significance of the state in the Western societies he studied, I view the Soviet state as a crucial center of power.[28] Soviet citizens employed the state's mandates for their own ends and also fought to regain control over their lives by resisting and reshaping the state's aspirations to total control of the population. This project uses celebration discourse and practices to analyze the ways that power was exercised in the Soviet Union in the 1930s.

Attention to alternative ideas voiced in the language of the dominant discourse reveals what James Scott calls the "hidden transcript"—the covert response of subordinates to domination.[29] One method of revealing the "hidden transcript," as we have seen above, is to read for Aesopian language and multiple meanings. Scott also argues that any dominant public discourse of legitimacy enumerates a number of promises to those who are dominated. These promises are often broken, but the population still can use the ideas represented in the dominant discourse to demand better treatment.[30] As Frederick Cooper and Ann Stoler have argued in their discussion of colonial discourses, there was not just "an official hermetic discourse of the colonizer" and a "set of hidden scripts among the colonized"; the process of creating and transmitting official accounts was much more complicated.[31] By identifying those places in celebration discourse where alternative ideas are in dialogue with official pronouncements, it is possible to examine contests for power and authority in Stalin's Russia.

The social histories of Fitzpatrick, Hoffmann, Kotkin, and Davies show that response to Soviet ideology was manifested by actions or practices as well as by language. While professing loyalty in the language of the dominant discourse, Soviet workers and peasants used such tactics as absenteeism, labor slowdowns, and theft of state property to assert control over their lives and their right to shape their own identities.[32] Holiday practices also reveal contests over the meaning of the New Soviet Man. While the actions of celebration participants were hardly aimed at overthrowing the Soviet government, the Soviet leaders' own discourse about enemies defined even the most trivial mistakes or non-conformist holiday behaviors and language as overt challenges to Soviet power.

Another method of reading the alternative meanings of Soviet celebrations is to document what happened when celebrations went awry. While official reports of failed celebrations are written within the dominant discourse, they reveal the official versions of the battles fought over the definition of celebrations and over control of the social practices that made up celebrations. A "failed" celebration (from the point of view of officials) could become carnivalesque in the way that theorist Mikhail Bakhtin defined this concept. In Bakhtin's analysis of early modern culture, carnival laughter is a highly subversive element of folk culture that liberates people from the prevailing official truth. In carnival, authorities are "uncrowned" and mocked, power relations are reversed, the world is inside out and upside down. Bakhtin argued that during carnival "thought and speech had to be placed under such conditions that the world could expose its other side. The side that was hidden and that nobody talked about, that did not fit the words and forms of the prevailing discourse."[33]

Although it was published much later, Bakhtin's very influential definition of carnival was written in the Soviet Union in the late 1930s and can itself be read as resistance to the Stalinist order. Bakhtin rejected official Soviet celebrations as the "official truth" and looked to popular culture for opportunities to overthrow the official discourse, at least temporarily. The discourse was overthrown by revealing the truth about Soviet life, but also by carnivalesque practices which challenged the imposition of Soviet cultural and behavioral norms. When an official harvest festival turned into a drunken, violent melee, for example, "folk" elements were at work in asserting freedom through a traditional form of holiday behavior.[34] This "celebration" revealed the ugly truth, suppressed by the official discourse, that although the Soviet state maintained repressive control over agricultural production (and perhaps *because* it maintained this control), it could not always effectively achieve "cultured" Soviet behavior in the countryside or transform traditional rural practices. Carnivalesque reversals and the sudden exposure of the hidden truth occurred not only through conscious resistance. Because of untrained cadres and an appalling lack of concern for the population's safety, celebratory events were as accident-prone as other aspects of Soviet life. Unsafe practices on the part of Soviet cadres caused accidents that reversed the meanings of celebration from joy to terror.

Key Categories in the Discourse of Celebrations

This analysis focuses on the creation of categories in the discourse of celebrations through inclusion and exclusion. Several recurring categories or themes form the core of the analysis: gender, nationality, history, culture, and heroes.[35] The tensions inherent in these categories reveal the possible openings for alternative voices in the language of celebrations.

Gender

The gendering of images or symbols created a variety of meanings in Soviet celebration discourse. For example, a word that was often used in celebrations to describe the Soviet Union as a country was *rodina*, motherland. The image of the female Soviet land giving birth to the citizen-sons who must protect her is one of the crucial concepts of Soviet identity expressed in Soviet celebrations in the 1930s. The discourse of celebrations thus used gender to define a system of relationships between citizens and country.

Celebrations also had implications for actual social relations between Soviet men and women and the definitions of male and female gender roles. In the mid-1930s many of the liberal policies on women and the family that had been established by the Soviet state in the 1920s were reversed. In 1936 abortion was made illegal and divorces became more expensive and difficult to obtain.[36] At the same time that the state tightened its control over family policies, however, it also encouraged women to join the labor force and to take on an ever-more responsible role in socialist construction. While the state defended and promoted enforced motherhood, it also proclaimed complete equality between the sexes. An examination of the celebration culture of this period provides insight into how the state promoted these contradictory gender policies and the opportunities that these conflicting policies offered to real women and men.

Nationality

One of the most significant aspects of the celebration culture of the 1930s was its reflection of Soviet attempts to create a unified country out of ethnically diverse and geographically dispersed territories. The policy of *korenizatsiia*, or the "rooting" of nationalities, which prevailed in the 1920s and early 1930s allowed for the economic and cultural development of individual nations, emphasizing the promotion of local industry, the creation of a native educational system, the codification of native languages, and the publication of literature in these languages.[37] In the mid-1930s, however, official nationality policy increasingly emphasized a Soviet "patriotism" based on a Russian imperial model.[38] While the Soviet government did not try to create a Soviet "nation" based on the assimilation of nationalities and the destruction of ethnic particularities, it did attempt to create a Soviet identity, a patriotic and holy allegiance to the Soviet motherland.[39] Belonging to the motherland required the ultimate loyalty: in the inevitable future war the entire Soviet *narod* (folk) had to be willing to fight and die for their country. Throughout the 1930s the attempts to create a particularly Soviet identity remained in tension with efforts to promote the development of the individual nationalities that made up the Soviet Union.

The definition of "Soviet" included an important geographic component as well as an ethnic or patriotic component. During celebrations Soviet authorities made great efforts to use not only print media but also documentary films, museum exhibitions, radio broadcasts, and popular songs to incorporate citizens from all walks of life and all geographic areas into the imagined Soviet land.[40] The connection between the celebration of Soviet achievements and the definition of the boundaries of a Soviet country was most apparent in the actions of the director of the Arctic Museum in December of 1939. He arranged for a portable exhibition celebrating the heroes of the Arctic to be sent to Western Ukraine and Western Belorussia, two areas that the Soviet Union had just annexed, under the terms of the Molotov-Ribbentrop Pact. The museum director argued that since "the visitors' book of the exhibition was full of enthusiastic testimonials," it would be "expedient" to send such an exhibition to the newly Soviet areas.[41] Soviet officials envisioned a direct connection between the spread of celebration discourse and the task of incorporating new citizens into the Soviet land.

History

In addition to the construction of a Soviet identity based on ethnicity or geography, celebrations articulated a temporal definition of what it meant to be Soviet. Celebrations provided a glimpse of future prosperity in the present and contrasted this glorious future with the evils of the Russian imperial past. In contrast to the 1920s, however, not all of the Russian past was rejected. Many pre-revolutionary Russian heroes, such as Pushkin, and even tsars Ivan the Terrible and Peter the Great became Soviet heroes and thus part of the "invented tradition" of the Soviet state.[42] This approach to the past created opportunities for ambiguity since the life of each historic figure had to be recast in the Soviet mold. The celebration of the pre-revolutionary past complicated the definition of "Soviet" by identifying the Russian imperial tradition as the inheritance of all of the Soviet nationalities.

One of the other remnants of the pre-revolutionary past that celebrations had to confront was religious tradition and practice. The discourses and practices of Orthodox Christianity, Islam, and other religions continued to exist alongside official Soviet discourses and practices. As a result, Soviet officials sought to discredit religion and replace religious holidays with Soviet holidays. The reintroduction of the New Year's tree in 1935 is an example of the co-optation of practices associated with a religious holiday by Soviet officials. Soviet officials also borrowed the forms of religious discourse, although there was no public acknowledgment that they were doing so. Soviet parades resembled religious processions; the portraits of the leaders were treated as icons; and the incorruptible body of the saint, Lenin, became the sacred center of the Soviet state. In Soviet celebrations there was always a tension between the rejection of the content of pre-revolutionary religious rituals and the adoption of their forms.

Culture

Soviet celebrations were created primarily under the auspices of cultural institutions such as schools, theaters, libraries, factory and collective farm clubs, and rural reading rooms. Soviet cultural workers of all types were responsible for the production of celebration discourse. As a result, it is not surprising that culture was a key concept in celebration discourse that was meant to attract not only Soviet cadres but the pre-revolutionary cultural elite. By celebrating a revered pre-revolutionary Russian figure such as Pushkin as a Soviet cultural hero, for example, Soviet officials encouraged apolitical or even hostile members of the intelligentsia to participate in bringing "culture" to the masses.

One of the stated goals of the Soviet state was raising the cultural level of its citizens and transforming them into New Soviet Men. Not only should the New Soviet Man be profoundly loyal to the project of socialism and a dedicated worker in Soviet production, but he should also have culture in two different senses. He was expected to be well-versed in the artistic culture of the pre-revolutionary elite—to recite the poetry of Pushkin and become a lover of opera—but on a more basic level, the New Soviet Man had to know how to behave in polite society. This second definition opposed "culture" with "nature" and meant that Soviet citizens were not supposed to spit on the floor, drink to excess, swear, wear dirty clothes, or live in dirty surroundings.[43] A major goal of Soviet holidays was to assist in the creation of New Soviet Men, but failure in the goal of transmitting "polite" culture often undermined attempts to promote loyalty, efficiency, and "high" culture. Celebration cadres themselves were often "uncultured" and the results of celebration were sometimes drunkenness and disorder or "tasteless" entertainment rather than socialist uplift. The idea of bringing both of these kinds of culture to the uncultured revealed the implicit power relations within Soviet cultural "missionary" efforts. Definitions of Soviet culture disdained many aspects of both Russian and non-Russian traditional, popular, and folk cultures. Singing in a church choir or living in a *iaranga*, a tent used by the native peoples of the Far North, were excluded from the category of "culture" in Soviet discourse and identified by Soviet cadres as practices that should be eliminated. Ironically, even though Soviet cadres disdained folk culture, they freely borrowed its form and drew extensively on the popular and patriotic culture of early twentieth-century Russia.[44] These contested definitions of culture reveal the complicated relationships between local cadres and the people they were expected to convert into "cultured" citizens.

Heroes

The dichotomy of hero and traitor is a crucial opposition of the 1930s in the Soviet Union that mirrors the paradox of celebration in a time of terror. In this unstable time of terror, many who had previously been viewed as revolutionary heroes were suddenly redefined by government prosecutors as traitors or spies. It was this sudden transformation that cost hundreds of thousands of people their lives. One of the ways in which the notion of traitor was articulated in celebrations and elsewhere in Soviet discourse was through the definition of opposition to the Soviet state. By 1937 the notion of "loyal opposition" was completely excluded from Soviet discourse. Either one was a "loyal citizen" (which, as we have shown above, could be a fairly fluid category) or one was a traitor. Celebrations simultaneously vilified enemies and gave examples of appropriate ways to be loyal to the state. They also defined those who, thanks to their extraordinary deeds for the state, exceeded the bounds of "loyal citizen" to become heroes.

In their depictions of Pushkin, the Arctic heroes Shmidt and Papanin, the pilot Chkalov, and, of course, Lenin and Stalin, Soviet ideologues created images of heroism that defined notions of legitimate authority and were supposed to be respected and imitated by the population. The larger-than-life status of these real men, however, created contradictions and tensions between their actual deeds and their mythic accomplishments, and created goals that were impossible for ordinary men to meet. The creation of a pantheon of Soviet gods valorized hierarchy in what was supposed to be an egalitarian society. The relationship of heroes to Stalin also produced tensions. On the one hand, celebratory representations linked Stalin to the heroes, suggesting that all of their glory stemmed from him. On the other hand, the popularity of heroes (and particularly that of Lenin) was a threat to Stalin's symbolic identity as the caring, concerned, all-powerful, all-knowing leader, father, and friend.

Celebrations and Social Practice

From the first days of the revolution, the Soviet leadership recognized the importance of celebration culture. The Party created a cycle of yearly holidays that both embraced pre-revolutionary socialist holidays (such as May Day and International Women's Day) and commemorated important dates in Soviet history (such as the October Revolution and, later, the death of Lenin). Soviet leaders transformed the demonstrations of protest that had marked May Day in the pre-revolutionary period into joyous celebrations of Soviet victory. They also organized elaborate mass festivals in honor of revolutionary anniversaries. On the third anniversary of the October Revolution, for example, thousands of Red Army soldiers participated in a dramatization of the storming of the Winter Palace; 100,000 people viewed the spectacle.[45] James von Geldern argues that the Party used mass festivals to "develop new identities that would legitimize its rule and assist its difficult transition from a revolutionary underground inspired by ideology to a ruling power."[46] Festivals of the Civil War period encompassed a wide variety of artistic styles, a large infusion of popular culture, and a great deal of theatricality and spontaneity.

During the years of the New Economic Policy, spectacles were organized from below by local amateur theater clubs, while demonstrations became more routinized.[47] Some celebrations focused on particular social issues; International Women's Day became an occasion to reflect on the special needs of women and on the removal of impediments to their political and social development. This celebration enabled activists to recruit women to the Bolshevik cause, promote their welfare, and reward their achievements.[48] Celebrations in the 1920s encouraged popular participation and were a vital part of the Bolshevik project of transformation.

Soviet holiday culture was profoundly changed by Stalin's ascent to power. Theorists of Soviet celebration culture tend to agree that by the end of the 1920s increased control from above had eliminated popular spontaneity from the demonstrations that took place on mass holidays. Describing the transformation of demonstrations, Richard Stites noted that "the stiffening elements of ritual tightened from 1928 onward. The parade in Moscow and other cities became more rigidly organized, politicized, militarized, and standardized." Christel Lane observed that mass ritual "had ceased to be the expression of any popular mood."[49] As celebrations became less spontaneous, they also increased in scope. The major Soviet holidays of May 1 and November 7 were celebrated with demonstrations on a larger scale, and physical culture demonstrations also became more prominent in the 1930s.[50]

The Soviet government also promoted many new celebrations—both one-time events and those that were to be repeated annually.[51] The upswing in celebration was most pronounced in the last months of 1935. About a month after Stalin announced in November 1935 that "life has become more joyous" the Soviet government reintroduced the New Year's tree for Soviet children and announced its intention to commemorate the hundredth anniversary of Pushkin's death in February 1937. In 1936, the celebration of the new Stalin Constitution brought forth a series of campaigns focusing on public discussions of the draft constitution and preparations for elections that lasted from June of 1936 through December of 1937. Although the first major celebration of Arctic and aviation achievements occurred in 1934, when the passengers of the *Cheliuskin* were rescued by Arctic aviators, such endeavors became particularly prominent in the summer of 1936 and especially during the summer of 1937. The focus on Arctic and aviation feats continued throughout 1938. In 1937, the celebration of the twentieth anniversary of the October Revolution was planned on a much grander scale than the usual October celebrations. Finally, several new holidays in the 1930s reflected the Soviet state's growing preoccupation with the issue of military preparedness. In addition to the holidays of Red Army Day and Border Guard Day, established in the 1920s, the Soviet state designated Air Force Day (the third Sunday in August, beginning in 1933,) All-Union Railroad Worker Day (the first Sunday in August, beginning in 1936,) Navy Day (the last Sunday in July, beginning in 1939), and All-Union Physical Culturist Day (second Saturday in August, beginning in 1939) as new Soviet holidays in the 1930s.[52]

In the first part of this book I explore holiday discourses and practices that promoted mass participation in the Soviet project through the creation of a Soviet popular culture.[53] Holiday and physical culture demonstrations, the celebration of Arctic and aviation exploits, and New Year's Day engaged large numbers of Soviet citizens in activities that were intended both to entertain and to build loyalty to the Soviet state. In the second half of the book my focus shifts to the attempts of the intelligentsia and the political elite to transform Soviet citizens into New Soviet Men and Women. The Pushkin Centennial of 1937, the twentieth anniversary of the October Revolution, and the promulgation of the Stalin Constitution provide insight into processes of Soviet cultural production and efforts to bring social and cultural enlightenment to the population.

While the contents of Soviet celebrations varied, almost all celebratory events were modeled on the mass meeting. During such meetings, groups of Soviet citizens, usually at their school or workplace but sometimes in communal living quarters, gathered together to hear Soviet officials articulate the meanings of the holiday and its connection to the current political situation, praise (and possibly reward) those who had achieved something significant for the Soviet state, and exhort the crowd to even greater achievements in the future. These meetings were usually followed by entertainment and refreshments. On major holidays local mass meetings occurred on the eve of the holiday and were followed on the holiday proper by the demonstration. A demonstration was a special kind of mass meeting in which the entire city or town's enterprises and military garrisons gathered together for a parade. The demonstration was reviewed, in the tradition of a pre-revolutionary military parade, by the highest-ranking Party, government, and military officials of the locality, who stood together on an elevated tribune. In addition to marking the major annual holidays and physical culture day, demonstrations could be used to show popular support for specific political decisions such as the death sentences meted out in the purge trial of August 1936. Mass meetings took place to commemorate the achievements of Arctic and aviation heroes, to discuss the new constitution, and in honor of holidays such as International Women's Day. The celebration of the Pushkin Centennial and New Year's Day sometimes provided the entertainment associated with a mass meeting without its overt political content. These events nonetheless gathered Soviet citizens to celebrate the advanced culture and prosperity of life in the Soviet Union.

Celebrations and Prosperity

The crash industrialization and collectivization programs of 1928–1932 produced mass upheaval. Collectivization brought severe repression and famine to the countryside and millions of starving peasants came to the cities to become workers. A strict rationing system was introduced in the cities to provide a very basic minimum for industrial workers. Virtually all Soviet citizens faced hunger and extreme deprivation in these years, especially in 1932–1933. By the beginning of 1935, the situation had stabilized enough that the government was able to do away with the rationing system for basic items. Few regained their 1928 standard of living, however, and the failure of the 1936 harvest created severe food shortages in the winter of 1936–1937.[54] In stark contrast to reality, festivals of the mid-1930s redefined the end of famine as "prosperity."

The Soviet holiday calendar was an important tool in regulating economic production, just as the religious calendar regulated agricultural production in Russian peasant tradition. The state attempted to use the yearly cycle of holidays both to mold its citizens into productive workers and to reward this productivity.

Cycles of alternating plenty and scarcity were a significant part of Russian peasant culture. The rhythm of the seasonal cycles of agricultural labor encompassed both the intense activity and the abundance of harvest time and the inactivity and sometimes destitution of the late winter and early spring.[55] The agricultural festival calendar was punctuated by a series of fasts followed by feasts.[56] In contrast to peasant tradition, the new Soviet laborer was expected to work steadily all year round. A significant aspect of Soviet ideology in the 1930s, including celebrations, was to discipline peasants newly arrived into the city into industrial work rhythms.

Despite its supposedly modern, industrial nature, Soviet society also operated within a yearly rhythm of alternating scarcity and plenty. Soviet officials created a rhetoric of mythic plenty that was supposed to exist year-round and then used holidays to back up this myth with the periodic and temporary appearance of goods. In addition to reinforcing old patterns of scarcity and plenty, Soviet holidays also intensified traditional peasant work cycles of alternating periods of intense productivity and times of inactivity. Managers would push for production plans to be fulfilled before a holiday because their production achievements would determine where their factory would march in the holiday demonstration. Then the celebration of the holiday would interrupt regular production for several days. Ironically, Soviet holidays, which were supposed to aid in the construction of new men and women and help transform the Soviet Union from a "backward" peasant society to an advanced industrial one ultimately reinforced traditional labor and consumption rhythms. In their efforts to gain support for new leaders and policies, Soviet officials perpetuated some of the ancient folkways they were trying to destroy. The practices associated with Soviet celebrations, then, were a bridge between traditional and Soviet cultural forms.

Soviet celebrations were special times during which the very limited material resources of the Soviet government were distributed. The discourse and social practices of Soviet celebrations reveal ways in which the Soviet government offered certain material benefits to its citizens. Soviet claims of prosperity and abundance were made tangible by the sudden appearance of food and consumer goods in the weeks before May 1st, November 7th, January 1st, and other holidays. Decisions about food procurement for holidays were made at the very highest levels. In January 1938, for example, the Central Committee decided to "improve the diet of Red Army soldiers and Red Fleet sailors" on February 22nd and 23rd in honor of the twentieth anniversary of the Red Army.[57]

The appearance of food was particularly significant in times of extreme deprivation. In the terrible conditions of 1932, a Hungarian Communist living in Russia bitterly commented about the May Day celebration, "Well those Russian *duraki* (fools), they will dance the whole day long for you if you fill their stomachs once a year. You see, they got some eggs and pot cheese on April thirtieth. That is why they were so happy. Give them one good meal and they forget about the whole year's starvation."[58] While one good holiday could hardly make people forget about a whole year of deprivation, the sudden appearance of goods around the holidays forced Soviet citizens into "celebrating" at the times that the government demanded that they do so even if their definitions of celebration were radically different than that of the government. H. G. Friese, a university student in the mid-1930s, remembered that before the holidays, "the stores are suddenly filled with hitherto unobtainable goods. The food in the dining halls becomes abundant. The whole country is in a heightened pre-holiday mood."[59] The appearance of food could create a mood of celebration that was significant in the lives of Soviet citizens, even if they were not otherwise inclined to applaud the achievements of the Soviet government.

Celebrations were always set against a backdrop of scarcity. Sometimes the special atmosphere of prosperity surrounding the holidays was created by enforced deprivation in the weeks before the holiday: one foreign worker pointed out that butter disappeared from shops in the fortnight before May 1st so that stores would be "able to release plenty on that occasion."[60] Whether or not they genuinely celebrated the victory of the Soviet regime on its official holidays, the Soviet people were compelled to take notice of days of plenty amid general want and acknowledge that they were special or different from the rest of the year.

The appearance of an abundance of goods during holidays and the promise of a bright future existed in a context in which very few people had access to accurate information about living conditions in the depression-stricken West. Many Soviet citizens believed that living conditions were worse in the rest of Europe than in the Soviet Union.[61] The lack of a real standard against which to measure their prosperity strengthened the power of the discourse of plenty in the mid-1930s and made the practice of increased consumption during Soviet holidays a significant way of exerting power on the population.

The nature of Soviet holidays as brief, carnivalesque periods of abundance in a time of great scarcity led to excesses in the celebration of official Soviet holidays. Soviet officials as well as the population at large indulged in these excesses. During holidays, Soviet institutions were authorized to spend resources on entertainment and food. Resolutions of the Sovnarkom (Council of People's Commissars) and the Politbiuro (Political Bureau of the Central Committee of the Communist Party) in October 1937 show that the administrators of institutions were sometimes overzealous in their commitment to celebrations. Because of "the expenditure of excessively great sums on the carrying out of holidays," the Politbiuro limited the amount of money that enterprise directors could spend on the October celebrations and Sovnarkom restricted the budgetary sources from which such expenditures could come. Sovnarkom also demanded that holiday expenditures "should take place with the observance of the greatest economy."[62] This admonition implies that enterprise directors freely allocated scarce resources for celebrations. The interference of the Politbiuro in the financial organization of celebrations suggests that holiday celebrations provided an opportunity for the squandering of state funds. When officials arranged things so that they personally benefited from celebrations, the actions of enterprise directors and Party and factory committees undermined the government's purpose in celebrating holidays. Some of the increased expenditures for holiday celebrations may have "trickled down" to workers, who, in conditions of scarcity, no doubt took full advantage of whatever material resources were available to them.

To what extent can festivity create satisfaction and belief in prosperity in a population that is suffering deprivation? Did the feeling of prosperity created during Soviet celebrations carry over to everyday life when poverty held sway? An analysis of the economic, cultural, and political aspects of celebration reveals the variety of arenas in which allegiances were created and destroyed in the Soviet Union in the 1930s.

Soviet Holidays and Traditional Culture

An analysis of records left by Soviet cultural cadres reveals the persistence of Orthodox religious practices and holidays throughout the 1930s. Sheila Fitzpatrick argues that the celebration of religious holidays in a rural context increased dramatically in the 1930s to justify the "evasion of fieldwork" on the collective farm.[63] By celebrating Soviet holidays, cadres hoped to decrease the power of religious celebrations to attract the population. Ultimately, however, they may have only succeeded in blending the two together. In April 1937, a Party official asked a worker at a leather factory in Moscow's Sokol'nicheskii District, "Are we preparing for Easter or for May 1st?" The worker answered, "We are preparing for both holidays."[64] Soviet holiday culture was a syncretic mixture of traditional and Soviet holiday practices.

The Party hoped to use holidays to raise the cultural level of the population, but this intention was often frustrated by the persistence of pre-revolutionary cultural practices. A 1936 report to the Central Committee described collective farm clubs as sites of "drunkenness, brawls, hooliganism, [and] sexual decadence," where young people "first sing about a girl stabbed by her villainous lover and second about a girl who poisons herself when dishonored by a fellow."[65] Nadezhda Krupskaia called this tendency of rural reading rooms to forego Soviet education in favor of depoliticized entertainment (that was often of pre-revolutionary origin), the *balalaechnyi uklon* (the balalaika deviation). By promoting non-political culture that conformed to Soviet visions of propriety, cadres tried to compete with traditional cultural practices. This contest with traditional culture shaped Soviet holidays in the 1930s.

Soviet officials themselves sometimes adopted identities that were antithetical to the Soviet culture they were supposed to promote. In September 1936, for example, the Balandinskii district committee of the Komsomol (Communist Youth League) in Saratov Territory spent funds allocated for International Youth Day on a banquet and alcohol for district Komsomol activists. As a result, the district celebration of International Youth Day was replaced by a dance and the activists got drunk and had a knife fight.[66] If local Soviet cadres did not adopt the definitions of Soviet holidays that Moscow officials wanted to promote, it was unlikely that their constituents would become cultured as a result of Soviet holidays.

The didactic functions of Soviet celebrations, like those of traditional peasant holidays, were sometimes marred by violence, drunkenness, and arson. Despite an official rhetoric of sobriety, alcohol was nevertheless an important part of Soviet celebrations. Like the appearance of scarce commodities and depoliticized culture at holiday time, the availability of alcohol represented both an enticement to and a compromise with the Soviet population. If the population was willing to participate in official Soviet events, food and alcohol would be made available for it to purchase. The collective farmer Frolov not only celebrated the anniversary of the October Revolution, he planned this celebration in advance. On September 9, he wrote: "Today I got my hands on a case of straight spirit for the holiday."[67] While the celebration of the holiday succeeded in encouraging this collective farmer to explicitly celebrate the founding of the Soviet state, his own

definition of this holiday was as an opportunity to get drunk. The agents of
the state succeeded in getting Frolov to pay homage to its founding, but he
retained some control over the form the celebration would take.

An anti-Soviet peasant who was released from a Soviet labor camp in
1936 after seven years of imprisonment described in his diary the after-
math of the October celebration in the town of Tiumen:

> The celebration is over, but the festive mood remains: with the state the
> workers are in, work is out of the question. You can still hear singing;
> some people are still out staggering around in the streets. Washing down
> the holiday with holy water. It's all literally come down to that: all anyone
> talks about is their holiday escapades. All the political hoopla was drowned
> in a blatant flood of drunkenness.[68]

This passage reveals the multiplicity of the meanings of Soviet celebration and the negotiations between three distinct groups: the central government that set official policies on celebration, the Soviet cadres who controlled celebrations at the local level, and the people who participated in
them. The state had access to massive coercive power yet it could not use it
when the purpose of celebration was to get citizens to identify voluntarily
with the state. State and local officials sacrificed productivity in their quest
to use celebrations to promote Soviet ideology. The people agreed to be
exposed to the ideological components of holidays if propaganda was accompanied by time off from work, food, and alcohol. Soviet citizens may
have willingly participated in the celebration of the anniversary and rev-
eled in their "holiday escapades," but they may not have imbibed all of the
"culture" and political knowledge which government officials intended.
Ideal conditions of citizen participation did not include massive drunkenness, for example, but the cadres who organized celebrations in practice
condoned this behavior for themselves and others. The central government
and Party therefore had to compromise with its local cadres and with citizens during celebrations. Social practices thus shaped the discourses of the
six celebrations featured in this book even as the creators of celebration
discourses endeavored to shape social practices.

Part One

Soviet Popular Culture
and Mass Mobilization

2

PARADING THE NATION

DEMONSTRATIONS AND THE
CONSTRUCTION OF SOVIET IDENTITIES

Describing the 1937 physical culture parade in Moscow, *Pravda* proclaimed, "It was as if the whole country unfolded in front of the spectators, and they felt that in every corner of the country, no matter how far away, creative work was boiling, amazing human material was springing up whose equal did not exist anywhere else in the world."[1] The Soviet press asserted that spectators interpreted the physical culture parade as a representation of the Soviet Union in microcosm and that the parade enabled Muscovites to envision the achievements of Soviet power in all regions of the country. Demonstrations, the ubiquitous symbols of Soviet holiday culture and the centerpiece of many 1930s celebrations, indeed represented the Soviet Union in microcosm. They created an image of perfect order, but beneath this appearance of order, rivalries, confusion, and indiscipline flourished.

Despite the egalitarian element of mass participation, the demonstration was one of many institutions in the Soviet Union in the mid-1930s that reinforced the idea that strict hierarchy and careful attention to precedence were appropriate ways of organizing society. Soviet parades organized their participants into hierarchies based on a variety of factors, including age, appearance, gender, nationality, Party membership, place of residence, social status, and occupation. A person's position within a parade indicated his or her individual status in society. From 1937 on, Moscow physical culture parades also symbolized the integration of the individual republics into the Soviet Union by including delegations from the ten non-Russian republics. Individual gymnastics displays defined and articulated the national identities of each republic and represented their collective belonging to the Soviet Union.

Beginning in the late 1920s, many of the carnivalesque and spontaneous elements of earlier Soviet demonstrations were suppressed.[2] As demonstrations became less popular, local Party officials often compelled participants to attend. Whether or not citizens wanted to show up, their appearance at the demonstration symbolized enthusiastic popular participation in Soviet life and loyalty to the Soviet state. In the 1930s even civilian parade participants demonstrated their discipline by marching in precise military formations. In her analysis of Soviet rituals, sociologist Christel Lane has argued that the regimented and controlled body movement of parades in the 1930s revealed "a striking correspondence between the physical and social body in Soviet society." She notes that "both in symbolic body movement and in socio-political activity the emphasis is on the mobilization of the masses, on the self-control of each constituent individual, and on a subjection of the individual to the collective pursuit."[3] While Lane is certainly correct that the synchronized body movements of the parade created representations of an ideal Soviet social order, this emphasis on the discipline of the parade fails to recognize two crucial aspects of Soviet life in the 1930s.

Too much emphasis on discipline reduces the significance of the parade to one official meaning. The creation of hierarchies in the parade elevated some groups at the expense of others. The parade's allocation of symbolic power created different meanings for different segments of the Soviet population. Examination of the process of constructing hierarchies allows an exploration of the relationships of the more and less privileged groups to each other and to Soviet officials and identifies the conflicts and tensions that hierarchies produced.

Planning to create perfect synchronization and order is not the same as actually doing so. Parade organizers could not always successfully produce a symbolically disciplined citizenry, never mind an actually self-disciplined one. The language of bodies marching in precision had the potential to communicate the state's success in mobilizing the population, but confusion in the ranks also transmitted more ambiguous messages about the nature of Soviet power.

Defining Hierarchies

Location, Audience, and Status

The act of ordered marching has a long and varied history in the Russian Empire. There were at least three types of Russian parades that lent meaning to the Soviet demonstration: political demonstrations, military drills, and religious processions. Workers' demonstrations in tsarist Russia expressed the population's spontaneous articulation of a collective identity and their political and economic opposition to factory owners and to the state. After the revolution, the Soviet government redefined the demonstration as a celebration of the power of the proletariat, but demonstrations protesting state policies did not entirely disappear.[4] Richard Stites has argued that tsarist rulers were obsessed with military drills and parades because of their desire to create an "administrative utopia" in which the "geometrization of space, rationalism, and the military ethos of order and obedience" were fused with an "iconography of happiness." Stalinist parades were also an embodiment of this vision of military-administrative utopia.[5] Although Soviet officials vehemently rejected the content of Orthodox Christian rites, they sometimes adopted their form. Ritual processions with icons to celebrate a religious holiday or to pray for a good harvest were also progenitors of the Soviet parade. As in church rituals, Soviet marchers marked out sacred and communal spaces while carrying revered pictures, now of political leaders rather than of saints. The varied origins of Soviet parades enabled them to create a wide variety of meanings for their participants.

The Soviet demonstration created hierarchies not only by ordering its citizens according to their relative importance, but also by moving them across a carefully defined geographic space and by creating a small but extremely important audience of Soviet officials to view the parade. The route of Soviet demonstrations marked the ceremonial centers of Soviet cities and towns as paraders from outlying districts converged at one central point, usually the seat of Soviet power.[6] The repetition of Soviet rituals obscured the pre-revolutionary history of these places by associating them with a Soviet holiday tradition.

In the late 1920s and 1930s, the Sovietization of centers of power was sometimes achieved by the physical destruction of historic landmarks and the erection of new monuments. Moscow Party boss Lazar Kaganovich had several old churches pulled down in order that "the demonstration processions from the six districts of Moscow should all pour into Red Square at the same time."[7] The simultaneous display of loyalty from all directions to the reconfigured center symbolized not only the city of Moscow's dedication to the Soviet project but also the support of citizens from every corner of the Soviet Union.

Moscow parade participants moved through the main square of ancient Muscovy, but it was now dominated by the mausoleum containing the embalmed body of Lenin.[8] Stalin stood atop Lenin's mausoleum to witness the symbolic representation of the entire country parading before him.[9] According to official rhetoric, Lenin's presence was also felt in this sacred place. One Turkmen delegate at the 1939 physical culture parade announced, "At his full gigantic height stood before us the form of the great Lenin, who is lying now right here in this mausoleum."[10] The Moscow parade was the place to see and be seen by Soviet leaders living and dead.

The opportunity to see Lenin and Stalin and be seen by them was granted only to certain Soviet citizens. Approximately 10,000 people, including leading Party and government officials, NKVD and army officers, newspaper correspondents, diplomats, and other specially invited guests, had the honor of viewing parades near Stalin in front of Lenin's mauso-

Demonstration enters Red
Square. From *Moskva
rekonstruiruetsia* (1938).

leum on Red Square.[11] The audience of the parade on Red Square was made
up of the highest-ranking members of the ruling elite. Less exalted Soviet
citizens received the honor of appearing in the parade. In the Moscow physical culture parade, military garrisons and physically fit industrial workers
from Moscow marched with athletes who had distinguished themselves
as "masters of sport," students from physical culture institutes, and specially picked delegations from the non-Russian republics. The appearance
of these groups in Red Square denoted their special status as residents of
the capital or skilled athletes who were honored guests from outlying regions. Because of their place in the Soviet social hierarchy, they came into
Lenin's presence and into visual contact with the great Stalin and other
illustrious members of the Soviet elite while the rest of the population was
excluded.

In Moscow demonstrations, when the columns reached the mausoleum the commander called out an order for an ovation and the marchers
responded with a powerful "Hurrah" in perfect unison.[12] Thus, the marchers, whose "hearts beat in one rhythm," became a symbol of the whole
nation, and gave Stalin unanimous and simultaneous acclaim.[13] Yet according to the Soviet press, the parade also produced a variety of personal meanings for participants.

It is canonical in any biographical account of a parade participant to dwell on the special significance of the moment in which the marcher caught a glimpse of Stalin and was seen by him. Georgian gymnast A. Dzhordzha-dze described his excitement at performing his gymnastics routine in front of Stalin: "I could not tear my eyes away from his dear face. I experienced such a lift, such a surge of strength, that I could have easily fulfilled any gymnastics maneuver. I think only about the fact that Stalin is watching me."[14] According to official discourse, being watched by Stalin empow-ered Soviet citizens to perform great deeds.

The eyes of Stalin could also create discord, however. A poem for chil-dren described the moment of contact with Stalin: "Mama, today I saw Stalin. / I marched with a detachment in the parade. / He looked just like he does in my little book. / He cheerfully waved his hand at us. / . . . . Mama, Stalin smiled at me, / but Volod'ka quarreled with me and said that Stalin smiled at him."[15] Here the desire to achieve personal communi-cation with Stalin, to be singled out above the crowd for Stalin's special notice, created dissension between two young boys. This poem revealed the tensions that were produced as Soviet hierarchies were defined. In their quest to improve their own status, citizens competed against one another and reduced possibilities for collective action.

Receiving the parade instead of marching in it was a mark of special status or of political power all across the Soviet Union as well as in Mos-cow. Soviet demonstrations identified the social and geographic centers of power in all Soviet towns and cities. Just as Stalin standing atop Lenin's mausoleum in Moscow was the acme of the social and political pyramid of the Soviet Union, the Party bosses of the provincial cities stood on their own elevated tribunes at the top of their towns' hierarchies. A Komsomol member, describing the first May Day demonstration he attended in 1929, recorded the reactions of the neighborhood boys, who were children of workers in a tobacco factory, to the demonstration. "The boys . . . spent the whole of the following week playing at demonstrations. The younger ones marched about the yard, roaring out songs and waving paper flags left over from the great day, while the older ones climbed onto a cart that was standing nearby and reviewed the parade."[16] The game of these children revealed not only their enthusiasm for the form of the Soviet holiday but also that they fully understood the hierarchy implicit in the demonstra-tion: the older boys got to play the role of the more powerful leaders of the Party and government. This game showed that the boys understood the key element of the demonstration—that the demonstration was about the relationship between the "reviewers" and the marchers and that a demon-stration would not be a demonstration without leaders watching the march-ers from "above."

Viewing the Party leadership could cause resentment as well as repro-duction of hierarchy. An émigré described his participation in the 1932 October Revolution demonstration in Kiev where he "saw the sleepy and indifferent faces of the Party leaders." His companions conjectured that the leaders "probably were getting drunk all night long, and now they're working off their hangovers."[17] Rather than representing the symbolic harmony between people and Party, this demonstration became an opportunity to visualize the distance between the rulers and the ruled.

The Order of the March

The Moscow demonstrators who made their way from the outskirts of the city to the center of power marched in an order that indicated their places in the Soviet social and economic hierarchy. The Soviet military marched first, denoting its overarching symbolic and strategic importance in Soviet society, its pivotal role as a model of discipline for the rest of the marchers, and its significance as an institution that united men from all social groups and all areas of the Soviet Union. In Moscow parades, military forces were followed by the industrial workers and students of Moscow and by collective farmers from Moscow Region. The Soviet government's subordination of agriculture to the military and industrial sectors was thus communicated repeatedly in the marching order of most Soviet parades.[18]

After the military marched industrial workers. The trade union physi-

"The ranks of sunburnt athletes of the Red Army. . . ." From *A Pageant of Youth* (1939).

cal culture movement incorporated military formations into the physical culture parade in 1932, at the height of peasant immigration to Moscow. Workers were supposed to observe the chain of command, follow commands quickly, and march rhythmically in unison "with a military bearing, a harmonious and beautiful placement of the head and torso, an observation of the correct distance between rows."[19] Physical culture organizers thus employed a military model to assist in the transformation of large numbers of pre-modern agricultural laborers into efficient modern industrial workers. By marching in precise military formation, workers symbolized their willing participation in a new industrial order where the scientific organization of labor and industrial tempos replaced rural tasks and rhythms.[20]

Industrial workers in demonstrations displayed newly created urban and industrial identities and "practiced the etiquette of urban living in public."[21] Parade participants and commanders were instructed to show "mutual respect, politeness and culture."[22] These directions suggest that participants had not yet fully internalized the desired norms of courteous behavior. Despite Soviet attempts to foster internalized disciplines based on political consciousness, the force of Bolshevik will, and discourses of culture and purification, a military model of discipline remained dominant.[23] The persistence of this model suggests the limitations of internalized discipline in the 1930s.

The placement of Soviet workers in a parade was directly connected to their roles in industrial production. The May 1st and October Revolution demonstrations were not just a spectacle of support for the Soviet project but a yearly "report card" in which production achievements determined the precedence among marchers. The hierarchy of the demonstration reflected the performance of each district, factory, and workshop in fulfilling the yearly production plan. Shock workers and Stakhanovites took the lead as factory workshops marched in order from the most to the least productive. The specific place of each participant in the parade thus reflected his or her status in the production hierarchy. This process was repeated on a larger scale within the demonstration itself as the most productive factory in the district carried the district banners and the most productive districts in the city marched closer to the mausoleum.[24] Marching in the parade provided opportunities for expressing workshop, factory, or district patriotism. In the formation of any parade, organizers and participants had an opportunity to measure themselves against others who stood before and after them, closer to or further from the mausoleum, outside the parade altogether, or on the tribune above them. The parade's physical articulation of social position created meanings for individuals beyond an affirmation of loyalty and devotion to the state.

The demonstration was also a crucial moment in the definition of the status of factory Party organizers who monitored fulfillment of production quotas. In April 1937, one Party member at the Dinamo metal works in Moscow noted proudly, "There has never been a holiday on which the Dinamo Factory marched in the demonstration with an unfulfilled program."[25] The marching order in a demonstration revealed which Party committees had been effective in organizing the production of their factories and which had failed. In the tense atmosphere of the purges, when failure in production was often followed by arrests, the holiday demonstrations served as an important production deadline and as a focal point for the ambitions and anxieties of Party members.

Within the factory, the orchestration of the order of the demonstration gave the Party committee an opportunity to publicly humiliate the least effective production units of the factory. The enmity between the factory administration and the Party committee at Moscow's Dinamo factory became clear during the preparation for the November 7th demonstration in 1937. The Party committee announced that the very last workshop to march in the demonstration would be the "factory administration," indicating that the administrators were the least productive workers in the factory.[26] The holiday demonstration thus reflected rivalries and hostilities within individual factories and demonstrated the victory of some local officials over others. The creation of hierarchies was a ubiquitous element of Soviet demonstrations, but the formation of these hierarchies was not simply an articulation of centralized power. The social meaning of hierarchies was generated within each Soviet institution and reflected localized social relations.

Bodily Hierarchies

Physical culture parades, which made their first appearance on Red Square in 1931, were different from holiday demonstrations in that their hierarchies were determined not by skill in production or Party status but by the physical appearance and level of physical fitness of the participants.[27] These parades posed different problems for their organizers and produced different meanings for participants than holiday demonstrations. Because they were more selective and more popular than holiday demonstrations, organizers had to decide which workers would be allowed to participate in physical culture parades instead of exhorting as many workers as possible to come. In 1936, a representative from the Union of Metal Workers asked Moscow Region physical culture parade organizers if he could bring more than his allotted 1,250 workers, since the parade was "such a popular event that all of our factory committees have asked us to include their people."[28] In 1937, the number of workers allowed to march in the Moscow parade was significantly reduced, creating a more select group of athletes.[29] Being chosen to participate in the physical culture parade gave workers enhanced personal status, since not every worker who wanted to attend was considered fit to participate.

The participation of Soviet citizens in physical culture parades was inextricably connected to their physical appearance and condition. Physical culture organizations strove to emulate the well-organized and well-conditioned Red Army contingent with its "naked bodies, chocolate from an even and healthy tan."[30] The ideal male participants were to be young, healthy, tall, and suntanned. The ideal women were to be healthy and athletic, and while they too were defenders of the country, they sometimes appeared in the parade as mothers carrying their children on their shoulders. While Soviet ideologues professed equality of the sexes, the military preoccupations of physical culture organizers led them to focus primarily on the display of the healthy male body. Yet the inclusion of women in physical culture parades was significant because women tended to be excluded from other militarized aspects of society.

In preparation for the 1936 physical culture parade, local trade union officials were expected to "pay attention to the people on the right-flank of the first division in every platoon, in every company. There should stand a strapping, healthy, suntanned Communist or Komsomol."[31] These were the elite physical culturists who would stand closest to Stalin. The ravages of years of hunger and repetitive factory labor made such athletes a scarce commodity in Moscow factories in the 1930s and all the more desirable because the very shape of their bodies refuted the difficulties of Soviet life. The demand for "strapping" athletes led to tensions between trade union officials and Party activists. Trade unions were required to send some of their athletes to march in the parade under the banner of the Party District Committee. One organizer was afraid that the Party Committees "do not want to let down their district and would pick out the best people and teams."[32] The most talented and physically attractive athletes were a scarce resource over which various institutions competed. Forming the ranks of the physical culture parade thus shaped regional and institutional identities as it boosted the egos and enhanced the individual status of the most sought-after athletes.

The physical culture parade elevated strong, physically fit workers and athletes over weaker and less attractive Soviet citizens who were purposely excluded from the parade. Trade union physical culture officials in Moscow Region cautioned local cadres: "When you are forming up your ranks, do not include people who are particularly small, even if they are people with merit, because we need to show a healthy, tanned person, a Stalinist athlete."[33] The parade created a disruption in established social hierarchies because the usual criterion of dedication to the state and Party was subordinated to the display of brawny physique.

This process of selection produced dissatisfaction among both local athletes and physical culture cadres and radically transformed the meaning of the parade for the excluded athletes. One local organizer complained:

> We had to conduct some very unpleasant work before we approved the physical culture columns. We made a special trip to various districts and removed the people who were not suitable by their exterior form and

Mother and child in 1939
physical culture parade.
From *A Pageant of Youth*
(1939).

physical characteristics for participation in the physical culture parade.
This was a very awkward task. People were offended. They had already
devoted some time to rehearsing when we dismissed them.[34]

These athletes had willingly agreed to participate in a spectacle of discipline and loyalty to the Soviet state, but were now told that the higher
authorities did not want them to take part because of the way that they
looked. Instead of fostering support for the Soviet project, the physical culture parade might have alienated some potential supporters. Soviet officials
sacrificed their goal of mobilization to create a spectacle of joyous Soviet
life.

Body and Nation

An important goal of the annual physical culture parades beginning in
1937 was to show how a Soviet identity was formed out of the collective
identities of loyal citizens from eleven ethnically distinct but equal republics. In the physical culture parade, Soviet bodies, shaped by the "expert

sculptor," Stalin, created a bodily symbolism, where naked tanned flesh and well-developed muscles stood for the might of the Soviet nation.[35] In the 1930s, both Nazi Germany and the Soviet Union drew on European traditions that linked the disciplined development of the male physique with the unity and strength of the nation.[36] In both Nazi and Soviet sports, young men exemplified the nation, but as literary scholar Hans Günther points out, "If for Bolshevik heroes, an iron will or a consciousness of steel stands in the foreground, then National Socialist heroism sees its ideal in the armor of soldiers' bodies."[37]

Because of this difference in the focus on the body, Nazi and Soviet male bodies also varied in their degree of sexuality. While the hardened body of the ideal male Nazi evoked both sexual prowess and homoeroticism, the erotic component of the Soviet physical culture movement was more muted.[38] This downplaying of sexuality during the celebration of physicality is representative of the literary, artistic, and scientific discourse of the 1930s, in which the open discussion or display of sexuality was uncommon.[39] On the other hand, physical culture parades took place at a time in which the body of the individual began to play a central role in Soviet art. The "body-as-machine" images of the First Five Year Plan were succeeded by classical figures made of flesh and blood, masculine muscles, and feminine curves.[40] Artists now rarely created trim and muscular women; the female figure became soft and moderately fleshy.[41] Unlike the 1920s, which literary critic Eric Naiman has termed a period of "revolutionary anorexia," the culture of the 1930s celebrated male and female embodiment.[42] The physical culture parade was thus a site of bodily discipline and self-control that also allowed for the possibility of bodily fulfillment and pleasure.[43]

In *Nationalism and Sexuality*, George Mosse argues that nationalism diverts repressed sexual and homoerotic energies into feelings of loyalty toward the state. Mosse believes that the idea of nationalism demands that "the love between male friends should not be projected upon each other but on the nation; in this way, homoerotic temptation would be overcome. The national stereotype symbolized such conquest, drawing unto itself homoerotic desires, only to transcend such passions."[44] Soviet sexological discourse of the 1920s explicitly articulated the idea of sublimation, arguing that sexual "abstinence has acquired such special value now as the key to the source of great reserves of social energy."[45] The display of physically attractive male and female bodies in the 1930s physical culture parade thus promoted patriotic loyalty to the Soviet state. During training for physical culture parades, feelings of both heterosexual and homosexual bodily pleasure could be transmuted into a passionate attraction to the Soviet state. Yet these pleasurable feelings could also promote a sense of self not related to patriotism as sought-after and attractive athletes celebrated their personal successes and garnered romantic conquests.[46]

The attempts of Soviet authorities to create modern industrial workers and transform physical attraction into patriotism took place in the context of a body culture that did not have a strong tradition of nudity. In Germany, late nineteenth-century social movements emphasized the naked body, but few such movements existed in the non-Russian republics or the Russian village.[47] The public appearance of young Russian men and women in shorts and tank tops symbolized the modification or displacement of traditional rural attitudes about the body.[48] One activist conducting physical culture classes in Gorkii Region explained that "it was noticeable at the beginning that the boys and girls felt shy about exercising in shorts and tank tops, but we gradually overcame this superfluous bashfulness. They first started getting used to practicing in their uniforms in the field and then they even performed on the stage at their club."[49] The attitude toward dress and the body that was standard in an urban physical culture parade was alien to at least some young inhabitants of rural Russia. The appearance of Moscow workers marching un-selfconsciously in shorts and tank tops reaffirmed their urban and modern image but also increased the possibilities for erotic excitement during the parade.

The physical culture parade's challenge to traditional body culture was most evident in the marching of bare-armed, unveiled women in the Central Asian delegations. Their very appearance proved conclusively that these women had rejected native traditions and adopted a Soviet way of life. The presentation of their uncovered faces and bodies to the crowd symbolized the victory of the Soviet state over traditional Muslim authorities. In the Muslim cultural context, however, the appearance of women without veils symbolized a lack of respectability and an open sexual invitation.[50] This attitude toward the female body also shaped people's physical attractions to one another in the parade.

In contrast to the focus of German gymnastics on the healthy bodies of the superior Aryan race,[51] in physical culture parades the Soviet Union celebrated the physical strength of Europeans and Asians together. Slavic, Caucasian, and Asian men all marched bare-chested in the parade, and publicists emphasized racial difference in the parade. An account of the 1937 parade celebrated the "swarthy faces, black like tar, the braids, the blinding smiles and the bold, free step" of the Central Asian participants.[52] Parade organizers literally foregrounded the Asian athletes. In their recommendations after the general rehearsal of the 1940 physical culture parade, Komsomol officials instructed the delegation from Kirghizia to "bring the indigenous inhabitants forward to the front line."[53] European migrants to Kirghizia hindered the symbolic representation of Asian inclusion and were moved to the back of the delegation.[54] From 1937 on, the Soviet physical culture parade was a celebration of racial diversity, but like Soviet official pronouncements about the equality of women, a public discourse of racial equality was contradicted and undermined by official and unofficial discriminatory practices.

Female Uzbek athletes in 1939 physical culture parade. From *A Pageant of Youth* (1939).

The Soviet Union Embodied

The inclusion of republican delegations in the parade "was an incarnation of the Stalin Constitution,"[55] demonstrating that the Soviet Union was a "union state, formed on the basis of the voluntary association of equal Soviet Socialist Republics."[56] Yet the location, form, and content of the parade belied this emphasis on equality. Delegations from the ten non-Russian republics were summoned to the "imperial" capital of Moscow[57] to represent their symbolic integration into the Soviet Union by swearing a "great oath to Comrade Stalin," pledging "their loyalty and their readiness to defend the sacred borders of the U.S.S.R. "[58] As the borders of the Soviet Union changed because of the Hitler-Stalin Pact and the Russo-Finnish War, so did the country's depiction in the physical culture parade. The 1940 parade included a delegation from the new Karelo-Finnish Republic and celebrated the incorporation of Western Ukraine and Western Belorussia into the Soviet Union.[59]

The delegation of the Russian Federation led the nationalities section of the July 1939 physical culture parade, carrying a banner that read "First Among Equals." This oxymoronic slogan beautifully captures the contradiction that was at the heart of the nationalities section of the parade. All of the republics were declared to be equal, but some were more equal than others. The "national" gymnastics displays were planned and executed under the direction of the All-Union Committee on Physical Culture and Sport. The content of the gymnastics exhibitions delineated the subjection of the non-Russian republics to the central Soviet authorities and articulated a precise hierarchy among the eleven Soviet republics. Officials of the committee's sector of *pokazatel'nykh vystuplenii* (demonstration performances) sent out their first directive about the parade in February of 1939, dispatched delegations to the republics in March, organized regional meetings in Central Asia and the Caucasus in April, and reviewed the plans of the republican delegations and ordered changes in the scripts in the middle of May.[60] Here is an excerpt from *Pravda's* description of the results:

> The Uzbeks showed the construction of the Liaganskii Canal, which provides water for their cotton fields. On the "irrigated" Square appears an enormous boll of cotton which opens to reveal a dancing [female] student from the Tashkent Pedagogical Institute. . . .
>
> Turkmen physical culturists with rifles come running out of a vineyard. They construct a harvest holiday on the Square, skillfully combining work in the fields with complex sporting maneuvers. They conduct a battle with bayonets. The sportsmen leave the Square with a song about Stalin. . . .
>
> The delegation of Armenian physical culturists depicts two episodes from the life of the Armenian people. A thousand years ago, Arabs carried out an armed incursion against the Armenians. Led by the popular/national hero David of Sasun, the Armenians were victorious. . . . The audience is transported a thousand years ahead. A painting tells of the achievements of present-day Armenia. . . .
>
> Six girls in bright, elegant, costumes run toward the mausoleum. They carry large branches, heavy with clusters of grapes. These branches spell out the word "Georgia. . . ." Georgia's physical culturists begin their presentation. They reproduce episodes from the history of their republic, they stage the harvesting of tea leaves, with great spirit they dance national dances, they present the popular game "lelo."[61]

In these gymnastics displays, republican nationhood had nothing to do with political sovereignty; instead, the republics were defined by their economic or military contributions to the Soviet Union. This definition of the nation by its function in the Soviet system was covered by a thin veneer of national "folk" costumes, traditions, and music, which were themselves sometimes Soviet rather than national constructions.[62]

In its gymnastics presentation, the Uzbek nation was reduced to a giant cotton field; the flowering of the nation was represented by a young man and woman dancing on a gigantic boll of cotton. Cotton was pervasive in the Uzbek presentation; even the uniforms of the Uzbek female gymnasts reflected this cotton theme. The women wore short-sleeved T-shirts with cotton boll emblems over their hearts and flowing full-length trousers that had a distinctly "Eastern" look.[63] These women from a Muslim republic served as a powerful symbol of the defeat of religious "superstition" by scientific socialism and of the liberation of Muslim women. The use of cotton as the primary emblem of the Uzbek nation signified the central Soviet government's domination of Uzbekistan. During the First Five Year Plan, Uzbek farmers were forced to expand their acreage of cotton at the expense of cereal crops, thus becoming dependent on grain imports from the north. The cotton grown in Uzbekistan was not processed there but was sent back north for industrial production, so that the economic relations of Uzbekistan to Russia in the late 1930s resembled those of a colonial economy.[64] Cotton was a symbol of Uzbek dependence on Moscow and the designation of cotton as the defining Uzbek national symbol reinforced notions of Uzbekistan's economic integration into and dependence on the Soviet Union and its loyalty and obedience to Moscow. The gymnastics exhibitions of Tadzhikistan and Azerbaidzhan also featured cotton growing and signaled their dependent economic relationship to Moscow.

The Turkmen delegation had originally planned a gymnastics exhibition on the theme of "friendship of peoples," but this idea was rejected by Moscow physical culture authorities. The Turkmen delegation was not permitted to represent the other ten republics by carrying their emblems or to build an emblem of the Soviet Union out of the emblems of the eleven republics.[65] Instead, this theme of "friendship of peoples" structured the entire parade as central authorities exercised their power by orchestrating the union of the eleven individual republics into one nation. The Turkmen delegation eventually adopted the much more general theme of harvest holiday, as did Kirghizia and Kazakhstan.

Armenia's presentation, unlike that of Uzbekistan and Turkmenistan, focused on an historical event from the tenth century.[66] This gymnastics display defined Armenia by its geographic position on the border of the Soviet Union and assigned Armenians the role of defending the Soviet Union from Middle Eastern attacks. While Moscow officials allowed the Armenian people to celebrate their ancient history, they would not approve a gymnastics display based solely on the exploits of David of Sasun. Moscow officials instructed the Armenian delegation to add a second scene showing the achievements of Armenia in the Soviet period.[67] The important defense functions of the republics on the borders of the Soviet Union were highlighted in the presentations of Ukraine and Belorussia as well. The Ukrainian delegation portrayed historical battles against Polish nobles in 1648 and against the Germans in 1918 to illustrate Ukraine's defense of the border "in close friendship with the great Russian people,"[68] but the

Georgian delegation in 1939 physical culture parade. From *A Pageant of Youth* (1939).

Belorussian presentation consisted solely of a dramatized alarm at the border followed by the defeat of the enemy invaders. Belorussia was reduced to border posts and Belorussians to border guards the way that Uzbekistan was reduced to cotton bolls and Uzbeks to cotton growers.

The Georgian presentation used gender difference to illustrate the dual identity of the Georgian nation as obedient to central authorities and defiant of foreign aggressors. Georgian women displayed grapes and harvested tea leaves, the crops which Georgia had been directed by Moscow to produce. Symbolizing fertility and submissiveness, the women offered up the fruits of their labors to Moscow, while the Georgian men represented their ability to defend the Soviet nation in a militarized dance. The Georgian presentation also alluded to a Georgian history of a very particular kind. The presentation celebrated the development of an underground Bolshevik newspaper edited by the young Stalin, suggesting that the most significant event in the history of Georgia was Stalin's contribution to the development of socialism.

The presentations of Armenia, Georgia, and Ukraine differed from the presentations of the Central Asian nationalities in that the Christian nations were allowed to display specially selected scenes from their national histories, while the Muslim nations could display only their fertile harvests and the specific goods they produced for the Soviet economy. While all of the national presentations carried the message that the national populations were ready to defend the Soviet Union, only three Christian nations, Armenia, Belorussia, and Ukraine, had their contribution to the Soviet Union specifically defined as military service in defense of the borders. Soviet hierarchy divided the Christian republics from the Muslim, the Slavic and Caucasian republics from the Central Asian. The parade also privileged the eleven nationalities who had their own republics over dozens of other nationalities who were not represented at all. [69]

The *Pravda* article, which described the presentations of the "fraternal republics," specifically mentioned the gymnastics routines of ten national delegations. The nationality that was not singled out by *Pravda* under the category of nationality was, of course, Russian.[70] The Russian Federation did, however, march under its own banner in the parade itself. The Russian banners displayed a rhetoric of advanced culture, claiming, for example, that "the great Russian people are a people of heroes, a people of talents." These heroes included "Lenin and Stalin, . . . Kirov and Kuibyshev, Pavlov and Chkalov, Pushkin and Mendeleev, Lomonosov and Timiriazev, Chernyshevskii and Mechnikov, people who personify the culture and pride of the Russian people."[71] As Soviet rhetoric elevated Russia above the other republics, it lauded Stalin as a Russian cultural hero despite his Georgian origins. With the blessing of Soviet authorities, the Russians in the parade asserted their leadership over the other nationalities. Like the citizens of the other republics, however, they lost the possibility to represent specific attributes of their ethnicity.

What was promoted by the Soviet state as a universal and simultaneous outpouring of support for Soviet power was in fact a complex mixture of local politics, individual rivalries, and personal preferences and ambitions that took a state-decreed form. Participants and audiences of Soviet parades drew a wide variety of meanings from their individual positions in the demonstration. The Stakhanovite worker carrying his factory's banner; the much sought-after athlete; the anxious Party organizer; the disgraced factory administrator; the star-struck republican visitor to Moscow; the short, pale, sickly man excluded from the ranks of the physical culture parade; and the Russian worker holding a sign in praise of Russian culture all emerged from the parade with distinct points of view about the Soviet Union and their place in it. Some of these views forwarded the state's goals of mobilization, conformity, and discipline while others had the potential to undermine them. Soviet demonstrations enabled citizens to envision their relationships to the Soviet state and to other Soviet citizens. These events alternately produced feelings of enthusiasm and estrangement as participants gloried in their inclusion in the community or resented the social distinction granted to others.

The Meanings of Disorder

A crucial element of the All-Union Physical Culture Parade was its representation of the voluntary and joyful subservience of both Moscow workers and national minorities to Moscow authorities. Those leaders on the tribune watching the precise and ordered movements of the parade could visualize how their orders were being carried out in every corner of the nation. Because of the weakness of the Party in rural and non-Russian areas, this kind of discipline was quite rare. Since the parade symbolized state control over the country, imperfections in the demonstration cast doubt on the government's ability to transform the citizens of its borderlands into New Soviet Men and Women. Mistakes and confusion in the organization of the parade, even if they were viewed only by the organizers and the organized, raised questions about the Party's leadership role and the special relationship between the citizens and the Party.

Soviet cadres had difficulty in executing even the symbolic representation of ideal order. For instance, in preparation for the 1939 parade, the Turkmen physical culture authorities received directives in February, consulted with Moscow officials in March and April, and still failed to submit acceptable plans to the Moscow authorities in May. When the delegation arrived in Moscow a few days in advance of the parade, Moscow organizers complained that the athletes were "weakly prepared" and they had to be specially drilled in the rifle exercises immediately before the parade.[72] Like other Soviet officials, Moscow physical culture officials could only gain full control over the gymnastics exhibitions when republican representatives arrived in Moscow, because their directions to the provinces were not effectively carried out.[73] The Soviet records that I examined did not reveal how well the Turkmen athletes actually performed their rifle exercises on Red Square, but a less-than-perfect performance might have enabled some viewers to envision the limits of Soviet power in Turkmenistan.

The Committee on Physical Culture and Sport evaluated the performance of each of the trade union delegations after the 1939 physical culture parade. In contrast to photographic and filmic depictions of this parade that emphasized its perfection, these reports revealed frequent lapses in discipline and order in the ranks of the parade, even at the critical moment of their appearance on Red Square.[74] Physical culture organizers noted that the delegation from the Bolshevik sports society was "slovenly in carrying its banners and slogans"; Arrow delayed the march of the parade by six minutes; as the participants of the Torpedo and the Kommunard clubs were marching across Red Square, "conversations and noise could be heard"; the marchers from the club Energy were aligned poorly and out of step. Metallurgist's participants "got confused"; Builder's and October's answers to the greeting were weak. Due to a traffic jam at the entrance to Red Square, Proletarian Victory had to appear without any props.[75] Even while performing on Red Square, the behavior of the parade participants was less regimented, more individual, and more chaotic than the physical culture ideal. In spite of organizers' best attempts to create discipline, the parade fell far short of the desired goals.

The Soviet parade's emphasis on discipline and coordinated movement was not always compatible with its promise of an opportunity to participate in an uplifting mass ritual, to see the great Stalin and be seen by him. One organizer of the 1939 October Revolution demonstration complained: "Everything goes well until the columns are on Red Square, but as soon as they go past the mausoleum, everyone is carried away by the sight of the tribune. A breach occurs and all of the columns get mixed up."[76] At the critical moment when the marchers were supposed to be a spectacle of order and strength, their participation as audience to the Soviet leaders created spontaneous disorder and confusion. The perfection of the parade broke down because of the tension between the competing goals of discipline and emotional transcendence.

While spontaneous awe of Stalin was celebrated by Soviet officials, cadres worked ceaselessly to eliminate other forms of spontaneity from parades. In 1938, a Party leader in Krasnopresnenskii District explicitly forbade friends and relatives of the marchers from out of town to join the October Revolution demonstration because "every participant must know how the demonstration is ordered."[77] This admonition shows that while marchers attempted to use the parade as an opportunity for socializing and visiting, Party officials viewed the demonstration as a display of Muscovite discipline.

This same Party official insisted:

> You must instruct people that no kind of costumes or disguises will be permitted in the columns because they often pervert and distort reality. People from Tambov, Riazan and other provincial people dress themselves up, and people who know everything in its real color, as it is, will say that they have never seen such ugliness. . . . In the column of demonstrators there will be people who are wearing national costumes, no one is forbidding this.[78]

The official celebrated the superiority of modern Muscovite workers over "backward" provincials to eliminate rural practices such as mummery from the parade. Only controlled "folk" customs such as wearing national costumes or performing dances were now permitted by Party officials. Spontaneous folk forms were unwelcome; this Moscow Party official did not encourage construction workers from the environs of Moscow who "walk around in bast sandals" to attend the parade.[79] The official's concern with preventing mummery, merry-making, and peasant clothing reveals that despite increasing control over the parade, Soviet citizens continued throughout the 1930s to introduce elements of rural culture and holiday practice into Soviet celebrations and invest Soviet holidays with personal and familial meanings. Spontaneity was not completely conquered and folk culture competed with that of modern Moscow.[80]

Like most other aspects of Soviet life, the organization of demonstrations was riddled with inefficiencies that transformed the ways that participants experienced them. For example, central authorities gave permission for the 1938 physical culture parade only two to three weeks in advance, causing "haste, superfluous spending of government funds, difficulties with supply."[81] While this problem was solved in 1939 with the designation of the second Saturday in August as Physical Culture Day, lack of preparation time fostered disorganization in the 1938 parade.

While marching in front of the tribune could be exciting for paraders, waiting for a turn to march rarely was. Valentina Bogdan, an engineer from Rostov who emigrated from the Soviet Union during World War II, described the demonstration as "a tedious and unpleasant task. We have to gather at our institution several hours in advance, they form us up into a column and they lead us to some little side-street where we wait our turn to go past the tribune on Theater Square."[82] Marching in the demonstration was, for Bogdan, a moment in which she clearly perceived the power of the Party members at her place of work, who compelled her to waste her time waiting on a back street. Although factory Party activists were criticized by district officials for assembling workers for the demonstration so early that the marchers became tired, cadres continued to err on the side of caution and force marchers to wait for hours.[83] The demand to organize a disciplined spectacle caused Soviet cadres to create conditions that dampened popular enthusiasm and popular mobilization.

The successful enactment of a demonstration required the discipline not only of the rank-and-file participants but also of Party and government cadres. For May 1st and October Revolution celebrations, the Party leaders of various institutions were supposed to "bring out" a certain number of workers, but it was difficult to mobilize demonstrators without consistent and sustained agitational work and the cooperation of the factory administration.[84] Many Soviet citizens would participate in demonstrations only when they were subject to the direct surveillance of Party cadres.[85] When such surveillance was weak, Soviet citizens exercised personal choice and did not appear for demonstrations. When overcommitted Party cadres failed to devote enough attention to the parade, its ranks were thinner.

The organization of parades could also interfere with factory production. When factory administrators decided to keep the factory in operation despite the holiday, Party cadres had difficulty filling the ranks of the demonstration.[86] When the choice was between going to work and going to the demonstration, however, workers might be more enthusiastic than usual about attending the demonstration.[87] The creation of a joyous mass affirmation of loyalty to the Soviet state sometimes necessitated the sacrifice of work productivity and always required the focused attention of Party cadres.

The behavior of Party cadres themselves during May 1st and November 7th demonstrations also affected the images of discipline and order that the parade produced. The files of the Party Committee of the Dinamo factory in Moscow revealed that Party workers were frequently chastised for their own indiscipline during demonstrations. Party members were punished for not showing up to the demonstration at all, for arriving late, for leaving early, for bringing alcohol to the demonstration, and for showing up so drunk that they had to be ejected from the parade.[88] Party cadres failed to produce order when they transgressed it themselves. This behavior on the part of Party cadres indicates the types of infractions that probably occurred even more frequently among non-Party workers, who were less concerned with upholding the policies of the state. The existence of a double standard of behavior soured worker-Party relations. As one cleaning woman from Moscow's Dinamo factory complained in May 1937, "They drive us to the demonstration but they don't go themselves."[89] Violations of parade discipline undermined both the image of a dedicated and disciplined Party and the legitimacy of local Party leaders.

During physical culture demonstrations, the very top ranks within the parade made mistakes and exhibited indiscipline. In the 1940 parade, a top physical culture official, V. V. Snegov, usurped the role of commander and issued the "illiterate" command, "march festively." The commander of the parade noted that "this time it was good that the commanders of the detachments showed indiscipline and did not carry out the unreasonable command."[90] Another Red Army commander refused to obey the head of the parade and delayed the march by two minutes. The commanders of the Republican delegations deliberately disobeyed orders to march close together because they "tried to show the face of their detachments and did not want to maintain [the proper] distance."[91] Confusion, indiscipline, and disobedience shaped the organization of the parade at the highest level as well as among the rank-and-file participants.

Because of the paranoid political atmosphere created by the purges, Party organizers were under a great deal of pressure not only to suppress disorder but also to ensure that no overtly anti-Soviet messages were transmitted by parades. Party organizers were directed to keep parade decorations under "political control" and make sure that enemies could not sabotage them.[92] In the minds of Soviet party officials, every slogan or portrait carried a message that could be easily subverted. Officials worried that even a misplaced comma could change the meaning of a slogan.[93] Party leaders themselves identified the parade as a site of dangerous communication and conspiracy and articulated how the parade could express messages of disloyalty.[94]

Party officials saw the hand of the enemy in every mistake, and because of the lack of qualified cadres and heightened vigilance, there was no shortage of real and imagined blunders. In preparation for May Day in 1934, a workers' club in Leningrad hung its May Day portrait of Stalin upside down, literally turning a symbol of respect for the leader into an "inversion" of power.[95] Badly executed portraits frequently made Soviet leaders unrecognizable or the objects of laughter. In connection with the purge of the All-Union Radio Committee in November 1936, Ia. A. Iakovlev, the director of the Agriculture Section of the Central Committee, denounced one of the announcers of the 1936 May Day parade. Reporting on the procession of a canine patrol unit through Red Square, the announcer said, "I am sorry that you cannot now see this touching spectacle: the well-trained dogs taking part in the parade."[96] Iakovlev interpreted this innocuous comment as a critique of the mindless discipline of the entire parade, and it is possible that other listeners did as well.

The purge trials also transformed the meaning of demonstrations in Red Square when some of the defendants at the Zinoviev-Kamenev trial were forced to confess that they planned to assassinate Stalin at the 1936 May Day parade. The trials suggested that the parade could thus turn into a "demonstration" of the ultimate disloyalty. At planning meetings for the International Youth Day demonstration in late August 1936, Moscow Party leaders anxiously discussed parade security. One Party leader from Kirov District warned, "We are in the second column from the mausoleum and we must take into account the court testimony of one of the traitors who declared, 'I did not shoot only because I was too far away from Stalin.'"[97] A Party leader from Krasnogvardeiskii District expressed his feeling of helplessness: "We are now talking about vigilance but is that any guarantee that some *svoloch'* (scum), excuse the expression, won't attempt something?"[98] Party leaders were afraid that if they did not organize the security of their columns carefully the whole district might be forbidden to march in the parade and they would then be in disgrace.[99] These comments reveal the instability of the demonstration's meaning in the minds of local officials. What was supposed to be a show of loyalty could suddenly become a manifesto of treachery and an attempt to overthrow the government.

The show trial defendants were probably forced to confess to an attempt on Stalin's life at a demonstration because the demonstration was one of the few places where anonymous Soviet citizens could have had access to Stalin. The lack of qualified artists to paint portraits of leaders and the low level of literacy among many Party and trade union propagandists guaranteed that at every demonstration there were bound to be at least some substandard portraits and illiterate slogans. The unintended consequences of claiming that an assassination attempt might have taken place at a demonstration or of calling every mistake in a portrait, slogan, or speech an intentional act of treachery was that Party leaders themselves created an alternative meaning of the demonstration as a site of chaos rather than of discipline.

Party cadres constantly juggled competing goals as they tried to create an ordered parade that encouraged the spontaneous emotions of the population toward their leaders but hindered other kinds of popular expression. The unofficial spontaneity that continued to permeate parades despite efforts to stamp it out, the many failures in discipline that marked the organization of the parade, and the official representations of indiscipline as disloyalty to the state multiplied the number of meanings that were constructed by Soviet parades. While parades celebrated the disciplined conformity of the individual to the collective, they were also sites of individual and non-conformist behavior that challenged Soviet discipline.

H. G. Friese, a Soviet university student in the 1930s who later emigrated to the West, described participating in demonstrations in his memoirs. He wrote, "Most of the [demonstration] participants—including Komsomol members—felt some inner resistance, something akin to embarrassment and humiliation, at the necessity of carrying 'Bolshevik icons.' . . . Sometimes one's sense of humiliation would suddenly give way to an opposite feeling—a sense of extreme pride and feverish enthusiasm."[100] This testimony reveals the complexity and contingency of the meanings of Soviet parades to their individual participants, despite their seeming uniformity. These parades were manifestations of the power of the state to impose social hierarchies and identities, but they were also sites of contested meaning as individuals sought to define their own status in a wide variety of ways. Many aspects of contestation in the parade served to reinforce Soviet power as officials tried to outdo each other in fulfilling the plan, individuals strove for personal excellence in their desire to capture Stalin's attention, or organizers co-opted the display of personal happiness as proof of the legitimacy of the state. Yet parades also produced moments when state officials publicly displayed their own insubordination, their fears, and their inability to create discipline. These incidents disrupted the production of the symbolic images of the "iconography of happiness" and created knowledge about the actual rather than symbolic workings of state power.

The parade organizers' attempts to construct images of equality clashed with their desire to represent order. The parade ultimately reflected a variety of hierarchies: men over women, center over periphery, Russians over non-Russians, Christians over Muslims, military over civilian, worker over peasant, city over countryside, Soviet culture over folk culture, and Stalin over all. These hierarchies defined the territory and sovereignty of the Soviet Union and the legitimacy of its leaders.

3

IMAGINING THE MOTHERLAND
THE CELEBRATION OF SOVIET AVIATION
AND POLAR EXPLOITS

While Soviet demonstrations sought to define the Soviet Union and to mobilize citizens to support the country and its leaders by physically including them in a tangible community of marchers, Arctic and aviation celebrations tried to achieve these goals by appealing to the imaginations of citizens and their desires for adventure. When Valerii Chkalov, the "Russian Lindbergh,"[1] flew across the North Pole to America or Arctic explorer Ivan Papanin spent nine months drifting on an ice floe, they captured the attention and the devotion of the Soviet public. As in Europe and America in the early twentieth century, Soviet aviation and polar exploits of the 1930s were closely tied to the articulation of national identities and to the creation of popular nationalism or patriotism.[2] The Soviet state celebrated these heroic exploits in part to create a geographically and ideologically based Soviet identity.[3]

Soviet authorities sought to create an "imagined community" in the way that Benedict Anderson has described, through the dissemination of print and other kinds of media across a defined geographic space.[4] The widespread celebration of aviation exploits was used as proof of the close and organic connections among distant parts of the Soviet Union. The celebrations projected an image of the Soviet Union as a harmonious and inclusive community in which every Soviet citizen had the potential and the opportunity to excel in his or her chosen field and become a hero. It is obvious that this mythic harmony, equality, and universal heroism did not exist in Soviet reality. It is worth examining, however, how a discourse that was intended to celebrate harmony and equality also revealed the contradictions, tensions, fractures, and fault lines of life in the Soviet Union in the 1930s.

Arctic and aviation celebrations revealed tensions about questions of authority and legitimacy. In the Soviet context, unlike the European or American one, the definition of the Soviet Union and its heroes was inextricably linked to the affirmation of the legitimacy of the Soviet state and its leaders. Leadership during heroic adventures modeled how legitimate authority in the Soviet Union was supposed to work. Interactions between the Soviet people and heroes represented the ideal relationship between Soviet citizens and authority figures. Celebrations also defined the Soviet Union's territorial legitimacy by delineating the geographic boundaries of Soviet authority and creating symbolic images of the country to which citizens should be loyal. Thus the relationships of heroes, leaders, and citizens in aviation and Arctic celebrations reveal how Soviet ideologues depicted the bonds that united the diverse peoples and vast territories of the Soviet Union into one country under the leadership of Stalin and the Communist Party.[5] A close reading of the celebrations' definitions of legitimate authority reveals the complexities of hierarchical rule in a supposedly egalitarian state. Encoded within the symbolic definitions of the Soviet Union is a justification for the use of force both to defend and to subdue the country.

Despite the attempts of Soviet Arctic and aviation narratives to be all-inclusive, they revealed who was excluded from the Soviet community. Gender is a key category for exploring inclusion in and exclusion from the Soviet community.[6] The gendered imagery of the Soviet Union as the motherland was a crucial part of the way that Arctic and aviation celebrations represented inclusion in the geographic and symbolic Soviet communities and imagined the bonds between citizens and the Soviet land. The symbolic depiction of the motherland in aviation and Arctic celebrations also illuminates the dominance of the masculinized center over the feminized periphery and the masculinized city over the feminized countryside. Both male and female Arctic and aviation heroes were celebrated in accordance with Soviet claims of gender equality. The different ways that narratives included male and female heroes in the Soviet community illustrate hierarchies of gender and the ways in which women's power was circumscribed in the 1930s.

Nationality is another category that provides insight into inclusion in the Soviet community in the 1930s. On a symbolic level, nationality, like gender, was extremely important in the construction of the Soviet motherland as a legitimate multinational state. Yet the narratives of Arctic and aviation celebrations did not embrace all nationalities on Soviet territory as fully Soviet. The interactions between Europeans and native peoples of the Far North in aviation and Arctic celebrations illustrate hierarchies of nationality and reveal the boundaries of the label "Soviet."

A third tension in Arctic and aviation celebrations concerns the supposed perfection of the Soviet heroes who were to gain mastery over the land and people of the Soviet community. The conquest of nature in heroic and record-breaking endeavors was not guaranteed, and these achievements often came at the cost of human lives. Accidents and failures during Arctic and aviation celebrations reveal the complexities of depicting real men and women as mythic heroes and the limits of Soviet control over nature.

Soviet Discourse Creates
the Soviet Union

The history of Arctic and aviation exploits in the 1930s was punctuated by disasters and dramatic rescues as well as by great achievements. In 1933, the *Cheliuskin* expedition, headed by Otto Shmidt, attempted to cross the northern sea route in one navigational season but became trapped in the ice. In February 1934, the ship was crushed by pack ice and sank, leaving 104 Soviet men and women stranded on an ice floe. The Soviet government organized a dramatic rescue by air in March and April and the seven aviators who saved the Cheliuskinians were decorated as the first "Heroes of the Soviet Union." The rescue of the Cheliuskinians was the first of a series of spectacular aviation and Arctic feats that the Soviet government transformed into mass public celebrations.

Public attention then turned to record-breaking aviators such as Valerii Chkalov, who flew across the Soviet Union from Moscow to Udd Island in July 1936. The next summer, as Stalin's purges intensified, publicity surrounding aviation exploits reached its peak. While some scholars have suggested that these aviation achievements were intended to divert attention from the purges, these record-breaking flights of international significance were also timed to coincide with the Paris International Exhibition.[7] In June of 1937, Soviet pilots landed four airplanes at the North Pole. They left Arctic explorer Ivan Papanin and his crew on the drift ice to conduct scientific experiments. In July, Chkalov and Boris Gromov made historic flights across the North Pole to the United States. In August, however, Sigismund Levanevskii was lost over the North Pole in his attempt to repeat this feat.

In February 1938, a second polar rescue was prominently featured in the Soviet news media. Papanin and three other polar explorers were recovered near the coast of Greenland after their ice floe began to break apart. Later that year, female aviators Valentina Grizodubova, Polina Osipenko, and Marina Raskova broke a world distance record. Unfortunately, their plane, the *Rodina*, ran out of fuel short of its planned destination, and the crew had to parachute to safety. The three heroines were stranded in the taiga for several days before they were located and rescued by other "heropilots." In 1939, pilot Vladimir Kokkinaki crash-landed in Canada on his way to the New York World's Fair. His highly publicized and embarrassing failure to break the world long-distance record and Europe's drift toward war ended this era of aviation and Arctic exploits.[8]

Because aviation and Arctic celebrations were a means of imagining and describing a unified Soviet country, they emphasized transportation across the Soviet Union and communication among Soviet citizens. The technology of aviation in reality gave Soviet authorities greater access to remote areas, and narratives about aviation discursively connected Moscow with the Arctic and Far East by tracing heroic exploits and victorious returns. Celebrations emphasized how advanced communication techniques such as telegrams, radio, film, and high-circulation print media spread heroic narratives across the entire country.

Attempts to bring the vast geographic area of the Soviet Union closer together played a crucial legitimating function. One of the most profound problems facing the Soviet state in the 1930s was the weakness of local administration. While authorities imagined a nation where directives would easily travel to their local destinations and instantly be carried out, the reality was much more chaotic. The creation of a myth of perfect communication over vast distances was crucial in maintaining the legitimacy of a state that failed to govern outlying regions effectively.[9]

Aviation and polar celebrations received a great deal of attention in the central press and radio, and Soviet authorities carefully monitored press coverage and other publications.[10] Newspaper correspondents accompanied all of the major polar expeditions. When Papanin and his men were left on the ice floe, they themselves became special correspondents for *Pravda, Izvestiia, Komsomolskaia Pravda*, and other local newspapers. They were barraged with requests for articles about their lives on the ice floe.[11] In his documentary film about three pilot-heroines, director Dziga Vertov constructed film collages of ordinary Soviet citizens reading about the pilots in their newspapers. These scenes showed "average" Soviet citizens eagerly following the fate of the pilots in the course of their rescue.[12] At least some Soviet citizens avidly followed the fate of Soviet pilots in the newspapers. A 1937 letter to Chkalov's wife from an economist at a machine tractor station in Uzbekistan explained that "in remote Kishlak, the central newspapers arrive on the sixth day," but he wanted her to know that "distant Uzbekistan is not indifferent to the name and deeds of Valerii Pavlovich."[13] This official, Netrebenko, had a Slavic surname and was a representative of Soviet power in Uzbekistan. While Netrebenko's statement that Chkalov was popular among Uzbeks may be questioned, it is clear that through the commemoration of an aviation feat, at least this Soviet official celebrated his own inclusion in a Soviet community, despite the thousands of kilometers that separated him from Moscow.

Because aviation and Arctic rescues were celebrated while in progress, these news events were like penny-press serial novels or radio soap operas. Each day the newspapers and radio reports brought the latest installment of the adventure, and the final outcome was not yet known.[14] A teacher wrote in the visitor's book of a 1938 museum exhibition on the Arctic that it

> reminded me again of the time when we did not sleep nights, awaiting the return of the Papanintsy, who are dear to all of us. All of the adults and children, in all of the distant and remote corners of the country, waited to hear news on the radio; I remember how my three little children woke up

in the night to hear the latest news about the Papanintsy. It is impossible
to describe the happiness of the elderly, the children, and all citizens, when
they were saved.[15]

This testimony revealed the power of the unfinished adventures to fasci-
nate a loyal Soviet cadre who explicitly identified being happy about the
Papanin rescue with having a Soviet identity. This teacher used the Papanin
expedition to imagine herself as part of a unified Soviet country.

Graphic artists, photographers, and cameramen also accompanied
major polar and aviation expeditions and recorded their heroic returns.[16]
Noted directors such as Dziga Vertov produced both documentary films
and dramatizations of heroic aviation feats.[17] Newsreels brought Soviet
citizens to the Arctic, over the Pole, to the Far East, and back again to Moscow. The showing of these films made the physical reality of the celebratory
journey to Moscow visually accessible to people in other parts of the Soviet Union. Soviet film audiences could vicariously travel across the Soviet
Union into Moscow, along Moscow's most famous street, and, ultimately,
to the gates of the most important geographic location in the Soviet Union,
the Kremlin. This kind of visual pilgrimage helped to promote Moscow as
the center of the Soviet nation.

Newsreels also demonstrated model responses to Arctic exploits. A 1935
newsreel showed kindergarten children playing *Cheliuskin*. One child acted
as Captain Voronin steering the ship, another played Shmidt, and a third
was a cameraman taking pictures of the scene. The rest of the children
moved supplies off the sinking *Cheliuskin*. The narrator of the newsreel
proudly announced, "The heroic epic of the *Cheliuskin* has become a beloved children's game."[18] By filming children playing *Cheliuskin*, Soviet
propagandists tried to show that Soviet children recognized the importance of the *Cheliuskin* and integrated Soviet heroes into their daily lives.
The children who viewed the newsreel were expected to imitate the actions of the children pictured.

Collective radio listening was another way in which the distant parts
of the nation were drawn together by communications technology. Local
Party organizations in all parts of the Soviet Union organized meetings at
which Soviet citizens would listen to important radio broadcasts from
Moscow. Ivan Papanin's diary also demonstrated the importance of radio
communication in bringing important Moscow events and celebrations to
the rest of the Soviet Union. The four Soviet men on an ice floe "listen[ed]
avidly" to the radio on the morning of November 7, 1937, in order to hear
the military parade on Red Square that marked the twentieth anniversary
of the October Revolution. They heard the Kremlin chimes, the hooves of
Budennyi's horse, his report to Voroshilov, and Voroshilov's speech. They
were rewarded by hearing Voroshilov call their expedition a "great victory." At midnight on New Year's Eve, the Papaninites turned on their
radio to hear the traffic on Red Square, the Kremlin chimes, and the "In-

ternationale."[19] The great Moscow holiday ritual of the military parade and the audible symbol of the center, the Kremlin chimes, were thus made accessible to anyone, anywhere in the Soviet Union, who was within reach of a radio.

On the occasion of the Papaninites' six-month anniversary on the ice floe, the Moscow Radio Committee prepared a special program in their honor which included greetings from their wives, a concert by the popular Utesov jazz band, a radiogram from Papanin to his Petrozavodsk electorate (Papanin was a candidate in the December 1937 elections for the Supreme Soviet), and a speech from Petrozavodsk in response. By listening to this broadcast, citizens around the Soviet Union could hear what the explorers' wives had to say to them and listen to praise of the great deeds of "the northernmost citizens" of the Soviet Union.[20] The listeners became part of a network of national communication that included Moscow, Leningrad, the Arctic, and Petrozavodsk.

In October 1938, people in Vladivostok heard radio broadcasts of the ceremony welcoming the crew of the *Rodina* to Moscow. The heroines, who had recently set off from that city, were now in Moscow, but the citizens of Vladivostok could still take part in the celebratory events. That a broadcast of the celebration could be heard in the Far East affirmed the propaganda theme that Moscow's influence reached the Pacific. This theme took on an added significance in October 1938, because Moscow's control of the Far East had been challenged only two months earlier when the Soviets clashed with the Japanese over the borders of the Soviet Union at Lake Khasan.

The final words of a newspaper report about the Vladivostok broadcast noted that "the audibility of the broadcast was good."[21] That this fact needed to be reported pointed to the unfortunate problem that good radio reception could not yet be taken for granted and that Moscow's transmission of propaganda to the Far East and other parts of the country was not always successful for technical reasons. Despite claims of bringing "culture" to the entire Soviet population, access to film and radio in the Soviet countryside was circumscribed by the Soviet Union's limited material resources. The vivid sounds and images of Moscow as the center of the nation reached urban and Russian audiences much more frequently than they reached other parts of the Soviet Union.[22] While radio broadcasts about aviation and Arctic adventures celebrated a united nation, their impact, particularly in the periphery, was limited by lack of access to radio sets. While Russian-speaking cities had at most 40 to 50 radios per thousand inhabitants, Russian villages had only 4 to 6.5 per thousand and national republics and districts about 8 to 10 per thousand.[23] The opportunities to imagine a national community were thus most numerous in Russian-speaking cities.

While the teacher and the head of the machine tractor station envisioned themselves as a part of the Soviet community through polar and aviation exploits, other Soviet cadres could not. For example, only one out of five Party members at a political discussion in Saratov Territory in September 1936 had heard of Chkalov's flight to Udd Island or of the pilots who were named Heroes of the Soviet Union after the *Cheliuskin* expedition.[24] While pilots and Arctic explorers were extremely prominent in the Soviet media, many Soviet citizens were beyond the reach of Soviet film, radio, and newspapers. These citizens did not have opportunities to construct a Soviet identity based on aviation and Arctic exploits.

Those who did receive the state's message about aviators and polar explorers through the media reacted in a variety of different ways. The reminiscences of one Soviet boy suggest that although some Soviet children pretended they were Soviet heroes, Soviet propagandists might not always have approved of the results; a fourteen-year-old Soviet boy explained, "In our yard, we play at the flight of the ANT 25, and at being Chkalov, Baidukov, and Beliakov, but it always ends in a fight because everybody wants to be Chkalov."[25] The fact that Chkalov was more popular than other aviation heroes turned a game that was supposed to glorify Soviet collective achievements into a quarrel about individual status.

The game remembered by author Mikhail Alekseev in his autobiographical novel *Drachuny* (*The Ruffians*) showed that the enormous difference in prestige between hero and victim created tensions for children playing *Cheliuskin*. After their local river froze over, the children of Alekseev's village set up a camp and called it the *Cheliuskin*. Then, "All day we rescued the girls, whom we insisted had to play the role of passengers of the 'sinking ship.' The boys were, of course, the pilots. Since the idea for this serious game came from me, I got the right to pick the name of a hero-pilot first."[26] Just as the identification of Soviet heroes reflected hierarchies in Soviet society, so also playing at heroes revealed hierarchies in the children's society. Children playing at *Cheliuskin* or other such games may have started out by adopting officially sanctioned ideals of heroism and community, but in play they transformed these models to fit their own social worlds. The results were the adoption of a variety of fluid identities loosely based on official culture. By encouraging children's play on patriotic themes, Soviet officials invited a spontaneity that could substantially transform the state's goals.

Letters to Soviet heroes also revealed a variety of responses to their achievements. Some echoed the language of the central press, lauding the pilots as Stalin's sons who "are capable at any moment and under any circumstances of fearlessly repulsing the enemy," while others were written in a more personal language.[27] An aspiring geologist wrote to aviator A. Beliakov, who flew with Chkalov over the North Pole to the United States in 1937. She told him of her dreams of heroic work, affirming her readiness to endure difficult conditions in the Kolyma region. She concluded, "This letter is the tribute of my generation to your courage, which I cannot help but give. But it is addressed personally to you Aleksandr

Vasil'evich, do not let anyone else read it."[28] The letter-writer sought to create an intimate personal relationship between herself and the pilot based on their common dedication to heroic labor. For this geology student, the celebration of aviation achievements had acquired a deeply personal, inspirational, and probably romantic meaning. Inspired by her personal connection to Beliakov, this student promised to bring Soviet science to distant Kolyma.

While those who felt included in the Soviet community could gain inspiration from the Arctic pilots, those who considered themselves already excluded could have an entirely different reaction. The diary of a peasant who had been imprisoned as a *kulak* contained a scathing critique of the 1937 landing of explorers on the North Pole:

> They'll slide around on the ice up there, pocket their extra travel money, run up an incredible expense account and fly on home, where the fools will shower them with flowers, and as a result the state will have to increase its budgeted expenses for scientific discoveries and add a kopeck or two to what they charge the poor slobs who don't go up in airplanes. What is there to gain from sliding around on the thick polar ice? If you ask me, not a thing. But bragging, portraits, the names of great men in the newspapers, no shortages here. Well, let them amuse themselves.[29]

For this observer, the aviation exploits epitomized the hierarchy and inequalities of the Soviet Union. "Poor slobs" or ordinary working men and women were forced to pay for the grand and ultimately useless exploits. The pilots and explorers became famous and rich, but the disenfranchised people gained nothing. The extent to which the celebration of Soviet aviation and Arctic feats made people feel as if they belonged to a Soviet community varied widely. Some Soviet citizens remained beyond the reach of celebrations. Others responded to the aviators in a personal manner, defining their communities in ways other than the Soviet government intended. Still others completely rejected the vision of community that Arctic and aviation celebrations offered.

Gendering the Soviet Union

Aviation and polar achievements played a crucial role in creating a new symbolic geography of the Soviet Union in the 1930s. A central aspect of this new geography was the gendering of the Soviet land as the "motherland." The notion of motherland, which had been commonly invoked in pre-revolutionary patriotic culture, disappeared from Soviet official discourse during the 1920s but re-emerged in the mid-1930s. Despite the fact that the word *rodina* is gendered female in Russian and was therefore already understood as motherland, in the late 1930s the word "mother" was sometimes appended to motherland, making it even more explicit that the

Soviet land was the mother of her citizens.[30] The official discourse of the mid-1930s embraced several concepts that had been rejected in the 1920s, including nationalism, an emphasis on traditional family structures and gender roles, and pro-natalism. The image of the motherland combined nationalist and traditional family discourse in the definition of the nation. Through this gendering of the country, Soviet ideologues attempted to foster patriotism by creating an emotional attachment to the Soviet land. Arctic and aviation celebrations depicted the Soviet motherland by demonstrating familial relationships between heroes, citizens, and the country.

The notion of motherland also affected how the territory of the Soviet Union was imagined. James von Geldern has argued that in the 1930s, representations of the Soviet Union expanded its social and geographical boundaries to include vast expanses of the country that had been excluded during the Cultural Revolution. The periphery was no longer characterized as savage and hostile, and folk cultures were no longer portrayed as backward.[31] Representations of the motherland in Arctic and aviation celebrations emphasized inclusivity and tamed nature to display the submission of the entire country to Soviet rule. Aviation and Arctic celebrations and other Soviet cultural production created an image of the motherland as an entity to love and to dominate.

The image of the motherland created a link between the country and the family. As Katerina Clark has shown in her work on socialist realism, one of the central myths of the Soviet Union in the 1930s was that of the "great family."[32] Soviet publicists often represented the Soviet Union as a family with Stalin as grand patriarch and the Soviet people as Stalin's children. A song of this era, for example, represented the Soviet republics as "eleven sisters" in the Soviet family. The only maternal image, however, was the country itself, the motherland. Stalin's "fatherly concern" was complemented by the care of a personified motherland who gave her children everything "like a tender and concerned mother."[33]

In 1936, the "Song of the Motherland" from the movie musical *Circus* became the unofficial anthem of the Soviet Union. This song was ubiquitous in the late 1930s. Pilot Polina Osipenko reported, for example, that she and fellow pilot Valentina Grizodubova sang this song to keep their spirits up after they crash-landed in the taiga and were lost.[34] The song declared:

> Broad is my native land. / It has many forests, fields and rivers. / I don't know of any other country / Where a man breathes so freely.
>
> From Moscow to the very borders, / From the southern mountains to the northern seas, / A man walks as the master, / of his immense motherland. . . .
>
> But we will knit our brows severely, / If the enemy wants to break us. / We love the motherland as we would our bride. / We protect her as we would our affectionate mother.[35]

The poet and composer defined the Soviet nation through its natural beauty and geographical features such as forests, fields, and rivers. This emphasis on nature reinforced the notion that the Soviet land was gendered female. The song also mapped out the political geography of the nation by identifying the capital city of Moscow and the borders of the Soviet state as significant symbolic locations.[36]

The "Song of the Motherland" created an intimate relationship between male citizens and the female nation by declaring "we love the motherland as we would a bride." The introduction of this song in the film *Circus* reinforced the romantic connection between the Soviet "everyman" and the motherland.[37] The handsome Soviet hero who has just returned from the military, Martynov, teaches the song to the film's heroine, American circus performer Marion Dixon, as he plays the piano and she sits on top of it. The placement of the actors suggests the singing of a love song, and during this musical interlude Martynov and Dixon realize that they are in love. After several plot twists, the two lovers are united and sing the song again as they march triumphantly in the May Day parade on Red Square. After panning the crowd, the camera focuses on Martynov as he turns to his "bride" and sings the line, "we love the motherland as we would a bride." The relationship of the two film characters symbolizes the emotional commitment of the Soviet man to his motherland.

The protagonist of the "Song of the Motherland" took pride in his freedom to explore and feel at home in all corners of the motherland. As the *khoziain* (master) of the motherland, he was her owner and husband and also her defender should the enemy attack. The song thus articulated a contract with Soviet male citizens, promising them mastery of the motherland in exchange for her defense.

The celebration of Arctic and aviation exploits helped to define the motherland as nature that could be mastered by Soviet citizens. Aviation and Arctic adventures extended the motherland by proving that the Arctic and the Far East were *rodnye* (native) to Soviets. Even inhospitable ice floes could become native to the Cheliuskinians. According to one member of the expedition, the support and guidance of members of the Party "made the drifting ice beneath them as firm as the solid land of our native country."[38] The treacherous ice on which the Cheliuskinians stood became harmless because of their Communist convictions. When Soviet navigator Marina Raskova was lost in the taiga for ten days, she asked herself: "What was there to be afraid of? Was this not her own, native, Soviet soil, the soil of her own country?"[39] The implication was that the "soil of her own country" could not hurt her. When Ginkin, a mechanic on the North Pole expedition, was told by his commandant that if he volunteered for the expedition he would be risking his life, he said, "I was very much perplexed. What sort of a place was it in the Soviet Union where I could lose my head? There wasn't such a place."[40] Arctic and aviation heroes were inspired to achieve great deeds on the territory of their motherland. By virtue of their Soviet identities, they claimed almost supernatural power to conquer the elements in their native land.[41]

An animated cartoon for children about the adventures of the three pilot-heroines in the Far East, *Friends in the Taiga,* emphasized the pilots' connection to nature by depicting how the animals of the taiga helped the heroines to collect the supplies that were parachuted down to them. The airlifted "presents of the motherland" reflected the care and concern of the country for the pilots, and the help of the animals showed that the Far Eastern taiga was a tamed and friendly part of the Soviet land.[42] Arctic and aviation discourse defined all parts of the motherland as safe, secure, and nurturing places that did not hold any dangers for their citizens.

The representations of the Soviet Union as a nurturing mother yielding everything to her children and Stalin as pater familias suggest that the power dynamics between Stalin and his country were like those of a husband and wife in a patriarchal social order. During collectivization, when the Soviet state used violence to extract grain from the countryside and to gain control of the fruits of the land, Soviet propaganda began to depict peasants as female much more often. As sociologist Victoria Bonnell has pointed out, this "feminization" of the countryside showed the hierarchy of urban over rural Russia.[43] The famous statue by Vera Mukhina, *Worker and Collective Farm Woman,* also represented rural Russia as feminine. This symbolic depiction of the Soviet Union showed the marriage of city and countryside, the marriage of Soviet citizens to the motherland. In these "traditional" marriages, the husband had control over the fertility of the wife and the reproduction of the family. Von Geldern argues that the new social geography of the Soviet Union in the 1930s helped to foster social stability through inclusivity.[44] These more peaceful nurturing and female images of the Soviet countryside emerged, however, only after it was subjugated to the Soviet state through collectivization. The symbolic marriages of Stalin and Soviet male citizens to the motherland showed their power over the country.

The Pilgrimage to Moscow

After each heroic feat, aviators and Arctic explorers made their way across the Soviet Union for a triumphant return to Moscow. Their progress through the Soviet Union helped to construct the symbolic geography of the country by showing the physical and emotional bonds that linked the country together. Both the Cheliuskinians in 1934 and the pilot-heroines in 1938 traveled by train from Vladivostok to Moscow and participated in dozens of local receptions en route. The return voyages of the Cheliuskinians and the pilot-heroines marked the distance "from Moscow to the very borders" of the nurturing and controlled motherland. The pilot Ivan Doronin,

Scene from *Days in the Tiaga*. From *Soviet Films, 1938–1939* (1939).

who rescued the Cheliuskinians, explained, "We traveled right across our country, and the country applauded us. Our train united all stations on the line, large and small."[45] It was the passage of the heroes across the railroad line that transformed the individual towns into a united country. A poem dedicated to the pilot-heroines described their journey: "From mile to mile, from Kerbi to the Kremlin, *Sovetskaia zemlia* (the Soviet land) brought forth flowers to meet them."[46] The fertile Soviet earth of the entire country gave blossoms to the heroines just as it was expected to yield grain and sovereignty to the Soviet authorities. The participants were depicted as traveling through a united, fertile, and loyal countryside.

In their descriptions of celebratory meetings en route from Vladivostok to Moscow, publicists emphasized the emotions of citizens. *Pravda* reported that the three pilot-heroines "were greeted by tens of thousands of Soviet citizens. They came to the pilots' train, congratulated them on their victory, and spoke to them about their feelings of love and admiration. They asked them to give their warm regards to Comrade Stalin—inspiration for all of the heroic deeds of Soviet people."[47] Just as lyrics of the "Song of the Motherland" sought to translate emotional attachment to the Soviet land into willingness to defend it, the central press described the enthusiasm for the heroines in emotional terms and then displaced these emotions onto other aspects of Soviet life. Newspaper articles translated love and admiration for the three aviators into love for Stalin and linked their achievements to the successes of the October Revolution.[48]

The Soviet press described meetings between both male and female heroes and the population as charged with emotion. One Cheliuskinian noted that each of the local communities they visited on the way to Moscow "had something distinguishing it from all the others, but in one thing they were all alike—in the warm comradely feeling and love shown."[49] This emotion affected both citizens and heroes. A carpenter from the expedition reported: "At meetings in Petropavlovsk, in Vladivostok, . . . the previously illiterate carpenters in vain tried to hide their tears of joy."[50] Aviator Vasilii Molokov confessed that at a reception in Vladivostok, "I got away aft to hide the upset which had taken hold of me. We had not quite understood just what we had done in the Arctic."[51] Doronin explained:

> At one tiny halt near Sverdlovsk an old collective farmer came up to me and clapped me on the shoulder and said, "Fine, lad, oh, fine!" And there were tears in his eyes. I doubt whether I was ever so moved in my whole life as at that moment. I felt I had so much to tell that old man. But I was too moved to speak.[52]

In this case it was the aged collective farmer who held back tears while Doronin became speechless with emotion. The power of these emotions was conveyed by the weeping of heroic men who tried manfully to hide their tears.[53] The achievements of Soviet heroes were supposed to be felt rather than thought about and to transform even the most masculine, heroic, and courageous Soviet citizens into spontaneous, fiercely emotional Soviet patriots.

These gatherings mobilized local populations to celebrate Soviet achievements and to experience the presence of Soviet heroes in their own localities. The luminaries thus forged a link between the communities they visited and the centralized state in Moscow. By energetically welcoming the heroes, local officials demonstrated the loyalty and submission of their communities to Moscow and their eagerness to participate in Soviet public culture. Moscow was thus a constant presence in the discourse of the celebratory journey.

The Cheliuskinians wrote to Stalin:

> Tomorrow we will be in Moscow. Tomorrow we will stand upon the soil of the capital of our great motherland. From the ice of the Sea of Chukotsk, saved by the steel birds of the five year plan, we have passed across one third of the earth. And so from Chukotsk, Kamchatka, the Far East, from Siberia and the Urals, we find ourselves in Moscow, where the Central Committee of our Party works, where our government works, where you live and work, our dear and beloved leader who is always close to us.[54]

The Cheliuskinians' voyage confirmed that the "one third of the earth" across which they had traveled was Soviet land, rightfully governed by Stalin and the Party. As they neared the capital, the pilot-heroines also wrote a greeting to their "native Moscow," calling it the "heart and brain" of the great fatherland of workers. Echoing the "Song of the Motherland," they emphasized that it was from Moscow that they had set out, "to fly past the mountains, plains, rivers and lakes of the immense country."[55] The heroines' great deeds were inspired in Moscow but encompassed the entire expanse of the Soviet Union.[56]

In his autobiography, Cheliuskinian Peter Buiko identified the image of Moscow as a source of inspiration at a time of extreme difficulty. After being taken off of the ice floe by airplane, Buiko was trapped in a blizzard as he traveled by sledge from Cape Onman to the Soviet outpost at Wellen. As he walked on "a purgatorial path over masses of broken-up, glass-like sheets of ice," he mused,

> What can a man think of in such moments? When our feet managed to pick on a smoothish floe, the Red Square in the sunlight came to our minds. And it was worth striving, worth forcing the pace, to see that again. We forced the pace, and still forced it. . . . Moscow! Red Square! Sunlight! . . . . Hurrah for the mainland, for the shore, for our coast, for our Soviet Union.[57]

In this passage, the vision of Red Square provided Buiko with the strength he needed to survive. Smooth ice was transformed by his imagination into the holy and perhaps even heavenly ground of Red Square in Moscow, and this vision enabled him to endure in his struggle with the elements. Buiko's victory over nature also allowed him to assert that this distant Arctic territory was controlled by Moscow.

When the heroes finally arrived in Moscow, their victorious return to the place that inspired all great deeds had a ritualized ceremonial form. On October 27, 1938, Grizodubova, Osipenko, and Raskova returned to Moscow after they successfully exceeded the women's international straight line distance record by 1,500 kilometers in their plane, the *Rodina*. [58] Here is how *Pravda* described the heroines' homecoming:

> On the platform of the railway station, an honor guard of prominent aviators forms up to welcome the pilot-heroines. The aviators stand silently in formation, looking out into the distance. . . . Relatives of the pilots with big bouquets of flowers walk along the carpet covering the entire railway platform.
>
> Among those meeting the pilot-heroines are L. M. Kaganovich, N. S. Khrushchev . . . and Heroes of the Soviet Union, Papanin, Gromov, Chkalov, Shmidt, and Molokov. . . . The long-awaited heroines hurriedly leave the train. Relatives and people bearing flowers step aside as Valentina Grizodubova and Marina Raskova rush to their children. All are moved by this touching meeting with the children.

The crew of the *Rodina.* From *Soviet Aviation* (1939).

>   Comrade Kaganovich hugs and kisses Valentina Grizodubova, Polina
>   Osipenko and Marina Raskova. Then the pilots fall into the arms of their
>   relatives and friends.
>
>   Valentina Grizodubova receives the report of the commander of the
>   honor guard and the pilots move to the square where thousands are await-
>   ing their appearance. . . .
>
>   The commander of the *Rodina,* V. S. Grizodubova, gives a speech. . . .
>   She speaks loudly, passionately, as if she wishes to invest each word with
>   the strength of her feelings, all of her gratitude for the help, the attention,
>   the warmth, the kindness, which surrounded the pilots from the first day
>   of their flight.
>
>   The meeting is over. . . . The pilots and their families get into automo-
>   biles that rush along a decorated and joyous Gorkii Street toward the Krem-
>   lin where the heroines are to meet with the leaders of the Party and gov-
>   ernment.[59]

In this description of the celebration there is a tension between militarized
discipline and emotional spontaneity. The event was depicted as both a
controlled, ordered, militarized ceremony and an emotional reunion of
endangered mothers with their children and other family members.[60]

The "ordered" elements of the celebration, including official speeches, the honor guard's solemn stance, and its report to Valentina Grizodubo-va, suggest the connections between this celebration and the crucial theme of national defense. The ceremony affirmed the idea of a military chain of command, since it was the commander of the *Rodina*, Grizodubova, who formally recognized the honor guard and spoke to the public on behalf of the crew. She proclaimed, "If the enemy dares to attack our sacred borders, we will wipe them off the face of the earth."[61] The celebration also reflected the standards of discipline expected of the Soviet military: the honor guard stood at attention while the relatives spontaneously rushed forward with bouquets. The pilots were honored for successfully following orders un-der the most difficult conditions.

The celebration highlighted the patriotism of Soviet women; a greet-ing sent to the aviators from the editorial board of the journal *Woman Worker* called the pilots the "daughters of the motherland" and claimed that "in our country nothing is dearer than the interests of the native land."[62] The celebration emphasized that the women of the Soviet Union were ready, willing, and able to participate in the defense of their country, and that the enemy in a future war would have to contend with the mobilization of the entire Soviet population.

The emotional and spontaneous elements of the celebration stemmed from the women's roles as mothers; demonstrative family reunions played a critical role in the ceremony. The sequence of events after the women left the train reveals a hierarchy in the definition of family. The first and most important reunion for Grizodubova and Raskova was with their children. Next Kaganovich hugged and kissed them in an "official-familial" greet-ing. Only then were the pilots reunited with rest of their families. The rela-tionships of the women to their husbands and their biological, rather than spiritual, parents were acknowledged, but they were the least significant in the symbolic ordering of the celebration.

The relationship of the heroines with their children played a crucial role throughout the day. Grizodubova held her son Sokolik (little falcon) when she appeared at the podium to give her speech. She thus represented both military commander and devoted mother, both a disciplined defender of the Soviet borders and a loving woman emotionally transported by her reunion with the little child who she feared she might never see again. This emphasis on motherhood coincided with the state's adoption of pro-natalist policies in the mid-1930s.[63] At the Kremlin reception later in the day, the children remained at the center of the activities and were seated between Stalin, Molotov, and Voroshilov.[64]

The tension between order and emotion within this celebration paral-lels an opposition that Katerina Clark has argued is the defining character-istic of any socialist-realist plot: the spontaneity/consciousness dialectic.[65] According to Clark, in socialist-realist aviation plots, the aviators, Stalin's sons, are spontaneous daredevils who are successful because they gain a measure of political consciousness through the tutelage of father Stalin.[66] When the most popular Soviet pilot, Valerii Chkalov, returned to Moscow after his flight to the Far East in August 1936, the central moment in the ceremony was not his reunion with his son, but his reunion with "father" Stalin. Like the relatives of the *Rodina* pilots, Chkalov's wife and family waited in the background while the symbolic father and heroic son were reunited. When Chkalov rushed toward Stalin to give him an official report of the flight, the two embraced and kissed instead, thus resolving the tension between order and emotion.[67]

While this same tension existed in the "plot" of the women pilots, the women were not depicted as daredevils; instead their spontaneity stemmed directly from their identities as women and mothers. Through political consciousness, they overcame their feminine and maternal natures. By focusing on spontaneous maternal emotion, this celebration represented a gendered variation of the fictional master plot of Soviet society. It produced meanings both because of its connections to a familiar pattern and because of the pilots' unique identities as mothers.

While Kaganovich was the highest-ranking official that met the female pilots in October 1938, Stalin and the entire Politbiuro welcomed the re-

Mal'tsev, *Meeting the Heroic Crew.* From *Russkaia istoricheskaia zhivopis'* (1939).

Ticker-tape parade for North Pole pilots. From *Soviet Aviation* (1939).

turning members of the all-male North Pole expedition at Tushino Airport near Moscow in June 1937. According to *Pravda* correspondent Lazar Brontman, "The members of the expedition passed from embrace to embrace. Stalin, Molotov and Voroshilov congratulated, embraced and kissed each member of the expedition in turn."[68] After the obligatory political meeting at the airport, the airmen took part in a "triumphal procession" through Moscow to the Kremlin in cars decorated with flowers. Brontman described the scene: "Stalin, Molotov, Kaganovich, Voroshilov, Kalinin, Zhdanov, Ezhov, Andreiev, Mikoian, Chubar, Kossior, the leaders of the Party and of the Government drove with the airmen through the streets of Moscow, and were received everywhere with enthusiastic cheers."[69] Thus the circle of polar comrades was extended to include the leaders of the Party and government: the exclusive club of hyper-masculine conquerors of the Arctic now welcomed the Moscow elite into its ranks. The most important Soviet officials became linked with the heroic deeds of the male pilots and explorers as they traveled along Gorkii Street. Brontman's description leaves ambiguous, however, whether the crowd was cheering for the airmen or for the government. Through this carefully planned ceremony, the glory of the courageous nature-conquering Arctic heroes was to be displaced onto Soviet officials in public. While these "displacements" may not have been successful, this tactic provides insight into the ways in which authorities sought to create a Soviet community in the 1930s.

Other Soviet aviation heroes played a crucial role in the celebration of the return of the heroine-pilots to Moscow. The most famous Soviet pilots personally greeted the heroines at the railway station and congratulated them publicly in the pages of *Pravda*, which celebrated the interaction between the pilot-heroines and their "friend-heroes."[70] The Kremlin reception located the three women among the "best people of the Soviet Union." At the reception, other "glorious pilots" who had already been named "Heroes of the Soviet Union," such as Beliakov, Chkalov, Gromov, Baidukov and Serov, "stood up one after the other speaking about their ideas, their feelings and their experiences in honor of the victory of the troika of fighting women comrades."[71] Here the pilot-heroes spoke about their own achievements rather than those of the female pilots who they were honoring. Soviet leaders also used the Kremlin reception to promote other technological achievements. In his speech, Stalin congratulated Papanin, other polar heroes, and the pilots who saved the crew of the *Rodina*. These ceremonies affirmed the status of the new initiates by celebrating the achievements of the entire fraternity of aviation and Arctic heroes.

Accounts of the Kremlin reception for Grizodubova, Osipenko, and Raskova depicted aviation heroes as a lofty yet comradely group of companions, enjoying the friendly and homey intimacy of drinking toasts with Stalin and other Soviet leaders. The monumental deeds of Chkalov, Beliakov, Osipenko and Raskova were symbolically transferred to Molotov, Voroshilov, Kaganovich, and Ezhov during the aviators' toasts to them at the Kremlin reception.[72] The closer connections between the male heroes and high Party officials and the image of the "best people" as a club of drinking companions suggest that the top of the hierarchy was more congenial to men than to women. In fact, there were few women other than these pilots whose deeds were great enough to gain admission into the "club."[73] It was harder for females to bridge the enormous gap between citizen and hero, and the form of valorizing heroes prevented women from achieving the full status of their male counterparts.

The role of the male aviators in this celebration speaks to their popularity and their personal authority. These figures, who had attained a larger-than-life, quasi-mythical status in Soviet celebration discourse, were instrumental in the induction of the women into the "pantheon" of Soviet heroes. They used the authority given to them by popular acclaim and by the state itself to support the Soviet state and to help popularize and legitimate other heroic figures. These pilots were official but popular spokes-people for Soviet power. They represented publicly the aristocracy of the deed and promised equal access to glory for all at the same time that they reinforced the idea that a select group of leaders deserved to be set apart from the people they led. While anyone could, hypothetically, become a member of the "best people," the achievements of this group were represented as superhuman.[74] The rhetoric of equality in the Soviet community was belied by the very portrayal of the new elite; the contrast between a few extraordinary heroes and crowds of ordinary onlookers revealed a culture of extreme inequality.

The pilot-heroines were relatively accessible to the "ordinary people" who met them along the railroad tracks from the Far East to Moscow. They "shook the hands of hundreds of workers,"[75] kissed babies, and personally accepted bouquets of flowers. Once in Moscow, however, the heroines were whisked past the crowds along Gorkii Street on their way to the Kremlin. The celebration thus revealed two conflicting notions of a hero: a person from the people who was intimately connected with them and a magnificent magical figure who was a tamer of the elements and was worthy to be the "comrade" of the most important people in the Party and government. While the pilots were in the periphery, the populist definition of "hero" was dominant; once they reached status-conscious Moscow, the crucible of elite formation, the heroes became so exalted that they lost touch with the people who venerated them.

Leaders and Communities

The Soviet media portrayed the polar communities of the Cheliuskin-ians and the Papaninites as microcosms of the Soviet nation, reflecting its achievements and the virtues of the socialist way of life. Press accounts showed how people who faced intense hardship and an uncertain fate participated in a Soviet community. Under the leadership of the Party, they held meetings, read Pushkin, and celebrated holidays as if they were in an ordinary Soviet town and not floating on an Arctic ice floe. These depictions of Party leaders interacting with their communities reveal both the ideal of the Party leader and some of the challenges that he faced in the 1930s.

The leaders of the *Cheliuskin* expedition believed that the behavior of Party members was crucial to the maintenance of order in their community. The first issue of the camp's wall newspaper, *We Will Not Give In!* admonished Party members to set a good example by obeying orders, believing that the group would be rescued, and allowing, "No rumors, no panic, no privileges, no advantages: The Communist is always united with the masses."[76] That Party members had to be reminded not to expect privileges reveals the stratification of Soviet life that was taking place in the

1930s. Under Arctic conditions, Party members had to lead in a way that did not divide them from the rest of the community.

In media accounts, Party-led Arctic communities possessed the power to transform ordinary people into New Soviet Men. Several members of the *Cheliuskin* expedition were uneducated construction workers who had been hired to build houses on Wrangel Island.[77] These men were raw material to be "forged" by the Party. During the long polar nights, they acquired culture by learning how to play chess and read Pushkin, and they also mastered the language of Party politics. One carpenter, Berezyn, was ashamed of his "darkness" before attending "polar school," but he explained, "Now you can ask me anything you like: how many republics do we have, and what are the nationality politics of Soviet power, or what did the 17th Party Congress teach us, I can explain it all."[78] This carpenter had a crash course in "speaking Bolshevik" and gained new authority and advantages because of his ability to express himself in Soviet political language.[79] This narrative of transformation was intended to inspire Soviet people to remake themselves. On the "mainland" this transformation was much more difficult to achieve because there was less Party supervision and there were many more activities to compete with political studies.

In official representations, communities of heroes developed strong emotional ties with each other in the course of their exploits. Depictions of heroic comradeship were prominent in accounts of the Soviet conquest of the Arctic. Despite the fact that Otto Shmidt had publicly declared that it was appropriate to include women in Arctic crews, in 1937, when he headed an expedition to set up Papanin's polar station on drift ice at the North Pole, there were no women among the thirty-five explorers. Brontman's narrative of the expedition described how the extreme dangers that the men faced created a powerful and emotional sense of community that precluded any kind of conflict or tension.

Like the bond between Stalin and Chkalov, relationships in the Arctic often took a familial form. When the navigator of the second airplane trying to land at the pole located the first airplane already on the ground, the deputy chief of the expedition, M. Shevelev, "threw his arms round the neck of our startled navigating officer, kissed him warmly and shouted in his joy, 'Alioshka, you devil! You've done it.'"[80] Shevelev's interaction with his subordinate showed the paternal nature of his authority. By hanging on the navigator's neck and calling him by the pet name "Alioshka," Shevelev rewarded the navigator for his success with the kind of warm emotional and physical contact that might occur between father and son.

Brontman also painted an idyllic picture of the masculine comradeship of Soviet polar heroes. The polar expedition left four men on the drift ice to conduct research: I. Papanin, the leader of the four; E. Krenkel', the radio operator; and two scientists, P. Shirshov and E. Fedorov. These extraordinary men formed the core around which the comradeship of the rest of the expedition was defined. Brontman reported, "Whenever Papanin and his mates turned up, soon there were roars of laughter, merry shouts and a hail of jokes."[81] Thus Brontman described a community of thirty-five men who took part in a convivial and boisterous community of heroes.

Whether or not it was true to life, in Brontman's official account heroic victories were celebrated by the men's declarations of allegiance to Stalin and their affection for one another. When the pilot Vodopianov's airplane successfully landed on an ice floe near the North Pole, "the air was filled with shouts in honor of Stalin. The members of the expedition embraced and kissed each other in their joy."[82] Through invoking Stalin's name and warmly embracing one another, the explorers expressed the powerful emotions stemming from their own achievements in the face of danger. By reciting Stalin's name, the community of male heroes, who seemed to thrive in this homosocial environment, included Stalin as one of their own and displaced their glory onto him.

Descriptions of the emotional farewell between the expedition members who returned to Moscow and the four who remained on the ice revealed the deep-rooted bonds of the Arctic brotherhood. Papanin reported, "We have become greatly attached to the remarkable men of the expedition—courageous, self-sacrificing men of the Stalin mold. They have become our very close friends, and we are very sorry to part with them."[83] The love, affection, and mutual admiration of these "men of the Stalin mold" enabled them to accomplish great deeds. The loving relationships of these men were portrayed as the cement that held their polar community together, and by extension, it was this ideal of heroic masculine affection that was to bind together the Soviet Union.

By comparing the representations of polar leaders Shmidt and Papanin in the Soviet media, one can explore the publicly expressed ideals of Soviet leadership. In official accounts, Shmidt possessed some of the same "larger-than-life" qualities that separated Stalin from ordinary men and women. Shmidt's vast erudition made him an ideal Soviet mentor: "Shmidt would expound to eager listeners the theory of Freud, the works of the philologist Marr, and about the Pamirs. That man's stock of knowledge seemed inexhaustible. He was able to answer any question you liked to put, and all attempts to stump him failed."[84] This statement showed that Shmidt's store of knowledge gave him great authority and legitimacy as a leader. His subordinates both recognized this authority and explored its boundaries by trying to ask him questions he could not answer. Shmidt could answer every question and thus proved his authority to be unlimited.

In the materials published about the voyage of the *Cheliuskin*, Stalin and Shmidt were representations of one another. Shmidt's secretary, S. A. Semenov, recalled that the daily news report was always read by Shmidt, "And how Comrade Shmidt knew how to relate the measures being taken by the government! Before our eyes was the might and power of our Gov-

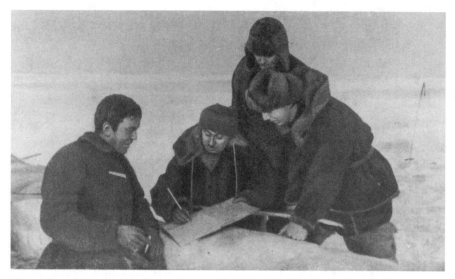

Papanin and his crew write a report to Party leaders. From *Deviat' mesiatsev na dreifuiushchei stantsii "Severnyi Polius"* (1938).

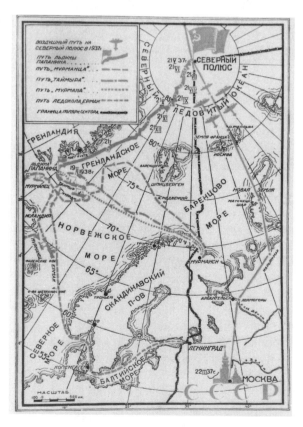

Map of North Pole Expedition. From *Deviat' mesiatsev na dreifuiushchei stantsii "Severnyi Polius"* (1938).

ernment and we were filled with . . . a passion for our country."[85] On the ice
floes, Shmidt was an incarnation of the power of the government.

Because life on an ice floe was extremely precarious and uncertain, the
linkage between Stalin's authority and Shmidt's authority had unintended
consequences. As the leader of the expedition, it was Shmidt's sacred duty
to be the last person rescued from the ice. When Shmidt became very seriously ill with a lung inflammation, Kuibyshev, the Politbiuro member in
charge of the rescue effort, ordered Shmidt to hand over leadership to his
deputy and leave the ice floe immediately.[86] The personification of the
government's authority turned out to be vulnerable to illness. The official
narrative of life in the Arctic revealed, despite Soviet rhetoric to the contrary, that the ice floe was not a nurturing motherland and that Soviet leaders could not always control the effects of the elements on their bodies.

Ivan Dmitrievich Papanin was not a distinguished professor like
Shmidt; he was an ex-sailor and lathe operator and had worked his way
up through administrative positions in Soviet government agencies during the 1920s. The other three members of Papanin's crew were technical
specialists; Papanin's role was to lead the group, provision the camp, and
repair household items. Paradoxically, the head of the expedition had to
undertake the most menial labor, including the unheroic task of cooking.
Although Papanin found kitchen work "dirty and dull" and felt that "only
housewives can appreciate my position," he persevered with his menial
labors so that the others could pursue their scientific work.[87] Papanin repeatedly described his kitchen work as "women's work." He proclaimed
that housewives would laugh at him for the way he made biscuits but that
they would be envious to have a kitchen as snow-white as his.[88] Papanin
was a different type of leader than Shmidt.

Unlike Shmidt, who guided politically illiterate carpenters through their
transformation into New Soviet Men, Papanin was not particularly active
in developing the Party consciousness of his three companions. Although
Papanin did accept Shirshov as a candidate member for the Party, leading
his crew in intense study of Party politics was not his first priority. He
wrote: "It is a pity we cannot get started on our study of the history of the
Party; everyone is so occupied with his work."[89] Papanin thus openly discussed a dilemma faced by many overburdened Party officials, who were
torn between achieving their production goals and educating their cadres.

Since playing chess was a symbol of culture and civilization in the So-
viet Union, when radio operator Krenkel' taught Papanin how to play chess,
the roles of student and mentor were reversed. To make matters worse,
Papanin was not a particularly good student. He recorded in his diary:
"Krenkel' and I played a game of chess, and, as usual, I lost to him."[90]
Fedorov, the magnetologist, remembered Krenkel' saying to Papanin:
"Guard, Ivan Dmitrich! See you don't lose your queen."[91] The extent of
Papanin's despair at ever winning a chess game became evident when the

icc underneath the living tent began cracking during a chess match with Krenkel': "We decided not to end the game at once— it seemed to me that I had chances of winning—but when it became clear that my game was hopelessly lost, we pricked our ears and listened."[92] Like many officials who had risen through the Party ranks, Papanin was a mentor who was less educated and "cultured" than those whom he was supposed to teach.

The Soviet censors' concern with enhancing Papanin's status as leader is evident in a change that was made to the 1938 version of Fedorov's autobiography in *Deviat' mesiatsev na dreifuiushchei stantsii "Severnyi Polius"* (*Nine Months on the Drift Ice Station "North Pole"*) as compared to the version published the same year in *Na vershine mira* (*On Top of the World*). In *On Top of the World*, Fedorov described a close encounter with a polar bear at Cape Cheliuskin in 1934: "Papanin, who was asleep, felt the touch of the bear's nose, woke up and asked me sleepily why I did not let him sleep. I replied that a bear had called. Papanin immediately jumped out of the tent and fired at the bear, which ran away. We rushed after it, but it was too quick for us."[93] The version of Fedorov's autobiography in *Nine Months on the Drift Ice Station "North Pole"* read "Ivan Dmitrievich [Papanin] immediately jumped out of the tent, shot and killed the bear."[94] The second version depicted Papanin as a powerful, courageous, resourceful, and effective leader.

Papanin's diary *Zhizn' na l'dine* (*Life on an Ice Floe*)[95] records his reaction to depictions of his expedition in the Soviet media:

> We are being glorified as valiant knights and heroes. We laugh, asking one another which of us is the knight. I am five feet four inches tall. Krenkel' is the tallest. Nevertheless we have cast ourselves for these roles; Ernst [Krenkel']—Il'ia Muromets, Peter [Shirshov]—Alesha Popovich, Zhenia [Fedorov]—Solovei Razboinik and Papanin—Ruslan and Liudmila.[96]

This passage mocks the Soviet propaganda that called these men *bogatyrs,* or Russian epic heroes. Papanin's self-deprecation is particularly pointed. He could not be Il'ia Muromets, the valiant warrior, because he stood only five foot four. The taller but subordinate Krenkel' was more suited to this role. They cast Shirshov as a warrior and Fedorov as a bandit. Papanin took the roles of the male fairy tale character Ruslan *and* the female character Liudmila, alluding to his girth and possibly to the fact that his work transgressed gender boundaries.[97] This passage reflects the polar explorers' discomfort and feelings of inadequacy when the Soviet media attempted to transform them into mythic figures.

Although Shmidt and Papanin were both celebrated as leaders and mentors, they practiced different kinds of leadership, the one intellectual and the other charismatic. Shmidt's vast education and intelligence enabled him to develop the minds of those in his charge. Although he did not have technical expertise, Papanin knew how to inspire his men to work, keep them in good spirits, and prevent tensions in their small community through a kind of humor that often made him the butt of his own jokes. The two leaders were both reflections of Stalin's symbolic leadership. The image of Shmidt echoed the many reports of Stalin's great knowledge on virtually any subject. The image of Papanin mirrored depictions of Stalin's earthiness, gruff good humor, and joie de vivre.

The actions of Shmidt and Papanin revealed some of the complexities of leadership in the Soviet Union. Each leader balanced the demands of educating his cadres and achieving his assigned tasks in different ways, but the goals that both men set out to accomplish were extremely ambitious. Although Shmidt succeeded in showing strong leadership during the trials of the *Cheliuskin,* he would have been an even better leader if he had realized that it was too risky to take a vessel like the *Cheliuskin* across the northern sea route. Papanin's men could have been removed from their ice floe in December, before the situation on the ice floe became dangerous, but Papanin believed that they could hold out until the spring. The cult of the Soviet leader often led real-life leaders to overestimate the capabilities of their subordinates and their own personal stamina. In leading others through danger, Shmidt overtaxed himself and became so ill that he had to be flown to Alaska. Papanin also constantly complained of heart pains, fevers, and headaches. The burden of leadership pushed both men to the limits of their personal endurance. The leaders' overestimation of what it was possible to do and their overconfidence in fighting the "battle with the elements" could, and sometimes did, lead to disaster.

Women as Heroes

In the 1930s, Soviet women were given opportunities to excel at their professions and achieved prominence in many fields. Female aviators and Stakhanovites provided examples of strong and successful women who were willing to struggle in order to achieve their goals. To understand the many difficulties and barriers that these strong women had to overcome, however, one must contextualize these female images as part of a gender system that professed equality and valorized some women's deeds but gave priority to heroic masculinity.

The role and status of women in Arctic expeditions and aviation exploits was difficult for Soviet officials and the Soviet media to define. Otto Shmidt's discussion of the population of the *Cheliuskin* at the time of its destruction shows his complicated attitude toward his female subordinates. Shmidt declared, "The crew also included four women—to do the chores. In my opinion, the participation of women in such expeditions is completely permissible. To speak plainly, I should only prefer to have men for such hard work as cleaning ship."[98] While Shmidt refuted the idea that polar exploration should be an exclusively male arena, the role that he assigned to women was a traditional and menial one. Shmidt also noted that some of the scientific workers who were supposed to have been dropped off at Wrangel Island had brought their wives.[99] What he neglected to mention was that at least two of these women were scientists in their own right: Ol'ga Komova was a meteorologist and Anna Sushkina was an ichthyologist. There was also a third female scientist, P. Lobza, the expedition's hydrochemist, who was no one's wife.[100] Thus, the women who peopled Shmidt's heroic narrative were auxiliaries to the men: menial workers and wives. Shmidt excluded from view the female scientists who took part in exploration as experts.

The uneasy fit between "explorer" and "woman" became even clearer after the *Cheliuskin* sank and the 104 survivors were encamped on an ice floe waiting for rescue. When the Cheliuskinians engaged in the heroic labor of clearing runways so that they could be rescued by air, "The women and weaker comrades, unfit for heavy labor, took over glove-making, some cutting, others sewing."[101] The contribution of women scientists and workers to the heroic labor of survival was circumscribed to the most feminine activity of sewing gloves.

The first rescue plane successfully landed on March 5, 1934, and Shmidt ordered the women and children to leave on this plane. Ichthyologist Anna Sushkina complained, "I must say that some of us were dissatisfied to be taken off first just because we were women. But Comrade Shmidt was adamant."[102] The women's identities as explorers came into conflict with Shmidt's unspoken assumption that men, even sick or weak men, could face danger better than women. Although the women's argument that they should not be privileged simply because they were woman corresponded to the Party line on gender equality, Shmidt ignored official pronouncements about equality when they clashed with his gendered definition of hero.

Shmidt was not alone in harboring contradictory and un-Soviet feelings toward the women in the camp. Sushkina reported that when the women and children departed, "our comrades waved to us from the ice, and the satisfaction on some faces was really a little too much, not at all fitting for a farewell."[103] Here Sushkina directly confronted the ambiguous position of women explorers. The Soviet system gave women the opportunity to become scientists and explorers, but the actions of both politically educated and politically illiterate males prevented these women from achieving full status as heroes. The male explorers defined heroism as an exclusively male preserve. The narrative of the *Cheliuskin* did not acknowledge the women who had endured the same trials as their male counterparts as heroes. By Shmidt's orders, these women were physically separated from the ranks of the heroes at the first opportunity.

Some Soviet aviation narratives of the 1930s suggested not only that women could not be heroes, but further that they prevented men from

Female Cheliuskinians
sew gloves. From *Pokhod
Cheliuskina* (1934).

becoming heroes. When the pilot Levanevskii heard that the *Cheliuskin* had
been crushed, he informed Moscow that he was "ready to fly to their assistance." Levanevskii reported, "When they learned of this my wife cried
and my children also set up a wail."[104] Levanevskii portrayed his wife as a
brake on his development as a hero. The attachment of a woman had to be
overcome for Levanevskii to become a hero.

The pilot Baidukov described the conspiratorial discussions that he
and Valerii Chkalov had while planning their flight over the North Pole
to America: "Late into the winter nights Valerii and I sat up talking, hush-
ing our voices to commonplace shop talk when our wives and children
began to be suspicious."[105] The pilots were afraid that their wives and children would interfere with their glorious but dangerous plans. In Baidukov's narrative, the unity of purpose of the two male comrades, their overwhelming desire to get permission to carry out the flight, and their bonds
of friendship and trust showed that the relationship between the men took
precedence over their relationships with their wives and families. Male
comradeship was a weapon to prevent women and children from wreck-

ing their heroic plans. The spontaneity of these "sons of Stalin" could occur only outside of their family circle, while the spontaneity of female pilots took place in the context of their dual roles as mothers and heroes.

Despite public proclamations of gender equality, women were depicted as incapable of understanding the importance of heroic action. Their love for their men caused them to prevent the enactment of heroic deeds; the men's love for each other, on the other hand, spurred them on to heroic action.[106] This same type of heroic friendship was much more difficult for women heroes; in her diary, one eleven-year-old girl revealed her understanding of the boundaries of heroic friendship: "I want to be friends with Ellie all my life. Boys say that only men can be friends like Petka and Chapaev, but that's not true. . . . Of course, we haven't yet been able to test our friendship in battle, but all the same it's a real one. We both want to be pilots, and want to learn to fly together."[107] To be a female hero of the Stalin era one had to actively combat male assertions that heroism and comradeship were exclusively male domains.

In addition to creating a rhetoric that downplayed women's heroism, Soviet policymakers placed concrete obstacles in the paths of women who hoped to train as pilots. A. V. Kosarev, the leader of the Komsomol, declared in a meeting of the organization's executive committee that there was little practical use for training female parachutists. He argued: "Imagine a woman in the position of fighter pilot on a U-16, flying at 400–450 kilometers an hour. What would become of her? Aviation is intensifying and not every man can endure the speeds; all the more reason why a woman cannot adjust to these speeds." Despite the objections of one of the women present, Kosarev recommended that "in the resolution we write 8–10 percent [of parachutists trained will be women] but in the instructions, I propose not to train a single one."[108] This document reveals Kosarev's sexism and the ease with which he circumvented official policies that promised equal opportunity for women. Since Kosarev's instructions would be received and implemented by predominantly like-minded male officials, it was unlikely that anyone would call him to account for the discrepancy between his public pronouncement and the internal directives.

Grizodubova, Osipenko, and Raskova were the only female aviation or polar heroes that the Soviet government celebrated. The heroines' narrative differed from the male narratives in that their status as mothers was central to their identity. The female pilots also had less control over their own narratives than other heroes. The story of the Rodina was told in the third person by L. Brontman and L. Khvat. While Brontman included autobiographies of Papanin and his men in his North Pole volume, he and Khvat composed biographies of the female pilots for the Rodina book. Vertov's dramatization of the Rodina flight focused on the command center that organized the rescue of the Rodina rather than on the actions of the three heroines during their adventure.[109] The narrative did not emphasize the comradeship of the three women in the same way that it emphasized the male friendships of the Arctic explorers and aviators and the heroic personas of the three women were not individually defined.

The celebration of aviation and Arctic feats revealed two competing sets of ideas about gender equality. While the achievements of women pilots elevated them to the level of the "best people of the Soviet Union," the biographical account of the pilots' adventures also included exemplary images of other women performing traditionally female labors. Some women in Vladivostok prepared sandwiches and hot cocoa for the pilot-heroines, and others, identified only as the wives of laborers and white collar workers, decorated the heroines' railway car.[110] The journal *Krestian'ka* (*Peasant Woman*) published a letter from Maria Babushkina, the wife of Arctic pilot Mikhail Babushkin, in which she described her role in the North Pole expedition of June 1937. She "tried to create circumstances under which Mikhail Sergeevich could calmly work and study" and also "worried about a few little things" like sewing gauze handkerchiefs for her husband.[111] These women were shown to be supportive to Arctic and aviation exploits only in domestic and trivial ways. The actions of the women who braved the Arctic themselves, like the Cheliuskinians, were muted in the expedition narratives to strengthen the male definitions of scientist and explorer. Soviet rhetoric about the equality of women and the affirmation of their participation as full citizens of the Soviet state clashed with an officially sanctioned "traditional" rhetoric in which women's participation was limited and controlled by men.

The official proclamations of women's equality were challenged by social practices as well: "traditional" attitudes and outright sexism both within the Party and in the population at large created barriers for women's participation in public life.[112] The accounts of Soviet female polar and aviation heroes reveal the gender tensions in the Soviet Union in the 1930s and the limits of the Soviet government's state-sponsored gender revolution.

Native Peoples as Heroes

According to the official ideology of the Soviet Union in the 1930s, people of all nationalities were supposed to be equal. This myth of the "friendship of peoples," however, masked repression, inequality, and the development of quasi-colonial relationships between the peoples of the periphery and the Soviet center. Tensions in Soviet attitudes toward the "small peoples" of the Far North and Far East shaped the way that these native peoples appeared in accounts about Soviet exploits.

A poem written about the three pilot-heroines in *Pravda* in 1938 claimed that "fishermen on the shores of the Amgun' river received all three as they would their own daughters."[113] These native fishermen were thus portrayed as part of the great Soviet family; having attained Soviet consciousness, they welcomed Moscow's heroes. The native population of the Chukchi Peninsula played a more active role in the *Cheliuskin* adventure. Chukchi teamsters took part in the rescue, transporting members of the expedition from the coast to the Soviet outpost at Wellen. Chukchi villagers also gave shelter to pilots Kamanin and Liapidevskii after they were forced to land because of bad weather and mechanical difficulties. Without the help of the Chukchi, the pilots would not have been able to rescue the Cheliuskinians and might have lost their own lives as well.

Interactions between Chukchis and the mostly Russian explorers provide an opportunity to examine the definition of becoming "Soviet" in the Far North.[114] Soviet publicists compared the horrors of tsarism's colonial conquest of the Arctic with the cultural and economic progress achieved by the peoples of the North in the Soviet period. They contrasted the Siberian slave trade and the exploitative bartering of fur pelts for vodka in tsarist times with the introduction of new written languages, the building of schools and "Red Tents," and the development of agriculture in Soviet times. According to one Soviet official, the advancement of the northern peoples disproved "fascist theories about the races."[115] Yuri Slezkine has argued that although Soviet cultural work in the North was not successful, "the cultural revolution in the north was proclaimed victorious" nevertheless.[116] While Soviet discourse about the Far North in the 1930s claimed that the native peoples had already become "Soviet," this transformation had not actually taken place.

Soviet media depictions of the relationship between Russians and non-Russian peoples in the Far North were similar to the portrayals of Russian friendship with non-Russians elsewhere in the Soviet Union; Russia was a kindly elder brother helping his less-developed younger brother. Soviet narratives tried to show that the northern peoples had attained a Soviet consciousness and had thus become an integral part of the Soviet Union. This celebration of the progress of the nationalities of the Far North differed sharply from nineteenth-century European colonial rhetoric that sought to maintain difference between white colonizers and the non-white subjects.[117] Soviet discourse instead proclaimed sameness while differences continued to exist.

The autobiographies of Arctic pilots in the Far North proclaimed the advancement of the northern peoples but also provided details that cast doubt on such assertions. Liapidevskii wrote that in the Soviet outpost of Wellen "Soviet civilization is rapidly penetrating. . . . They are learning to read and write."[118] Liapidevskii put this modest achievement into context when he described a remote village where he was forced to land his airplane: "That was a dead end of a place! The Chukchis there had preserved all of their ancient habits and peculiarities, and only now did we get an idea of what the Chukchis were under tsarism." These customs, according to Liapidevskii, included dining on half-decomposed walrus meat, a general lack of cleanliness, and going "practically naked" indoors.[119]

Despite the supposed Soviet advancement, Liapidevskii described the Chukchis as frozen in time. His narrative combined the past, present, and future. He was able to observe "what the Chukchis were under tsarism" in 1934 but also hailed the cultural advancement that was still part of the future.[120] Liapidevskii thus revealed that Soviet media accounts which compared the evils of tsarism to the accomplishments of the present day were exaggerated. His account called into question the ability of the Soviet state to transform the Arctic.

Liapidevskii's diary also cast doubt on the idea that the Arctic belonged to the Soviet nation. The relationship of Liapidevskii with the Chukchis was not like that of the pilot-heroines with the Amgun' fishermen who became their symbolic fathers. Although the Chukchis welcomed Liapidevskii as an honored guest and helped him reach the Soviet outpost at Vankarem, Liapidevskii excluded the Chukchis from his Soviet family. When a party of Cheliuskinians arrived in the same village, Liapidevskii said that he was probably happier to see them than they were to see him "when we first flew to them on the floe." The arrival of the Cheliuskinians, with whom he shared a Soviet identity, rescued Liapidevskii from a Chukchi village that he viewed as more desolate than a barren ice floe. When Liapidevskii discovered that the Soviet government was going to decorate him for his efforts in saving the Cheliuskinians, he noted, "We understood that even while we had been there, in those huts, cut off from them all, lonely and helpless, the country had not for a moment forgotten us."[121] This statement echoed a common theme in Arctic narratives: the concern of the Soviet government for all of its citizens. This statement contradicted another common theme of Arctic narratives, however: that the Arctic was Soviet territory, and its people were Soviet people. Liapidevskii felt that he had been cut off "from them all," from the whole country. The Chukchis, then, were not Soviet comrades. The pilot's account revealed the "otherness" of the Chukchis and their exclusion from his definition of Soviet. If the Chukchis still lived as in tsarist times and were not part of the Soviet family, then Soviet rule was not brotherly assistance from a more advanced nation to a less advanced one. The narrative thus revealed the colonial nature of Soviet rule in the Far North.

Liapidevskii's story was not the only *Cheliuskin* narrative that subverted the ideal image of the Soviet Arctic. When Peter Buiko was traveling in a blizzard, led by Chukchi guides, he fantasized about meeting "living people, people who could understand us." Buiko's remarks suggest that he did not consider the Chukchi guides to be "living people," not to mention "Soviet" people. The teamsters who drove the sledges were made invisible by his narrative. Buiko, like Liapidevskii, excluded the Chukchis from the Soviet community.

When Buiko finally reached his destination of Inmitauen, he was "met by Silber . . . the first Russian for 300 kilometers of traveling. . . . Without more ado he handed us out a can of condensed milk each. . . . That was our resurrection!"[122] Although it was the Chukchi teamsters and guides who led the expedition over those 300 kilometers and brought them safely to Inmitauen in spite of a blizzard, Buiko's "resurrection" was attributed to a Russian man and a symbol of "advanced" civilization: canned milk. The Chukchis' contribution to the survival of the expedition, like their identities, were erased from Buiko's narrative.

Both Buiko and Liapidevskii obscured their dependence on the local Chukchi population. Although Liapidevskii denigrated the customs of the Chukchi villagers with whom he stayed, their hospitality and half-rotten walrus meat kept him alive. When the pilot Nikolai Kamanin was forced to land his airplane near a Chukchi village, he refused to go inside the *iaranga* (Chukchi tent) at first, because he thought it smelled terrible. But the tent of the Soviet men was blown away by a snowstorm and they would probably have frozen to death but for the shelter of the *iarangas*. Kamanin remarked, "Now a *iaranga* seemed to us something like the Peterhof Palace."[123] Instead of bringing advanced Soviet culture to the Chukchis, the Soviet men were saved by a Chukchi "palace."

Despite the fact that Kamanin's account explicitly, if not very graciously, acknowledged the importance of the Chukchis to the Soviets' survival, the Soviet government did not promote the Chukchis as heroes for saving the pilots. The Soviet definition of heroism excluded the local Chukchi population just as it excluded the female scientists on the *Cheliuskin*. The Soviet government in Moscow granted its highest honor of Hero of the Soviet Union only to the pilots who saved the Cheliuskinians and not to the Chukchis who saved the pilots. While several Chukchis received the Order of the Red Star for their part in the *Cheliuskin* rescue, they were not identified as individual heroes in the literature.[124]

The Soviet media defined heroes as masculine carriers of an advanced Soviet culture. Despite contributions to Soviet exploits, most women and all Chukchis were excluded from the ranks of the heroes and framed as the "other" against which heroes were measured. When the "other" turned out to be as heroic or more heroic than the Soviet men, narratives tried to suppress this fact but could not always do so completely. While Soviet women were usually depicted as inferior members of the imagined Soviet community, the Chukchis were often excluded from the community altogether.

Unpredictable Arctic/Unpredictable Discourse

All of the adventures the Soviet government employed to create Soviet patriotism were predicated on risk and danger. The constant danger that helped to make citizens into heroes also introduced an element of uncertainty into the propaganda. Severe Arctic conditions and the desire to

Ethnographical image of a
"typical Chukchi girl."
From *Pokhod Cheliuskina*
(1934).

create heroes led Soviet propagandists to construct the beginnings of narratives whose endings had not yet been determined, and sometimes the
ending turned out to be disaster. The utopian nature of Soviet socialist-
realist discourses, which conflated the future and the present, made it
difficult for them to accommodate failures. The Soviet aviation hero was
simultaneously mastering technology and already supposed to have mastered it; he was in the process of being perfected, yet already perfect.[125] The
failures of Arctic and aviation heroes were troublesome for Soviet propagandists because they revealed that the perfect future did not yet exist.

One of the most important claims of Soviet publicists about Arctic and
aviation exploits was that these achievements were evidence of Soviet
science's conquest of nature. Otto Shmidt proclaimed: "Nature subordinates herself to man when he knows how to arm himself for the fight and
when he does not come out alone, but in a large group supported by the
warm love of millions of citizens."[126] When supported by the Soviet community, male citizens supposedly gained the power to tame female land
and nature and bring them under Soviet control. However, even when pilots and explorers were supported by the "warm love of millions of citi-

zens," and even when Soviet technology reduced risks to a minimum, the nature of the Arctic could and did resist being incorporated into Soviet geography.[127]

In Soviet celebrations, the theme of Arctic conquest coexisted with a second important motif: the concern of the Soviet government for pilots and other heroes, who were seen "not merely as record-breakers but as human beings."[128] Given the widespread indifference to the value of human life in the Stalin era, this theme was particularly ironic. Assertions of the conquest of nature and concern for human life conflicted with reality and with each other. Stalin indirectly acknowledged this contradiction at the reception for the heroine aviators in the Kremlin in October 1938, when he "warned about the necessity for particular caution and care with the most valuable things which we possess—with human lives and particularly with the lives of our courageous, sometimes too impetuously courageous, hero-pilots."[129] By calling the pilots "too impetuously courageous," Stalin attempted to shift the blame for the danger the pilots encountered onto their own shoulders and away from himself and his government. This speech acknowledged that the government's pursuit of thrilling aviation feats and world records routinely put pilot-heroes in harm's way.

The fact that aviation exploits played a key ideological role sometimes caused Soviet officials needlessly to endanger the heroes in their endeavor to create a spectacle of the Soviet state's authority and legitimacy. In June 1937, when the aviators who took Ivan Papanin's expedition to the North Pole victoriously returned to Moscow, Stalin himself wanted to meet the heroes at the airport. The aviators were instructed to land in Moscow at "5 p.m. sharp."[130] The airplanes, which had been especially designed for Arctic flying, ran the risk of overheating and engine failure if they flew during the hottest period of the day. The pilots flew overnight to Kalinin and then risked only a short flight to Moscow in the warm part of the day. As they were taking off in Kalinin, severe thunderstorms broke, but the planes could not wait for better weather, given their 5 o'clock deadline.[131] The very ceremony that was meant to show the government's care and concern for the aviators caused the pilots to risk their lives. While praising the exceptional skill and preparedness of the pilots in any situation, Brontman's account revealed that some of the dangers that Soviet pilots faced were caused not by nature but by Moscow's inflexible demands.

The wreck of the *Cheliuskin* exposed the expedition organizers' indifference to the safety of the passengers. Otto Shmidt himself admitted that the *Cheliuskin* was "intended for more restricted trips than the passage of the northern route."[132] Nevertheless, Shmidt and the Soviet government risked the lives of 113 people, including an infant and a pregnant woman, to discover if the *Cheliuskin* could survive such a journey. The success of the widely publicized and dramatic rescue of the Cheliuskinians underscored the fact that they had been calamitously set adrift on a polar ice floe in the first place. While the Soviet ideologues turned their failure into a public media success, they did so at a great cost. Sovnarkom estimated that the Soviet government spent over 11 million rubles on the rescue of the Cheliuskinians.[133] All but one of the Cheliuskinians were saved, but the narratives of the expedition revealed both the Soviet failure to control the harsh Arctic elements and the carelessness of the Soviet government with its financial and human resources.[134]

Despite Soviet boasts about the easy conquest of a feminized nature by Soviet male heroes, the shape of Arctic and aviation narratives revealed the constant dangers that heroes faced and their frequent impotence in their battle with the elements. Attempts to rescue the Cheliuskinians were marred by mishaps, crash landings, and missing aviators. Only two of the squadron of five planes sent out under the command of Nikolai Kamanin actually reached the Cheliuskinians and took part in the rescue.[135] The Cheliuskinians were trapped on the ice for two full months before rescue parties could reach them, revealing the complexity of the rescue operation and the inability of the Soviets immediately to master Arctic weather conditions.[136] While the *Cheliuskin* rescue was represented by the Soviet media as a great Soviet victory, the narratives reveal that nature could easily have won this battle.

At first, the establishment of Ivan Papanin's winter camp on an ice floe in May of 1937 was quite successful. In a telegram to Moscow, Shmidt declared, "We have now taken revenge on the elements for the loss of the *Cheliuskin*."[137] Nine months later, however, Papanin and his men were themselves at the mercy of the elements; they had to be rescued by icebreakers when their ice floe "cracked to pieces" during a storm.[138] Like the rescue of the *Cheliuskin*, this rescue operation was also marked by significant setbacks. Thirteen people were killed when a dirigible on its way to save Papanin crashed, and one icebreaker was seriously damaged.[139] The rescue attempts were ultimately successful but did not prove the inevitability of Soviet mastery of nature.

Papanin's diary about his nine-month battle with the elements at the North Pole recounted the daily struggles and unceasing labors of his men. Despite a whole year of planning, Soviet science could not provide the expedition with equipment that worked properly. Their fresh meat spoiled, their silk tents leaked badly, their primus stoves exploded, and their lanterns smoked so much that their eyes teared. Papanin eloquently expressed the uncertain nature of their life on the ice floe: "Life makes radical corrections both in our plans and our theoretical premises."[140] Both science and Bolshevik planning had to submit to Arctic forces.

In his diary, Papanin also reflected on his own mortality. He made sure to send the scientific observations of the expedition to Moscow periodically so that the data would not be lost if all perished. When the icebreakers were already on their way, Papanin wrote about the tragic death of

Captain Scott on his return from the South Pole. Unlike Scott, Papanin claimed that he was not worried about who would take care of his family if he died. He knew that behind him stood, "the whole Soviet people, our Party, and our Government."[141] Papanin acknowledged however, that, like Scott, he could become a victim of natural forces beyond his control.

A number of Soviet adventure narratives did not have happy endings. By publicizing dramatic rescues while they were in progress, Soviet propagandists risked public failure. When Sigismund Levanevskii and his crew disappeared while flying over the North Pole to America, the Soviet government organized a massive and highly publicized rescue with the help of Soviet and American pilots. Levanevskii was never found, and news of the failure of this New Soviet Man spread all over the Soviet Union and the world.[142]

The fallibility of Soviet aviation was also evident during the celebration of Aviation Day. Aviation Day exhibitions became more and more elaborate throughout the 1930s. Because of a scarcity of cadres and equipment and chronic inefficiency, carelessness in the preparations for and execution of Aviation Day often led to accidents that marred the festivities. A parachutist was killed when his parachute failed to open at the Moscow Aviation Day celebration on August 18, 1935. Organizers admitted that the rehearsals of parachutists took place at the last moment, saying "tomorrow is the holiday and today they conducted the preparation of the parachutists," and bemoaned the absence of responsible people to supervise this training.[143] The death of the parachutist occurred in public with an audience of over 40,000 people watching.[144] This sudden reversal from celebration to tragedy served as a powerful and unavoidable reminder that Soviet aviation achievements came at a cost and that Soviet technology was not in the utopian realm of the perfect future.

NKVD reports in the days before the 1936 celebration of Aviation Day revealed the difficulties organizers faced in displaying "the latest achievements in aviation technology."[145] The NKVD noted that there was not one spare airplane and no spare parts. Despite instructions that each parachutist must have had five jumps before taking part in the holiday, the majority of the parachutists had taken three jumps or fewer. During rehearsals there were numerous accidents and injuries. For example, one female jumper panicked because she "took to heart the death of her girlfriend," parachutist Nata Babushkina.[146] Celebrations sought to hide the Soviet reality of insufficient technological and human resources, but accidents caused by pushing the existing resources to their limits revealed what celebrations were organized to obscure. The numerous public accidents and deaths all too loudly proclaimed that Soviet claims of scientific superiority and boasts of having developed a new breed of technologically skilled heroes were both unfounded. After Nata Babushkina and another female parachutist were killed in March 1936 while trying to capture a free-fall record, the

Central Committee forbade jumping for records and free-fall jumps without special instructions from the Central Committee. They also forbade the civil defense organization Osoaviakhim to send parachutists to jump at any kind of celebration.[147] From late 1938 on, Stalin would only allow the pursuit of world records in "rare and extreme circumstances."[148] Stalin thus resolved the contradiction in the celebration of aviation and Arctic exploits by preventing further exploits, but numerous accidents undermined the official meanings of technological celebrations before he did so.

Memoirs, letters of citizens, and reports of Soviet cadres show that Arctic and aviation narratives were extremely popular among both adults and children. The popularity of tales of Arctic and aviation heroes assured that the images of the nation they contained gained at least some currency among the population. The ability of the Soviet government and cultural cadres to spread these narratives across the country was linked to the strength of communication technologies and the skill of Soviet cadres. These myths, therefore, were most successfully communicated in Russian-speaking urban areas. They functioned to affirm the leaders' authority in the center rather than in the "inaccessible" provinces. The Soviet Union was most easily imagined by the workers and officials who had invested in it. Remote villages and non-Russian areas were thus imagined by others to be part of the nation but were given few opportunities to imagine themselves as Soviet.

Soviet depictions of a harmonious, unified, and loyal community were also weakened in many other ways. While seeking to foster the power of Soviet leaders, celebrations could undermine their legitimacy. Mythic depictions of the great Arctic leaders Shmidt and Papanin as well as NKVD reports of Aviation Day showed that Soviet leaders pushed their technological and human resources to their limits in trying to achieve spectacles of technological superiority. These spectacles may have served a powerful legitimating function when they succeeded as planned. Arctic and aviation narratives often revealed, however, that happy endings were a product of chance rather than of Soviet know-how, that Soviet planning could not conquer all, and that Soviet leaders needlessly placed the lives of their subordinates at risk. These narratives raised doubts about the concern of the Soviet leaders for their people, and therefore about the legitimacy of Soviet rule.

Arctic and aviation celebrations did not envision all Soviet citizens as equal members of the community. By creating superhuman heroes, they elevated these leading citizens above the population. While Soviet heroic rhetoric sometimes included both men and women in the symbolic nation, aviation and polar exploits most often created a masculine vision of the nation and its citizens. Although the heroine aviators were honored, and offered an alternative model of inclusion in the nation, they were never as independent, as popular, or as heroic as male heroes such as Chkalov and Papanin. Like many other nationalisms, at least one strain of Soviet nationalism was based on the exclusion of women from the intimate circle of heroic male comrade-citizens that made up the country. Male comrade-citizens were to be inspired to greatness by their tenderness and love for a female country. These men were depicted as both conquerors and protectors of their motherland-bride. In contrast to official rhetoric about the equality of all races, the heroes created by aviation and Arctic narratives were also overwhelmingly European. The natives of the Far North who took part in Arctic rescues were written out of the heroic narratives. Despite a rhetoric of inclusivity, the Soviet Union as imagined in Arctic and aviation discourse tended to be exclusively male and European.

The vision of the Soviet Union as the fertile motherland who voluntarily yielded up the fruits of the land to her children and to Moscow was challenged by Arctic and aviation adventures. These exploits gained their emotional edge from the dangers that heroes faced and captured the imagination of Soviet citizens precisely because of the extreme difficulty of aviation in the wilderness or survival on an ice floe. Both Soviet and European Arctic and aviation narratives emphasized risk because the heroes' flirtation with death appealed to audiences.[149] Narratives of Soviet exploits were intended to arouse the spontaneous emotions of the population in order to foster a conscious Soviet identity. The use of danger to create excitement, however, threatened to undermine the celebration of Soviet technology and legitimacy. Soviet exploits differed from European adventures in that New Soviet Men were already supposed to have achieved the conquest of nature. When Soviet adventurers failed, they revealed the incomplete nature of the mythic Soviet transformation and the limits of Soviet power. The Soviet community as portrayed in Soviet Arctic and aviation celebrations revealed both Soviet fantasies of power and legitimacy and the struggle of Soviet citizens for equality and autonomy.

4

FIR TREES AND CARNIVALS

THE CELEBRATION OF SOVIET NEW YEAR'S DAY

While marching in physical culture demonstrations and dreaming about aviation and Arctic adventures were entertaining activities that the Soviet state hoped all citizens would enjoy, such celebrations appealed particularly to Soviet youth. The focus of these holidays on attracting youth to the Soviet cause was reinforced by Soviet bureaucratic practice. In the mid-1930s, physical culture parades and Aviation Day were organized under the auspices of the Komsomol, the Communist Youth League. A third holiday for which the Komsomol was responsible was New Year's Day, a celebration that underwent a profound transformation in the mid-1930s.

On December 28, 1935, a month after Stalin announced that "life has become more joyous," the Second Secretary of the Ukrainian Communist Party, Pavel Postyshev, called for the return of the fir tree (*elka*) to celebrate New Year's Day. In an article in *Komsomolskaia pravda*, Postyshev noted that before the revolution "through windows, the children of workers looked with envy at fir trees sparkling with multi-colored lights and the children of the rich enjoying themselves around the tree"; he argued that Soviet children should not be denied this pleasure because some "left deviationists" considered it a "bourgeois undertaking." Postyshev proposed that the Komsomol and local Party and government leaders should help organize "collective" fir trees in "schools, orphanages, Pioneer palaces, children's clubs, theaters and movie theaters."[1] Postyshev's pronouncement accelerated the transformation of New Year's Day into an official Soviet holiday that emphasized entertainment, merry-making, and the creation of a joyous atmosphere of prosperity.

In the first years of Soviet power, there had been debates about whether or not it was appropriate to preserve the fir tree tradition as a part of the New Year's celebration. V. I. Lenin and N. K. Krupskaia believed that the fir tree was suitable as long as it was "freed from its Christmas interpretation." They themselves took part in public fir tree festivities during New Year's celebrations in 1918, 1919, 1923, and 1924. The opposing viewpoint, held by the cultural left, was that the fir tree had direct connections with the church and bourgeois culture and should not be promoted.[2] In 1928, at the start of the Cultural Revolution, Soviet officials attacked the fir tree because of its alien bourgeois origins. The anti-religious journal *Bezbozhnik* criticized the fir tree as part of the bourgeois commercialization of Christmas in the West and used pictures of Christmas trees in Berlin and Warsaw to denounce the divisions between rich and poor in capitalist countries.[3] In addition to being exposed as a "bourgeois prejudice" in the late 1920s, fir trees were also rejected on practical grounds. Anti–fir tree propaganda argued that the destruction of young fir trees was an economic evil.[4] In 1928 the fir tree was banned and the Russian Santa Claus, Grandfather Frost, was "unmasked as an ally of the priest and *kulak*."[5]

During the First Five Year Plan, New Year's Day was a production- and accounting-oriented holiday with many carnivalesque elements. In 1930, the entertainment at a New Year's Day event at a major Moscow factory included a brigade from the Meierkhol'd Theater that sang to the workers about waste in the factory. Their song asserted, for example, that if 1,000 people were to choose not to come to work on a religious holiday it would cost the factory 48,000 rubles. The event also included a dramatized meeting at which the report of the worst workshop in the factory was accompanied by a street organ, bringing "comradely laughter." The shortcomings of the last economic year were also put on trial and then buried.[6] In 1930, the theme of production was the core element of a celebration that could be characterized as carnivalesque. The celebration endorsed the mockery of those who did not work efficiently and incorporated the traditional carnival element of the burial of the old year. The leaders of the Cultural Revolution, who promoted this kind of politicized entertainment, believed that the purpose of culture was to advance political and production goals. Non-political entertainment was thus rejected as anti-Soviet. Cultural leaders also sought to eliminate "bourgeois" cultural influences such as jazz music and the fox trot from adult amusements because their "erotic" and "narcotic" nature lured citizens away from socialism.[7]

In 1935, the New Year's holiday changed dramatically. According to the memoirs of his son L. P. Postyshev, it was Pavel Postyshev's idea to reintroduce the fir tree in 1935. His son remembered him complaining,

> Now that we have the opportunity to give the children of workers this joyful holiday, we ourselves forbid the fir tree, as a priest's prejudice. But we ourselves cannot think up a good, happy holiday for children's handlers. By the way, our priests were smarter. The fir tree is not a Christian custom, but it crossed over to us from paganism . . . and priests did not begin fighting with it, but instead used it in their interests.[8]

Postyshev argued that the origins of the holiday, which were pre-Christian in any case, were less important than the benefits it could bring to Soviet children. He wanted the Soviet state to adopt this holiday to advance its own interests. The adoption of the fir tree was thus a pragmatic decision to promote an already established urban holiday tradition throughout the entire Soviet Union to fill a void in the Soviet holiday calendar and mobilize support for the Soviet state.[9]

By 1935, the carnivalesque mockery so central to the 1930 adult New Year's celebrations was almost entirely gone. A winter carnival for Archangelsk lumbermen and their families, held on January 1, 1935, in honor of both New Year's Day and *Den' Udarnika* (Shock Workers' Day), consisted of entertainment that was purged of any critical or mocking elements. Production was still a central theme at a separate New Year's Eve gathering where speakers "summed up the successful fulfillment of the plan" and the most productive workers received the title of "shock worker" and were given prizes.[10] Rewards for good service had replaced mockery for inefficiency; entertainment had replaced carnival.

In the next few years many of the production aspects of New Year's celebrations were pushed even further into the background and were even more sharply separated from holiday entertainment. During the celebration of the 1936 New Year, the first year of the official Stalinist New Year's tree and the first New Year's Day after the founding of the Stakhanovite movement, the Stakhanovite Busygin was faced with a dilemma; he was so popular that he could not decide which social event to attend on New Year's Eve.[11] A January 1937 newsreel showed heroes of Soviet production not at a New Year's Eve production meeting, but at a ball with banquet tables laden with delicacies, fruit, and champagne.[12] Model Soviet citizens now listened to jazz music, danced the fox trot, and enjoyed depoliticized leisure on New Year's Eve.

The changes in New Year's Day were in keeping with other decisions of the Soviet leadership at the same time. In the mid-1930s, the Soviet government backed away from the radicalism of the First Five Year Plan era and the use of coercive methods against the peasantry and sought to promote social stability and increase economic productivity by allowing a limited market for collective farm produce, providing workers with material incentives, and reincorporating selected elements of Russian Imperial patriotic and cultural discourse into Soviet life. Like the fir tree, these elements were not in accord with a socialist worldview, but were nonetheless employed to generate support for the Soviet project. The reintroduction of the fir tree and masquerade balls followed the defeat of the hard line on culture which had excluded both bourgeois art and non-proletarian artists from the Soviet cultural scene.[13] In the mid-1930s, artists from all class origins were welcomed back into the Soviet fold as long as they supported the Soviet state, and it became possible to create works of art that did not have an explicitly political message.

New Year's Day was thus a site of negotiation both among cadres and between cadres and citizens. The introduction of a mobilizing event without overt ideological content created disagreement among Soviet cadres

New Year's ball in the Central House of the Red Army. From *Pravda*, January 2, 1937.

about the extent to which New Year's Day should be politicized. Conflicts about how New Year's Day should be organized illuminate ongoing debates about the role of culture in mobilizing the population to participate in the Soviet project in the 1930s.

New Year's Day also offered the population something new; by promoting a holiday that had its roots in pre-revolutionary bourgeois urban religious culture, the creators of New Year's festivities mobilized citizens to participate in official Soviet events because of their entertainment value rather than their ideological messages.[14] In authorizing official public celebration of the fir tree, the Soviet government also sanctioned private and familial fir tree celebrations which had been forbidden since the beginning of Stalin's Cultural Revolution. New Year's celebrations thus created new opportunities for domestic and depoliticized leisure in Soviet society. Like most other Soviet "compromises," however, the ultimate goal of New Year's celebrations was to increase officials' control over the population. Having enhanced the possibilities for Soviet citizens to participate in a private and home-based holiday, Soviet cadres set about defining the content of such celebrations and circumscribing the private and non-political spaces that they had just created.

Because New Year's Day did not have an established form like the annual revolutionary holidays, Soviet cadres created a wide variety of celebrations with diverse political content and target audiences. For children, cadres decorated trees, organized lively games, and provided costumes, candy, and presents. For adults they organized dinners, carnivals, and masquerade balls. While some New Year's celebrations emphasized entertainment, others explicitly promoted loyalty to Stalin and the Soviet state.

Negotiating Fir Tree Celebrations

In the mid-1930s, Soviet cultural officials debated whether culture had to be explicitly political in order to mobilize the population. A. V. Kosarev criticized the politicization of leisure in the Soviet Union. The protocols of the Central Committee of the Komsomol reflect Kosarev's belief in mobilizing Communist youth through providing depoliticized entertainment. In 1934, for example, he argued that it was better to sing a pretty song than an explicitly Komsomol one.[15] Kosarev believed that the activity of singing rather than the content of the song did the ideological work of creating a unified political movement. He also railed against bureaucratic collective entertainment that created "ersatz" leisure and criticized the attempts of the leaders of the Pioneers, the Communist youth organization for children aged nine to fifteen, to create "minutes of organized laughter."[16] He believed that this trend toward bureaucracy made Komsomol activities less effective in fostering the loyalty of youth to the Soviet cause. Kosarev's attempts to depoliticize leisure were particularly evident during the first New Year's celebrations. Kosarev forbade the Komsomol from organizing any kind of political meeting during the winter holidays of 1935–1936. At fir tree celebrations, he did not allow "any sort of lectures about the activities of the school, about the common goals of the coming year and so forth."[17] He wanted the fir tree festivities to be pure entertainment.

A brochure published by the Komsomol of the Western Siberian Territory in December 1936, "A New Year's Tree for Our Children," also emphasized the creative and artistic aspects of the New Year's celebration rather than the political aspects of the holiday. Of course, few official Soviet events were ever completely apolitical; the Komsomol brochure mentioned the "Soviet country's care for its children" and expressed hope that after the New Year's celebration, the grateful Soviet children would study harder. Some costumes at the masquerade ball were to feature heroes from the Civil War period in addition to characters from fairy tales and classical Russian literature. Komsomol activists were to encourage the children to participate in the invention of a "creative fantasy" that included Soviet heroes but did not privilege them over the other fairy tale characters. The main focus of the brochure was to create a celebration that the children would remember for as long as they lived. The New Year's holiday was "a great and joyous present to the children from their happy parents."[18] As in much Soviet discourse from the mid-1930s, the "happy parents" were, for the most part, projections into the future. Such attention to creating joy for children, however, may have enabled "happy parents" to materialize in the present, at least temporarily.

Material about the New Year's tree published by the Moscow City Committee of the Komsomol for elementary school students also contained few references to politics. While it recommended that Grandfather Frost should tell the children gathered around the fir tree that in the recent past only the children of the rich had fir trees, the vast majority of the fir tree activities focused on nature, fairy tale characters, and forest animals. The dramatis personae of this winter holiday were rabbits, bears, foxes, wolves, Grandfather Frost, his helper Snow Maiden, Red Riding Hood, Sleeping Beauty, Pierrot and Columbine, ballerinas, clowns, and snowflakes. The only representatives of contemporary Soviet life who were acknowledged at the New Year's tree were the pilots and parachutists featured in the children's songs. At the New Year's tree, the children were to dance and sing, run relay races, play freeze tag, and receive gifts.[19]

The collection *Elka: Sbornik statei i materialov (Fir Tree: Collection of Articles and Materials)*, which was published by the toy committee of Narkompros (People's Commissariat of Enlightenment) in 1937, also emphasized the non-political nature of the New Year's tree. The lead article by the editor of the volume, E. Flerina, did not emphasize official slogans such as "the children's gratitude to Stalin for their happy lives." Instead, it focused on the practical considerations of preparing a fir tree for young schoolchildren. The main thrust of the article was to show teachers how to delight the children by decorating a New Year's tree. All political concerns were secondary to the main goal of making the children feel "happy, celebratory, . . . free, joyful, and easy." Like the pamphlet from Western Siberia, this collection saw the fir tree as a means of developing the children's aesthetic sensibilities and giving children "material for their imagination, and for the flight of their fantasies."[20] Flerina called for freedom and easiness during the fir tree celebration and protested against a "dry, *kazennogo* (bureaucratic)" organization of the fir tree ceremony in which "strict order" inhibited the children.[21] By emphasizing the children's creativity and free movement, Flerina raised her voice against the cultural models in place during the Cultural Revolution, the tendency toward regimentation in Soviet life, and the uniformity that Soviet authorities increasingly imposed on holiday ceremonies and political demonstrations during the 1930s.

The depoliticized fir tree seemed to strike a chord among Soviet officials and citizens alike. Flerina complained that the novelty of the fir tree was wearing off because "some parents, in the space of six days, managed to take their children to see ten New Year's trees."[22] This "complaint" shows that the fir tree was able to mobilize parents and children more success-fully than many official Soviet events. Nina M. Sorochenko, a nursery-school teacher, described the preparation for the first official New Year's tree as "strikingly different from that for 'revolutionary holidays' of previous years" that had been "colorless and stereotyped." Sorochenko explained that everyone became preoccupied with "finding something with which to make tree decorations." Her solutions to this problem included bonbon-nières, baskets, cornucopias, little houses made of straw, red holly berries, and fruits and vegetables made out of painted cotton.[23] Sorochenko's de-scription of the 1936 New Year's ball organized at her school reveals its apolitical nature. The little girls were dressed up as snowflakes and the little boys as bunnies. The children received bags of sweets, nuts, and apples, and "even responsible Party workers danced the fox trot and tango."[24] The cultural workers in the nursery school used the celebration of other Soviet holidays as a time to teach parents slogans and to make sure that they had subscribed to the state loan.[25] The New Year's celebration focused instead on creating a beautiful holiday world for the children. Even "responsible" Party officials felt free to participate in this world of celebration.

While some officials were overjoyed at the promotion of a popular fam-ily-centered tradition, other officials were less pleased at the encourage-ment of a celebration that had such strong connections with the pre-revo-lutionary past. Because of the "Sovietization" of the fir tree, Soviet officials had to cope with the contradictions inherent in the self-conscious adapta-tion of a "bourgeois" tradition connected to the religious past by a self-avowed proletarian and atheist state. Negotiating the multiple Soviet, reli-gious, and popular meanings of the fir tree and its decorations often put Soviet officials at odds with Soviet citizens and with each other.

The mixture of old and new symbols led to conflicting interpretations and differing opinions about which symbols constituted appropriate deco-ration for a "Soviet" New Year's tree. Nina Sorochenko described a De-cember 1935 visit to her nursery school by representatives of Narkompros and the Section of Public Health, who found fault with the school's fir tree. The children, relying on traditional fir tree methods, had festooned the tree with chains that they had made out of colored paper. The visitors demanded that the teachers remove these chains, insisting, "How can there be an emblem of slavery on a Soviet fir tree, on the first joyous socialist fir tree?"[26] The unexpected reaction of the officials shows how even the simplest artis-tic expression could convey multiple and conflicting meanings. It also in-dicates that certain Soviet officials, who could not help but be aware of the contradictions inherent in the introduction of a Soviet Christmas tree, were on their guard against any further concessions to the old order. Two years later, however, *Fir Tree* ignored the political association of the chain with slavery and encouraged the festooning of the New Year's tree with paper chains. In an article devoted to homemade fir tree decorations, which were often the only kind available, E. Bykovskaia advocated the fashioning of multicolored paper chains for hanging on the fir tree. She was particularly enthusiastic about the chains because "chains are generally a very worthwhile subject around which to organize collective work."[27] Bykovskaia implied that rather than representing slavery, chain making was a way of teaching children to labor collectively in the socialist state.

In *Fir Tree*, the authors consistently defended all "traditional" tree decorations except explicitly religious ones. Flerina argued against the politicization of fir tree ornaments, and thereby against the politicization of the New Year holiday. Flerina praised a set of New Year's tree ornaments that featured images of socialist construction such as the Metro, Dneprogas, a traffic light, and an oil well, but she rejected one official's proposal to do away with "old" fir tree decorations and to create fir trees with only socialist decorations. Flerina remonstrated, "It is wrong to say that sparkles, golden stars, animals and birds . . . are 'old images.' These are decoratively shaped life images which are familiar and entertaining for the child."[28] Flerina's defense of old celebratory traditions and non-political decorations was consistent with a view of the New Year's celebration as a vehicle for children's happiness, not for their political indoctrination.

The recommendations from Komsomol and Narkompros leaders about organizing a New Year's celebration that focused on the pleasure of Soviet children rather than on their political education illustrate a significant trend among those who participated in the redefinition of the New Year's holiday. These leaders did not worry unduly about the earlier association of the fir tree with the religious holiday of Christmas. Nor did they concern themselves with the possibility that they were replicating an alien bourgeois culture. Rather, these groups focused on the entertainment and the stimulation that exposure to a beautifully decorated tree would provide the children. These benefits were not related to the children's political education. Instead, they furnished stimulus to the children's imagination and brought some brightness into their often drab and difficult lives. This nonpolitical attitude toward the fir tree, while dominant, was not universally held. The proposal to eliminate any kind of tree decoration except those connected to socialist life and the attack on the nursery-school teachers for festooning their tree with chains revealed that some Soviet officials contested Narkompros's interpretation of New Year's Day.

Other Soviet officials linked the celebration of New Year's Day to the ongoing struggle against religion. They felt that official fir tree celebrations competed directly with the religious rituals and traditions of the Christmas season. Komsomol officials in Kuibyshev Territory in 1936, for example, categorized the organization of fir trees in all of the schools of the territory during the Christmas holidays as "anti-religious" work.[29] The goal of their fir tree celebrations was to steal some of the thunder from the private commemoration of the Christmas holidays. These Soviet organizers wanted children to be delighted during the winter holidays by a civic rather than a religious celebration, a public rather than a private one. Through the reintroduction of the fir tree, some Soviet officials sought to gain control over the festivities of the winter holiday period.

The new fir tree celebration became a site of contestation between citizens and the state about the way that Christmas would be celebrated. While the fir tree celebration gave new autonomy to the family, it made celebrating New Year's Day in the home an affirmation of Soviet holiday traditions. No longer could a secret fir tree celebration be an avenue of resistance.[30] Soviet officials' designation of January 1 as the appropriate date for fir tree celebrations was an attempt to diminish the celebration of Christmas. New Year's celebrations used children to change their parents' holiday calendar and private family traditions. Valentina Bogdan, an engineer from Rostov who remembered the Christmas trees of her youth with great nostalgia, resented the fact that the newly allowed Christmas trees had to be lit up on January 1 rather than on Christmas Day, January 7. She felt that the officially sponsored fir trees in public places forced parents to light their own private trees before Christmas: "The children, seeing that the time for the fir tree had arrived, did not want to wait another week for their trees at home." Bogdan complained, "Lighting the tree before Christmas, I felt that I had taken something away from the true holiday."[31] She reported that Soviet authorities did not permit trees to be sold after January 1, and they cautioned the population that keeping fir trees after New Year's Day created a fire hazard. Bogdan resisted the state's redefinition of the holiday season by keeping her tree up until Christmas Day and inviting the children of friends and neighbors over on Christmas Day to "take down" the fir tree.[32] In this particular case, rather than supplanting Christmas, the reintroduction of the fir tree actually enhanced the private celebration of Christmas with friends at home.

The celebration of the holiday with friends at home could also lead to behaviors that were considered anti-Soviet. Private parties on New Year's Eve were sites of heavy drinking. Galina Shtange wrote in her memoirs that when her son returned home from a New Year's Eve party on January 1, 1938, he was "pale as death, cold and with a barely detectable pulse." She stayed awake all night, afraid that he would die.[33] The promotion of a private holiday provided opportunities for drunken revelry and the commemoration of Christmas to occur in the homes of individuals, beyond the control of Soviet officials.

Although Narkompros did not advocate the politicization of New Year's Day, it still sought to exert control over the production of New Year's toys and tree ornaments. An article by S. Bazykin, a co-editor of *Fir Tree*, was directed at the factories and cooperatives that produced fir tree ornaments and toys. In addition to discussing the specifications for various ornaments, Bazykin complained that the ornament producers stuck to pre-revolutionary forms and did not think that they needed the input of trained artists. Bazykin demanded that in order to avoid "ruin[ing] the children's aesthetic taste" it was time for "production organizations to stop holding the harmful opinion that toys and tree ornaments can be made by amateur craftsmen." The "artistic" input that Bazykin demanded, however, would also allow education authorities to increase their control over the production of New Year's toys.[34]

The lack of control of Party and educational officials over ornament production led to the creation of objects that Soviet cadres considered to be lacking in "culture." One organizer of New Year's celebrations complained about the production of "negative" masks that portrayed identities such as a drunkard, a swine, an ass, or a freak.[35] He advocated, instead, the creation of masks with positive Soviet identities. Kosarev was greatly displeased when the Moscow Cooperative of Wine and Spirits produced miniature pitchers filled with syrup and matching shot glasses as New Year's toys in late 1936. He railed, "This is *sploshnoe golovotiapstvo* (complete, stupid bungling). . . . This accustoms children to alcohol. Why should we give children such toys?"[36] The celebratory nature of New Year's Day and the increased production of toys for the occasion created new opportunities for Soviet agencies and individuals to reproduce artifacts of a traditional popular culture that clashed with Soviet holiday goals.

Despite the fact that the content of the New Year holiday was rarely politicized and private aspects of the holiday were officially sanctioned, Soviet officials nonetheless sought to oversee the New Year's holiday. Officials lost control over what happened in individual homes, but they gained the power to affect the timing of the holiday. Although they did not demand that all ornaments have a political theme, they nonetheless tried to strengthen their regulation of ornament production. And although they embraced pre-revolutionary holiday culture as a way to mobilize the population, they sought to filter out aspects of traditional culture that they found objectionable. The New Year's holiday in some ways made Soviet power more effective and in other ways gave Soviet citizens more freedom. The discussions about New Year's Day also showed the ongoing disagreements among cultural cadres about the place of bourgeois culture in Soviet society and the best way to gain the loyalties of Soviet citizens.

Politics and Children

Not all official fir tree celebrations remained apolitical. The Moscow Trade Union Council organized a fir tree in the Hall of Columns from January 1 to January 12, 1937. During this twelve-day period, there were twenty-two separate celebrations in the Hall of Columns in which 26,800 children and 8,000 adults participated.[37] An article in *Fir Tree* described the fir tree

Hall of Columns Fir Tree, 1937. From *Elka: Sbornik statei i materialov* (1937).

festivities in the Hall of Columns with many references to their gaiety and only one reference to the political content of the celebrations. This "political" reference noted that the Hall of Columns was adorned by a portrait of Stalin among children.[38]

The detailed description of the fir tree celebration, which was sent to the Moscow Trade Union Council by the celebration's organizers, however, was filled with political language and references to the political content of the ceremonies. One reason for this difference was, of course, the different audience for the document. The purpose of the second document was to prove to the Trade Union Council that the money spent on the celebration was worthwhile and that the celebration had been effective in transmitting its message to children. The organizers described this effect on the children not in terms of the development of their aesthetic sensibilities or the stimulus to their imaginations, but in terms of their dedication to Stalin and Moscow Party boss Nikita Khrushchev. This politicized fir tree celebration for children both illuminates the workings of the Stalin cult and reveals transformations in the social organization of Stalinist society in the mid-1930s.

The report to the Trade Union Council described the creation of a children's wonderland in the Hall of Columns. During the celebration, the children wandered through the Hall of Toys, the Hall of Pushkin's Fairy Tales[39], and the Hall of Animals, or they frolicked in a Winter Park decorated in a northern theme. After the children had played for a time, they were summoned to watch the lighting of the fir tree. Then the children broke up into groups for games and contests and finally were gathered together again at the end of the celebration so that prizes could be awarded to the contest winners.[40]

In the two segments of the celebration during which the children were all gathered together, the children sang explicitly political songs. The organizers noted that the children sang the last stanza of "The Holiday Song" in an especially uplifting way. This stanza included the lines "We are proud of our native country. / We sing happy songs. / The beloved name of Stalin, / We carry carefully in our hearts." The children also sang "Thanks to the great Stalin for our miraculous days."[41] While songs and poems about Stalin were missing from the article on music in Narkompros's *Fir Tree*, the organizers of the Hall of Columns celebration reported their enthusiastic participation in promoting the cult of Stalin.[42] The report focused on how the celebration fostered love of Stalin by associating him with miraculous deeds and acknowledging his supreme role in the creation of the children's happy lives.

The final segment of the Hall of Columns holiday even adopted a form that was explicitly political. This part of the holiday included some of the standard features of an adult political meeting. A group of Pioneers proposed to send Stalin a "pioneer greeting" and to send Khrushchev a letter from all the children participating in the holiday celebration. According to the organizers, "The children received this proposal with rapture." The letter to Khrushchev had been prepared beforehand in the form of a song. The first verse of the song began:

> Nikita Sergeevich, we hurry to say from the soul,
> As we are gathered beneath the beautiful fir tree,
> Thank you very much for the fir tree, for the happy holiday.
> We want you to tell Comrade Stalin,
> Today, from all of the Pioneers of Moscow
> Thank you, our beloved Stalin.

The three subsequent verses, which elaborated on the New Year holiday, happy childhood in the Soviet Union, and studying hard in school, each ended with the words "Thank you, our beloved Stalin."[43]

The organizers of the Hall of Columns fir tree celebration closed their report by reproducing three letters purportedly written by the children who had participated in the fir tree celebration. The organizers claimed that these letters were the best evidence of the "usefulness of the enormous work that we undertook." The first letter was from Nina Mukhina: "I didn't want to go home. This fir tree will remain in my memory for the rest of my life. Thanks to the great, dear, Comrade Stalin for all of his concern about us." This letter reflected the writer's recognition of the fantasy aspects of the holiday and of its political side. The second letter was from Elena Morgenstern, whose mother told her, "Now you see, daughter, how the Party, the government and dear Comrade Stalin are concerned about you. And when you grow up, you will stand up in the defense of our dear socialist motherland." The third letter-writer, Lidia Lopatina, noted, "We are very happy that we have such a happy childhood" and enclosed a poem: "We don't know worries and sadness. / The genius loves children. / He ordered life to be happier. / The genius swept away all sadness from our path. / We romp and we sing, / We call out his name. / This genius is our beloved Stalin."[44] The fir tree organizers thus demonstrated how the educational and fantasy aspects of the holiday promoted political loyalty to Stalin and the Soviet state.

An incident at the toy exhibition that the organizers of the Hall of Columns celebration included in their report provides some information about the identities of the children at the celebration. The organizers noted that at the toy telephones located at either side of the hall, "fans of telephone conversations carried on a *delovoi* (business-like) conversation. 'Sasha, do you hear me? I will ask papa to buy me a telephone like this one.' The answer carries from the other end of the hall. 'Me too.'"[45] Whether or not the children's fathers could really afford to buy these expensive toys, the use of the adjective *delovoi* by the fir tree organizers underlined the fact that real telephones were important tools used by the cadres who ruled the Soviet Union. Toy telephones were even categorized as "defense toys" by Soviet officials.[46] The organizers proudly reported the children's emulation of adult political meetings and Party work. The implication was that these children would become devoted Party and government officials. In describing the children's behavior in a fairyland of wonder, the authors of the report focused not on the tremendous privilege that such an afternoon's entertainment represented in a time of widespread deprivation, but on how New Year's Day festivities would enable Party bureaucrats and political officials to replicate themselves in the next generation.

The organizers of the Hall of Columns fir tree, who had to justify spending significant public resources on a children's fantasy world, represented their celebration as political to those in charge of giving them funding. They emphasized political mobilization and adherence to the "cults" of Khrushchev and Stalin in describing the same event that Narkompros officials depicted as an apolitical fantasy world. By omitting rather than emphasizing the political aspects of the celebration, Narkompros officials strengthened their stance against a "dry" and "bureaucratic" celebration.

Narkompros and the Hall of Columns celebration organizers each high-lighted the aspects of the celebration that would be most helpful in pro-moting their ideals or their careers.

The trade union organizers' emphasis on politics in the Hall of Col-umns fir tree celebration and their claims that this politicized message was adopted by the young participants reveal that this celebration was unlike most fir tree celebrations. The nearly 27,000 Moscow children who partici-pated in this particular celebration received a political message that was either cursorily addressed or completely absent from other fir tree celebra-tions. The way trade union cadres described the political aim of this cel-ebration was completely different from the way Narkompros cadres ex-plained the educational aims of the fir tree celebrations in much of the pamphlet literature. Given the location, the very high quality of the event, and the fact that the organizers emphasized the children's emulation of political and bureaucratic forms, it is likely that the Moscow children who were granted access to the fairy-tale atmosphere of the most wonderful fir tree celebration in the country were the best Moscow students and the chil-dren of the Moscow elite.[47] Among these children in particular the fir tree was used to foster loyalty and devotion to Stalin. These were the children who were being groomed to be the next generation of Soviet leaders; these children received special privileges and special indoctrination.

Not only were the children of the elite feted at lavish public celebra-tions, but these children also had fir trees in their homes. Galina Shtange, who was an active member of the *obshchestvennitsa*, or wives' volunteer movement, of the mid-1930s, and whose husband was a professor at the Moscow Electromechanical Institute of Railroad Engineers, recalled in her diary that "everyone has a New Year's tree now, though there was a time when they were completely banned. I remember a time in Udelnaya when I wanted so much to decorate a tree, but we didn't dare. But now people do everything they can to make sure every child has the chance to enjoy a New Year's tree."[48] Shtange's desire for a New Year's tree even when they were still forbidden explains her enthusiastic reception of the fir tree; on January 1, 1938, she decorated a fir tree and had a party for her grandchil-dren. When Shtange said that "everyone" had a tree, she referred to those in her relatively privileged milieu. The celebration of New Year's with one's own tree was a mark of status among the new elite in Moscow in the 1930s.

Valentina Bogdan, another privileged Soviet engineer, reported that in the city of Rostov a large number of toys and decorations for the New Year's tree were available. She noted that "despite their high cost, the most beau-tiful and interesting toys were sold out very quickly."[49] Whimsical tree deco-rations, which had not been available for several years, were joyfully snatched up by the eager Soviet shoppers who could afford to pay for them. Attractive decorations on one's private tree were thus a sign of status and an indication that one could afford to purchase items that were not neces-sities.

Lidia Chukovskaia's novella about the 1930s, *Sofiia Petrovna*, includes an incident at a fir tree celebration in a Soviet office in 1937 which reveals how the fir tree celebration marked the status of a certain group of Soviet children. The title character, Sofiia Petrovna, was in charge of organizing the fir tree for all of the children in her editorial office. The chair of the Mestkom (local trade union committee) became offended when her son's present was only a drum while the son of the Party secretary received wooden soldiers. Sofiia Petrovna had also purchased a special present for the director's daughter: a "pretty little trumpet with a fluffy tassel."[50] Sofiia Petrovna's ranking of the children according to their parents' positions and the chair of the Mestkom's desire to be treated as an equal to the Party secretary suggest some of the ways in which Soviet fir tree celebrations awarded status and reinforced hierarchy, particularly among the children of the Soviet elite.[51]

The New Year's Day celebration's emphasis on consumption also linked it to the creation of new social hierarchies. While the purchase of food, alcohol, and tree decorations was intended to show the improved standard of living of all Soviet citizens, special holiday purchases were only possible for the elite urban citizens who had access to and extra money for holiday luxuries. Bogdan was very surprised to find oranges, the traditional fir tree decoration and treat, in the stores in the city of Rostov before New Year's Day 1936. Since oranges usually had to be bought abroad and paid for with hard currency, they had not been available for many years.[52] According to *Pravda*, a wide variety of holiday foods was available in Moscow before New Year's Day 1937. A January 1 article announced that in Moscow pre-holiday purchases of champagne, wine, kolbasa, smoked fish, cakes, cookies, and fruit brought in 35 million rubles on December 30 and a record 45 million rubles on December 31. Moscow stores also sold 4 million rubles' worth of tree decorations.[53] Since Soviet factories only produced 12 to 15 million rubles of tree decorations in 1936, virtually a third of the supply of decorations for the entire country went to stores in Moscow.[54] The sales of champagne, smoked fish, and festive decorations testified to the purchasing power of *znatnye liudi* (notables) in the Soviet capital and other urban areas. New Year's Day as a holiday of consumption differentiated the Soviet urban elite from the rest of the population.

Newsreels transmitted Moscow images of abundantly stocked delicatessens, stores full of new consumer goods such as pianos and other musical instruments, and elite holiday merrymaking to the rest of the Soviet Union. The New Year's newsreels of this period interspersed images of the year's socialist construction and achievements with glimpses of prosperity and gaiety.[55] The newsreel *Happy New Year*, which ushered in the 1936 New Year, ended with a song declaring that "we live happily today" and promising that "tomorrow will be happier still."[56] These news documentaries carefully selected images of elite Soviet citizens and broadcast them as examples of how the Soviet people lived. The films depicted the prosperity that was a cornerstone of Soviet myth but that was fully enjoyed only by a tiny group. The disparity between myth and reality was bridged in the newsreel by the implicit promise in the film that those who had yet to live happily today could hope for a tomorrow that was happier still.

Soviet Carnivals for Adults

In the mid-1930s, the organizers of New Year's celebrations explicitly acknowledged the separation of politics and play. In December 1937, an article in the journal *Klub* suggested that propagandists organize discussions highlighting the most important events of 1937 on December 29 and 30 since "at the New Year's evening itself you will hardly succeed in organizing such . . . discussions."[57] The phrase "hardly succeed" suggests that the atmosphere of the New Year's celebration was no longer conducive to political discussions. New Year's Day was celebrated in full accordance with two trends in 1930s celebration: the separation of official political celebrations from light-hearted entertainment and the promotion of a "tamed" carnival.

Rosalinde Sartorti has argued that Stalinist carnivals in the mid-1930s corresponded to the worldview of certain Stalinist elites who staged an "illusionary world of art" in order to confirm their own positions. According to Sartorti, however, these carnivals lacked spontaneity and failed "to create an emotional involvement, an identification with the new norms and values expressed on this occasion" among the rest of the population.[58] Sartorti's conclusion that Stalinist control and lack of spontaneity destroyed the carnivalesque nature of Soviet carnivals needs further examination. While I do not believe that carnivals in Stalinist Russia represented Bakhtinian carnival moments when "official truth" was overthrown by folk resistance, I explore the extent to which Soviet official carnivals created a space for limited social critique and for activities that did not comfortably fit into the official Soviet worldview.[59]

G. D. Kremlev, the organizer of the major Moscow summer carnivals in Gorkii Park, was also the creator of a prototype of a New Year's carnival that was to take place in Railroad Clubs and Palaces of Culture throughout the Soviet Union.[60] This scenario was reproduced in ninety copies in 1938 and, presumably, distributed to the heads of railroad clubs across the Soviet Union. It met with some success because 350 more copies were printed in 1939. While it is impossible to know how many of Kremlev's carnivals actually took place, it is certain that the carnival scenario was aimed at an audience of Soviet cultural cadres.

Kremlev was aware that "routine" and "cliché" condemned a masquerade ball to failure and he acknowledged that the ball's "success was defined by the degree of creative invention and resourceful activity" of the organizers.[61] Nevertheless, Kremlev's official carnival had a bureaucratized form and included elements that Kosarev might have criticized as "moments of organized laughter." By developing plans for gaiety, organizers risked undermining their attempts to create a happy celebration since enforced gaiety only underscored the absence of joy.

The language of official Soviet carnivals revealed the organizers' overriding concern that the participants be joyful. At the 1937 New Year's ball for Stakhanovites and other heroes of Soviet production, a placard proclaimed in rhyme: "All are strictly cautioned to leave their sadness outside."[62] The prototype of the railroad workers' carnival contained plans for a "cloakroom for bad moods." A sign proclaimed: "It is strictly prohibited to be sad or to despair." Further directions included: "Check your bad mood. Go out on the dance floor and try to lose your receipt. Note: Pleasant moods may not be returned."[63] These signs are remarkable in a number of ways. The first significant aspect of these placards is their implicit recognition that the guests at these New Year's balls might be weighed down by sadness when they arrived. The guests might be in a bad mood or even in despair. The organizers of carnivals for the Soviet elite suggested that the territory of the carnival was distinct from the difficulties, worries, and fears of the participants' everyday lives. It was the carnival's special role to bring them joy and to dispel their unhappy feelings, even though Soviet discourse proclaimed that all citizens were already happy.

These signs also show that the carnival organizers described emotional life as if emotions were concrete objects that could be physically manipulated by their possessors. Participants could leave their sadness outside or at the coat-check along with their boots and umbrellas. While happiness was not as "concrete," the carnival organizers believed that it could be found on the dance floor and in the company of others, since "according to masquerade rules, it is strictly prohibited to remain alone."[64] The proposition that emotions could be physically manipulated reflected, in exaggerated form, Soviet ideas about the ability of humans to control their environment through strength of will. This objectification of emotion reflected the superficiality of the carnival atmosphere.

In order to help people to follow the rule of not "remaining alone" the author of the New Year's carnival for railroad workers proposed an organized mingling of male and female guests. To help people become acquainted, the cultural workers were to hand out envelopes of one color to men and another to women. Inside each envelope was a postcard that had been cut in half. The carnival participants were to approach members of the opposite sex in order to find the other halves of their postcards; the first twenty couples who matched up received prizes. Kremlev thus envisioned gaiety being created by association with the opposite sex. Happiness was to be found in personal relationships rather than in service to the state. In regard to this activity, however, he warned cultural workers "not to use postcards on serious subjects for this game."[65] This admonition shows that

Kremlev feared that someone might mistakenly create a highly subversive situation in which carnival participants raced around matching up the parts of dismembered portraits of political leaders. The need for this admonition reminds us that Stalinist culture's attitude of enforced reverence toward political symbols led to numerous opportunities for accidental or intentional political subversion.

Another form of entertainment at New Year's carnivals was fortune-telling, which had been a widely practiced New Year's Eve custom in pre-revolutionary Russia.[66] A contemporary observer noted in his diary in January 1937 that "fortune telling is all the rage among young people—so much for their consciousness."[67] But in the mid-1930s, fortune-telling was not just a private activity; this traditional custom appeared in the journal *Klub* as a recommended component of a New Year's carnival.[68] The railroad carnival prototype also endorsed fortune-telling as a carnival activity. The author suggested that carnival organizers prepare written fortunes in advance, but that they could allow a fortune-teller to improvise if a "cultured, resourceful and witty performer played the role."[69] The Soviet carnival of the mid-1930s incorporated carefully controlled but ideologically alien elements in the name of fun and entertainment. As the contemporary observer implied, fortune-telling constituted a carnivalesque inversion of the Soviet political ideology of "scientific socialism." The fad for fortune-telling also underscored the anxieties of Soviet life as prominent Soviet citizens feared that they could be turned into enemies overnight. Under these circumstances, official fortune-tellers' promises of a happy future might have reassured uneasy Soviet cadres.

The game that matched up couples, fortune-telling about future love, and a carnival booth called the "loves me, loves me not machine" encouraged the development of personal relationships as a means of entertainment. These games were encouraged by carnival organizers and cultural workers despite the fact that they sometimes contradicted socialist ideals, could easily get beyond the organizers' control, and put pressure on the borders of acceptable public behavior in Soviet society. The emphasis on romance as an antidote to the difficulties of the world outside the carnival acknowledged the significance of private life. The privileging of the private was a rare occurrence in the official discourse of the 1930s in which the division between public and private was officially denied; the private gained a more prominent place in Soviet culture during World War II and in the post-war years.[70]

While Soviet carnival was fragile and could not easily fulfill its task of creating gaiety, it is possible to detect some carnivalesque elements in the form of the New Year's ball. The organizers of Soviet carnival chose to adopt a didactic trope in carnival pronouncements. They communicated to carnival participants by "strongly cautioning" them to leave their sadness behind or "strongly prohibiting" them from despairing. One reason that they did so was because of the rigid parameters of Soviet discourse. Soviet political language did not offer many possibilities for articulating ideas about leisure, relaxation, or merry-making, so cadres had to fall back on a pervasive bureaucratic discourse. A polite invitation which offered the participants the choice of whether or not to take part was rare in political discourse; the participants had to be "strictly cautioned" to have fun. The way organizers employed Soviet didactic and bureaucratic language in inappropriate situations made these statements ironic. The organizers in some sense engaged in self-parody as the purveyors of silly rules; they created an implicit critique of the myriad rules and regulations, great and petty, of the bureaucratic state.

The encouragement to check one's sorrows and lose the receipt, for example, was particularly significant in a society in which passes, permits, and receipts were ubiquitous indicators of the operation of the bureaucratic and political systems. The loss of a pass, permit, or receipt could cause a great deal of inconvenience or even serious trouble for Soviet citizens.[71] By making the loss of a receipt bring happiness instead of sadness and frustration, carnival planners turned one bureaucratic value upside down, creating a carnivalesque reversal. The parody of rules gains another level of meaning because the carnival rules that sought to control people's emotional states, along with many other Soviet rules and regulations, were unenforceable. Carnival rules pointed to the limits of Stalinist decrees.

In addition to using bureaucratic language to try to accomplish the impossible tasks of changing people's moods, the author of the railroad workers' carnival also parodied the heroic language that was used to acclaim great Soviet achievements of the 1920s and 1930s. Kremlev planned that between two and three o'clock in the morning all participants should be on the dance floor. He called this time the "hour of the liquidation of dance illiteracy."[72] By evoking the familiar heroic slogan of "liquidating illiteracy," Kremlev emphasized the desirability and necessity of learning how to dance but trivialized literacy campaigns.

The mocking of Soviet heroic language was especially evident in one proposed carnival booth. A curtain was set up so that carnival participants could not see the contents of the booth. A sign on the outside majestically proclaimed "Mystery Chamber: Dream or Reality?" and "The age-old dream of humanity is accomplished. The transmission of thoughts over distance." When the participants entered the chamber they found only an ordinary mailbox. A second variant promised "Novelty: Fire in your Pocket. The achievements of chemistry at the service of humanity." Inside the chamber was a box of matches.[73] Through traditional carnival humor, this booth revealed the illusory nature of highly vaunted technical achievements and could be interpreted as a critique of Soviet tendencies to idealize technological achievement. While it could be argued that the showcasing of the postal service and matches proved to carnival participants that they had advanced technology at their fingertips, the enormous promise on the exterior of the booth followed by the ordinary products inside mirrored the experience of Soviet carnival participants who discovered in the course of their daily lives that well-publicized advances in Soviet technology did not always yield the promised results. The carnival booth played on the enormous distinction between Soviet myth and reality, between the external appearances and the internal workings of Soviet life.

While the carnival for railroad workers parodied some of the bureaucratic and heroic language of Soviet life, it also used Soviet heroic language in a straightforward manner in club decorations, in the creation of production-oriented slogans, and in commemorating the most solemn moments of the New Year's ball, the arrival of midnight and the toast to Stalin. The serious use of heroic language and the parodying of that language coexisted in the carnival evening; carnival organizers displayed their political loyalty and played with the parameters of that loyalty at the same time.

The actual form of the masquerade also played with some of the conventions of Stalinist society. Kremlev insisted that at the New Year's ball everyone should wear a mask. Part of the enjoyment of the evening was to come from concealing one's own identity and taking on another one. These images of a full-scale Soviet masquerade ball in the mid-1930s seem incongruous because of the concurrent rhetoric of Stalin's purges. The purges were all about the "unmasking" of enemies and traitors who had disguised themselves as loyal citizens. Contemporaneous with this treacherous masking and deadly unmasking, the masquerade ball became fashionable entertainment and privileged Soviet citizens played at disguises. Soviet carnival provided an opportunity for Soviet citizens to deny or diffuse their fears.

In the publicity promoting the masquerade ball, Kremlev touched on another sore spot in Soviet society: the way in which the victims of the purges simply disappeared from their homes. One of the model advertisements for the New Year's ball gave a description of a man who has "ushel iz doma (left home)." The advertisement continued, "Please do not worry. He will return on the morning of January 1. He will be at the masquerade ball. Why don't you come too?"[74] This play on the disappearance and reappearance of a carnival participant reflected the fears of the Soviet elite and tried to reassure them that their lives would continue normally despite the turmoil that surrounded them.

The emphasis on teaching carnival participants to dance and the parodies on bureaucratic and technical language provide some clues about the intended audience for the railroad carnival. Railroad workers were singled out as a privileged group in Stalinist society. In 1936, they became the first civilian industry to be granted their own special holiday.[75] The prototype carnival proposed by the Central House of Culture of Railroad workers was elaborate in nature and required a considerable staff and a large amount of money to organize. Railroad clubs and palaces of culture, like the clubs of other key industries, tended to be better funded and staffed than other clubs; because of their special function, transport workers tended to be better paid than other workers. Transport workers and managers were designated as elite. The New Year's carnival was to provide established elites and those rising in rank with cultural trappings suitable to their positions. They were to mingle and establish ties with one another in a social situation, to partake of light and harmless entertainment such as fortune-telling, and to learn classical ballroom and western dances.

In creating entertainment for the bureaucratic-technical elite, the carnival author parodied bureaucratic-technical culture in a self-critical way. While not directly critical of the political order, the carnival's ambiguity provided an opportunity to explore the meaning of the rules and regulations of the railroad bureaucracy's own political culture and the general political culture of the Soviet state. By manipulating the concepts of masks and masquerades and even playing with the ideas of disappearance and reappearance, the carnival's author revealed his anxieties about the terror in Soviet life and about the tenuous links between Soviet myths and realities. While the carnival did not turn the social hierarchy upside down, it did provide an opportunity for those who occupied the middle of the hierarchy to play with the conventions they were usually obliged to follow and to test the limits of their own authority.

Fir Trees and Disaster

Attempts to create a fantasy world of holiday entertainment were sometimes ruined by the Soviet realities of a lack of qualified cadres and the tendency to ignore instructions from Moscow, republican, regional, and district centers. There were a number of fires at public New Year's celebrations in 1937, the first year that Soviet institutions organized fir trees for children on a wide scale. Despite the propaganda emphasis on the power of electricity to transform Soviet life and culture, many public fir trees were still lit with candles rather than electric lights.[76] Two articles in *Pravda* on January 2, 1937, publicized terrible accidents at New Year's celebrations. In Sverdlovsk 400 people celebrated the New Year in a hall that should only have accommodated 120. Disaster struck when a " hot candle fell on the head of a child who was wearing a bunny costume made of cotton. The cotton caught fire and soon other children's costumes were burning. The children panicked and ran away from the fir tree, while in their panic their parents ran toward them."[77] Thirteen children were burned, three were seriously injured, and one child died. The horrible image of innocent children wounded or killed by the bunny costumes that were supposed to bring them delight underscored the nightmare of celebration turning into terror.

Pravda reported a second incident that occurred near Kirov in the city of Slobodskii. An eleven-year-old girl who was dressed up as Grandfather Frost burned to death after a candle fell on her costume. Four other students also received burns. The final paragraph of this article revealed the atmosphere in which these articles were written: "Workers in the school and in the city department of education, who allowed criminal negligence in the preparation of the fir tree, will be held responsible."[78] The appearance of these articles in *Pravda* indicates that high government officials considered fir tree accidents to be a serious problem. The direct or indirect assignment of blame to negligent organizers in both articles suggests that these incidents were publicized as warnings to other fir tree organizers about the danger of fire at fir tree celebrations, and the need for cadres to follow directions and exercise strict control over these events.

Fir tree accidents were a common occurrence in January of 1937. The Central Committee of the Komsomol, which was responsible for the organization of fir trees, received reports of fourteen accidents in which children were killed or severely burned. Komsomol figures show that thirty-nine children died and eighty were seriously hurt in these incidents.[79] The Komsomol figures do not include mishaps that resulted in only minor injuries; fir tree accidents may have been even more widespread. These tragic events underscore two issues that are critically important to the analysis of Soviet celebrations of the 1930s: the disorganization of Soviet cadres and the unintended consequences when Soviet officials lost control over the events they were supposed to supervise.

In 1935 the Central Committee of the Komsomol encouraged schools and other Soviet institutions to organize fir trees, and pushed for the inclusion of tree ornaments in industrial production plans, but it did not put a lot of emphasis on the basic rules of fir tree safety until dozens of children were killed.[80] This was in part a result of the hectic pace of central Soviet administration in the 1930s, when plans for celebrations and other events were hurried and not thought through completely. When assigning blame for accidents in January 1937, Kosarev admitted that they should not have released flammable toys or cotton for use in fir tree celebrations.[81] Thus, central authorities were negligent because they organized holiday production without the safety of children in mind. Although letters were sent out forbidding children to be dressed in cotton or gauze where there were candles on the fir tree, these instructions were ignored by local officials, and the central administration of the Komsomol did not effectively monitor local fir tree safety.[82] As recent discussions of the bureaucratic culture of Soviet local administration show, orders from "the center" or from regional authorities often did not reach or were disregarded by local officials.[83] In January 1937, carelessness on the part of local officials led to the deaths of children. These incidents prompted Narkompros to draw up strict guidelines concerning the prevention of fir tree fires in November, 1937. The new regulations included injunctions against candles, overcrowding, and the hanging of decorations or the wearing of costumes that had not been made fire resistant.[84]

As the *Pravda* articles show, the blame for accidents was placed primarily on the local organizers of fir tree celebrations. The central authorities delegated the organization of New Year's celebrations to local officials who could not cope with them. It required only common sense to prohibit overcrowding where there were candles on the tree or to prevent children who were wearing flammable costumes from coming too close to the tree. Kosarev admitted in early January of 1937 that the fir tree campaign *"predostavili samotek* (had been allowed to take its own course)," and that the Komsomol had "allowed anyone who wanted to engage in this matter" to organize a fir tree. Kosarev further explained, *"kakaia-nibud' mamasha* (some mother) came and supervised, and what did she know about how to do this? If we had appointed a real commandant, then these sad things wouldn't have happened."[85]

Kosarev's reaction to the accidents reveals a great deal about Soviet administration and the organization of fir tree celebrations. It was not uncommon for the Communists to blame backward women for their own failures, and this case was no exception. The fir tree accidents were blamed on "mothers" who did not know how to control crowds. In fact, responsible Komsomol and Communist officials did not always handle emergencies well. In Novo-Nikolaevskii District, the district secretary of the Komsomol was dressed up as Grandfather Frost and giving out candy to children when his costume caught fire. Although the chairman of the District Executive Committee and the district prosecutor were present, they "did not take action" and the director of the District Department of Pioneers, who was also dressed as Grandfather Frost, caught fire as well as he tried to help his colleague. Soviet attempts to mobilize the population through non-political entertainment were marred by incompetence of state and Party cadres at the local level. The very informality and relative decentralization that made New Year's celebrations appealing to Soviet citizens also created the possibility that they could be dangerous. The apolitical fantasy of New Year's Day was sometimes turned into a nightmare by negligent cadres.

The return of the New Year's tree in the 1930s reflected some Soviet cadres' public rejection of the radicalism and austerity of the Cultural Revolution. The content and form of the fir tree celebration revealed tensions between Soviet organizers and citizens who sought to make the holiday political and those who wanted to emphasize apolitical entertainment and education, between cadres trying to control public celebrations and citizens opting for private ones. The "apolitical" camp was usually more successful in promoting their version of the holiday; the celebration of New

Year's Day in the 1930s was less regimented and more diverse than the commemoration of the November 7th or May 1st festivities. During New Year's Day celebrations there were new possibilities for private and non-political festivity. Memoirs, published accounts, and archival materials all suggest that this move toward sponsoring entertainment was enthusiastically embraced by many Soviet cadres and the population.

The reintroduction of the fir tree gave special attention to young children, and this aspect of the celebration also seemed to attract women. The fir tree occupied a more prominent place in the memoirs of women than those of men.[86] Women were engaged in fir tree celebrations both in their private roles as organizers of family festivities and in their professional roles as teachers. Kosarev's complaint about "mothers" taking charge of New Year's celebrations also indicates that women actively participated in organizing public fir tree celebrations. The actions of Lidia Chukovskaia's fictional everywoman of the 1930s, Sofiia Petrovna, are emblematic of women's participation in this holiday. While Sofiia Petrovna had only the vaguest notions about Stalinist politics, she was thrilled when she was asked to organize her office's fir tree celebration and worked diligently to create a happy occasion.[87] This evidence suggests that the fir tree may have enjoyed particular success in mobilizing women to participate in official Soviet events. Like Arctic and aviation adventures and the excitement of demonstrations, this new festivity broadened the appeal of official Soviet culture.

New Year's Day celebrations reveal the ways in which Soviet cadres and citizens could resist state control or use official discourse to explore aspects of Soviet life that were supposed to remain hidden. The celebration of New Year's Day offered Soviet citizens the possibility of celebrating in private, and those who had enough material resources to afford trees, decorations, and special food created New Year's festivities in the home. These private practices meant that some families could defiantly celebrate Christmas while others marked out their status as part of the Soviet elite by displaying their prosperity. The holiday sanctioned the participation of citizens in traditional New Year's practices such as drinking, fortune-telling, and masquerading. While cultural cadres sought to regulate these practices, they could not always do so. The reintroduction of the holiday thus enabled a multiplicity of private practices with private meanings.

New Year's celebrations created a wide variety of public meanings as well. During New Year's Day, the children of the elite were groomed to be the next generation of leaders, and railroad workers aspiring to elite status acquired social skills such as dancing. New Year's celebrations thus fostered the creation of Soviet hierarchies. Not all public celebrations successfully communicated the precepts of official ideology. Traditional holiday practices also penetrated public festivities. The railroad carnival, for example, offered romance and fortune-telling as antidotes to the unhappiness and uncertainty of the 1930s, and cultural official Kremlev also used carnival to articulate some of his concerns about the purges. New Year's Day sometimes affirmed official culture and at other times called it into question. The horrifying image of children being burned to death in their bunny costumes reminds us of the fact that the plans and scenarios of celebration could often go seriously awry. The regimentation and order reflected in Soviet discourse about celebrations could and did give way to chaos in practice, a chaos that completely undermined the compromises between citizens and cadres and radically transformed the meanings of the holiday. Like parade marchers out of step and parachutes that did not open, fir tree fires revealed that Soviet order often existed only in myth and not in reality.

Soviet New Year's Day represented a series of small compromises with Soviet cadres and the population in the interest of promoting mobilization. During New Year's Day, scarce resources were distributed to create images of prosperity, and a religious custom became the centerpiece of Soviet winter holiday practice. New Year's Day reflected the syncretic nature of Soviet culture and identity and the ways in which a brutal and repressive state conceded a small measure of cultural autonomy to its cadres and citizens. Like citizens who marched in parades or were captivated by Arctic and aviation adventures, those who celebrated New Year's Day both were mobilized to participate in Soviet life and used the celebration to achieve their own personal goals.

Part Two

The Intelligentsia and
Soviet Enlightenment

5

A DOUBLE-EDGED DISCOURSE ON FREEDOM

THE PUSHKIN CENTENNIAL OF 1937

The profound changes in Soviet culture in the mid-1930s led to disagreement among Soviet cadres about how best to transform the population into ideal Soviet citizens. Cadres and the intelligentsia not only debated the organization of New Year's Day but also argued over the shape of other Soviet celebrations. The next three chapters focus on the role of the intelligentsia in constructing celebrations.

In 1935, Soviet officials identified aspects of the pre-revolutionary past that, like the New Year's tree, could be reclaimed and celebrated as part of the Soviet cultural heritage. In December of that year, the Central Executive Committee of the USSR announced its plans to commemorate the hundredth anniversary of the death of the nineteenth-century Russian poet Aleksandr Sergeevich Pushkin. The 1937 anniversary established Pushkin as a central symbol of Soviet culture and celebrated his status as the "great Russian poet, the creator of the Russian literary language and the father / founder (*rodonachal'nik*) of new Russian literature."[1]

From December 1935 to February 1937, when the anniversary took place, the All-Union Pushkin Committee, under the auspices of Narkompros of the Russian Soviet Federated Socialist Republic (RSFSR) and chaired by Andrei Bubnov, the People's Commissar of Enlightenment, coordinated the celebration of the life and works of Pushkin across the entire Soviet Union.[2] The official preparations for the centennial were extensive; every Soviet school was to incorporate Pushkin into the literature curriculum[3] and every Soviet theater was to perform a Pushkin play or concert on the anniversary of Pushkin's death.[4] The planners of this commemoration, like the creators of New Year's Day festivities, realized Stalin's slogan that life was becoming "more joyous" by promoting carnivals, costume balls, ice sculptures, jokes, and crossword puzzles on Pushkin themes, and even by the sale of special Pushkin cakes.[5] A more serious and scholarly aspect of the celebration resulted in the publication of countless newspaper and journal articles and over 13 million copies of books by and about Pushkin in Russian and many other languages of the Soviet Union.[6]

The article in *Pravda* announcing the plans for the Pushkin Centennial proclaimed:

> Speaking about the significance of the best poet of our Soviet era, Maia-kovskii, Comrade Stalin recently said, "Maiakovskii was and remains the best, most talented poet of our Soviet epoch. Indifference to his memory and to his works is a crime." These words about Maiakovskii raised the question of the significance of our poetry to the very highest level, and the resolution of the Central Executive Committee of the USSR about the Pushkin committee continues the line indicated by the words of Comrade Stalin.[7]

This declaration pointed to one of the fundamental features of the Stalin era, the explicit imposition of a hierarchical model of order in all fields of endeavor. Just as Stalin was the supreme leader who lesser leaders should emulate, Maiakovskii was the preeminent Soviet poet and Pushkin was to be the archetypal Russian poet.[8] This pronouncement also reminded the Soviet population about the serious repercussions of not taking part in this celebration. Indifference to the works of Pushkin was defined as a crime. Despite the fact that the Pushkin Centennial was an attempt by the government to reach out to educated and cultured Soviet citizens, the official rhetoric of the centennial also contained a thinly veiled threat against those who resisted cooperation with the state.

The Pushkin Centennial took place just after the second show trial of Radek, Piatakov, and others members of the "Anti-Soviet Trotskyite Center" ended. While the newspapers lauded the cultural advancement of the Soviet citizens who read and studied the works of Pushkin, they also celebrated the execution of the "Trotskyite" traitors. The concept of vigilance crept into the discourse of the centennial as well; a *Pravda* article published on the anniversary of Pushkin's death declared: "The base crime of the Trotskyite bandits is the direct reaction of counter-revolutionary bourgeois exploiters in our country. But across a hundred years Pushkin extends a friendly hand to us in solidarity. . . . He would happily applaud the destruction of the exploiting classes."[9] The Pushkin Centennial thus enables us to gain insight into the complex relationship of terror to celebration.

The Pushkin Centennial of 1937 must be understood in the context of two contradictory trends of the mid-1930s. The decision to celebrate the Pushkin anniversary was an invitation to the pre-revolutionary intelligentsia to participate actively in Soviet celebration culture. This policy was a continuation of the official rapprochement with independent and non-Party writers that was begun with the founding of the Union of Soviet Writers.[10] Because the persecution of the non-Communist intelligentsia during the

Cultural Revolution caused chaos and failed to produce artistic works of high quality, the Soviet government sought to re-establish ties with previously excluded cultural figures. The anniversary delivered yet another blow against the cultural radicals who had vehemently rejected Pushkin before 1932. By adopting Pushkin as a symbol of Soviet official culture, the designers of the Pushkin Centennial hoped to translate the old intelligentsia's reverence for Pushkin into support for Soviet political and cultural activities. On the one hand, then, the Pushkin Centennial was a celebration of the inclusion of the intelligentsia in the Soviet state. On the other hand, this inclusion of the intelligentsia occurred at the same time that the political repression of the Soviet elite was gaining intensity. The Pushkin Centennial stood at the crossroads of contradictory discourses of inclusion and exclusion, of celebration and terror. The relationship between the individual and the state articulated in the centennial reveals how members of the Soviet elite who had access to print and other media imagined Pushkin's place in the tsarist state and their own place in the highly restricted and regimented Soviet order in 1937.

The main tendency in the centennial's depictions of Pushkin was to portray him as a fervent revolutionary, a "singer of the love of freedom" who fought for the liberation of the common people and opposed the evils of tsarism to his dying day.[11] Commentators emphasized his connections to the Decembrist movement, the radical poems he wrote in his youth, and his six years of exile from the capitals.[12] It was more difficult for literary critics to portray Pushkin as a revolutionary in the last decade of his life, when Pushkin held an official position at court and was financially dependent on the tsar. Soviet scholars nonetheless generally maintained that Pushkin remained a revolutionary throughout his life and, in the tradition of the nineteenth-century Pushkin myth first articulated by Mikhail Lermontov, represented Pushkin as a martyr to autocracy.[13] The Soviet press asserted that D'Anthès, who killed Pushkin in a duel, was a mercenary in the pay of Nicholas I.[14] Pushkin did not die because of his passion for his wife or while defending his manly honor; instead he was a victim of the repressive autocratic regime of Nicholas I.[15]

Marcus Levitt has argued that the Pushkin Celebration of 1880 "came to mark a neutral zone, to stand for Russian society's independence both from the state and from the self-proclaimed radicals of the left."[16] While the notion of an "independent society" is inappropriate in the Stalinist 1930s, the special cultural space of the 1937 centennial enabled various groups of Soviet intellectuals and cultural cadres to express notions of culture, citizenship, and patriotism during a time of instability and upheaval. Soviet officials faced significant challenges in mobilizing the population during the Pushkin Centennial and the execution of the celebration produced some unanticipated results.

Official Goals of the Pushkin Centennial

Mobilizing the People and the Intelligentsia

The Pushkin Centennial, the most significant and sustained cultural campaign of the mid-1930s, was designed to encourage the Soviet masses to reforge themselves into socialist men and women as they participated in the transformation of the Soviet Union from a backward to an advanced country.[17] A key aspect of the New Soviet Man or Woman was his or her acquisition of culture, defined both as good manners and as mastery of the elite culture of pre-revolutionary Russia and the West. The Pushkin Centennial was different from other campaigns of the 1930s in that cadres mobilized the population to attain culture of both kinds through entertainment and a wide variety of non-political activities. Although the content of Pushkin celebrations was more political than that of fir tree celebrations because of the politicization of Pushkin's biography, the Pushkin Centennial still offered a wide variety of opportunities for concentrating on the literary works of Pushkin as art. The centennial was, nevertheless, a Soviet campaign. In the absence of sustained political work among the population, Soviet cadres jumped from one special campaign to the next, collecting money to build new aircraft, encouraging citizens to earn civil defense badges, selling government bonds, or celebrating Pushkin. Soviet cultural authorities complained that the problem with this approach to mobilization was that as soon as attention was focused on a new project, Soviet cadres lost all interest in promoting the goals of the previous mobilization efforts.[18] Despite the significant resources devoted to it, the Pushkin Centennial was also a temporary campaign.

The enthusiastic celebration of Pushkin was depicted in the central press as a "remarkable all-national cultural movement" that was "closely tied with the general cultural improvements of the Soviet Union, with the victory of socialism and the creation of a new society."[19] *Pravda* proudly announced that "millions of workers now have the possibility to study the works of our great national poet in depth."[20] Official centennial discourse celebrated not only the increased access to Pushkin provided by the Soviet government but also the use that the Soviet population made of Pushkin "from below." Soviet newspapers applauded amateur choirs and drama circles that performed the works of Pushkin and Stakhanovite workers who held Pushkin readings in their homes. The study of Pushkin became proof of the cultural advancement wrought by socialist transformation.

The rhetoric of the centennial demonstrated how through their own initiatives model representatives of the Soviet public formulated new identities as cultured Soviet citizens by embracing Pushkin. Soviet workers and peasants affirmed that reading Pushkin opened up new pathways to knowledge and culture. One worker explained, "Having liquidated my illiteracy, I made Pushkin's works my first companion." Another recommended, "If you want to be a poet, writer or a cultured person, study Pushkin." A third proclaimed that after reading Pushkin, she "became attracted to singing."[21] A fourth announced that after an excursion to Pushkin's last apartment and the Lycée in Detskoe Selo, "I felt that I have grown up significantly."[22] These workers represented the study of Pushkin as instrumental in their transformation into cultured Soviet men and women.

Because Pushkin was supposed to be accessible to even the semi-literate, his works were often described as "simple." A letter from a collective farmer published in *Vecherniaia Moskva* declared that "Pushkin is the national pride of the Russian people. The brilliant simplicity of his work is understood by millions."[23] The traits of simplicity and realism linked Pushkin to the prevailing literary style of the time, socialist realism. In reality, however, Pushkin's language was often subtle and complex and far beyond the capabilities of the newly literate. The unwillingness of the authorities to acknowledge this fact distorted the poet's legacy and made it even more difficult for citizens to acquire culture by reading his work.

By emphasizing, and at times exaggerating, the population's access to Pushkin, Soviet cultural workers contrasted the egalitarianism of Soviet society with the strict class hierarchy of pre-revolutionary Russia: "Extremely great achievements of culture, available earlier to only the classes of oppressors have become the property of millions of people."[24] By celebrating the people's access to Pushkin, Soviet cadres defined a significant break with the past, but they also acknowledged the tremendous power of pre-revolutionary Russian culture. The Soviet cultural campaigns of 1937 were not organized around the life and works of Maiakovskii, Gorkii, or some other Soviet literary figure, but around the life and works of Pushkin. Unlike earlier Soviet cultural officials who rejected pre-revolutionary Russian culture as a culture of class and ethnic oppression, Soviet cultural cadres consciously redefined Pushkin as a Soviet poet.

Soviet authors also tied the Pushkin Centennial to Stalin's 1935 slogan that "life has become more joyous." They depicted Pushkin as a hero because of his undiminished happiness and optimism despite great struggle and suffering.[25] This use of Pushkin implicitly acknowledged the political and economic struggles of the Soviet population and tried to instill the message that one should be optimistic about the future despite one's material and social circumstances. One student, for example, stated:

> Indeed, if you remember in what circumstances Pushkin lived and worked, then you are more amazed about how he brought such power into his poetry. . . . In our time, when we are given so much, not all of us know how to value what we have and we do not approach everything with the same seriousness and optimism as Pushkin did.[26]

The Pushkin Centennial was one way that Soviet propagandists tried to bridge the gap between an official rhetoric of plenty and a reality of poverty and oppression. Despite the difficulties that they faced in their daily lives, the Soviet people were supposed to keep working to guarantee future prosperity.

The Pushkin Centennial also provided a different kind of answer to the question of how plenty would be achieved in the Soviet Union. A letter in *Vecherniaia Moskva* from a collective farmer stated:

> I confess. I only recently took a liking to the books of Pushkin. Living became better. Worries about bread were dispelled. Everything became abundant. And I am reading more. To read Pushkin is pure delight. You simply rest and feel like you are advancing. I love Pushkin for many things: for his works, for his love toward the people. Although Pushkin lived many years ago, it is as if he is walking with us on the same path right now. Thanks to Soviet power, thanks to it, because it opened up all of Pushkin to me.[27]

The discourse of the centennial publicly acknowledged one of the burning issues of the 1930s, the material poverty and uncertainty of life in the Soviet countryside. The collective farmer's assertion of the miraculous ability of Pushkin's words to transform poverty into prosperity was most likely a reflection of the newspaper editor's exalted views of literacy, a reverence shared by both the pre-revolutionary and Soviet intelligentsia.[28] The "magical" solution to Soviet prosperity that this article described, however, only widened the gap between Soviet discourse and economic realities.

The collective farmer asserted that Pushkin seemed like a Soviet contemporary, "walking with us on the same path right now." This idea permeated many of the writings and speeches of the centennial. One worker affirmed, for example, "Pushkin is more our contemporary than he was the contemporary of his own generation."[29] This notion of Pushkin as contemporary could be taken quite literally. An article in *Pravda* on February 8, 1937, wistfully proclaimed, "it is useless to dream that in our time, in Leningrad, someone with a wound like Pushkin's would have a 50–60 percent chance of being saved by an operation."[30] This statement highlighted the material and technical advances of the Soviet period that might have enabled Pushkin to defy death, but also sought to conjure up the image of a living Pushkin in Leningrad. By claiming Pushkin as a contemporary, these writers asserted his immortality.

The religious aura surrounding Pushkin originated with intellectuals who drew on pre-revolutionary cultural traditions to express their thoughts and ideas. In her memoir *Hope Against Hope,* Nadezhda Mandel'shtam described the poet Osip Mandel'shtam's intense reverence for Pushkin. When Mandel'shtam was arrested, he was interrogated by a man who had the same patronymic as Benkendorf, the chief of police in Pushkin's time who was responsible for the "official persecution of Pushkin."

The interrogator certainly had a name hallowed in Russian literary tradition: Christophorovich. Why didn't he change it, if he worked in the literary section? Perhaps the coincidence appealed to his fancy. M[andel'shtam]
was always very angered if one even pointed such things out: he was very
much against the frivolous mention of anything connected with Pushkin.
Once, when I was ill, we had to spend two years in Tsarskoe Selo and we
actually took one of the apartments in the old Lycée, which were quite
good and comparatively cheap. But M. was terribly upset by what for
him was almost sacrilege, and at the first pretext he insisted we clear out
and revert to our usual homeless existence. So I was never able to sum-
mon up the courage to discuss the name of the interrogator.[31]

This quasi-religious veneration of Pushkin created a link between intelligentsia figures who worked within the Soviet cultural establishment and
those who remained outside of it.

The festivities in honor of Pushkin tried to mobilize segments of the
intelligentsia that had not been attracted by other aspects of official Soviet
culture. One non-Party intellectual who participated in the centennial because of her devotion to Pushkin was the poet Anna Akhmatova. Akhmatova was not allowed to publish her own poetry between the revolution
and World War II, but she wrote at least one article about Pushkin in 1936.[32]
By adopting Pushkin as a symbol of Soviet official culture, the designers of
the Pushkin Centennial sought to translate the old intelligentsia's reverence for Pushkin into support for Soviet political and cultural activities.

The pre-revolutionary intelligentsia's respect for Pushkin could also
create complications for the organizers of the centennial, who felt obligated
to produce an homage to Pushkin that would rival pre-revolutionary
Pushkin celebrations. V. P. Stavskii, the general secretary of the Union of
Soviet Writers, wrote to the Politbiuro in November of 1936 asking for permission to hold a plenum of the Union of Soviet Writers devoted to Pushkin.
Stavskii wrote:

Naturally, writers should say something about their relationship to Pushkin
and these speeches should be at a very high level. This is made all the
more difficult because all of the comrades who will speak will necessarily
have to look back at the speeches about Pushkin made by Dostoevsky and
Turgenev half a century ago. For this reason we must set to work preparing the plenum immediately.[33]

The centennial was an opportunity to prove that Soviet writers were
as talented and as devoted to Pushkin as their pre-revolutionary counterparts. V. Kirpotin, one of the most politically influential literary critics active in the Pushkin Centennial, stated in regard to the All-Union Pushkin
Meeting, "It is necessary that speeches like the speech of Dostoevsky remain. That was a cultural event."[34] The high standards that the writers set
for themselves were extremely difficult to attain in the troubled atmosphere
of 1937. Thus, for some Soviet cultural figures, the centennial may have

served to heighten the distinction between the exalted achievements of pre-revolutionary high culture and their own accomplishments.

Soviet ideologues glorified Pushkin as a way of celebrating the achievements of the Soviet state and mobilizing both intellectuals and less well-educated people to participate in official Soviet culture. In doing so, they fostered a quasi-religious discourse about an immortal and hallowed Pushkin whose words performed magical deeds.

Pushkin and the Making of a Soviet Elite

Despite the rhetoric of equality that pervaded the centennial, the Pushkin celebration was one of the many ways in which the Soviet government sought to create distinctions within its population in the 1930s. One special group singled out by Soviet authorities in this period consisted of Stakhanovite workers.[35] In exchange for their loyalty to the regime and as a reward for overfulfilling production norms, these workers were given special material and cultural privileges. In early 1937, the Stakhanovites' ability to master Pushkin and transmit their knowledge to other workers proved that they had attained "culture." They hosted Pushkin evenings in their homes and gave speeches about Pushkin. The Stakhanovites' role as mentors to other workers in their acquisition of culture gave them a sense of pride in their achievements and authority over the other workers.

Unfortunately, Stakhanovites were sometimes barely literate and were often not fluent in the language of literature and culture that they were supposed to speak at these Pushkin evenings. Unqualified Pushkinists were the subject of a satire by Mikhail Zoshchenko in the journal *Krokodil* in early 1937.[36] Although the *Krokodil* piece targeted academics and not Stakhanovites, Zoshchenko directly addressed the theme of speakers given the right to lecture others out of privilege rather than because of their expertise. In the "First Speech about Pushkin," the speaker continually wandered off the subject and voices from the audience admonished him to "talk about Pushkin" and corrected his many factual mistakes.[37] In the "Second Speech about Pushkin," the speaker confused Pushkin and Lermontov and spoke gibberish, announcing to the audience that the words of Pushkin were "simple and *malovysokokhudozhestvennye* (unartistically artistic)."[38] These two satirical pieces by Zoshchenko are another example of the ambiguity of the discourse of the Pushkin Centennial. While on the one hand Zoshchenko mocked incompetence in a straightforward manner, he also revealed the falsehoods in the rhetoric of the centennial. Pushkin was not "simple" and accessible to everyone. Some Pushkin specialists had not attained culture, they had just been given license to speak nonsense because of their privileged positions in Soviet society. And worst of all, the true artistic and literary value of Pushkin was lost because it was not understood by the speakers and therefore could not be transmitted to the audience.

While the Pushkin Centennial created opportunities for the rising Soviet elite to adopt a cultured and educated identity, it also provided the members of the top echelons of Soviet society with occasions to distribute material resources among themselves. The Pushkin Centennial provided Soviet writers with special opportunities to gain material privileges and benefits. For example, in order to "provide the best conditions for their work," the Uzbek Pushkin Committee sent a select group of poets and prose writers to a resort at Chilegan so that they could translate the major works of Pushkin into Uzbek in time for the centennial.[39] In 1936, the Pushkin Committee requested that 646,000 rubles be allocated by Sovnarkom to renovate Pushkin's estate at Mikhailovskoe and turn it into a rest home for the Academy of Sciences.[40] The Pushkin Committee made provisions for approximately 100 special guests to travel around European Russia and attend several events during the ten-day Pushkin festivities. They were scheduled to attend the Pushkin meeting at the Bolshoi Theater in Moscow and the dedication of Pushkin's apartment-museum in Leningrad and then visit Mikhailovskoe. The projected costs for travel, accommodations, and food for these guests was over a quarter of a million rubles. In Moscow, this select group was also invited to celebrate with the Party and government elite at a banquet for 700 people at the Hall of Columns with a projected cost of 84,000 rubles for refreshments alone.[41] For this one evening of entertainment the Pushkin Committee requested that Sovnarkom give them approximately 280 times the average monthly wage of a factory worker. During the celebration of the centennial, the very top levels of Soviet society marked their elite status by participating in lavish, by-invitation-only state-sponsored events.

Since the Soviet government gave the All-Union Pushkin Committee a limited amount of money, expenditures for the Pushkin celebration were a zero-sum game. Money that was spent on 100 special guests would not be available to organize festivities or publications for the rest of the Soviet population. The centennial was thus shaped by the priorities of the cultural authorities at the top of the hierarchy, and very often their tendency was to spend money for the elite commemoration of Pushkin rather than for the dissemination of Pushkin to the wider public. One member of the Pushkin Committee complained in late 1936 that publishing houses decided "to provide for the publication of luxurious editions while they cut the number of mass editions or do not provide them by the deadline."[42] The organization of a Pushkin celebration that could mobilize the wider population thus faced a double challenge; resources tended to be allocated toward the top of the Soviet Union's hierarchical structure, and even when they were not, the chronic delays and inefficiencies of production in the Soviet Union made it exceedingly difficult for materials about Pushkin to be distributed in time for them to be used in the celebration of the centennial.

Despite detailed publication plans that provided for the completion of most of the Pushkin materials by the end of the 1936 calendar year, many publishers raced to release their materials before the centennial began. The directors of the publishing house Izogiz, which published posters, prints, postcards, and other pictorial materials for the centennial, had to ask the head of the Pushkin Committee to authorize overtime work for their typographers in January 1937.[43] Records of the Pushkin Committee show that a large number of works were not ready for release until the 10th or 11th of February 1937, when the centennial celebrations were already underway.[44] These works were published too late to play any role in the preparation for the centennial, and they were not likely to reach destinations outside of Moscow until months after its conclusion.[45] While considerable resources had been put into the publication of works for the centennial, the impact of these works was diminished by their late arrival. Because of the dynamics of Soviet campaigns, Pushkin circles were likely to be disbanded after the centennial, just when literature by and about Pushkin was appearing in the provinces. The time lag diminished the impact of the resources that had been invested in the centennial for the purpose of mobilizing the population.

Even when Soviet cadres had resources available, they did not always use them effectively. In March 1937, the judges of the Union of Leather Workers' contest for the best Pushkin issue of a factory newspaper, for example, awarded no monetary prizes because the entries were dry and monotonous and "newspaper editors did not display sufficient creative initiative toward the publication of an interesting, colorful, and lively issue worthy of the memory of the great poet."[46] The lack of committed cadres at the local level weakened the efforts of the central committee of the Union of Leather Workers to promote the Pushkin Centennial in leather processing factories. Without active cadres in the factories, the Pushkin Centennial was just another campaign on which overburdened cultural cadres spent a minimum of time and effort.

The forced pace and chronic inefficiency of Soviet industry and the shortage of educated cadres who could effectively carry out cultural work led to the production of Pushkin materials of low quality that compromised attempts to create the newly cultured Soviet Man and Woman. Only ten days before the centennial, the All-Union Pushkin Committee complained about the "completely unsatisfactory quality" of portraits and posters for the centennial. They demanded that "the print runs of successful portraits be increased at the expense of stopping the production of the unsuccessful ones."[47] Pushkin publications were often shoddily produced and full of mistakes and misprints. A satirical verse published in *Vecherniaia Moskva* criticized the publishing house Kniga za Kniga (Book after Book) for the poor quality of its edition of Pushkin's fairy tales. The verse suggested that since there were so many mistakes the series be called "Misprint after Misprint."[48] One critic attacked the State Literature Publishing

House's mass edition of Pushkin's plays for having over 600 mistakes in diction and punctuation. He explained that "there are so many mistakes that it unintentionally creates the impression that the editor couldn't care less about the literary heritage of the great poet or about the mass reader."[49] Lack of supervision and carelessness also marred the festive atmosphere. V. Bonch-Bruevich, the head of the State Literary Museum, complained to Bubnov in May 1937 that the bronze commemorative Pushkin medal he received came in an "untidy" box, "packed with scraps apparently swept up from the floor or the street, strips of dirty paper, used candy wrappers, and so forth."[50] The low quality of production called into question the "culture" of the centennial in both of its meanings. The Soviet people could hardly become acquainted with the heights of literary culture if Soviet editors produced books that were riddled with mistakes, and Soviet people would not learn to be tidy and have good manners if the example that cultural cadres set was the careless and slovenly packaging of commemorative medals in dirty paper.

When discussing hierarchy in the Soviet Union in the 1930s, one must think not only of administrative or prestige hierarchies, but also of the geographic hierarchies which privileged urban over rural and elevated the residents of the city of Moscow far above the rest of the population of the Soviet Union. Despite Pushkin's close connection with the city of Saint Petersburg, Moscow was the site of the All-Union Pushkin Exhibition, the All-Union Pushkin Meeting, and the Pushkin Plenum of the Union of Soviet Writers. For the ten days of the celebration, every theater in the capital was supposed to produce either a work of Pushkin's or a Pushkin concert. One member of the Pushkin Committee thought that perhaps ten days of Pushkin productions in Moscow might be excessive and wondered if "Muscovites simply won't bear it and the halls will be half empty?"[51] If things had gone according to plan, Muscovites would have had too many theater productions to attend, while people in provincial cities would have had limited access to theater and those in rural areas none at all. As it turned out, the Moscow theaters failed to fulfill their plans for the Pushkin Centennial. Only three Pushkin plays were produced in Moscow, and only one of them in time for the centennial.[52] The tendency toward privileging Moscow led to a waste of resources and diminished the capacity of Soviet cultural cadres to mobilize the wider population.

The preparations for the Pushkin Centennial also revealed the Soviet government's tendency toward centralizing control over the resources of the rest of the country. Part of the preparation for the All-Union Pushkin Exhibit consisted of locating documents about Pushkin that were housed in provincial and local archives. In early 1937, the Politbiuro confirmed Sovnarkom's decree ordering local archives to send their original documents to Moscow to be displayed in the All-Union Pushkin Exhibit and forbidding all other museums from organizing exhibits without the permission of the All-Union Pushkin Committee in Moscow.[53] Thus, the Historical Museum in Moscow added to its collection at the expense of local museums and these museums could not display their original documents about Pushkin or anything else without Moscow's approval. This appropriation of local Pushkin materials likely dampened the enthusiasm of local museums for creating their own individual displays about Pushkin and thereby decreased the participation of provincial citizens in the centennial.

The supply of Pushkin literature to Moscow and Leningrad was far superior than to other urban areas in the Soviet Union. An article in the journal *Plamia* on January 2, 1937, revealed the apprehensions of the cultural authorities in Stalingrad, a major provincial city of half a million people. The author noted that by January 2, 1937, the city had received only 1,300 books by or about Pushkin with which they had to serve six city bookstores, 450–500 libraries and 40 district bookstores. They received no portraits of Pushkin at all and only 300 posters of Evgenii Onegin, but they had to provide 2,000 schools and 1,000 rural reading rooms with materials.[54] While the Pushkin Committee's attention to this article may have assured Stalingrad the delivery of more Pushkin materials, these books and posters would have arrived only a week or two before the centennial, if at all.

Letters that were sent to the Pushkin Committee by rural teachers illustrated the extreme dearth of Pushkin materials in rural areas. N. G. Pudyshev from the Solovetskoi Village Soviet in the far northern Vokhomskii District, wrote:

> We are located 45 kilometers from the district center, and a huge distance from any city at all. The nearest railway station is 150 kilometers away. There is not one bookstore near our school. If something appears in the bookstore of the district center, of course, nothing is put aside for us. As a result, in preparation for the Pushkin days, we are left with absolutely nothing. . . . We burn with the desire to conduct the celebration so that our students will always carry with them the image of the poet, so that the name of Pushkin will be dear and understandable to them. . . . Our school is poor. We would be very grateful for the smallest donation of materials to the school. If you cannot do this, we will buy anything that you can give us, using the personal funds of the schoolteachers.[55]

This remarkable letter reveals both the dedication of the schoolteachers, willing to spend their own funds to commemorate Pushkin when their institution had no money to spare, and the vast disparity between the way that the Pushkin Centennial was celebrated in Moscow and in the hinterlands.

A Narkompros report about the teaching of Pushkin's works during the third and fourth quarter of the 1935–1936 school year confirms that the capability of Soviet ideology and instruction to reach various segments of the population varied significantly by region. The report noted that the instructional plan was carried out in territorial and regional centers and in the biggest district centers, but that the majority of "distant" districts and "remote" village schools did not receive the plan on time.[56] This letter and report provide insight into the enormous scope of the problem of transforming people into New Soviet Men and Women. While the process of mobilization was relatively easy among elites and in Moscow, the reach of Soviet ideology was compromised in rural areas by sheer distance, lack of infrastructure, and shortages of material resources. Without the few dedicated members of the rural intelligentsia that happened to teach school in remote villages (and such cadres were in very short supply across the Soviet Union), the children in Solovetskoe and villages like it would never have read Pushkin or heard about the Pushkin Centennial.

Aleksandr Kosarev, the outspoken leader of the Komsomol, also questioned the priorities of the centennial in a December 1936 meeting of the Central Committee of the Komsomol. In political education courses for collective farmers who were learning technical skills, lessons were given about "Pushkin and modernity." Kosarev complained, "I'm for Pushkin, but I can't understand why . . . [they are studying] 'Pushkin and modernity.' Now what about 'illiteracy and modernity,' don't you think that that is an urgent question?"[57] In view of the very limited resources of the Soviet state and the disintegration of the educational networks set up for liquidating adult illiteracy in the 1930s, Kosarev questioned the use of time and energy on promoting Pushkin when basic literacy was neglected. The numerous testimonials of peasants who claimed that Pushkin helped them on the path to literacy, like the claims that Pushkin made the harvests more plentiful, were part of the mythology of the Pushkin Centennial. But could peasants really read Pushkin when the resources to teach them basic literacy were lacking? Did the emphasis on the Pushkin Centennial, paradoxically, slow progression toward the creation of cultured New Soviet Men?

How then can we evaluate the success of the Pushkin Centennial as a means of mobilizing the population of the Soviet Union and aiding in their transformation into cultured Soviet Men and Women? On the one hand, it is clear from letters of complaint from rural areas that the Pushkin Centennial was more visible in Moscow and Leningrad and other "Pushkin places" than anywhere else and that few of the resources allocated for the Pushkin Centennial reached provincial cities and rural areas in time to be of use in the preparation of the centennial. The "campaign" nature of the centennial also suggests wasted effort and resources that might have been better used to develop more permanent educational institutions such as libraries, reading rooms, and literacy schools.

Yet it is clear that the Pushkin Centennial did strike a chord with some rural schoolteachers and other segments of the Soviet population. The Pushkin Committee received a variety of letters from citizens who wanted to name schools and airplanes after Pushkin and from people who found mistakes in the materials published for the centennial or who critiqued the artistic productions prepared for it.[58] The members of the Pushkin Society, a voluntary association formed in Leningrad in 1931, wrote to the Pushkin Committee seeking an active role in the celebration.[59] In Moscow and Leningrad, there was a strong demand for activities and publications related to Pushkin. At an All-Union Pushkin Committee meeting in 1936, Kirpotin rejected the suggestion that the committee should send letters to Soviet organizations to raise their level of activity:

> The fact that I am a Pushkinist has turned into a misfortune for my family, since there is not a single factory, publishing house, or institution that has not requested a lecture. I gave a few lectures at the Polytechnic Museum, and there the tail of the line remained at the box office after all of the tickets were sold. Therefore, there is no need to raise the level of activity.[60]

Kirpotin's problem and the fact that subscriptions to Pushkin publications quickly sold out reveal that there was considerable interest and "activity" surrounding Pushkin that was not generated by Party or government fiat, but rather by the voluntary participation of segments of Soviet society.[61] Through their mobilization for the centennial, educated citizens voluntarily engaged in Pushkin activities and entertainment, and they also carried out cultural work that would, over time, create the educated and cultured population that the Soviet government sought.

At a meeting of the All-Union Pushkin Committee shortly before the centennial, one organizer noted that "the report of the Western Regional Executive Committee and the Kirov Regional Executive Committee and so forth, about preparation for the Pushkin Days bear witness to the fact that this matter has unfolded with significantly more breadth than we could have imagined."[62] This candid remark was part of a meeting protocol rather than an official report, and its implication that the centennial organizers had doubts about how successfully the celebration would be carried out in the provinces was clearly not for public consumption. This statement reveals that the dedication and seriousness of some provincial cadres in carrying out the celebration of Pushkin surprised even the centennial organizers in Moscow. While the centennial did not meet with success everywhere or come anywhere close to creating the cultured men and women that the state wanted, it did mobilize segments of the population to participate voluntarily in an official Soviet holiday, which exposed them to a discourse about Pushkin that articulated the major themes of Soviet ideology.

Pushkin and the Image of the Soviet Union

Like the tsarist-sponsored Pushkin celebration of 1899 that saw "the emergence of a new kind of 'official nationality,' which used Pushkin as its banner," the 1937 celebration of Pushkin created possibilities for defining what it meant to be Soviet both within the Soviet Union and abroad.[63] The celebration of Pushkin was directly linked to the promotion of a Soviet patriotism that contrasted the Soviet Union with the rest of the world. Through the Pushkin Centennial and many other public pronouncements in the mid-1930s, Party and government officials sought to define being Soviet as possessing a patriotic love for the Soviet Union and being willing to die for it. Access to the advanced culture of Pushkin was one of the proofs that the Soviet Union was worth dying for. According to academician V. Komarov, the president of the Academy of Sciences of the USSR, the love of Pushkin actually strengthened the defensive capabilities of the country at a critical moment:

> Dark clouds are hanging in the east and in the west. Fascism is bloodily advancing on labor and culture. . . . But we are calm. Our culture, our great brotherhood of laborers will be preserved by the unconquerable Red Army, that same Red Army which is more interested in Pushkin than the liberal-bourgeoisie of the past who had a monopoly on education ever was.[64]

Furthermore, the love of advanced culture was defined as love of country. A *Pravda* article displaced the love of the Soviet people for Pushkin onto the Soviet motherland: "Love for the motherland, born in the struggle for her freedom, for her happiness, for her independence from all enemies of the people, is strengthened by love for the wonderful, extremely rich, popular, native work of Pushkin."[65] To love Pushkin, therefore, was to be a patriot ready to die in order to protect advanced Soviet culture.

The centennial enabled the Soviet Union to compare itself to other European nations and to identify foreign friends and foes. According to articles in *Vecherniaia Moskva*, the Pushkin days were celebrated "in all cultured countries." However, "Fascist Germany and Italy . . . keep silent about the anniversary date of the great Russian poet who is the pride of all progressive humanity."[66] These statements identified the Soviet Union as a cultured European country united with progressive forces in Europe against fascism. The articles define the fascist states of Italy and Germany as "other" through their lack of culture and their failure to celebrate Pushkin.

The organizers of the Pushkin Centennial believed that the celebration could play an instrumental role in shaping world public opinion regarding the Soviet Union. Official plans to organize a Pushkin festival in England proclaimed that "the Pushkin days in the Soviet Union undoubtedly call forth great interest among progressive representatives of the foreign intelligentsia. It follows that it is politically expedient to ensure the upcoming celebration the most significant possible resonance in world public opinion."[67] The organizers intended to use the celebration both to inculcate Soviet pride and patriotism at home and to strengthen democratic forces against fascism by winning the approval of European and American intellectuals.

The organizers of the Pushkin Centennial wanted the celebration to be associated with Europe, culture, and progress. They carefully selected the images to be displayed to foreign and domestic audiences. Because Pushkin had an African ancestor, William Patterson, a member of the Anglo-American sector of the Executive Committee of MOPR (International Organization for Aid to Revolutionaries) suggested in 1936 that "Negroes in the whole world, especially in the United States, considered Pushkin their national hero" and that there should be an exhibit of African art during the Pushkin Centennial. Bonch-Bruevich reacted negatively to this suggestion, arguing that there had never been an occasion when Soviet cultural authorities celebrated a writer "not only for his literary activities but also because he came from some nationality or other."[68] Since the Soviet press repeatedly described Pushkin as "the pride of the Russian nation," Bonch-Bruevich's argument is not very convincing. Despite the official doctrine of racial equality, Soviet cultural authorities were not anxious to identify Pushkin as African. Pushkin represented the cultured, conscious, European New Soviet Man and not the spontaneous African with a "stormy temperament."[69]

The definition of Soviet in the 1930s was created by opposition to a variety of other terms that articulated differences in geography, time, and nationality. Cultural authorities contrasted "Soviet" with "fascist" and "African" in the context of the Pushkin Centennial in order to affirm that to be Soviet was to be progressive, European, and cultured. A more complicated relationship existed between the definitions of "Soviet," "Russian," and other nationalities within the boundaries of the Soviet Union. The discourse of the Pushkin Centennial emphasized that Pushkin's appeal to the population was "all-national." The lead article in *Pravda* on December 17, 1935, recalled Pushkin's poetic dream:

News about me will travel all around Great Rus',
And my name will be called by every one of her tongues,
By the proud grandson of the Slav, and Finn, and the presently savage
Tunguz, and the Kal'myk, friend of the steppes.

The article continues: "This dream, impracticable in a bourgeois system based on the oppression of savage tongues, is realized in the Soviet country with its exceedingly rich development of national cultures, with its great friendship of peoples." The introduction of the slogan "friendship of peoples" occurred as the Soviet government was abandoning its policy of *korenizatsiia* that gave limited cultural autonomy to nationalities.[70] In 1937, Soviet rhetoric celebrated "the development of national cultures," even as the NKVD was accusing national elites of "bourgeois nationalism" and arresting them. Christel Lane has suggested that "a deterioration in actual nationality relations became disguised by a ritual presentation of harmonious relations between the different national groups of the Soviet Union."[71] Yet the "ritual presentation of harmonious relations" during the Pushkin Centennial did not so much disguise tensions as reveal the ways that Pushkin as a representative of Russian culture was being deployed by Soviet ideologues in the creation of a Soviet empire.

While *Pravda* declared that Pushkin's longing to be known throughout Rus' showed the "international traits in his poetic nature," in fact the poem reveals Pushkin's embrace of the nineteenth-century notion of empire and his dream of conquering the great expanse of the Russian Empire with his fame. By promoting Pushkin among the non-Russian peoples, the Soviet government revealed its affinity with pre-revolutionary imperial aims. The article in *Pravda* contrasted the Soviet promotion of so-called savage languages to the pre-revolutionary oppression of them yet did not acknowledge that identifying Pushkin as the height of poetic and literary culture and using scarce resources to translate Pushkin's works into dozens of non-Russian languages was a reflection of the imperial ethos of the superiority of the ruling culture. In the official discourse about Soviet nationality in the 1930s, the transformation of nationalities from "savage" to "cultured" occurred when nations embraced Soviet ideology. During the Pushkin Centennial, Russian literature was the vehicle through which nationalities overcame their savage natures. Although literary accomplishments of other nationalities, such as the work of the Georgian poet Rustaveli and the Armenian folk epic David of Sasun, were also commemorated in the late 1930s, no writer was celebrated or disseminated as widely as Pushkin.

While Pushkin's works supposedly taught Russian citizens to read and to acquire culture, they taught non-Russian citizens to love Russian language and literature. One Belorussian worker affirmed that "Pushkin's style teaches us to understand the beauty of the Russian language."[72] In February 1937 an article in *Pravda* declared that "all of the people of the Soviet Union unite in brotherhood toward this holiday of Russian literature because this literature has become close and native to them."[73] This assertion that Pushkin was "native" to the non-Russian peoples suggests more than a transformation from savage to cultured; it implies that the non-Russians had become native "Soviets." In addition to celebrating the development of national cultures, the rhetoric of the Pushkin Centennial also articulated a model of "Sovietification" not unlike nineteenth-century Russification. According to Willard Sunderland, the imperial Russian racial ethos held that "people of lesser developed races could always be improved by the acquisition of culture."[74] By embracing the advanced Russian culture of Pushkin, formerly "savage" nationalities could become Soviet.

The Soviet intelligentsia who organized the Pushkin Centennial were not unaware of the implications of using Pushkin to spread Soviet "civilization." In his address at the Bolshoi Theater on the anniversary of Pushkin's death, I. Luppol, head of the Gorkii Institute of Literature, boasted that "Pushkin is translated into a greater number of languages than the Bible was in several hundred years by tsarist and imperial missionaries."[75] By arguing that the Soviet authorities were more successful disseminating Pushkin than imperial missionaries were in propagating their faith, Luppol affirmed the Soviet goal of imposing "superior" Russian culture on the less advanced peoples within the Soviet Union. While this statement overtly praised the achievements of Soviet power, it also implicitly acknowledged the imperial nature of the Soviet civilizing mission.

Pushkin festivities among national minorities served as evidence of the success of Soviet power in transforming previously "backward" cultures and therefore justified continued Soviet control over these areas. Non-Russian performers and writers were invited to Moscow to participate in the Pushkin celebration, acknowledge their debts to Russian and Soviet culture, and affirm their loyalty to the Soviet state. Summoning non-Russian cultural authorities to appear in Moscow, however, weakened the celebration of the centennial in the periphery. If republican cultural leaders were called to Moscow, they could not supervise the celebration in their own republics. Although detailed plans about how the centennial should be organized were sent from Sovnarkom to the republican Commissariats of Enlightenment and their Pushkin Committees, it is likely that the Pushkin Centennial, like many other campaigns, weakened as it moved from the Russian center to the non-Russian periphery.[76]

It was easier to arrange for the publication of Pushkin's works in Russia than in the non-Russian republics. An article in *Pravda* in September 1936 criticized the non-Russian publishing houses and republican state organs for not making the Pushkin Centennial a top priority:

> Not all of the nationalities' publishing houses and sometimes state organs as well, correctly understand their task: to provide maximally all the material resources (paper and other materials) apportioned by the yearly plan for the publication of the works of Pushkin. All organs of planning and supply, all publishing houses and printers knew about this task on time. They must fulfill it.[77]

Whether from general inefficiency, lack of material resources, the complexity of producing high-quality literary translations, or conscious resistance, republic officials were very slow to fulfill Moscow's plans for translations of Pushkin. This criticism in *Pravda* communicated Moscow's dissatisfaction with the efforts of the republics to publish Pushkin in translation.

One publishing house in Khar'kov, Ukraine, used the opportunity of the Pushkin celebration to publish the work of the Ukrainian national poet, Taras Shevchenko, by reprinting a book first published in 1859 called *New Verses of Pushkin and Shevchenko*. An article by S. Reiser in the journal

Literaturnoe obozrenie first praised the numerous translations of Pushkin into Ukrainian and then proceeded to attack this one particular publication:

> In front of us is a pulp publication of thirteen poems: six by Shevchenko and seven by Pushkin (out of which, incidentally, three do not belong to Pushkin). . . . The book itself has no interest or worth, and a photographic reprint of a defective edition in a luxurious velvet cover at an inordinate cost calls forth amazement and bewilderment.[78]

The critic was bewildered because he could not understand why this particular volume of poetry was reprinted. One possible explanation is that the Ukrainian editors wanted to publish a book that celebrated not only the Russian national poet but also the Ukrainian poet Shevchenko. This publication may have been an expression of resistance against the cultural imperialism of Soviet Russia, against the implication that the poetry of Pushkin deserved more attention than the poetry of Shevchenko. What is certain is that a Ukrainian editor chose to reprint an 1859 edition that put Shevchenko and Pushkin on equal footing.

The Pushkin Centennial defined "Soviet" culture as an advanced, progressive, European culture, based on Russian culture, that had the power to transform the less advanced non-Russian cultures of the Soviet Union. The definition of Soviet was open to contestation, however. Foreigners and fascists questioned the efficacy of Soviet culture from the outside. Within the Soviet Union, the intelligentsia and cultural cadres of the non-Russian republics, who were necessary for the success of the centennial, did not always comply with Moscow's wishes.

The Pushkin Centennial's Ambiguous Meanings

Pushkin's Contradictory Identity

Many of the debates surrounding the Pushkin celebrations of 1880 occurred because "to proclaim Pushkin a world-class genius meant in some measure to sanction Russia's oppressive political, economic, and cultural order."[79] Soviet Pushkinists also had to cope with the contradiction of a poet of genius who emerged from the ruling class during an extremely repressive period of Russian history. They had to come to terms with many inconvenient facts about Pushkin's private and family life that did not fit well with their depiction of Pushkin as a revolutionary and a people's poet. As a noble and a serf owner, he was an oppressor of the Russian peasantry. His familial and personal relationships also did not conform to the ideal Soviet images of son, husband, and father.

Detaching Pushkin from his noble family was a major aspect of official

N. P. Ul'ianov, *Pushkin and His Wife at a Ball*, 1936. From *Sovetskaia zhivopis'* (1939).

attempts to reclaim Pushkin as a socialist hero. In lectures and articles aimed at Soviet children, authors emphasized Pushkin's unhappy childhood and dismal family life, and contrasted them with the happy childhoods of Soviet children.[80] His aristocratic parents did not love him or pay any attention to him. As in nineteenth-century Pushkin mythology, the poet received affection and inspiration only at the knee of his serf nanny who imbued him with a love for the common people that enabled him to become a people's poet. By portraying Pushkin as spiritually orphaned, the official mythmakers denied the class character of his upbringing.

Soviet sources also tended to blame Pushkin's wife, Nataliia Nikolaevna Goncharova, for the fact that Pushkin moved in elite court circles and had close social interaction with the tsar. Soviet accounts tended to place the most emphasis not on Pushkin's married life but on his circle of friends at the Lycée and his relationship with the young radical thinkers of his time and the Decembrists. Although Goncharova's life at court ruined Pushkin financially, and D'Anthès's obsession with her led to Pushkin's public humiliation and the duel that killed him, Soviet accounts did not blame Pushkin's death on his unhappy marriage. The Soviet myth of Pushkin, not unlike pre-revolutionary myths, saw him as a public man. In this mythology Pushkin struggled to free Russian society from the bonds of autocracy; he was not a seeker of private individual freedom or a desperately unhappy and jealous man whose personal life caused his tragedy. Since the New Soviet Man was not supposed to allow his personal life to interfere with his social goals, Pushkin would have been a failure had he allowed his private life to destroy his great artistic and literary talent. The Soviet Pushkin myth, therefore, took great care to give Pushkin's death social meaning by asserting that the autocracy hatched a plot to kill him.

At the time of the Pushkin Centennial, Soviet definitions of public and private were in flux. "The private" was a narrow yet expanding category in Stalin's Soviet Union. Repressive Soviet policies forced citizens to make personal sacrifices for the good of the state and Soviet ideology privileged public over private life. At the same time, some limited aspects of private life were affirmed in the mid-1930s, such as the strengthening of marriage as an institution, the glorification of motherhood, the celebration of the stay-at-home wife as a marker of elite status, and the acknowledgment of home-based celebrations such as the New Year's holiday. Since passion and sexuality were not included among the officially sanctioned private elements, inspiration for heroic actions could not stem from intimate relations between lovers. Filial love took precedence over romance, and any romantic love discussed in public was extremely chaste. The depiction of Pushkin's personal life during the centennial was circumscribed by Soviet definitions of private life, but it also challenged these definitions.

In the official version of Pushkin's biography, one woman whose love was instrumental in his literary and political development was his serf nanny. The organizers of the Pushkin Centennial provided Soviet women with the role model of the nurturing mother and showed that if mothers did their job well, they, too, could raise glorious sons. Defining the serf nanny as surrogate mother also allowed Pushkin to be "reborn" as a poet rooted in the common people, one who understood their trials and could be appreciated by them. Pushkin's love for his nanny was translated into love for the people. In the discourse of the 1930s, the love for mother and *narod* was directly connected to patriotic love of the Soviet motherland. The beloved nanny stood as a symbol for the country that the New Soviet Man was willing to give his life to defend.

It was implied, on the other hand, that Pushkin's relationship with his wife prevented him from achieving his full potential. It was his attachment to a group of male heroic comrades that led to his literary and revolutionary achievements. In Soviet cultural production of the 1930s, inspiration for great achievements often arose from such a circle of male comrades. Soviet heroes thrived in the homosocial environments of war, exploration, and, in Pushkin's case, a male boarding school. Both of the biographical films about Pushkin produced in 1937 located him in homosocial environments. *The Youth of the Poet* (*Iunost' poeta*) focused on Pushkin's years at the exclusive Lycée, and *Journey to Erzerum* (*Puteshestvie v Arzrum*) depicted his travels to visit his Decembrist friends in exile and his experience of the Russo-Turkish campaign of 1829.[81] Despite public affirmation of women's equality in the Soviet Union, public discourse tended to define heroism as a collective male activity.

Within this collective male domain, the role of the mentor or father who instructed his sons on how to become Soviet heroes was crucial, and, as Katerina Clark and others have shown, Stalin was the ultimate father-mentor. In the biographies created for the centennial, although Pushkin was sometimes encouraged by notable figures such as Chaadaev, Derzhavin, and Zhukovskii, in many Soviet depictions he lacked a strong male mentor. One authority figure who often held a central place in Pushkin's biography was Nicholas I. This relationship was one of conflict and surveillance rather than one of mentoring. As Pushkin's personal censor, Nicholas I circumscribed rather than enhanced Pushkin's ability to express himself. Their conflict was framed as the individual's struggle for freedom against the autocratic, repressive state. Unlike most cultural heroes of the Soviet 1930s, Pushkin was often depicted as the rebellious son rather than the obedient one. A central feature of the Pushkin myth ran against the current of Soviet culture by challenging rather than affirming patriarchal authority.

Although official biographers emphasized Pushkin's alienation from his noble roots, they still had to portray Pushkin as a member of the dominant class at the same time that they exposed the evils perpetrated by that class. While undomesticated sexuality was never shown in a positive light in Soviet public discourse, sexual abuse of serf women by noble men served as a powerful metaphor for the depravity of class domination. In the film *The Youth of the Poet*, Pushkin had an innocent romantic relationship with a serf girl who was a member of a serf theater. When the girl was sold to someone who desired her sexually, she wistfully remarked to Pushkin "If you'd been rich, you could have bought me."[82] The screenplay made Pushkin heroic but vilified the class to which he belonged because of its economic and physical domination of the peasantry. In 1937, Pushkin occupied the anomalous position of a class enemy turned hero at a time when purge victims were persecuted for concealing their "alien" class origins.

Pushkin's status as a Soviet hero was further complicated by the fact that his actual relations with serf women during his lifetime were far from chaste. In a December 1936 meeting of the All-Union Pushkin Committee, I. Luppol opposed the publication of the volume *Letopisi Gosudarstvennogo Literaturnogo Muzeia, kniga pervaia: Pushkin* (*Annals of the State Literature Museum, Book One: Pushkin*) in a print run of 10,000 because it included documents that were necessary only to the "top three hundred Pushkinists." Luppol wanted to shield the Soviet population from the fact that Pushkin fathered an illegitimate child by one of his serfs, Ol'ga Kalashnikova, the

Pushkin and serf actress Natasha in the film *The Youth of the Poet*. From *Iunost' poeta* (1937).

daughter of his steward. The documents in *Letopisi* revealed that Pushkin used his power as a noble and a landowner to satisfy his sexual appetites at the expense of a serf woman, and that his steward Kalashnikov "made fun of the peasants, ruined them, and Pushkin protected him."[83] The Pushkin Committee hoped to use censorship to prevent Pushkin's lax sexual morality from becoming public knowledge and to deny Pushkin's involvement in abuses of power over the peasantry. As Luppol put it, if the volume were widely circulated "you will send to factories Pushkinists who consider establishing that Pushkin had illegitimate children out of wedlock a more important phenomenon than his literary and general political significance."[84] *Letopisi* revealed that Pushkin was a class oppressor empowered by tsarism, its beneficiary rather than its victim. The volume was printed and distributed in 1936.[85]

Soviet mythmakers sought to compensate for Pushkin's social origins and social location in tsarist Russia by emphasizing his revolutionary credentials and his suffering at the hands of the autocracy. In order for the Soviets to reclaim Pushkin as a proletarian hero, he had to be oppressed by tsarism the same way that workers and peasants were oppressed. One of the main goals of the All-Union Pushkin Exhibit, for example, was to "uncover the politics of the tsarist government, which falsified Pushkin's political and literary character, held his works under the guardianship of an ignorant censorship, and restricted their dissemination."[86] The unintended result of transforming Pushkin into a victim was that official Soviet literary criticism created a fable of an artist of genius oppressed and ultimately silenced by an authoritarian government.

Testimonials of workers collected by the Central Committee of the Union of Workers of the Leather Industry during the centennial reveal that this image of Pushkin as a revolutionary and a victim of tsarism was current among factory workers. A worker from Kiev proclaimed, "Pushkin was exiled more than once, but when he was exiled he continued to write, criticizing the autocracy even more."[87] A Moscow worker described how the tsarist "*oprichniki* (political police)" killed Pushkin, noting that "in our time it is unthinkable that such a fate could befall a poet."[88] These statements glorify poets as defenders of freedom and make a direct comparison between the lot of poets in tsarist Russia and in the Soviet Union. While the irony of these statements may not have been obvious to the leather workers, it was clear to many Soviet writers that they were in increasing danger of becoming victims of the Soviet government.

In the 1937 film *Journey to Erzerum,* Pushkin visited his Decembrist friends in exile, was spied upon by tsarist agents, and wanted to flee the country but did not succeed. He also refused to write poetry to glorify the Turkish campaign. According to a book published in conjunction with the film, Pushkin did not cave in to pressure to write what the government demanded: "He does not excuse himself and he does not get down on his knees."[89] This depiction of the artist as prisoner who was spied upon, not allowed to leave the country, and forced to write in a certain way described the Soviet artistic community in 1937. Unlike Pushkin, many of these intellectuals were forced to "get down on their knees" and confess their mistakes. The writings of the centennial also emphasized the precarious position of the poet who endangered his life in order to exercise his literary and political freedom. This vision of the suffering artist, which was also a part of the nineteenth-century myth of Pushkin, became an important aspect of the centennial that was encouraged by high cultural officials. In December 1936, official reviewers of the film *The Youth of the Poet,* for example, wanted the scenarist Slonimskii to emphasize the theme of "the danger of Pushkin as poet" even though Slonimskii protested that this approach was historically inaccurate.[90] The film depicted Pushkin as a dangerous revolutionary who was ready to sacrifice his life for freedom, but it also raised the stature of poets and granted them a privileged position from which to speak the truth and criticize the government. Emphasis on the artist or writer as a symbol of political freedom and an enemy of the government was particularly provocative in the Soviet context as members of the intelligentsia watched their comrades being dismissed from their jobs and arrested for what they had written.

Pushkin and Debates about Freedom

Freedom was a central concept in the Pushkin Centennial of 1937 as well as in Soviet discourse of the mid-1930s. In 1936 the promulgation of the new Soviet Constitution brought the issues of rights, freedom, and democracy to center stage. Yet, in the tense atmosphere of the purges, Pushkin's definition of freedom and the freedom of Soviet Pushkin scholarship were hotly contested. In late 1936, Luppol criticized one scholarly work for suggesting that Pushkin's rebelliousness and free-thinking came from his position as a "nobleman who mourned for the prosperity he had once enjoyed."[91] The editors of the journal *Literaturnoe obozrenie* severely censured the literary critic Gorbov for "underhandedly garbling" Pushkin's "aspiration to free himself" from the gendarmes of Nicholas and Benkendorf by transforming this aspiration into the "counter-revolutionary demand for the freedom of the artist from the epoch, the revolution, the proletariat, and the popular masses."[92] Some Soviet publicists thus sought to limit the discussion of freedom by defining it narrowly as political struggle against Nicholas I, but more expansive definitions of freedom, such as the freedom of the artist and the freedom to achieve personal desires, co-existed and competed with this more limited one. These definitions of freedom contradicted official representations of the complete unity of the individual and the state.

The debates of the Soviet intelligentsia about artistic and political freedom show the ways in which a group of people under threat of terror and in conditions of tight censorship wrote about an issue that had direct relevance to their own lives. The conflicting interpretations of freedom during the centennial expose the extent of debate that was possible in the Soviet Union in 1937 and reveal the struggles of members of the Soviet literary establishment to write what they believed about Pushkin when their interpretations differed from officially sanctioned ones.

The most serious public challenge to the depiction of Pushkin as a revolutionary freedom-fighter despite his aristocratic origins came from Dmitrii S. Mirskii. A Russian prince who had fought on the side of the Whites in the Civil War and then emigrated to England, Mirskii became a Eurasianist in the 1920s, but by 1930 became convinced that the Soviet state was the only possible source of rebirth for Russia.[93] He embraced Marxism and returned to the Soviet Union in 1932, where he began to publish literary criticism that asserted that the class origins of the writer determined the type of literature produced.[94] This strict adherence to socio-economic categories, or "vulgar sociology" as critics called it, had fallen out of favor with the downfall of the Russian Association of Proletarian Writers in 1932. Mirskii's espousal of this particular type of Marxist literary criticism was dangerously behind the times.

Mirskii's 1934 article in the journal *Literaturnoe nasledstvo* set off a debate about Pushkin's relation to the people and to the tsar that continued over the next three years. Although Mirskii had softened some of the more controversial conclusions of his 1926 biography of Pushkin,[95] his article still challenged fundamental tenets of the Soviet Pushkin myth by claiming that the aristocratic Pushkin was a "lackey," and a "narrowly national poet," whose worldview was "alien to the proletariat" because of his class origins.[96] Soviet publicist D. Zaslavskii virulently attacked Mirskii's interpretation of Pushkin in a *Pravda* article, launching a public campaign against him in the Soviet press.[97]

In an article in *Vremennik*, Mirskii was forced to admit that his views of Pushkin were incorrect. His retraction was not contrite enough for the editor of *Vremennik*, however, who commented, "Unfortunately, the answer of D. S. Mirskii to his critics, despite the reservations made by him, shows that the error of his views is still not clear to him."[98] A review of *Vremennik* in *Literaturnaia gazeta* attacked both Mirskii and the editor of *Vremennik*: "It was hardly expedient to accommodate such an article even in the presence of an editor's reservation."[99] Mirskii was forced to recant once again, and in a completely abject manner. He wrote to the editor of *Literaturnaia gazeta* "I presented a vulgar-sociological understanding of the essence of Pushkin's work as 'bourgeois' with 'noble' vestiges. . . . I inevitably came to a formalistic understanding of the great poet as 'only an artist,' only a master of forms." In regard to his first apology, he noted: "This confession, rehearsed in a tone that only strengthened the original mistakes, provoked the *Pravda* article."[100] Mirskii's fate was similar to that of the victims of the show trials, who had to confess their sins publicly before they were executed. Mirskii's life history and his outspoken criticism of the Soviet literary establishment made him a likely target of the purges. *Literaturnaia gazeta* accused him of being "nothing but a filthy White Guard Officer," and he was arrested in June 1937. He died in 1939.[101]

Mirskii refuted the notion of Pushkin as a revolutionary who fought against Nicholas I until his dying day, and thereby cast doubt on assertions that Pushkin's definition of freedom was political rather than personal. All of the prominent Pushkin scholars active during the centennial went to tremendous efforts to refute Mirskii. When Mirskii called Pushkin a lackey, he struck a nerve among Soviet literary critics who themselves displayed a high degree of conformity to the dictates of Soviet power. It is possible that Mirskii even meant to provoke these Soviet literary authorities. Ironically, his critics proved their own servility by attacking him.

Mirskii's charge that Pushkin was a subservient toady to autocracy rather than a rebel was energetically refuted by V. Kirpotin. Kirpotin had been at the forefront of the Stalinist literary scene as the secretary of the organizing committee of the Union of Soviet Writers between 1932 and 1934, but he did not hold significant leadership positions after that time.[102] In his book *Nasledie Pushkina k kommunizmu* (*Pushkin's Legacy to Communism*), which was widely excerpted in journals and newspapers,[103] Kirpotin emphasized Pushkin's desire for freedom:

> Pushkin's welcoming hymn of happiness suppressed notes of sadness; it turned into a song of sorrow. One of the reasons for this transformation was the political regime of the country. A free man in the company of other free men could be happy. A despotic regime awkwardly and inhumanely interfering in the life of an individual self-realized person distorted his life's path, broke his hopes, deprived him of happiness. There is no happiness without freedom—Pushkin himself keenly understood this in his own way. Pushkin's poetry was freedom loving. In truth, one would have to possess the narrow vision of a *buntuiushchego stolonachal'nika* (mutinous bureaucrat) in order to claim that Pushkin's poetry is permeated by a spirit of servility.[104]

Kirpotin claimed that despotism interfered with Pushkin's concept of himself as a person and robbed him of his personal happiness. Although the concept of freedom was a part of official Soviet discourse, this emphasis on the private and internal construction of the individual personality was not. According to Kirpotin, it was Pushkin's "striving for personal independence" that gave his life "its freedom-loving, seditious character."[105] To define Pushkin as a rebel, Kirpotin argued that the quest for personal freedom and independence in and of itself was sufficient to challenge an autocratic government. Kirpotin's insistence on personal dignity and inner freedom revealed the limits of autocratic or Stalinist repression.

In dismissing Mirskii's charge that Pushkin was servile to autocracy, Kirpotin focused on Pushkin's unsuccessful struggle to maintain inner freedom. Kirpotin tried to reconcile Pushkin's supposedly anti-autocratic stance with the textual evidence of his glorification of the autocracy in such poems as "Poltava." Kirpotin acknowledged Pushkin's increasing sympathy with the autocracy toward the end of his life and the contradiction that it caused: "Nothing came out of his attempts to be the singer of an idealized autocracy. An unresolvable contradiction remained: Pushkin could no longer be the singer of freedom, but his genius also could not get on with absolutism."[106] The dilemma of the entrapped artist who could neither express his idea of freedom nor maintain good relations with political authorities was common in Stalin's Soviet Union.

While the dominant interpretation of Pushkin during the centennial emphasized the political nature of his desire for freedom, some authors were criticized for taking this conclusion too far. In an article in *Pravda*, scholar and literary bureaucrat M. Khrapchenko acknowledged that there were differences of opinion about Pushkin's role in Nicholaevan society that divided the Pushkin scholarly establishment. He criticized much of the writing in the centennial for its "vulgar sociologism," which he defined as attempts of Pushkin scholars to "present Pushkin as a consistent democrat, practically a revolutionary of the proletarian type. Marxism does not need such groping in the dark. The greatness of Pushkin will become clearer precisely when we reveal his real ties with his epoch, his development, going beyond limited social surroundings."[107]

While Mirskii was charged with "vulgar sociologism" for claiming that Pushkin was not a revolutionary, Khrapchenko indicted other scholars for the same crime when they did precisely the opposite. Khrapchenko argued for historicizing Pushkin rather than blindly asserting his revolutionary nature. In his view, Pushkin was neither a lackey nor a Marxist, but a nineteenth-century nobleman who held ideas about freedom. In late 1936, a member of the All-Union Pushkin Committee also complained about a lecturer who told his audience that Pushkin "was practically a Communist."[108] These criticisms reveal the ways in which the complex official interpretations of Pushkin's quest for freedom were misunderstood and vulgarized by the less-sophisticated writers and speakers of the centennial, creating even more contradictory meanings of the concept of freedom.

Retreat to Textology

While some Pushkin scholars sought to explore Pushkin's ideas of freedom, others fought to maintain their own freedom as scholars. Some Pushkin scholars resisted the reforging of Pushkin into a New Soviet Man. These scholars found ways to continue their careers without adopting official views of Pushkin; many Pushkinists working in Leningrad pursued textology. By working directly with Pushkin's manuscripts, they could continue to study his work without contributing to what they considered to be false scholarship. These Leningrad scholars prepared Pushkin's *Collected Works*, published by the USSR Academy of Sciences, in conjunction with the centennial. They sought to use their expertise on Pushkin to carve out a niche for themselves in the Soviet literary establishment. These scholars engaged in a struggle with political authorities to maintain their interpretations of Pushkin, even when these interpretations contradicted the new Pushkin orthodoxies.

Evidence of this struggle may be seen in the publication history of Pushkin's *Collected Works*. After the first volume (Volume VII) of the *Collected Works* appeared, its editors were criticized in the Soviet press for "not employing the Marxist-Leninist heritage" in their interpretations of Pushkin.[109] In late 1936 Sovnarkom decreed, and in February 1937 the Politbiuro confirmed, that Volume VII and all future volumes of the *Collected Works* would be published with textual variants and only minimal commentary.[110] At the same time, Sovnarkom ruled that the *Collected Works* be published in a deluxe version with high-quality paper and binding.[111] The high Soviet leadership restrained the Pushkin scholars from including their own interpretations of Pushkin's life in the *Collected Works*. Yet it was a matter of prestige that a luxurious edition of the *Collected Works* be completed, so the government continued to provide work and elite status for the textologists.[112]

Just as Pushkin was supposed to be politically engaged, Pushkinists were expected to dedicate themselves to socially useful work. Articles in the Soviet press criticized both textology and esoteric study of Pushkin devoid of clear political content. A joke called "About Pushkinists" published in *Vecherniaia Moskva* parodied a Pushkinist by having him say "About Pushkin himself, my child, I can't tell you anything. I'm a specialist on the close relatives of Pushkin's distant acquaintances."[113] This joke implied that specialized Pushkin scholars were trivial and useless.

The retreat to textology, genealogy, and esoteric branches of Pushkin scholarship was sometimes seen as subversive. Khrapchenko, in the article in *Pravda* discussed above, accused some members of the professional Pushkin establishment of writing about irrelevant topics. Khrapchenko cited articles on such subjects as "One Comma in *Evgenii Onegin.*" Khrapchenko explained: "This is not an evil invention, or a parody. A lot of so-called 'concrete' work appears in the collection *Zven'ia*, published by the fascist, bandit, and murderer Kamenev."[114] Soviet authorities thus identified non-politicized or non-conformist scholarship about Pushkin with enemies of the people. Writing about Pushkin in a way that did not conform to the expectations of Party leaders and the official Soviet literary establishment here becomes akin to a traitorous act. Nevertheless, some Pushkin scholars were able to use the Pushkin Centennial to discuss political freedom, the plight of the artist, and the dangers of becoming a lackey. Other scholars used the opportunities created by the Pushkin Centennial to maintain their careers as textologists. Party officials who sponsored the Pushkin Centennial sought to define Soviet freedom in a narrow political way, yet the centennial opened up spaces in which individual freedom could be both discussed and pursued.

Pushkin and Resistance

The Pushkin Centennial engendered multiple interpretations of heroism, freedom, and the individual. How can we interpret the repeated allusions to political and artistic freedom and the struggle of the individual versus the state in the rhetoric of the Pushkin celebration? The centennial's concepts of political and artistic freedom were a double-edged sword, creating possibilities for multiple and subversive readings of centennial discourse.

Centennial discourse seems to have fostered several kinds of subversive readings. The first possibility is that of multiple interpretations, in which

Soviet ideologues produced official representations that unintentionally created alternative meanings. In these cases, the instability of language and its polysemous nature enabled Soviet readers to interpret official documents in idiosyncratic ways that subverted their intent. A second possibility is unconscious subversion. In early 1937 the Soviet intelligentsia was under intense psychological strain because many people were being arrested. Under these extraordinary circumstances, members of the intelligentsia were drawn to the theme of artistic and personal freedom. Without reflecting on what they were doing, these writers unintentionally revealed their anxieties and registered their incomprehension of, and resistance to, government policies in their writings about Pushkin's life and works. A third type of subversive discourse is the conscious use of Aesopian language to create ambiguity.[115] For example, emphasis on the existence of censorship, the lack of political freedom, and the presence of lackeys and hypocrites surrounding the throne of Nicholas could simultaneously describe Stalin's rule. While these three possibilities emerged from quite different circumstances, they produced similar results: texts that could be read as opposition to the Soviet government and to Stalin's policies.

Pushkin's life and works were rich in allusions that provided an excellent field of play for Aesopian language, an art of which Pushkin himself was a master. Kirpotin analyzed the way in which Pushkin used Aesopian language in his poem "André Chénier":

> Chénier says about the leaders of the Jacobin dictatorship, "We chose a murderer with executioners as kings." But Pushkin always made an analogy between the tyrants of autocracy and the petty-bourgeois dictatorship in France. These words might especially refer to Nicholas I, the murderer of the Decembrists.[116]

The creation of Aesopian analogies was thus explicitly addressed in the discourse of the centennial.

The Soviet censors were also aware of the possibilities for Aesopian messages in the works of Pushkin. Although the Moscow Art Theater and the Meierkhol'd Theater prepared productions of Pushkin's *Boris Godunov,* both were prohibited from performing the play.[117] This drama about political legitimacy and the nature of political power inherently produced a variety of meanings that Soviet officials did not want to transmit. Furthermore, in the highly charged atmosphere of the purge years, Party and government officials feared that even typographical and grammatical errors might contain hidden messages.[118]

Like *Boris Godunov,* Pushkin's other historical works provided many possibilities for Aesopian analogy. Depictions of Peter the Great were an excellent source of Aesopian meaning because in Russian historical and literary traditions, Peter was a "strikingly bipolar" figure, loved for his modernization of the Russian state but hated for his enslavement of the peasantry.[119] The figure of Peter thus embodied the tension between the state and the individual. By the mid-1930s, official Soviet views of Peter emphasized his heroic transformation of Russia and endorsed his privileging of the state over the individual. Stalin invited the analogy between Peter's achievements and his own by authorizing positive depictions of Peter in literature, drama, and film.[120] While Soviet cultural officials sanctioned the analogy between Peter and Stalin, a long tradition of negative evaluations of Peter facilitated the creation of subversive meanings.

In "The Bronze Horseman" Pushkin lauds Peter for building the extraordinary city of Petersburg, but shows the human cost of Peter's triumph in the character of Evgenii, an ordinary clerk who is robbed of his personal happiness, indeed, of his sanity, when the Petersburg flood of 1824 kills his fiancée. The Peter theme in "The Bronze Horseman" provided Soviet citizens with the opportunity to praise the existence of a strong leader, thereby indirectly paying homage to Stalin. In a readers' poll about Pushkin conducted by *Literaturnyi sovremennik* in March of 1936, a district secretary remarked that he loved the strong character of Peter the Great. Another respondent particularly liked "'The Bronze Horseman' where the problem of personal versus public [obligations] is resolved in favor of the public."[121] This view of "The Bronze Horseman" affirmed the Stalinist ethos that the suffering and sacrifices of the ordinary man mattered little in comparison to the great achievements of the modernization of the state.

References to Pushkin's "The Bronze Horseman" could be much more ambiguous, however. In January 1937, the journal *Red Archive* (*Krasnyi arkhiv*) published archival materials and manuscripts relating to Pushkin's early years. The volume began with a brief but suggestive biographical article by E. N. Cherniavskii, whose work appeared frequently in this journal between 1936 and 1938.[122] He emphasized the ways in which the regime of Nicholas I oppressed Pushkin and suppressed the freedom of the individual.[123] The article quoted Pushkin on public life under Nicholas and showed how his views were reflected in "The Bronze Horseman":

> "Our public (*obshchestvennaia*) life is everywhere sad. This absence of public ideas, this indifference to all duties, to justice and truth, this cynical disdain for ideas and for human worth truly lead to despair."

> Pushkin tries to give the solution to these contradictions in his brilliant poem "The Bronze Horseman." Evgenii opposes the good of the government to his personal happiness, his interests. Having lost his bride, he threatens the Bronze Horseman and gazing into the metallic eyes of the terrible, merciless governmental strength, he runs away from the specter of this power and goes insane.

Cherniavskii then stated that Pushkin "knew that he was not insane," but that the "system" was "irrational."[124]

A common tactic of Aesopian language is to use quotation from an outside source to hide the narrator's responsibility for possibly subversive ideas.[125] Cherniavskii quoted Pushkin's attack on Nicholaevan society, but this critique could also be construed as a revelation of the despair and confusion that beset the intelligentsia in Stalin's time. In 1937 there was indeed reason to be concerned about "indifference to truth" and "disdain for ideas and human worth" in an "irrational system."

Cherniavskii's discussion of "The Bronze Horseman" focused on the political legitimacy of Nicholas's government:

> The very formulation of the question of the rights of the individual to contest the wisdom and stability of the supreme autocratic power presented a disastrous threat to [Nicholas I]. It was not Evgenii, a pitiful madman, that Nicholas feared. He feared those who could come after Evgenii and ask the idol of autocracy the same question in the name of the enserfed slaves, in the name of the abject people, in the name of those languishing in the depths of the Siberian mines.[126]

This passage raised the question of political opposition to the "supreme power" and listed grievances that were also applicable in Stalin's Russia. The use of the word "wisdom" (*mudrost'*) in connection with the autocratic government of Nicholas was a textual link to Stalin, since "wise" was one of the adjectives frequently used to describe Stalin as leader. One could thus read this selection as a call for someone to speak out in the name of the collectivized peasants, the oppressed masses, and, most strikingly, the political prisoners tortured in the forced labor camps of Siberia.

Once a reader began to read between the lines of Cherniavskii's article, many other passages could be interpreted as oppositional or subversive, despite their apparent adherence to the Party line. After his discussion of individual rights, Cherniavskii announced that only the "system of socialism" could resolve the contradiction between the individual and society. He began the next paragraph with the words "And only in our day,"[127] one of the clichés of the 1930s that created an opposition between Soviet Russia and the tsarist past. This formulation created a double entendre for any reader who was skeptical of the surface value of Cherniavskii's words:

> And only in our day, in the day of the victory of socialism and the Stalin Constitution, in our day, when the nations of the Soviet Union deeply feel the greatness and strength of their motherland—do the torment and the quests of this poet of genius become understandable.

Although Cherniavskii seemed to praise the accomplishments of the Soviet Union in raising the cultural level of the non-Russian nations, he may have been questioning the imposition of Soviet culture by force.

The quest for freedom played a prominent role in Cherniavskii's article:

Pushkin continued to work up until his last breath, seeing in front of him a great goal—the enlightenment of the people. In his work the idea of freedom was combined with the idea of a great motherland.

Freedom is unthinkable outside of a country where it can be realized. And the motherland cannot become great until she is free.[128]

Cherniavskii again attributed the ideas in this passage to Pushkin, but he put the second paragraph in the present tense and did not mention Pushkin at all. The change in tense moves the reader from the time of Pushkin into the present, suggesting that the Soviet Union could not achieve greatness until it achieved political freedom.

While in Cherniavskii's text a complex elaboration of ideas could be traced, clearly suggesting a conscious attempt to create double meaning, there were large numbers of other texts whose meanings were ambiguous in a less systematic way. The frequent emphasis on Pushkin's struggle for freedom led to many suggestive formulations about the role of the writer in society. These statements occurred even at the most prominent publicized Pushkin events. During the Pushkin meeting at the Bolshoi Theater, at which Stalin himself was present, I. Luppol gave a speech entitled "The Greatness of Pushkin." This speech was also printed in the April 1937 issue of *Oktiabr'*. In the speech, Luppol described the reign of Nicholas as "an age when 'it was dangerous to speak and disastrous to keep silent,' to use the just observation of one of Pushkin's contemporaries . . . But Pushkin was not silent, he spoke and he knew to whom he spoke."[129] As in other incidences of Aesopian language, Luppol carefully attributed his words to one of Pushkin's contemporaries. His speech emphasized, however, the necessity of speaking out against oppression despite the danger of doing so. These words about Pushkin could indicate Luppol's awareness of the precariousness of his own situation. Did these words mean that Luppol was bold enough to challenge Stalin in front of a whole theater full of people? Did these phrases resonate as politically subversive among the audience at the Bolshoi Theater that night? Or were they an affirmation of blind loyalty on the part of Luppol, who was proving he could make this statement without flinching? Could this statement just have been a straightforward report of conditions under Nicholas I? Or was it evidence of Luppol's subconscious desire to speak the truth at no matter what cost?[130]

In late 1934, Luppol helped Osip and Nadezhda Mandel'shtam survive by giving Nadezhda translating work, but three years later he refused to assist Mandel'shtam. By June 1937, Luppol and his wife would not socialize with Communists who they did not know.[131] This combination of facts suggests that Luppol was aware of the nature of events in 1937. In his speech, he may have given voice to his anxiety, confusion, and anguish about the purges by making a statement about the danger of keeping silent in the face of oppression. While this speech was probably not a direct cause of Luppol's arrest, he was arrested in 1940 and died in 1943.[132] His statement reveals that meanings in even the most high-profile public discourse of the Pushkin Centennial were fluid and open to multiple interpretations that questioned the status quo and protested the actions of the Soviet government.

It was also possible to read the contributions of other prominent Soviet writers to the Pushkin Centennial as containing double meanings. V. V. Veresaev began his literary career before the revolution and in 1917 considered himself a Social Democrat and a Marxist. As his biographer noted, however, Veresaev believed that "the Bolsheviks . . . hurried the revolution, the raging sea of the common people's passion, a passion that could sometimes be very inhuman and could ruin socialist ideals." In the early 1920s Veresaev lived through a crisis of conscience, during which he reevaluated his role as a writer.[133] *Sisters,* his novel about collectivization published in 1933, criticized Communist officials for ignoring their own consciences and violently repressing the peasantry. In the 1920s and early 1930s, Veresaev's works were widely published but often criticized in the press.[134]

During the Pushkin Centennial, Veresaev became the most prominent biographer of Pushkin. In late 1936, Bubnov even criticized the work of the sub-committee in charge of biographies, headed by Luppol, because of its reliance on Veresaev: "It disturbs me that you are releasing Veresaev in three forms, one and the same author, and three biographies."[135] Veresaev's *Life of Pushkin* was not only published in Russian in 50,000 copies, but it was translated into English, French, German, and Ukrainian as well and sent abroad.

In *Life of Pushkin,* Veresaev recounted the plot of *Scenes from the Times of Chivalry,* Pushkin's unfinished play about the end of feudalism, and then wrote:

> Here the written scenes end. The story was to have been concluded as follows: Berthold Shvartz, a monk and alchemist confined to the . . . dungeon as a sorcerer, during his imprisonment invents gunpowder. There is a rebellion of peasants who besiege the castle. The lord of the castle, who is supposedly invulnerable in his *steel* armor, is killed by a bullet. The impregnable walls of the castle, blown up by Berthold, rise in the air and crumble into dust. Faust arrives on the scene, riding on the tail of the devil. The synopsis concludes with the following words: "The invention of printing is a peculiar kind of artillery."
>
> Against the old world of privilege, armored in *steel* and fenced off by strong walls, there arise new forces-the enthusiasm of the oppressed, improved technology, widespread education. The *steel* is punctured, the impregnable walls crumble and the old flies to the devil.[136] (Emphasis added)

Here is Pushkin's original plan for the play:

In prison, Berthold takes up alchemy—he discovers gunpowder—there is a peasant revolt incited by the young poet. The chateau is under siege. [Berthold] blows it up. The lord of the castle—mediocrity personified—is killed by a bullet. The piece finishes with reflections and with the arrival of Faust riding on the tail of the devil. (The invention of printing is a different kind of artillery).[137]

Veresaev's work added details that had no basis in the original Pushkin. The passage created a lord behind "the impregnable walls" of his castle who was "supposedly invulnerable in his steel armor," and, through repetition, emphasized the idea of a walled-off world of privilege armored in steel.[138] Veresaev used the Marxist idea of the necessary historical progression from feudalism to capitalism to show that the defeat of the lord in steel armor was inevitable. Unlike Luppol and Mirskii, who were purge victims, Veresaev continued to live undisturbed in the Soviet Union and won the Order of the Red Banner of Labor in 1939 and the State Prize in 1943.

The texts of the centennial reveal numerous opportunities for alternative and subversive interpretations. The language of celebration offered Soviet citizens a wide variety of ways of thinking about the world in which they lived.

The Pushkin Centennial of 1937 illuminated the efforts of the Soviet government to affirm the accessibility of cultural advancement to all citizens of the Soviet Union. It attempted to use the magical, quasi-religious figure of Pushkin as a bridge between the newly educated masses of the common people and the intellectuals well versed in the culture and glory of Old Russia. In doing so, the Soviet state transformed official discourse by trying to appropriate the greatness and power of the Russian empire and incorporate it into its national image.

The Pushkin that emerged was both a symbol of the greatness of Russian culture and of the availability of this culture to Soviet citizens of all nationalities. This definition of Pushkin as a Soviet national poet expanded the realm of Russian culture into the non-Russian republics through a kind of cultural imperialism based on the man and his work. Yet there were substantial logistical, linguistic, and political barriers to the spread of Russian culture that made the Pushkin Centennial much more effective in the center than in the periphery. The attempts to make Pushkin accessible to the entire population tended to be more successful than entirely politicized Soviet holidays because the centennial captured the imagination of cultural cadres in a way that political celebrations did not. Nonetheless, the centennial was most effective in Moscow and Leningrad and among the Soviet elites. The goal of bringing culture to Soviet citizens who lacked access to it was compromised by the hierarchical structure of Soviet life. Paradoxically, the areas that were most "backward" by Soviet standards received the fewest resources, while the center and largest provincial cities received the lion's share of resources and most qualified cadres. Despite images of equality and unity that Soviet officials promoted during the Pushkin Centennial, the celebration revealed divisions between rural and urban, center and periphery; it also revealed vast inequities in the Stalinist system.

The decision to celebrate a revered intelligentsia figure, which enhanced the success of the centennial among cultural cadres, also introduced ambiguity into the celebration. In choosing a beloved figure from pre-revolutionary culture, the Soviet leadership played on the feelings of various segments of the intelligentsia and allowed them to participate in the centennial, so long as they seemed to be defining Pushkin in the way mandated by Soviet officials. Responses to the invitation of the official Pushkin Committee were varied. Some intellectuals categorically refused to play the game, while others played by their own rules. These scholars from various backgrounds and generations used Pushkin to express their own diverse and sometimes contradictory reactions to the Soviet government. Through official channels, they were given the opportunity to put their ideas into print. Soviet officials did not always acknowledge the extent to which "the invention of printing was a peculiar kind of artillery" for the intelligentsia. The writers of the Pushkin Centennial thus expressed a variety of opinions on freedom, truth, human worth, peasant rebellions, imperialism, travel abroad, state surveillance, party privilege, despotism, Stalin's leadership, and many other topics.

In 1936–1937, Soviet intellectuals, from respected pre-revolutionary writers to ordinary state functionaries, from obscure editors of historical journals to prominent scholars of the Stalin era, publicly examined and questioned the orthodoxies of the Stalin era. Even in the most repressive era of Soviet history, voices from different places in the Soviet system explored the meanings of freedom and questioned the relationship of the individual to the state through the medium of official celebration.

6

ANNIVERSARY OF TURMOIL

THE TWENTIETH ANNIVERSARY OF THE
OCTOBER REVOLUTION

In 1937, the Soviet cultural intelligentsia was mobilized to produce its own great works of art and literature to commemorate twenty years of Soviet power. Like the cultural production of the Pushkin Centennial, the art of the October anniversary was intended to define the relationship between Russian and Soviet history. The October anniversary also continued the work of the Pushkin Centennial and New Year's Day by attempting to reach out to the Soviet population. There was not, however, a consensus about how best to accomplish these goals. The chairman of the Committee on the Arts, the administrative body that supervised all Soviet artistic production, declared that artists had a crucial political and social role to play in the celebration of the twentieth anniversary of the October Revolution.[1] P. M. Kerzhentsev stated in mid-1937 that "the celebration of the jubilee is not just some kind of ceremonial meeting but a great political campaign, which not only celebrates our achievements after twenty years but simultaneously strikes a blow against our enemies . . . and strengthens the masses' consciousness of the correctness of the Lenin-Stalin line."[2] The organization of the celebration was complicated by the fact that this "great political campaign" took place while the purges were in full swing. Many of the celebration organizers discovered that the enemies against whom they were supposed to strike were themselves.

From 1917 on, there were tensions in Soviet arts policy between embracing the art of the past and creating new proletarian art; between the promotion of grand artistic masterpieces that required considerable artistic training and the creation of smaller art forms by and for the masses.[3] During the dominance of the proletarian writer's association (RAPP) in the late 1920s, the accessibility of art to the masses became more important than artistic talent, and proletarian art of "small forms" predominated.[4] The official adoption of socialist realism in 1932 overturned the hegemony of RAPP and permitted art forms that the proletarian movement had excluded. During the preparation for the October Jubilee in 1937, the Soviet cultural elite and bureaucrats actively defined and implemented socialist realism in the arts. They embraced widely diverging cultural forms, carefully selecting classical models for Soviet aesthetics such as Beethoven, Repin, and Pushkin, but also supporting the creation of Soviet popular and folk arts.[5] Whether socialist realism was packaged in a large or small form, it was supposed to be *narodnyi*, accessible to and appreciated by a mass audience.

Despite this official solution to artistic conflicts, tensions in Soviet arts policies still persisted in the late 1930s. During the preparation for the October anniversary, arts officials had to decide whether to allocate their limited resources and personnel to the production of a few major masterworks or to the creation of types of art in which the broad masses could participate. The creators of the anniversary negotiated these artistic and aesthetic conflicts in the midst of the heightened social, political, and economic pressures of 1937.

Just as the October anniversary was a critical moment in the ongoing definition of socialist realism, so it was also a watershed in the reconceptualization of Russian and Soviet history that occurred in the mid-1930s. Like RAPP, the school of history led by M. N. Pokrovskii was discredited in 1932 both for its abstract historical schemes that ignored individuals and for its exclusively negative evaluation of the Russian Empire.[6] The twentieth anniversary of the October Revolution occurred as Soviet governmental and educational cadres officially reinterpreted Russian, Soviet, and Party history by writing new textbooks. In preparation for the October jubilee, museum directors were expected to reorganize their exhibits to conform to new historical interpretations and periodizations.[7]

This reorganization of history reflected the defeat of the Pokrovskii school; some aspects of Russian imperial rule were now defined as progressive, and the heroic exploits of individuals, particularly the militarily successful and state-building Russian tsars such as Peter the Great and Ivan the Terrible, were lauded. Soviet rhetoric now linked the historical successes of the Russian Empire to notions of a multinational Soviet patriotism. Turning away from the internationalism of the 1920s, Soviet ideologues again embraced the pre-revolutionary concepts of motherland and the *narod* who would give their lives to defend it.

This reorientation of history led to a variety of ambiguities in the historical discourse of the October anniversary. As Lowell Tillett has pointed out, in the 1930s, "Soviet historians revised their views only on subjects about which they had specific instruction and retained older views elsewhere, leaving the contradictions for the future to solve."[8] The new historical interpretations promoted by the October anniversary thus co-existed and competed with older and conflicting viewpoints. Official articulations of the relationship between the past and present were shaped by competing historical interpretations and the disjuncture between Soviet discourses and Soviet realities.

The historical interpretation of the Russian Revolution of 1917 was, of course, a particular focus of the twentieth anniversary celebration. As Stalin consolidated his power and physically destroyed Party leaders who challenged his legitimacy, Soviet cadres constructed narratives about 1917 that affirmed his status as Lenin's sole heir. In these depictions, Soviet history became a constant battle between heroes and traitors, mirroring the turmoil of 1937. These histories both shaped and were shaped by the efforts of Soviet cadres to create popular support for the virulent campaigns against enemies of the people. The political upheavals of 1937 affected the practices of the October anniversary as well as its discourse since the very cadres needed to create a mass political holiday themselves became targets of the purges. The discourse and practices of the celebration of twenty years of Soviet power were thus transformed by the holiday's coincidence with Stalin's quest for legitimacy and with the purges.

Great Expectations

The plans of top Soviet cultural and political leaders for the celebration of the Twentieth Anniversary of October reveal that they considered the occasion to be an extremely significant moment in the history of the country. Soviet cultural authorities began to discuss anniversary plans over two years in advance of the holiday[9] and sought to differentiate the Twentieth Anniversary of October from "the ordinary carrying out of celebrations."[10] The plans to commemorate the anniversary differed from other celebration schemes in timing, scale, and quality.

The October Revolution Jubilee was to extend beyond the date of November 7th; in June 1937, Kerzhentsev encouraged dramatists, directors, and actors "to consider the entire year as a year to demonstrate the fundamental achievements of twenty years of Soviet theater."[11] Kerzhentsev also emphasized that literary works should reflect the overwhelming importance of the revolution as a transformative event:

> We should proceed from the position that we are holding the twentieth anniversary of the greatest revolution in the history of humanity. A new historical epoch in the life of humanity has begun. . . . If we approach questions from this tall snowy summit, they will be treated as great and profound questions because we stand before the immortalization of the most grandiose events in the history of humanity. I understand that this scale is very difficult. . . . We must show how people have changed.[12]

Kerzhentsev hoped to inspire writers to capture the essence of the revolution as a landmark moment in human history. He encouraged writers and artists to build the celebration on a grandiose scale, as a monument to the achievements of the revolution.

In addition to demanding that Soviet art attain "a higher plane" in honor of the anniversary, Kerzhentsev called on Soviet artists to "mobilize our art on a far more extensive front."[13] While he admitted that artists might have difficulty portraying the extraordinary transformations that the revolution engendered, he did not acknowledge that there was a fundamental tension between creating great art and making it accessible to the masses. In the grand plans for the anniversary, both goals were to be achieved at once. Yet individual pronouncements about the celebration usually focused on achieving one goal or the other. While N. A. Velilovskii, head of the Moscow Administration of the Arts, proclaimed that "the art of small forms" and the "amateur movement"[14] had "an enormous role" to play in the celebration of the October Revolution, V. M. Kirshon, head of the Union of Soviet Writers, urged authors to concentrate on "fundamental works and perhaps the best works of their lives."[15] The Malyi Theater's 1935 plan to produce a show for the jubilee, which highlighted "the best examples of all genres of literature," met with resistance from dramatists who wanted the theater to produce one full-length play.[16] For Kirshon and the other dramatists, the most important aspect of celebrating the jubilee was the creation of the great work of art. This insistence on the creation of larger forms limited the numbers of both actors and audiences who would have access to plays.

One of the most vigorous defenders of mass art was film director G. Roshal'. Five months before the jubilee, at a meeting of the Committee on the Arts, he attacked the committee for failing to provide "genuine" guidance about how to carry out the holiday. Roshal' imagined a holiday that would integrate all of the arts and unify artists and the population:

> Indeed we should celebrate the year 1937. We should create a protracted, perhaps week-long festival of the arts, uniting painting, music, and theater in a single program, in a genuine demonstration of our achievements as a unified whole. Moreover, this festival should be united with a beautiful mass holiday of Soviet art, which we have not yet once truly created. We are obligated in 1937 to make this festival a genuine, great, creative holiday of art. This is not utopia, this is a simple and very necessary thing.[17]

Roshal' also argued that mobile theaters should be able to produce their own plays and not have to copy the plays that larger theaters were producing. He asserted that "our work is founded not on snobbism but on contact with spectators."[18]

Roshal' objected to the separation of the arts from one another, the inaccessibility of the arts to the masses, elitism, and the lack of local autonomy. By emphasizing the need to create a mass holiday and promote "contact with spectators," Roshal' criticized the Committee on the Arts for its failure to bring art into the lives of ordinary citizens. Roshal' wanted the October Anniversary celebration to set a new course in arts policy, in which the arts community could rectify its past faults by creating a genuine mass holiday. Ultimately, however, this mass festival of the arts failed to materialize because Soviet officials instead privileged the production of individual films, plays, and concerts.

Even in the genre of the *estrada* (variety show) where, by definition, small forms predominated, there was a tendency toward hierarchy and away from accessibility to the masses. In August 1937, Moscow Administration of the Arts officials emphasized the significance of the special festival program made up of the best variety show artists. This concert was to be performed in Moscow's prestigious Hall of Columns for the leaders of the Party and government. Moscow officials asserted that "the All-Union Committee on the Arts attaches great importance to this performance which should be the star of the holiday."[19] The production of a "star" performance came at a price, however. A variety show official admitted that putting together this grand spectacle "at the peak of the holidays" meant "denuding" the clubs of their performers.[20] Despite their own insistence that the festival program become the star of the holiday, Moscow arts officials also criticized *Mosestrad* (the Moscow variety show administration) for paying too much attention to the one concert in the Hall of Columns and not enough attention to the thousand concerts that the organization was supposed to perform for the rest of the city of Moscow and its environs.[21] The dilemma of Moscow variety shows revealed how, in the mid-1930s, the central arts organizations put pressure on Moscow performers to serve the Moscow political elite at the expense of ordinary Muscovites. Local arts officials recognized this problem, but lacking political clout and financial resources, they could not rearrange their priorities to serve the local population better.

One of the clearest examples of this tendency toward privilege and luxury for the few was the government's decision to provide the Bolshoi Theater with an expensive new curtain in honor of the Twentieth Anniversary of October. An anonymous letter from artists of the Bolshoi to the Council of People's Commissars asked the government not to spend 350 to 400 thousand rubles on a new curtain, but instead to "to spend these funds in honor of the Twentieth Anniversary on the building of clubs or theaters in some villages, for peasants, and our theater would come there and present some opera."[22] The dream of the artists to take opera beyond the walls of the Bolshoi and out to the people clashed with the government's desire to make the premiere theater of the Soviet Union even more luxurious.

Since access to culture such as art, literature, and theater increasingly defined Soviet elite status in the 1930s, the question of what kind of works would be produced for the jubilee and to whom they were accessible was also a debate about the establishment of cultural, social, and economic hierarchies. Would the arts bureaucracy produce elaborate and expensive artistic productions that could be enjoyed by the select few or more modest productions that could be more widely disseminated? While accessibility to the masses was a watchword of socialist realism, only a minority of voices among the artistic elite emphasized the need to offer mass audiences the opportunity to participate actively in the creation of the October celebrations. These artists implicitly rejected the social hierarchies that were in the process of formation, but their voices were drowned out by a pronounced tendency of central arts organizations toward elitism; scarce resources were overwhelmingly channeled toward art for the *znatnye liudi*, or notables of the Soviet state. While arts officials frequently claimed that art now belonged to the masses, their financial and personnel decisions guaranteed that access to art remained a symbol of rising social status.

The Revolution as Turning Point

A key concept of the anniversary celebration of the October Revolution was transformation. The revolution was represented as a *perelomnyi moment*, a break with the past and a turning point in history. Much of the holiday rhetoric focused on a comparison of life before and after this momentous event. As a handbook for schoolteachers put it, "From a backward peasant country, the USSR turned into a country of powerful, advanced industry." Agriculture in the Soviet Union was transformed "from the plow to the tractor and combine, from crippled individual farming to prosperous life on the collective farm."[23] Soviet publicists employed the binary opposition of "before" and "after" in a systematic and conscious way,[24] contrasting the sadness and deprivation of life in tsarist Russia with the joy and abundance of Soviet life after Stalin's industrialization and collectivization campaigns. Cadres thus included Stalin's First Five Year Plan in their definition of the revolution.

This rigid pattern of binary oppositions that assigned a negative value to the pre-revolutionary era and a positive value to contemporary Soviet life co-existed with a more ambiguous historical discourse about the Russian past. In the mid-1930s, the top Soviet leadership began to identify certain aspects of the Russian imperial past as integral parts of the Soviet heritage. The military prowess of Peter the Great, the literary genius of Pushkin, and the creative power of "the folk" were now assigned a positive value. This change in orientation complicated historical interpretations of the past and of the revolution itself.

At the same time, the positive values assigned to life in the Soviet period clashed with the realities of material poverty and massive social upheaval that existed in 1937. Since the transformations that had taken place during the First Five Year Plan left the vast majority of the population worse off than they had been in the 1920s, proving Stalin's famous claim that "life has become better" required both reshaping people's memories of how they lived in the past and transforming their perceptions of the present. This rhetorical insistence that the revolution had transformed everyone's life for the better and that all social problems had already been overcome created difficulties for Soviet officials because the discourse of Soviet prosperity was constantly contradicted by physical reality. The actions of Soviet officials were also circumscribed by a discourse that afforded them few opportunities to articulate the myriad problems that they encountered daily. Trapped within an exclusively positive discourse about Soviet life, Soviet officials struggled to convince others that the future had arrived as they themselves battled the frustrations of the difficult present.

The Future as the Present

According to arts officials in Sverdlovsk Region, the main goal of artistic performances and other events during the celebration of the Twentieth Anniversary of October was to help every worker, employee, and collective farmer "to see graphically and feel with happiness those enormous changes which took place in the past twenty years in the life of the country, his factory, his collective farm and in his personal life."[25] Given this potentially difficult task, it is not surprising that the arts, with their appeal to emotions and their ability to project an alternative reality, played a major role in urging citizens to "feel" the changes in their lives "with happiness."

Soviet dedication to positivism and scientific method offered another means of proving the success of the Soviet Union. Moscow Region museum directors, for example, resolved in August 1936 that history departments "should be saturated with concrete and convincing historical facts underlining in principle the great significance of what has been accomplished in twenty years of Soviet power."[26] Soviet institutions such as schools, museums, theaters, libraries, reading rooms, factories, and collective farms created exhibits that documented Soviet construction using facts and figures drawn from local records and supplied by the State Planning Administration. By specifically and concretely documenting the local progress of Soviet construction, exhibits created undeniable images of changed urban and rural landscapes. Soviet cadres used these changes in physical environment as a stand-in for improvements in the lives of Soviet citizens.

The State Planning Administration prepared a volume of statistics for propagandists that compared production and cultural statistics from 1913 and 1937.[27] These figures were used by cadres to demonstrate that the Soviet Union had achieved significantly more than tsarist Russia in all fields of endeavor. Soviet cadres barraged citizens with numbers about schools, factories, workers, and production output and hoped their audiences would draw the conclusion that life had become better. They displayed these statistics to show that the main trend of twenty years of Soviet history was accelerated movement forward and that Soviet citizens had already arrived at a bright future. If local evidence of present construction was insufficient to prove that life had become better, Soviet cadres were advised to help their audiences to visualize future improvements. One instructional pam-

Growth in the number of maternity beds. From *Stalinskaia Konstitutsiia sotsializma* (1938).

phlet suggested taking students to new schools that were under construction so that the children could envision their futures.[28] By creating exhibits of Soviet history, museums affirmed the effectiveness, solidity, legitimacy, and endurance of the Soviet project. By using "concrete" facts and statistics about achievements, they hid the difficulties of everyday life behind a facade of new construction. Where achievements had not yet materialized, cadres focused on the promise of the future.

The many ways in which contemporary Soviet life contradicted the celebratory representations of Soviet cadres led not only to the suppression of problems that existed in the present, but also to the glossing over of certain problems from the past. While the rhetoric of the anniversary often contrasted the exploitation of the peasantry under serfdom with the happy and cultured existence of the peasantry under Soviet power, not all of the consequences of peasant oppression could be represented in museum exhibits. In 1936, instructions from the Moscow Regional Department of People's Enlightenment reminded local museums that villages under the yoke of serfdom contained more than just "filth" and a "lack of culture." They were sites of "folk creativity" and "native talents."[29] This anxiety about portraying villages as "uncultured" stemmed, on the one hand, from the trend to resurrect the concept of the *narod* as a source of political legitimacy and patriotism. On the other hand, in the detailed descriptions of the squalor of pre-revolutionary villages, museum visitors might recognize their own living conditions and the inability of Soviet power to create culture and prosperity in the countryside.

In literary works created for the anniversary, plots often revolved around the defeat of the old by new revolutionary forces. Such plots were easy to write about military and historic events but were much more difficult to create when their focus was the reconstruction of daily life. During the October jubilee, the Satire Theater planned to perform V. Shkvarin's play, *Simple Girl*, about the re-education of a Soviet citizen. This play had to be rewritten, however, after its first act was criticized by Moscow arts officials for "creating a repulsive picture of everyday life."[30] Shkvarin's play was rejected by cultural authorities because he depicted real social ills.[31] Even though the heroine victoriously overcame her problems, the play's acknowledgment of the need for profound transformation called into question the possibility of creating a perfect Soviet order. During the anniversary, the capability of Soviet artists to herald the victory of the new was limited by their inability to portray the persistence of negative aspects of the past.

Although one of the main purposes of all public celebrations in the 1930s was to improve agitational work that would mobilize the population to participate enthusiastically in Soviet construction, during the Twentieth Anniversary cadres could not admit in public discourse that there were shortcomings in their previous cultural work. In institutional meetings, however, some Soviet cultural leaders identified the celebration of the twentieth anniversary as an opportunity to make up for past inadequacies. At a September 28, 1937, plenum of the Cultural Section of the Moscow City Soviet, cadres from Moscow film and dramatic theaters confronted their failure to establish and fulfill plans for the Twentieth Anniversary celebrations. One Moscow cultural leader called the twentieth anniversary itself a "turning point" during which one could "put an end to the past with all of its shortcomings and ugliness and start a new life."[32] Another Moscow cultural worker declared that "for the twentieth anniversary we should rebuild all aspects of our life and I demand that for the twentieth anniversary a Rubicon be laid down."[33] This yearning to start over again and rebuild their lives revealed that these officials did not feel themselves to be living in the glorious socialist society they were charged with promoting. Although they were supposed to use the October anniversary to celebrate the victory of socialism, these officials re-interpreted the holiday as a different kind of turning point, a new revolution that this time would truly transform their lives. The Rubicon had not been crossed in 1917, and Soviet officials wanted to cross it in 1937.

The chair of the September 28th meeting was the new head of the Moscow Administration of the Arts K. P. Chudinova, a former district secretary who had been voluntarily demoted to cultural work after the arrest of her first husband in the summer of 1937.[34] She recognized the dangerous implications of calling the Twentieth Anniversary of October a Rubicon. She stated, "I consider fundamentally incorrect in the resolutions the idea that the October anniversary should serve as a turning point so that theaters would rise to the highest level. I consider that the theaters stand at a high level."[35] The plenum approved Chudinova's motion to alter the resolution. The demands of cultural cadres that their lives be rebuilt in honor of the October anniversary were thus rejected by the majority of officials at the meeting.

Chudinova's defense of the success of socialist construction illustrates the challenge Soviet cultural officials faced in 1937. They were not able successfully to organize the October celebrations because their institutions lacked resources and personnel, but they could not openly acknowledge the problems they experienced. Fearing for their own safety, officials proclaimed the success and affirmed the vitality of institutions that were in fact foundering. The actions of cultural cadres were thus circumscribed by their own discourse of success. Ironically, the purges offered new opportunities for cadres to discuss current problems; they could resort to a rhetoric of enemies and wreckers to explain their difficulties.

The Past Is the Present

In their eagerness to project the happiness and majesty of socialist life, Soviet cultural cadres did not draw exclusively on Soviet cultural models. The mass dramatic festivals of the 1920s and statistics of socialist achievements did not capture the grandeur that cadres sought to project during the holiday. In creating a festival to celebrate the solidity and legitimacy of the Soviet state, they returned to pre-revolutionary traditions. The Moscow Administration of the Arts allocated funds to purchase presents for the children who attended October anniversary theater and film performances. Moscow arts officials proclaimed that these presents "do not necessarily have to be standardized, but it is necessary that each theater gives a child some kind of present, so that he will remember this jubilee for his whole life." The inspiration for giving presents at the October jubilee came directly from the coronation ceremonies of the Romanovs. One of the arts officials had met an old woman who still preserved the tankard she had received at the coronation of Nicholas II. Moscow officials hoped that Soviet children would save their October anniversary keepsakes, as this old woman had, for the rest of their lives.[36] This conscious imitation of tsarist ceremony revealed the flexibility of 1930s officials in adopting new forms to glorify the Soviet state. When Soviet traditions and realities did not provide the necessary luster, authorities were willing to use pre-revolutionary models to create a shining celebratory moment.

The October celebrations also revived the heroic reputation of Tsar Peter the Great. The film *Peter I*, based on the novel by Aleksei Tolstoi, was one of two important historical films produced in conjunction with the Twentieth Anniversary of October.[37] The first part of the film was released in September 1937; the second series was supposed to appear in time for the October anniversary, but was not shown until March 1939. This production delay suggests the complexity of creating a Soviet version of Peter's life.[38]

B. Z. Shumiatskii, head of the Central Administration of the Cinema and Photo Industry, explained in a June 13, 1937, meeting of the All-Union Committee on the Arts that Tolstoi and screenwriter V. Petrov had made significant changes to the final scenes of the film. Tolstoi had concluded the novel with a political victory but a "failure in Peter's personal and family life" that included the "treachery of those close to him."[39] Shumiatskii here alluded to the fact that Peter's son was implicated in a plot to overthrow him, was tried publicly, and died in prison under mysterious circumstances. Shumiatskii argued that "to put the accent on the personal fate of the character would somewhat discredit the deeds that he conducted." The Soviet tendency to reject the existence of a dichotomy of public and private life thus forced the film directors to eliminate Peter's personal failures as the Pushkin Centennial eliminated those of Pushkin. Instead, the new ending "showed how Peter finished his wars" and "understood that the time had come when he needed to consolidate his position." The conclusion showed Peter as a "person who initiated strong ties with the governments that surrounded him."[40] Peter was thus redefined in 1937 as a strong national figure who won territory through war and defended it through diplomacy. He was lionized for the achievement of raising Russia to the status of a great power in the European arena.

Shumiatskii was quite aware, however, that Peter was a complex figure whose historical legacy could not be evaluated in a completely positive light. Although the first series of the film focused on Peter as a great reformer who created a European government, built a new capital, and created "cadres of statesmen," the film also acknowledged the "contradiction" that through Peter's reforms "the broad masses were not emancipated, but [were] even more oppressed."[41] The Petrine state's relationship to the people was portrayed in the film through a focus on an ordinary peasant Fed'ka, who represented the "independent line of the people's movement."[42] Fed'ka was not oppressed by Peter himself, but by the evil boyars serving the tsar. The film thus promoted the age-old myth of evil advisors who surrounded the tsar and prevented him from ameliorating the suffering of his people. Fed'ka eventually gained his freedom from tsarist oppression by running away to the south and becoming a Don Cossack.[43] By deflecting the guilt for repression away from Peter and by enabling Fed'ka to achieve freedom, the film glorified Peter's reforms and minimized the suffering that they caused.

Robert Tucker has argued that Stalin consciously emulated Peter as a leader and personally encouraged Aleksei Tolstoi to write about Peter with the "right historical approach."[44] Just as Peter the Great had overseen the construction of St. Petersburg and built industry in Russia, Stalin had supervised the reconstruction of Moscow and the industrialization of the Soviet Union at the cost of many lives. Stalin, like Peter, had trained new cadres to be statesmen. Like Peter in the final scenes of the film, Stalin in the mid-1930s ended the warlike atmosphere of the First Five Year Plan, consolidated his economic and political position, and negotiated with his European neighbors for "collective security." The film could thus be interpreted as a celebration of Stalin's as well as Peter's rule and as a justification of the hardships that the Soviet population had endured for future military and political victories. Even if the dominant message of *Peter I* was that both Stalin and Peter were great leaders, this biography of Peter the Great nevertheless acknowledged the cost to Russia of becoming a great nation and revealed the possibility of the coexistence of revolutionary reforms and oppression. Peter's life raised the issue of conflict between state and people, a theme that was at odds with the ideology but not the practice of Stalinism in the 1930s. This October anniversary film thus offered its viewers a complex and ambiguous vision of Russian and Soviet history.

Through the October jubilee, Soviet cultural officials sought to redefine history in ways that affirmed the legitimacy of the current Soviet leadership and the efficacy of their political, economic, and international decisions. They created a complicated and internally inconsistent rhetoric of nostalgia for aspects of the Russian past and bold claims about how much life had been transformed by the revolution. While the discourse of the celebration constantly juxtaposed Imperial Russia and the Soviet Union with the intention of glorifying the latter, it also sought to strengthen the positive image of the Soviet Union by associating it with triumphs of the Russian imperial past. Both positive and negative aspects of the Russian past thus penetrated the discourse of the October celebrations, although the Soviet present could only be discussed in positive terms. Contrasting the past and the present created opportunities for Soviet citizens to evaluate the changes in their lives. While cadres tried to avoid comparisons that cast the Soviet Union in a negative light, the extensive and contradictory use of history made some of the shortcomings of the Soviet Union visible.

Lenin, Stalin, and Legitimacy

One of the most important historical problems with which cultural officials grappled in 1937 was the redefinition of the revolution itself. The Committee on the Arts believed that the most important goal of the celebration of the twentieth anniversary of the October Revolution was to show the "leading role of the Party in the deeds of the October Revolution and socialist construction and the roles of Lenin and Stalin in connection

Moravov, *Lenin and Stalin.* From *Russkaia istoricheskaia zhivopis'* (1939).

with these events."[45] Illustrating the roles of Lenin and Stalin in the revolution required the identification of heroes and traitors both inside and outside of the Bolshevik Party. The historical accounts of the October Revolution written in 1937, like the new history of the Party, gave more prominence to the defeat of the socialist foes of the Bolsheviks than to the rout of bourgeois enemies.[46]

Furthermore, these new chronicles of the revolution depicted the Bolsheviks who opposed Stalin during the 1920s as enemies of the revolution from its inception. The new history of 1917 showed how Kamenev, Zinoviev, Bukharin, Trotsky, Rykov, and Piatakov all tried to undermine the revolutionary victory. By discrediting virtually all of the other revolutionary leaders, these narratives represented Stalin as Lenin's only possible legitimate successor. In these historical accounts, Stalin remained ever faithful to Lenin and coordinated the brilliant military victory in the Civil War. This version of the revolution both identified Trotsky as a traitor and credited Trotsky's achievements to Stalin.[47]

The celebration of the Twentieth Anniversary of October brought the actions of Lenin and Stalin during the revolution into focus and highlighted the relationship between the two leaders. Nina Tumarkin has argued that by 1934 "Lenin remained an object of organized reverence, but only within the context of the extravagant veneration of his 'worthy continuer.'"[48] Victoria Bonnell has demonstrated how visual representations of Lenin and Stalin underwent a gradual transformation in the early 1930s. While in 1930 Lenin was the dominant figure, he "was soon shown as the equal of Stalin," and "by 1933 Lenin's position vis-à-vis Stalin was adjusted to accentuate . . . the primacy of Stalin."[49]

In the few years before the Twentieth Anniversary of October, authoritative literary interpretations of the relationship between Lenin and Stalin were expressed most clearly and most often in the genre of official Soviet folklore, created by non-Russian bards such as Dzhambul Dzhabaev and Suleiman Stal'skii and by Russian singers such as Maria Kriukova.[50] Dzhambul, for example, wrote in his "Song of Stalin," "Lenin you are alive / you are in the full bloom of your strength / We in Stalin see your traits."[51] This poem boldly asserted an organic continuity between Lenin and Stalin.

While folklorists under direct political supervision routinely produced effusive and glowing praise of Lenin and Stalin as rightful leaders of the Soviet Union, other Soviet writers were slower to adopt this theme. Poet A. Bezymianskii complained in September 1937 that "among poetry about Lenin and Stalin . . . ninety-nine percent is written by poets from the fraternal republics, not by Russian poets. This is a very important and very sad fact which needs to be noted, and measures have to be taken to exert social pressure so poets feel all of the pain and shame of such a position."[52] When left to choose their own themes, many writers avoided the extremely politicized topic of the deeds of Lenin and Stalin and the hagiographic style in which works about these two men were often written.

In conjunction with the Twentieth Anniversary, however, the Central Committee of the Communist Party indicated that it expected major literary works about 1917 to focus on the heroic deeds of the Party's leaders. On March 19, 1936, the Central Committee invited ten playwrights and ten screenwriters to enter a closed competition for the best play and film scenario about the October Revolution as a "turning-point in the history of humanity." These authors were instructed to "show the role of Lenin in the preparation and carrying out of the October Revolution" and were officially given permission to include Lenin as a character in their films and plays. The contest entrants were offered considerable financial rewards for their participation. All of the playwrights who submitted plays were guaranteed ten thousand rubles. The winning playwright was promised forty thousand rubles; the second-place submission, thirty thousand rubles; and the third-place submission, twenty thousand rubles.[53] Despite the trend toward the dominance of Stalin, the Central Committee's plans for the Twentieth Anniversary devoted significant attention and financial resources to the creation of new images of Lenin. These Stalinist images of Lenin, however, were radically different than those produced in the 1920s.

High-ranking Soviet officials responsible for the production of images of Lenin in 1937 profoundly disagreed about how Lenin should be conveyed. While Shumiatskii argued that the task of the arts was "to interpret Lenin artistically" rather than to create photographic exactitude, Rabichev, the director of the Lenin Museum and official guardian of Lenin's image, insisted in August 1937 that Soviet works of art had to provide a faithful likeness of Lenin because "the notion, the image of the genuine Lenin is still too fresh in our memories."[54] Rabichev recalled his reaction to a poorly executed statue of Lenin that he chose not to exhibit at the Lenin Museum: "The first sensation is of horror and then comes the feeling that some kind of blasphemy had been committed."[55] Rabichev treated Lenin as a sacred figure, as a saint or deity whose incorrect depiction would be sacrilege. Because of the highly controlled nature of the medium, Soviet film was uniquely able to satisfy both Shumiatskii and Rabichev, creating a politically driven "artistic" interpretation of Lenin that also emanated a saintly aura.

Lenin in Film

A. Kapler's film scenario, *Lenin in October*, won the Central Committee's closed competition. The film was directed by Mikhail Romm. While *Lenin in October* was not ready for general release at the time of the anniversary, Stalin and the highest-ranking Party officials viewed a preliminary version in the Bolshoi Theater on November 6th, 1937.[56] The film was released with great fanfare on December 12, 1937, in conjunction with the elections to the Supreme Soviet. *Pravda* called the film "a thrilling, true, artistic, cinematic story about Vladimir Ilich Lenin" and an "enormous victory for Soviet film."[57]

While articles in *Pravda* emphasized the film's truthfulness, *Lenin in October* was, in fact, a radical revision of the narrative of the revolution, contending that Stalin was Lenin's chief assistant and advisor in 1917. It was also the only jubilee work in which Stalin allowed a fictional representation of himself to appear.[58] The film showed Lenin consulting with Stalin about key decisions at every opportunity. As soon as Lenin arrived in Petrograd, for example, he requested a meeting with Stalin. An on-screen caption reported that the meeting of the two leaders lasted for four hours.[59] In his study of Stalin's actions during the October Revolution, Robert Slusser has argued that Stalin's October meeting with Lenin was "an invention of Soviet historians of the Stalin era," to cover up the fact that Stalin had not played a role in the Soviet seizure of power.[60] *Lenin in October* thus transformed Stalin into a revolutionary hero and credited him with the achievements of others.

In *Lenin in October*, Kapler and Romm did not portray Lenin as a brilliant theoretician, a keen politician, or a tactical genius, but rather as a source of moral authority. The film created a likable, modest, genial, and grandfa-

therly Lenin who inspired the revolution but relied on Stalin to help organize it. This folksy and spiritual depiction of Lenin downplayed his intellect so that the film did not undermine Stalin's image as the wise and all-
knowing leader. By depicting Stalin as Lenin's faithful and active young
deputy, Kapler and Romm employed the sacred image of Lenin to bolster
Stalin's status as a revolutionary leader and to identify him as Lenin's only
legitimate successor.

This crass rewriting of revolutionary history revealed two important
aspects of Stalinist discourse. Even if Lenin was de-emphasized in relationship to Stalin in the 1930s and the revolutionary narrative was rewritten to show Stalin as his right-hand man, a heroic and holy image of Lenin
nevertheless remained inextricably tied to the creation of the Soviet state.
In a November 1937 letter reviewing *Lenin in October* and two jubilee dramas, Nadezhda Krupskaia, Lenin's widow, reminded Stalin that "even in
the most out-of-the-way, remote corners of our motherland, the masses
cannot imagine the struggle and victory without Lenin." When Lenin appears on stage, "a burst of applause rings out, the public becomes agitated
and stands up."[61]

Krupskaia's critique of the actors who played Lenin revealed the ways
in which the Lenin of 1937 not only affirmed Stalin's legitimacy but also
mirrored Stalin's mode of authority. According to Krupskaia, the jubilee
works misrepresented Lenin's relationship with workers and peasants.
Krupskaia claimed that Lenin "approached the workers, peasants, and comrades not in a didactic manner, not haughtily, but as equal to equal. The
edifying gesture immediately distorts Ilich's image."[62] Representations of
authority in the 1930s, however, expressed the innate superiority of the
leader and were almost always didactic. Two of the most prevalent epithets for Stalin, for example, were "father" and "teacher." Krupskaia also
objected to the way that workers were portrayed in jubilee works. She argued that they were drawn "schematically" and that "women appear only
as daughters, wives, and fiancées; women workers from the factories are
not shown even though they played a most prominent role in the October
Revolution."[63] Krupskaia contested a version of the revolution that transformed her husband into a Stalinist role model and exalted the Bolshevik
leadership while it underplayed the contributions of both male and female
workers to the victories of October. She contrasted Lenin's "simplicity"
and "intimacy" with the common people to Stalin's hierarchical and patriarchal mode of leadership.[64]

While Stalin denied rival leaders such as Trotsky, Zinoviev, and Kamenev their revolutionary accomplishments, he could not rewrite Lenin's central role in the revolution. Instead he had to put Lenin's positive image in
soft focus while he highlighted his own political acumen. In the 1930s, Lenin thus remained a model leader who citizens could compare with Stalin.
In August 1937, when the leaders of the Committee on the Arts discussed
banning the jubilee submission of Ukrainian playwright I. Mikitenko, one

"Let me go, father. . . . I am feeble-minded." Scene from *Peter I*. From
Sovetskoe kino (1937).

official wondered whether Mikitenko hadn't counterposed Lenin with Stalin
in his play *When the Sun Rises*.[65] Whether or not this accusation was true, it
revealed how continued reverence for the image of Lenin could pose a
danger to Stalin's self-representation as a great leader.

Second, *Lenin in October* revealed Stalin's preoccupation with political
legitimacy. The film depicted how the other revolutionary leaders made
themselves unworthy of being Lenin's heir, while Stalin remained loyal to
both Lenin and the revolution, earning his legitimate right to rule. The
question of legitimate succession to authority was a crucial theme in both
parts of the film *Peter I* as well.[66] In *Peter I*, Peter fathered a second son to
replace the one who had disappointed and deceived him.[67] In *Lenin in October*, Stalin was portrayed as Lenin's good son while Trotsky, Zinoviev,
and Kamenev betrayed the revolution. Both films thus celebrated the existence of a rightful heir, to whom legitimate authority could be passed in
an unbroken line, and attacked his illegitimate rivals.

Lenin on Stage

While *Lenin in October* and its sequel *Lenin in 1918* became Soviet film classics, playwrights and directors had far less success in creating an image of Lenin for the stage. On stage, the role of Lenin would be undertaken by multiple actors in different theaters, would vary at every performance, and could not be revised once executed. Under these difficult circumstances, playwrights struggled to create a Lenin that was both artistic and faithful to Lenin's holy image. Officials from the Committee on the Arts were not satisfied with the results of the jubilee drama competition. In June 1937, they criticized the playwrights for their "extremely timid" approach to Lenin, their failure to make Lenin an active participant in the dramatic composition of the plays, and their external rather than internal portrayals of the revolutionary leader.[68] Endeavoring to create a Lenin who would not blunder on stage, playwrights portrayed him statically, neither allowing his character to develop nor permitting his actions to propel the plot.

Rabichev, who was also the deputy chairman of the Committee on the Arts and the head of the jury for the jubilee play contest, agreed that the playwrights had failed in their task. He announced in August 1937 that the competition had been "wrecked" because only four acceptable plays had been submitted to the jury, and two of four required additional work.[69] While some members of the Committee on the Arts complained that playwrights had failed to give Lenin a central role in their plays, Rabichev, on the other hand, proposed limiting the amount of time that audiences would see Lenin. He explained "if Lenin appears on the stage or on the screen for a few minutes, then this will not astonish the viewer too much, but do you know what it means to play Lenin from the beginning to the end of a show? That is a labor completely beyond our strength, at least in 1937."[70] Rabichev's comments suggested that the image of Lenin was an elemental force that could escape from official control and produce unpredictable results.

Once the scripts of jubilee plays with the character of Lenin began to be circulated among Soviet theaters, central arts officials set additional restrictions on Lenin's portrayal. The scenes with Lenin were even removed from one of the jubilee plays, K. Trenev's *On the Bank of the Neva*. The Committee on the Arts announced in late August 1937 that amateur, collective farm, state farm, and traveling theaters would not be allowed to perform plays with the character of Lenin.[71] Officials also doubted whether regional theaters could properly portray Lenin and demanded that they obtain the special permission of the committee before doing so.[72] Even in Moscow and other major cities, no theater was permitted to play Lenin until a representative of the All-Union Committee on the Arts had personally approved the production and the actor.[73] Soviet arts officials understood that their influence on local and provincial productions had practical limits and they would not permit the character of Lenin to be performed beyond the boundaries of their immediate authority.

These actions of the committee revealed the belief of top cultural leaders in Lenin's sacred authority and mythic power. Because of the holiness of Lenin's image, they did not allow second-rate theaters and actors to represent him. Because of his mythic power, they did not permit Lenin to appear unsupervised in the provinces. In the 1920s Soviet fairy tales "Clever Lenin," and "Ilich Will Wake Up Soon," Lenin left his mausoleum from time to time to check on the progress of socialism.[74] While Soviet officials wanted to resurrect Lenin in 1937 to affirm that Stalin was the legitimate heir who had fulfilled Lenin's plans, they did not want provincial actors to appear as Lenin and assess local conditions. The arts bureaucracy strictly controlled the fictional embodiment of Lenin so that only they could claim Lenin's authority to evaluate the effects of twenty years of Soviet power.

Local arts officials also participated in the regulation of Lenin in jubilee productions. Chudinova, the head of the Moscow Administration of the Arts, acknowledged the "exceptionally serious task" of inspecting the production of A. Korneichuk's play *Truth* at the Theater of the Revolution. She asserted in September 1937 that "the slightest artificial note which . . . might slip into the actor's speeches would wipe out all of the political significance of the production."[75] Because of her anxiety about controlling the actor who played Lenin, Chudinova suggested that all of Lenin's lines in the third act of the play might have to be taken away, leaving him to appear silently.[76] Believing that "a bad play is a colossal scandal," Chudinova sought to decrease Lenin's activity on stage even when he was being played by a noted Soviet actor (M. Straukh) in a prominent theater.[77] Like central arts officials, Chudinova did not want to take responsibility for a performance that was beyond her personal control, and so she curtailed the appearance of Lenin. Because of fear, Lenin, the most potent spokesman for the legitimacy of the Soviet state was rendered speechless in jubilee plays.

The end result of this long process was that arts officials gave only two jubilee productions permission to include Lenin in their live performances, N. F. Pogodin's *Man with a Rifle* and Korneichuk's *Truth*. Just five actors were permitted to play Lenin, so he appeared in *Man with a Rifle* only in Moscow and Voronezh, and in *Truth* only in Moscow and two Kiev theaters.[78] Even after the plays with Lenin had debuted, they were scrutinized by high Soviet officials. The head of the Department of Culture and Propaganda of the Central Committee attended the premiere of *Man with a Rifle* on November 13, 1937, and sent a report about inaccuracies of B. V. Shchukin's portrayal of Lenin to L. Kaganovich and N. Ezhov. The official planned to visit the performance again in order to make sure that the actor's errors were corrected.[79] Because of the need of arts officials to exercise strict control over Lenin's image, the significant effort and financial resources that the central authorities expended to bring Lenin to life yielded extremely limited results. Relatively few Soviet citizens were exposed to a symbolic Lenin who legitimated the actions of Stalin in 1937.

The caution of playwrights and the unwillingness of arts officials to take responsibility for events that they could not control ultimately led to the creation of a Lenin that lacked a full-bodied living presence and to the censoring and silencing of Lenin's image. The Lenin that emerged during the twentieth anniversary lacked any internal complexity and more resembled the Lenin in the mausoleum than the Lenin who organized the revolution. Although Bonnell is clearly correct that in the 1930s images of Stalin were given primacy over images of Lenin, the scarcity of living images of Lenin during the October Revolution celebrations in 1937 was not caused by neglect. Rather, cultural officials considered Lenin so important that they feared the consequences of making mistakes in their portrayals of him. Reverence for Lenin's image and the tense political atmosphere caused Lenin to disappear from jubilee plays. Ironically, Lenin was not prevalent among the images produced in 1937 because he was so central to cultural officials' views of the revolution.

The Purges and the October Celebration

Writers and Editors

The mass arrests of Party and government leaders throughout 1937 hampered the abilities of the organizers of the October anniversary to create images of a happy and prosperous Soviet Union or to create new interpretations of revolutionary events. Even during the early stages of preparation for the October anniversary in mid-1936, writers were wary of producing works about the momentous events of October 1917. One dramatist, Volzhenin, who wanted to create an "interpretation of our reality where heroism has become everyday life," revealed his apprehensions about this task at a May 1936 meeting at the Union of Soviet Writers. He confessed, "The demands of creating an October repertoire are so serious that, to be honest, I am feeling some dread of picking up my pen."[80] The complexity of portraying transformations that were larger than life and did not correspond with the writers' own experiences of Soviet reality made writers doubt their own abilities and stifled their artistic creativity.

Soviet writers were also aware of how suddenly the dominant discourse about the revolution could be transformed. In May 1936, the dramatist Argo expressed his discomfort with writing a drama more than a year in advance of the anniversary date.[81] He declared, "How can I imagine the atmosphere that will exist a year from now? I cannot begin to write for the twentieth anniversary until after the nineteenth anniversary passes."[82] He noted that it seemed as if "worn out notions such as 'motherland,' 'patriotism,' and 'narod'" had "been swept off the earth fifteen years ago," and now "they are restored in new qualities."[83] Because of the frequent and sometimes dramatic changes in official discourse, writers were hesitant to commit themselves to creating works on themes that might later be perceived as outdated or even subversive.

While Volzhenin questioned whether he was personally capable of representing the theme of transformation and Argo did not want to write for the anniversary until he had a better sense of the ideological trends of 1937, dramatist Bill'-Belotserkovskii wondered whether the very genre of drama was adequate to express the revolution. Himself an active participant in the events of 1917, Bill'-Belotserkovskii said in January 1936:

> The theme of the twentieth anniversary is very agitating, especially for those who took part in the revolution and the preparation for it. . . . For this reason it is difficult for me to choose from the rich materials and abundant impressions which are still so vivid and fresh in my memory. It is difficult for me to confine this theme within the limits of theater.[84]

Bill'-Belotserkovskii announced that out of his many impressions of the revolution, he most wanted to focus on the theme of the leadership of the Bolshevik Party during the Moscow uprising and to emphasize the selflessness of Party leaders who took responsibility for the insurrection and did not worry about their own safety. Rather than creating a dramatic interpretation of these revolutionary events, Bill'-Belotserkovskii offered to write a memoir of his own personal experience of Party leadership. He thus narrowed and limited the scale of his work for the October anniversary. Bill'-Belotserkovskii completed neither the play nor the autobiography about Moscow during the revolution.[85]

Argo's fear that writers' ideas in 1936 might not be current in October 1937 was borne out and much of the preparatory work for the twentieth anniversary conducted in 1935 and 1936 was obliterated by the purges. On January 14, 1936, the Union of Soviet Writers compiled a list of twenty-eight plays that were being prepared for the anniversary by Russian playwrights. Only two of these twenty-eight Russian plays were actually performed during the October celebrations, Trenev's *On the Bank of the Neva* and Chekin's *Night in September*.[86] The other twenty-six plays disappeared in the intervening eighteen months. The situation in other genres of literature was similar. In September 1937, N. Nakoriakov, head of the State Literature Publishing House bemoaned the failure of the publishing house to complete its plan: "We had the intention to publish a series of new works on the theme of the Civil War, but the plan is one thing and the reality of our program another." He explained that "thanks to the fact that the majority of authors were late in handing in their works, we have no works on the theme of 'Heroics of the Civil War.'"[87] Under conditions of terror, many authors did not produce their works in time for the holiday.

Even if all of the authors had met their deadlines, however, few of the works that were submitted in 1937 would have been published because of the extreme narrowing of what was considered politically and artistically acceptable and the dire consequences for editors of making errors in judg-ment.[88] In Leningrad, for example, seventeen writers submitted work for a volume entitled *Two Five Year Plans,* but in March 1937 the editors of the volume reported that only two authors had contributed publishable work.[89] Despite great plans for the publication of the Kirghiz epic poem *Monos,* this work did not appear in time for the anniversary because it "required some purification." In September 1937, Nakoriakov explained, "In the Kirghiz text was hidden a spirit of Pan-Turkism and Pan-Islamism." These "nationalist" elements had to be removed before the text could be pub-lished.[90] Because their own lives and livelihoods were at risk, editorial boards were extremely cautious about accepting literary work.[91]

In the volatile political atmosphere of 1937, however, editors could not foresee what might suddenly become subversive. Writing about the revo-lution of 1917, for example, became increasingly dangerous in the spring and summer of 1937 as heroes were turned into villains by purges that targeted prominent Old Bolsheviks in the Party, government, and military. Mikitenko's play about the revolution in Ukraine, *When the Sun Rises,* por-trayed Ia. Gamarnik as a hero of the Kiev uprising. After Gamarnik was removed from his post of First Deputy Commissar of Defense in May 1937, after which he committed suicide, Mikitenko's play was banned by the Committee on the Arts.[92] Mikitenko was arrested and executed in October 1937.

When literary figures were excluded from the Party or arrested, the production of their work was halted. In late September 1937, the Moscow puppet theater had to cease its production of the play *The Blue Carpet* be-cause its author was excluded from the Komsomol.[93] An arts official ex-plained in August 1937 that production of the film *Brothers* could not pro-ceed despite the fact that "the scenario is excellent" because "the author was arrested."[94] The purges thus produced an enormous amount of waste and upheaval as half-finished plays and films had to be abandoned very suddenly.

The constantly shifting rhetoric and tense political atmosphere of the mid-1930s caused Soviet authors to experience "writer's block" and to cling to the familiar because they feared making mistakes. When literary work reached editors, they screened it extremely carefully for any kind of sub-version. The anxieties of these writers and editors were well founded; by the time the anniversary arrived, editors as well as authors had paid with their lives for their interpretations of the October events. This anxiety and turmoil caused the publication of artistic works about the October anni-versary to slow to a trickle.

Administrators

The purges had a profound effect on the cadres who carried out the October holidays. Several of the leading organizers of the October jubilee from all-union arts institutions were killed in the purges. Kirshon, for instance, was arrested in April 1937; Shumiatskii was removed from his post in early 1938 and killed in July of that year.[95] The purges also took a heavy toll on republican and regional cultural bureaucracies. By June 1937, arts officials had been arrested in the Azovo-Chernomor Territory, Armenia, Azerbaidzhan, Tataria, Cheliabinsk Region, Kalinin Region, and the Far Eastern Territory.[96] An administrator from Azerbaidzhan bemoaned the fact that recent arrests "could not help but affect the Union of Writers' work on the preparation of plays for the October jubilee."[97] In Kuibyshev Region, fifty of the eighty-eight Department of Enlightenment inspectors, whose duties included checking the readiness of schools and libraries for the October anniversary, were removed as enemies by late September 1937, and no new inspectors were hired.[98] Prominent cultural institutions also lost their leaders; for example the directors of Moscow's Bolshoi and Malyi Theaters were arrested in the spring of 1937.[99]

The fate of K. P. Chudinova illustrates how the purges transformed the lives of Soviet officials. After her first husband's arrest, Chudinova left her position as first secretary of a Moscow district committee to head the Moscow Administration of the Arts. Later in 1937 she was forced to leave her post again when her second husband was arrested and "it was impossible for her to remain in ideological work."[100] Because of Chudinova's precarious position, one can understand her insistence on a positive assessment of Soviet achievements and her caution in authorizing portrayals of Lenin. The briefness of her tenure at the Moscow Administration of the Arts also illustrates the upheaval of the times, or *tekuchka*. At every level of authority and in all kinds of institutions, key cadres who were involved in the organization of the October anniversary disappeared because of the purges.

Although the rhetoric of the purges valorized the promotion of new young cadres to take the place of "enemies," many of these new cultural cadres were not qualified to handle the tasks with which they had to cope.[101] Newly appointed provincial administrators demanded help from the Committee on the Arts in June 1937 meetings about preparations for the October anniversary. A cultural official from Saratov Region accused the committee of "not leading the periphery" and pleaded with Moscow officials to educate local cadres who "were working in the localities in very complex political conditions."[102] The director of the Orenburg Administration of the Arts begged the All-Union Committee for instructions on how to do his job and maintain "Party sharpness." He sought direction from Moscow on the "subtleties" of what made a play politically unacceptable and asked Moscow to send him October theses so that he would be able to lecture at ceremonial meetings. Without this training from Moscow, the official argued, "you don't feel yourself to be a boss, but just some kind of a *fitiul'ka* (midget), and you become ashamed."[103] The pleas of these local officials reveal that the purges wreaked havoc on provincial preparations for the October anniversary.

Things were not much better in Moscow; less than six weeks before the holiday, a Moscow official acknowledged that the state of the October repertoire for movie theaters was "frankly catastrophic." Engaging in *samokritika* (self-criticism), the official in charge of Moscow film distribution confessed that her organization "had not yet sufficiently thought up grand measures that would distinguish this year from all of the past years, as a jubilee year."[104] The October repertoire for variety performances was pronounced at best "monotonous" and at worst "hack-work." Out of 600 variety artists who would perform this repertoire, 520 had just begun work in late September and would not be well prepared for the holiday.[105] The plans for the 1937 October celebrations were haphazard and chaotic even in Moscow, where holiday events were usually much better coordinated than in the rest of the country. All across the Soviet Union cultural authorities lost control over the forms that the holiday would take as institutions that were responsible for organizing the October celebration were purged.

Unable to admit that the organization of the October holidays had slipped out of their grasp, officials explained their failures using the rhetoric of the purges that pervaded all of Soviet officialdom. Arts bureaucrats blamed "wreckers" for the shortcomings in the organization of the October holidays. The chairman of the Moscow Administration of the Arts complained in September 1937 that "the policy of wreckers in the field of literature consisted of making sure that nothing valuable in literature was produced by closing the road to fresh young forces."[106] This explanation for the failure to produce an October repertoire deflected guilt from the Moscow Administration of the Arts by placing blame on the Union of Writers. In September 1937, when Moscow arts officials failed to produce a jubilee plan for Moscow film theaters, they blamed Shumiatskii for allowing wreckers to disrupt the film industry.[107] These attempts of officials to shield themselves by blaming others could sometimes have very serious consequences. Shumiatskii lost his life because of these kinds of accusations.

While some Soviet bureaucrats used the concept of wrecking to explain why they were unable to do their own jobs properly, other officials threatened their subordinates by suggesting that their failures might be the result of wrecking. When, in August 1937, the music publishing house Muzgiz did not deliver October jubilee songbooks on time, Rabichev suggested that the heads of Muzgiz should check up on their production personnel because "it could very well be that the leaders do not know that sabotage can be observed in their organization."[108] Rabichev adopted the language of the purges to send a clear message to the leaders of Muzgiz to speed up production of jubilee songbooks. Rabichev's threats, however, only heightened the atmosphere of suspicion and fear that hampered Soviet institutions from doing their jobs in 1937.

While frightened officials used the excuse of wrecking to deflect criticism from themselves, officials like Rabichev actively embraced the purges as a means of accomplishing their organizational work. In August 1937, when cinema officials complained that projectionists in the countryside did not properly care for films and equipment, Rabichev suggested this:

> At the end of September or the beginning of October select a couple of instances when they are showing a torn, unrepaired, film and *trakhnut'* (screw) them as they ought to be. Prosecute them, declare them wreckers, in the newspapers strike fear into them, vilify them in front of the whole country so that the people will have been given a warning. That will keep everyone on his toes. We should not wait until the press tramples us, but we ourselves should start to strike at three to five locations.[109]

Later in the meeting, Rabichev reiterated that the Committee on the Arts should not wait until the press "thrashed them" and offered a prize to whomever found the first "victim." He justified his actions by saying "we will punish one or two and save dozens."[110] In order to appear vigilant and to avoid the press's accusations that local arts cadres were not doing their jobs, Rabichev was willing to sacrifice the lives of innocent people. Rabichev hoped that the arrests of one or two film projectionists would help the Committee on the Arts to gain control of the October holiday on the local level. In general, however, the effect of the purges was the disappearance of experienced cadres with no one available to take their places. It is unlikely that this destructive phenomenon could have improved the local celebrations of the October anniversary or central control over local arts administration.

The celebration of the twentieth anniversary of the October Revolution at the height of the purges revealed key characteristics of Stalinism in the mid-1930s. The organization of this holiday illustrated the ways in which officials increasingly allocated state resources toward benefits for the elites and away from improving cultural and living conditions for the majority of the Soviet population. Despite the demands of individual artists and writers to increase the access of ordinary people to the arts, the Committee on the Arts focused primarily on creating Soviet masterworks. While Soviet officials mouthed the slogan of guaranteeing culture for all, they spent most of their resources arranging cultural services for Moscow's political elite.

The trend toward hierarchy can also been seen in the artistic representations of the October Revolution produced at this time. Workers and women were pushed to the background as the works focused on the deeds of Party leaders. Lenin and Stalin, the fathers of the revolution, towered above ordinary workers. The power and authority of tsars such as Peter the Great and selected aspects of tsarist ceremonials were also valorized by the anniversary celebration. The recasting of Soviet political authority along hierarchical lines was thus clearly expressed in both the organization and the content of the celebration.

The second aspect of the 1930s that this holiday reveals is the simultaneously enabling and constraining nature of Soviet political discourse. On the one hand, the sudden incorporation of new historical elements into Soviet discourse and the new willingness to embrace aspects of the imperial past drew the attention of Soviet citizens to such issues as pre-revolutionary conditions in the villages, the costs of state power, and the nature of the authority of Lenin and Stalin. While those responsible for incorporating these new ideas into official rhetoric intended to bolster the legitimacy of Stalin and the Soviet state, the results were not always what they had intended. These additions to Soviet discourse allowed Soviet citizens, for example, to compare Lenin with Stalin, Peter with Stalin, and serfdom with collectivization. These comparisons created opportunities for citizens to reflect on the inadequacies and injustices of the Soviet system.

While the boundaries of Soviet discourse could thus be transgressed by some citizens, Soviet cadres found their actions limited by the very discourses they promoted. Cadres were often unable to discuss the problems they faced in mobilizing the population because of their own discursive strategy of declaring that socialist victory had already been achieved. One of the few ways to escape from this trap, blaming enemies and wreckers for failures, ultimately jeopardized their work even more than the rhetoric of success.

The political atmosphere of 1936–1937 prevented cadres from fulfilling their grand plans for the October anniversary. Elite writers, artists, musicians, and film-makers did not produce the great works that were expected of them. Publishers found little to publish and film theaters had few films to show. Cultural officials from the centralized arts bureaucracy were unable to provide the periphery with jubilee repertoire materials or guidance. Local and republican arts administrations lacked leaders to issue directions and cadres to carry them out. Failures at all administrative levels accounted for the lackluster celebration of the jubilee.

Considerable human and financial resources were channeled into the October Anniversary, but many of them were wasted because of the chaos the purges created in cultural institutions coupled with the tendency of the Soviet arts in the 1930s to devote resources to a few grand productions. As the effort to create fictional works about Lenin shows, the more important a cultural product was considered the more restrictions were placed on it and the more difficult it was to complete successfully. The end result was the worst of both worlds: a dearth of major holiday productions and an inability to organize the holiday effectively at the local level. The weakness of this celebration revealed that the Soviet state's achievements in 1937 were not as great as it proclaimed them to be.

7

CELEBRATING CIVIC
PARTICIPATION

THE STALIN CONSTITUTION AND ELECTIONS
AS RITUALS OF DEMOCRACY

While the organizers of the Pushkin Centennial and the Twentieth Anniversary of October sought to raise the cultural level of Soviet citizens, the cadres who organized the celebration of the Stalin Constitution attempted to raise the political literacy of the population. One of the many glaring contradictions of Soviet life in the 1930s was the disjuncture between official claims of the growing political consciousness of every New Soviet Man and Woman and the low level of political interest and knowledge among the population. Since the Party focused its limited agitational energies in the 1930s on production issues and on raising the consciousness of those in its ranks, the political education of the rest of the population suffered relative neglect.[1] In this context, the "nationwide discussion" of a draft constitution, the promulgation of the constitution, and the preparation for elections to newly created legislative organs played especially significant roles in educating the general population about how they should participate in Soviet political life. The Soviet government mobilized its citizens to participate in civic rituals of democracy at the same time that it denied them basic civil rights.

In February 1935, Stalin decided to amend the constitution of the USSR that had been promulgated in 1924. The draft of the new constitution, which was unveiled in June 1936, resembled the constitutions of Western Europe and the United States in that it guaranteed the citizens of the Soviet Union universal suffrage and basic civil rights. The constitution also restored the right to vote to so-called class enemies such as priests and *kulaks*. The Central Executive Committee of the USSR called for a "nationwide discussion" of the draft constitution so that Soviet citizens could propose changes. After several months of nationwide discussion, the Eighth Extraordinary Congress of Soviets approved the new constitution on December 5, 1936.[2] This constitution included forty-eight corrections that had been collected during discussions with the population.[3] One year later, on December 12,

1937, elections to the new Supreme Soviet were held with great fanfare. Despite the fact that there was only one candidate on each ballot, Soviet propagandists went to great lengths and great expense to ensure the participation of every eligible voter in the elections.[4]

Since the civil rights guaranteed in the constitution existed on paper only, most analysts have treated the constitution of 1936 as a propaganda ploy to prove to the West that the Soviet Union was a democracy. J. Arch Getty has challenged this position by arguing that Stalin's plans for constitutional reform, including contested elections, represented a fundamental change in political course. He suggests that Stalin had a last minute change of heart, canceled the contested elections, and trampled on a constitutional system that would have guaranteed Soviet citizens civil rights.[5] Whatever Stalin's political intentions were, the public celebration of the constitution and elections introduced a new political discourse within which Soviet cadres and citizens could articulate their goals and aspirations.

By creating a public discourse of democracy and participation, the Soviet government provided a space for the discussion of political issues such as equality, justice, and civil rights and a new language with which to discuss them.[6] Given the political pressure exerted on Soviet cadres and citizens, it is hardly a surprise that this discussion was comprised primarily of statements of support for the Soviet state. This state-sponsored invitation to talk about politics also elicited a variety of unanticipated responses, however, including protest against state policies both for being too "liberal" and too restrictive.[7] As Sheila Fitzpatrick has pointed out, Stalin never again repeated this invitation to the population to participate in open political discussion.[8]

The constitution of 1936, like the emancipation legislation of 1861, produced results other than those intended by the central government and, like Stalin's 1930 article "Dizzy with Success," created tensions between citizens and local cadres, and local cadres and their superiors. The Russian peasantry had a tradition of creative interpretations of official documents, and a widely held belief that official written documents could have the power to transform their lives for the better. Perhaps the most well known example of peasants' willful misreading of an official document is the uprising in the village of Bezdna in Kazan Province in 1861. The emancipation legislation of 1861 was a disappointment to the population, because, according to the head of the political police, "A majority of the peasants hoped to receive complete freedom from obligations to the *pomeshchik* [estate owner] and a free allotment of land."[9] In Bezdna, a literate peasant named Anton Petrov interpreted the emancipation legislation as offering the land and freedom that the peasants wanted, and the peasants flocked to hear him. The peasants claimed to believe that the real provisions of the emancipation decreed by the tsar had been distorted by landlords and corrupt local officials. The crowds were dispersed by tsarist troops who shot and killed many of the peasants and then executed Petrov.[10] Petrov's reading of the legislation offered the peasantry the opportunity to oppose their landlords while claiming loyalty to the tsar.

In 1930, Soviet peasants used a document from Moscow to protect themselves from local officials. Whatever the intention of Stalin's article "Dizzy with Success" in *Pravda* on March 2, 1930, it was a printed document which gave the peasantry a weapon against the local officials who were forcing them into collective farms. The peasants understood very well the implications of such a document from the center and, according to the journalist Maurice Hindus, "They rushed to the post offices and to the town to buy the newspapers that printed Stalin's letter. They paid three, four, five rubles for a copy of such a paper, that was how eager they were to see the letter with their own eyes."[11] Soviet peasants were anxious to gain access to official documents that proved that the power of the state was on their side.

Because of its rhetoric of democracy, justice, and equality, and its enumeration of specific economic rights, the Stalin constitution of 1936 caught the interest of many Soviet citizens. An August 1936 report from the Agitation and Propaganda Department of the Central Committee noted disapprovingly that in Kursk Region "in a great number of instances, collective farmers began reading and discussing the draft constitution themselves, without waiting for the Party organizations."[12] Central officials considered discussion of the constitution not directed by local Party leaders to be undesirable because it would enable peasants to construct independent interpretations of the constitution and publicly articulate them. Even when Soviet officials guided the reading of the constitution, the experience, in the words of a cultural official from Leningrad Region, "put an enormous number of political questions before the collective farmers that had never been put in front of them before."[13] This expansion of the peasants' political language enabled them to think and talk about their lives in new ways.

The celebration of the constitution and the elections was much more significant to the Soviet population than was ordinary Soviet political agitation. The new vocabularies of the Soviet constitution and election discourses elicited a wide variety of responses from both local officials and the population.

A New Audience

The audience envisioned by the Soviet state for the constitution and election campaigns was far wider than that of other Soviet holidays analyzed in this work. The Soviet government aimed to mobilize every adult Soviet citizen to participate in these campaigns, and the Central Committee kept detailed statistics on the number of citizens who took part. These statistics about the number of participants in the nationwide discussion of the constitution are inconsistent, however, ranging between 36 million to

75 million people, or between 40 to 80 percent of the adult population.[14] Election statistics claim that 98.61 percent of eligible voters participated in the elections to the Supreme Soviet in 1937.[15] These extremely high figures reflect local officials' desires to prove their efficiency and loyalty to the state rather than concrete realities, and in some districts the turnout was 10 to 15 percent lower.[16] Nevertheless, in 1936 and 1937, Party and government officials were repeatedly directed to mobilize their constituencies to discuss the constitution and participate in the elections, and their efforts were monitored by the central government.

The staying power of the celebration of the constitution and the elections was also far greater than most other Soviet holidays in the 1930s. Like most other Soviet "campaigns" of the 1930s, the discussion of the constitution draft was at first carried out for a limited time and then eclipsed by the campaign that followed. Unlike other campaigns, however, the Soviet government periodically renewed its instructions about the constitution and monitored the course of the discussions for several months after the first directives had been sent. As a result, the discussions were carried out in a series of waves. Local officials collected amendments and commentary on the draft constitution beginning in June 1936. Throughout June and July, the press criticized the progress of the local soviets in carrying out the campaign and the Central Executive Committee sent a directive criticizing local executive committee chairmen for their poor performance in organizing discussions.[17] In the fall of 1936, the Central Executive Committee collected bimonthly reports about the course of the discussion of the constitution in all parts of the Soviet Union. These documents suggest that constitution discourse reached the greatest number of people in the Russian Republic where, by November 1, 1936, 160,092 meetings about the constitution attended by 12,702,508 workers and peasants were reported to have been held.[18] An October 15, 1936, report to the Central Committee of the Communist Party claimed that over 70 percent of the voters in Moldavia and over 2 million people in Kiev Region had discussed the constitution. This report also indicated that the campaign was not going as well in Tadzhikistan, where discussions had only reached as far as district centers.[19] Like all Soviet political campaigns, the constitution campaign weakened as it spread from the center to the periphery.

Central authorities continued to press for the study of the constitution in factories and collective farms after it was ratified in December 1936. Stalin's speech to the Eighth Extraordinary Congress of Soviets became the most important political document associated with the constitution. In August 1937, the government ordered that this speech be reproduced in 20 million printed copies and on 5 million phonograph records.[20] While it is unlikely that this number of copies ever reached the population, it is clear that the political ideas expressed in Stalin's speech were intended to achieve an extremely wide currency and extend the constitution campaign.

Party organizations continued to monitor and promote study of the constitution in the early months of 1937.[21] In July 1937, the government published election laws for the Supreme Soviet elections and new efforts were made to promote the study of these laws along with the constitution. During the celebration of the Twentieth Anniversary of the October Revolution, the constitution was heralded as the embodiment of the achievements of twenty years of Soviet rule, and in December of 1937 voters were mobilized to show their support of the Soviet state during the elections to the Supreme Soviet.[22] The extension of the celebration of the constitution for eighteen months indicates its importance to the Soviet leadership. Because of the central government's persistent attention to the campaign, constitution discourse was far more widely disseminated than other political agitation.

During the celebration of the constitution and the elections, new segments of the population were targeted for political mobilization. Since virtually all Soviet political education and mobilization occurred at school or in the workplace, there were certain categories of people who were usually beyond the reach of Soviet propagandists. Constitution and election propagandists made a concerted effort to involve the "unorganized" population, including housewives, the elderly, and domestic workers, in Soviet politics. An elderly housewife from the city of Pushkin in Moscow Region announced at a women's meeting about the constitution on September 30, 1936, "Today is a holiday for us housewives because I do not remember another occasion on which they gathered us together to discuss issues."[23] This statement rings truer than most ceremonial speeches made at political meetings because it contained an implicit critique of past propaganda work. Although it is unlikely that the discussion of the constitution and elections actually reached all of the people that the government claimed it to have reached, it certainly placed political questions before segments of the population that had not been addressed in this way before. This appeal to the politically inexperienced or apathetic gave the government the opportunity to gain new support, and it also invited previously silent elements of the population to voice views that may or may not have corresponded with the views of the state.

A New Language

The celebration of the constitution and elections both transformed and expanded Soviet political rhetoric. The constitution transformed Soviet discourse by publicly refuting the notion that class enemies and other "former people" should be denied their civil rights. By extending the right to vote to all Soviet citizens "irrespective of . . . religious persuasion . . . social origin, property position and past activities,"[24] the constitution destabilized the old conception of "enemy" as one who was already marked and set apart from the community. In his speech to the Congress of Soviets, Stalin suggested that the old enemies had been completely vanquished, citing Lenin's 1919 call for universal suffrage after the "expropriators had been expropriated."[25] But he contradicted himself by acknowledging that the "expropriators" could still pose a threat if they were elected to the Supreme Soviet. Denying any possibility of a loyal opposition, Stalin proclaimed that "if our agitational work is conducted in a Bolshevik manner, then the *narod* will not allow hostile people into their supreme organs."[26] Only the vigilance of the propagandists and the electorate could prevent enemies from penetrating the Soviet community once more, undermining the elections and the entire Soviet state. By removing the juridical boundary between enemies and the rest of the population, the new political language of the Stalin Constitution allowed for the possibility that enemies could now be found anywhere in the Soviet state, even in the "supreme organs" of government.

The Stalin Constitution also expanded Soviet rhetoric by bringing western conceptions of civil rights to the forefront, guaranteeing freedom of speech, association, the press, and religion and offering protection against arbitrary arrest. It also identified universal, secret, direct, and equal suffrage as a central tenet of Soviet democracy. By emphasizing those parts of the new constitution that resembled the constitutions of the capitalist West, Stalin publicly charted a new political course. When Soviet institutions did not follow this course in practice, Soviet cadres were obliged to publicly promote new political ideals that were constantly contradicted by their own actions.

The promotion of new political goals caused disruptions in the state's public image. For example, when asked, "How can it be that priests will vote?" one chairman of a village soviet in Voronezh Region replied, "They will be deprived of the vote on Election Day,"[27] revealing the intention of local officials to subvert the execution of the new law. When confused officials had to steer the population through a new set of political contradictions that they did not understand or had not yet learned to disguise, they sometimes uncovered the arbitrariness of Soviet rule. The confusion of officials and the population revealed aspects of Soviet politics that had previously been excluded from public discourse and provided new ways of thinking about power relations in the Soviet Union.

The Stalin Constitution was not represented by Soviet officials simply as an enumeration of the civil rights and political responsibilities of Soviet citizens. In addition to introducing new and contradictory political language, the discourse of the constitution and election campaigns reflected propagandists' notions about the magic of literacy and writing. Official discussion of the constitution was couched in a quasi-religious discourse of mystery and wonder; like the proclamation emancipating the serfs or a heavenly letter sent by God, the constitution was a "golden book" and its words were written "in golden letters."[28] Cadres described the constitution as a powerful mystical force that could transform the lives and mentalities of Soviet citizens, bringing them political consciousness, prosperity, and happiness. That the constitution was identified as Stalin's creation enhanced its strength, since cadres represented the words of Stalin, like the words of God, as particularly powerful utterances.

In addition to the constitution, Stalin's speech to the Eighth Extraordinary Congress of Soviets was identified by Soviet propagandists as a particularly powerful text. In this speech, which was broadcast on the radio, filmed, printed, and recorded, Stalin provided a complicated theoretical discussion of the political underpinnings and significance of the constitution. He chronicled the evolution of the class structure of the Soviet Union since 1924 and discussed the relationships of workers, peasants, and the intelligentsia to the state under socialism. He proclaimed the victory of Lenin's nationality policies and explained the differences between Soviet democratism and bourgeois democracy. This dry and rather technical discussion of the constitution was aimed at an audience of politically educated Soviet citizens and the foreign press, and it was not universally appreciated even by this group. One memoirist recalled the reaction of his co-worker, "a pseudo–Young Communist and a fanatical careerist," who proclaimed that Stalin's speech was "nothing special. He talks like a Tatar

Svarog, *Comrade Stalin Gives a Speech about the Draft Constitution....* From *Russkaia istoricheskaia zhivopis'* (1939).

and doesn't command respect. I didn't like it and I stopped listening somewhere in the middle."[29]

Soviet ideologues described the spoken words of Stalin in an entirely different way; they represented Stalin's speech as a holy communication that spoke directly to every Soviet listener. The chairman of the Moscow City Department of Enlightenment described reactions to the radio broadcast of Stalin's speech: "A small pre-school child says: 'It is so interesting, it is almost as if it is for children.' . . . People listened to the simple and clear words of Comrade Stalin."[30] In the accounts of Soviet cadres, the words of the constitution and of Stalin's speech traveling over the "invisible waves" of the radio spoke simultaneously to every Soviet citizen at his or her individual level.[31]

According to these cadres, the constitution united leader and people in a mystical and personal communion with one another.[32] In a Moscow City Soviet meeting about the draft constitution, one of the speakers quoted an old Kazakh man's opinion of the draft: "It is as if Stalin himself overheard my thoughts."[33] The constitution thus both reflected and transformed the political consciousness of children, the elderly, and members of the non-Russian nationalities. Cultural and political officials represented ideal reactions to the constitution in a way that downplayed their own roles in the transmission of political consciousness. The sacred words of Stalin acted all by themselves.

The idea that the constitution and Stalin's speech were fascinating and immediately accessible to everyone was a product of socialist realist fantasy rather than reality. Since those who publicly depicted Stalin in any light but the most positive often paid for it with their lives, the portrayal of Stalin as a charismatic statesman and a mesmerizing speaker was inevitable. The representations of the speech as accessible, however, belied the fact that the speech was beyond the understanding of most Soviet elementary schoolchildren or the less-educated segments of the population and had to be explained to be understood. Despite official representations to the contrary, cultural intermediaries such as teachers, librarians, and propagandists were absolutely crucial in the communication of Soviet political ideas from the top leaders in Moscow to the rest of the population. By characterizing the speech as a direct communication between people and leader that did not require explanation, Soviet ideologues complicated the work of these teachers and rank-and-file propagandists, many of whom themselves did not understand the complexities of the constitution.

Teachers of a constitution class for seventh- through tenth-year students were sometimes not skilled enough to make study of the constitution compelling. A March 1937 Central Committee report about constitution teachers complained that "instead of interesting, entertaining explanations of the constitution in a form accessible to the children, in many cases, they give their students boring lectures and reports."[34] The divine words of Stalin lost their luster in the hands of mediocre cadres. In the same month, an education official raised the problem of a class of "mischief-making children" where there existed the "unhealthy and philistine opinion" that it was difficult to read Stalin's speech about the constitution.[35] Teachers could not openly acknowledge the complexity of constitution discourse and this made their task of explaining it all the harder. The reaching for the giant, the mystical, and the fantastic that was an integral part of Soviet life in this period and the use of religious discourse to build the cult of Stalin thus created contradictions that adversely affected the professional credibility of cultural intermediaries and lessened their effectiveness.

The words of the constitution were depicted as having the power to transform not only the consciousness but also the lives of its listeners and readers. At a July 1936 meeting of the Noginskii District Executive Committee in honor of the constitution, a female worker who was a member of her village soviet declared, "When I read the constitution, it was as if I received new strength."[36] In December 1936, a Moscow official reported the remarks of an elderly man: "I am getting younger; who says I am 72 years old?"[37] When collective farmers at the state farm Kudinovo[38] gathered to hear a report about the work of the Eighth Congress of Soviets, one collective farmer stated, "When they read the constitution, then you feel that you want to live and your heart works better."[39] In these instances, the words of the constitution became a healing and life-giving force. To assert the transformative power of the word, however, propagandists defined a "before" and "after" that offered a momentary glimpse at the realities of Soviet life. The collective farmer's statement implied that he did not want to live before he read the constitution. The assertion that the constitution had the power to heal led to the implicit acknowledgment that the population was somehow injured and sick at heart.

Soviet publicists depicted the constitution as ushering in a new era of prosperity. The rhetoric of plenty surrounding the 1936 constitution was one aspect of the government's efforts to convince citizens of the "continuously growing abundance which distinguishes the present moment."[40] At a meeting in honor of the new constitution in Moscow Region, one female collective farmer heralded the new prosperity brought by the constitution, proclaiming that the peasants now "all have cows and pigs and eat meat every day."[41] The poverty of the countryside had been miraculously transformed to abundance by the constitution.

Official propagandists sought to create loyalty to the state by employing a discourse of abundance, miracle, and sudden healing that had much more in common with backward "superstition" and religion than with scientific socialism. The attempt to use such a trope reveals that official Soviet discourse absorbed elements of older "irrational" discourses even as it claimed to eliminate them. This trope offered opportunities to appeal to the emotions of the population, but also complicated the work of propagandists by forcing them to make extravagant, far-fetched, and fantastic claims about the efficacy of the constitution.

Criticism of the Constitution

When the Soviet government published a draft of the new constitution and invited the population to submit suggestions for revision, it opened up a dialogue with the population and created space for comment on and criticism of state policies. While criticism of self and others was an ever-present part of Stalinist political culture in the late 1920s and 1930s, public criticism of a document associated with and endorsed by Stalin extended the boundaries of the usual culture of criticism. One puzzled official, for example, announced at a meeting of state farm workers that "suggestions for changes in individual articles or inserting additions into the draft is forbidden." When instructions from the center contradicted this official's experience of how politics in the Soviet Union worked, he ignored directions and behaved according to the dominant political model, entirely excluding the population from decision making. This habitual behavior was now censured by central government officials.[42]

The draft constitution elicited foreign as well as domestic criticism. Stalin admitted in his speech to the Congress of Soviets that the new constitution had been attacked in the foreign "bourgeois" press. By enumerating "bourgeois" criticisms and then responding to them one by one, Stalin disseminated a critique of the constitution to the far corners of the Soviet Union.[43] Stalin used humorous anecdotes and folk sayings to mock his enemies' interpretations, but he nonetheless explained their objections to the constitution in detail. Those Soviet citizens who had enough education and sophistication to understand the implications of Stalin's speech were informed that the constitution had been criticized both for being "an empty piece of paper" and for being a "rejection of the dictatorship of the proletariat."[44]

Stalin directly addressed the issue of whether the Soviet constitution was actually going to be enforced or whether it was just a propaganda ploy. According to Stalin, Fascist critics believed that the constitution was "an empty promise, calculated to pull off a well-known maneuver and deceive people."[45] Stalin rejected the German charge that the constitution was a deceptive "Potemkin village" by throwing the same charge back at the Germans. He accused them of trying "to hide the truth about the USSR from the people, to delude the people and deceive them."[46] The idea that a government might build up an elaborate facade to deceive its people thus became part of discussions about the constitution. The notion that propaganda could create an alternative reality was an element of public political discourse in the Soviet Union, appearing in the very rhetoric that sought to disguise Soviet reality.

Another charge that Stalin took great pains to rebut was the idea that the constitution was a "shift to the right," rejecting the dictatorship of the proletariat. This criticism from the left in Poland and the United States attacked the Stalin constitution for its resemblance to the constitutions of capitalist countries. Stalin did not reply substantively to this charge, but rather restated his position that the new constitution represented the "transformation of the dictatorship [of the proletariat] into a more flexible, . . . more powerful system of leadership of the State by society." He accused his critics of not understanding what the dictatorship of the proletariat meant and of not being able to tell left from right.[47] Stalin thus publicly defended the transformations in political language that complicated the lives of local cadres. Stalin's speech ensured that broad critiques of Soviet politics became part of a public political vocabulary that could be employed by those who opposed Stalin.

Discussion of the constitution provoked criticisms of the Soviet order and calls for better treatment from various segments of the population. Some Soviet citizens demanded rights based on the constitution's guarantees of freedom of conscience, assembly, speech, and the press and the inviolability of the person. Other criticisms focused on the constitution's definition of the economic and social status of workers, peasants, and employees and on the enumeration of the benefits guaranteed to these groups. National minorities used the constitution's protection of "the equality of rights of citizens of the USSR, irrespective of their nationality or race," to assert their individual rights.[48]

Freedom of Religious Worship

Article 124 of the constitution guaranteed "freedom of religious worship and freedom of anti-religious propaganda."[49] This article of the constitution brought forth a variety of reactions, both against religion and in favor of it, that alarmed Soviet officials. Interest in the religious issues raised by the constitution existed throughout the Russian Republic. Bulletins sent to the Central Executive Committee in the fall of 1936 documented numerous requests to open or repair churches based on Article 124.[50] Interest in religious questions was not limited to the Orthodox Christian population. A propagandist among the Khants and Nenets peoples in Omsk Region reported that in their discussion of the constitution, these peoples "were only interested in the questions of religion. They asked, 'And did the shaman receive rights? We have many shamans.'"[51] In one Muslim area, the population requested the re-opening of twelve mosques and the organization of a system by which mullahs would be paid a salary by the collective farm.[52] Discussions of the constitution brought forth proposals to allow priests, shamans, and mullahs to participate in the social life of their peoples;

to support religious leaders financially; and to provide new places of worship. These requests sought to incorporate religious institutions into the Soviet economic and social order.

The declaration of freedom of conscience was interpreted by those who had suffered religious persecution as a sign that religion would now be reintegrated into Soviet life. The clergy of the Viaz'ma diocese wrote a fulsome letter to Stalin, praising "the immortal historical document—the great Stalin Constitution."[53] Other priests offered to propagandize the constitution "from the pulpit."[54] The promulgation of the constitution brought people together for open religious worship as part of both Soviet and religious communities; in the Mordovskii Autonomous Republic, 500 people gathered for prayers to thank God for Article 124.[55] These actions illustrated some citizens' beliefs that there need not be a contradiction between religious worship and loyalty to the Soviet state.

Other Soviet citizens interpreted the separation of church and state guaranteed by the constitution to mean that local control over religious life was at an end. One citizen in Kuibyshev Territory asserted that because of the constitution, "the village soviet does not have the right to manage the church."[56] A bookkeeper in Zel'man Canton told the local population that priests "can freely assemble religious meetings, processions, and so forth, at any time, without the permission of the village soviet and the canton executive committee."[57] According to these interpretations, the constitution created a significant change in local power relations, diminishing the prerogatives of the local soviets as it strengthened the rights of churches.

Many individual Soviet citizens saw the guarantee of freedom of conscience in the constitution as an opportunity to restore religion to a more public and prominent place in their lives. At a meeting in Iaroslavskii Region to discuss the constitution, a cleaning woman said, "Now the constitution allows us freely to perform religious rites. We are grateful for all of this, but in order to perform religious rites, we have to go to the neighboring village. For this reason, please allow us to open the church." Although the speech was struck from the record, it could not be struck from the minds of the rest of the people gathered at the meeting.[58] Local officials either had to defy the new constitution in front of the whole gathered assembly or to acquiesce to more religious activity at the local level.

A worker at Moscow's Dinamo factory caught the attention of Party propagandists in October 1937 because he attended church and never attended meetings. When approached by Party workers, he defended himself by saying "belief is not forbidden."[59] The constitution provided this worker with a defense against the propagandists who were pressuring him to participate in the political life of the factory. The constitution thus destabilized the relationships between local officials and the population. Citizens and clerics now had the newly written law on their side, but local officials retained the means of repression.

Like the peasants during the Emancipation in 1861, Soviet citizens read the Stalin Constitution in a variety of idiosyncratic and highly imaginative ways. There were many misinterpretations of Article 124. In the Marinskii Autonomous Region, someone agitated that "the new constitution obliges everyone to pray to God and to sacrifice livestock." Because of this agitation, the peasants on one collective farm tried to slaughter the collectivized bull. In other places, the coming of the new constitution gave the collective farmers incentive to baptize all of the children between the ages of three and six.[60] In the Dagestan Autonomous Republic, a mistranslation turned the "freedom of anti-religious propaganda" clause into "freedom of religious propaganda," leading citizens to believe that an even more sweeping change in the state's attitude toward religion had taken place. There, rumors spread that the constitution encouraged the opening of mosques and learning of the Koran, but that "the village soviets do not want to promulgate this 'document.'"[61] As in the cases of the emancipation legislation and the "dizzy-with-success" article, rumors accused local officials of distorting legislation from the center and denying the people the freedoms that had been decreed.[62] In 1936, like in 1930, there was an element of truth to the assertion that local officials were unwilling to comply with the dictates of the very document that they were obliged to promote.

The freedom of religious worship guaranteed by the constitution drew criticism from elements of the Soviet population who had embraced the anti-religious doctrine of the Soviet state. These people openly opposed the rights that the constitution had given to priests. One Leningrad propagandist explained that in the course of discussions about the constitution, collective farmers in Leningrad Region proposed a variety of "undesirable corrections" that not only forbade priests to vote and be elected but proposed further limits on their civil rights and demanded that churches be closed.[63] A collective farm Party organizer explained to his audience that priests should not be allowed to vote because they lived off "unearned income."[64] Open hostility to Orthodoxy, which had up until the publication of the draft constitution been a marker of support for Soviet power, suddenly became a statement of protest against the government's policies. By espousing a liberal policy toward religion, even if it was only a policy on paper, the Soviet state placed some of its most vocal supporters at odds with official government doctrine and lessened the enthusiasm and effectiveness of some loyal cadres.

Freedom of Speech

The Stalin Constitution's espousal of freedom of speech also emboldened citizens to challenge local officials. One man in Moscow Region proclaimed, "Now according to the constitution, they cannot arrest me. Freedom of speech means that I can say whatever I want."[65] Because the constitution guaranteed basic civil rights at the same time that NKVD terror was reaching its height, those citizens who dared to claim the civil rights guaranteed in the constitution, were, ironically, in greater peril than ever of suffering arbitrary arrest.

The constitution's guarantee of freedom of speech was employed by peasants searching for a voice with which to express political and economic demands. Peasants from Sverdlovsk Region wrote about their difficult lives to a newspaper and invoked the constitution to increase the chances of their plea being heard. They wrote, "Freedom of speech and the press are inscribed in the new draft. And we *bedniaki* (poor peasants) ask the editors to write our letters in the newspaper."[66] These peasants combined the new political language of the constitution with the older category of *bedniak*, despite the fact that in current official language, the prosperous collective farm order was supposed to have already eliminated poor peasants. This letter, which challenged official depictions of the countryside, never appeared in open public discourse.

Even if it the guarantee of freedom of speech was not put into practice, the fact that it existed in Soviet public discourse was nonetheless significant. The constitution caused members of the political police to reflect on their activities and their role in the Soviet order. At a meeting of NKVD agents in Western Region to discuss the constitution, a dispute arose. One participant described the controversy: "Do we have freedom of criticism or not? Many considered that if we [do] have freedom of criticism, then it is forbidden to prosecute people for anti-Soviet conversations."[67] A Party official was sent to talk to this group and explain their "mistakes" to them. Of course, the agents were not mistaken. Arresting people for anti-Soviet conversations directly contradicted the constitution. The nationwide discussion of the constitution, with its emphasis on political rights, confused even members of the police and made them aware of the contradictions in their own actions. The language of democracy produced new knowledge that made Soviet citizens more aware of the political contradictions surrounding them.

Economic and Social Benefits

In addition to civil rights, the constitution enumerated the economic and social rights of workers and peasants. Articles 119 and 120 ensured "the establishment of annual vacations with pay for workers and employees and the provision of an extensive network of sanataria, rest homes, and clubs for the use of the toilers" and "the extensive development of social insurance for workers and employees at state expense."[68] These provisions promised Soviet toilers that in exchange for productivity, they would receive material benefits and a social safety net.[69]

One propagandist in the Dinamo factory in Moscow admitted that promoting the constitution was a difficult task; in January 1937, he noted that "many of our workers are still in a bad humor and they do not understand the fundamentals of the constitution. Indeed some workers quickly apprehend their rights, but forget about their obligations."[70] This propagandist acknowledged the low morale of Soviet workers and their rejection of the constitution's exhortations to work hard, protect socialist property, and defend the motherland. This propagandist also revealed that workers in the Dinamo factory were particularly receptive to the social welfare provisions of the constitution. The workers took the guarantees of benefits seriously and sought to use them to improve their economic status.

The very popularity of social benefits caused difficulties for Soviet propagandists. Another propagandist at the Dinamo factory in Moscow complained in August 1936 that "as soon as we begin to speak about [the government's] concern for people, then the first thing that pops into our people's heads is a *putevka* (a place in a sanitarium or on a vacation tour). But everyone knows that it is not possible to provide everyone with a *putevka*."[71] Soviet workers were quick to comprehend that rhetoric about prosperity, concern for citizens, and the "right to leisure" gave them the opportunity to request attractive social benefits. Since there were not enough resources for everyone, these demands led to friction between workers and factory organizers when organizers used the distribution of benefits to construct social hierarchies. The promises of the constitution raised workers' expectations of economic benefits that were slow in trickling down to rank-and-file workers.

The social benefits in the constitution were guaranteed only to workers and employees, excluding the peasants from even the possibility of receiving these privileges. The constitution thus reaffirmed the hierarchy of urban over rural and defined the peasantry as second-class citizens of the Soviet state. The inequality written into the "most democratic constitution in the world" was not lost on the peasantry. According to J. Arch Getty, in the discussion about the draft constitution, "one-fourth of all suggestions from Smolensk and one-third nationally" demanded equal status for the peasantry in vacation benefits and social insurance.[72] As one female collective farmer in Chernigov Region put it, "Collective farmers who work in the fields do not receive enough for their work compared to those who work in production. We work twenty hours a day, and they work eight hours. We have a common need for clothing and shoes, we walk around in torn dresses and shirts, and they, workers, are provided with everything in full. We don't have free places in resorts, but they do."[73] These provisions of the constitution created much resentment and jealousy, but nothing was done to redress this imbalance in the final draft.

Discussion of the welfare benefits promised by the constitution created conflicts among Soviet citizens. In April 1937, a propagandist from the Moscow Sharikpodshipnik factory reported a bitter interchange between a worker recently arrived from the countryside and more urbanized workers. An urban worker taunted the new arrival by mimicking a peasant's

complaint about Article 9 of the constitution that gave the land to the collective farms "free of charge."[74] He pretended to whine, "What do you mean,
'free land' when we pay such prices for bread?" The new arrival stolidly
insisted that "there's no benefit at all from the free land." An urban worker
shot back, "And what do you want, that they sell you bread at a cheap
price and sell it to workers at an expensive one?" A third worker chided
the others, saying, "Do you want there to be enmity between workers and
collective farmers in the Soviet Union?"[75] The grinding poverty of the Soviet Union set peasants and workers against each other as they sought relief from their desperate economic circumstances.

The reactions of younger and older workers to the constitution also
revealed a difference in their attitudes towards the Soviet state and their
resentment of one another. One young woman complained, "In the constitution it is written that abortions are illegal and they haven't made a lot of
nurseries." An older woman responded to this complaint by saying that
before "in the factory, pregnant women had to work until the last day [be-
fore the baby was born.]" The younger woman answered, "That was before, and now we all speak about [things being] better; that means they
should be better."[76] This interchange reveals the older worker's jealousy of
the welfare benefits received by younger workers. It also reveals that the
younger worker had high expectations of the Soviet welfare state because
of official rhetoric about improvements in living conditions. Discussion of
the economic and social welfare aspects of the constitution revealed tensions between cadres and citizens, between workers and peasants, between
the old and the young. Rather than illuminating the perfection and unity
of Soviet society, study of the constitution uncovered unresolved conflicts
and inequalities.

The Collective Farm Order

Discussions of the constitution also raised questions about the possibilities of farming outside of the collective farm. Article 9 explicitly permitted the "small-scale private economy of individual peasants and artisans
based on their personal labor." While the constitution thus acknowledged
that *edinolichniki* (individual peasant-farmers) had a right to exist outside
of the collective farm, it also affirmed that the "socialist system of economy
. . . shall be the predominant form of economy in the USSR," upholding the
centrality of collective farm agriculture.[77]

Government reports recorded a variety of creative interpretations of
this article of the constitution, however. Rumors circulated in Western Region that this article meant that "now individual peasant-farmers will be
the preference, and soon Soviet power will return to *kulaks* the property
that had been taken away from them." In Gorkii Region, it was rumored
that "individual peasant-farmers will be given a great deal of land and will
be freed from all taxes."[78] In Chernigov Region, a peasant proclaimed "there

will be no difference between collective farmers, individual peasant-farmers, and *kulaks*. All will receive full and equal freedom."[79] In the mid-1930s, the peasants circulated the same kind of rumors about land and freedom that they had spread eighty years before. As a result of these kinds of rumors, some people who had been deprived of their property during the collectivization drive asked for it to be returned. Other people decided to leave their collective farms.[80] The arrival of the constitution in villages across the Russian Republic inspired peasants to grasp at freedom by interpreting the constitution as the embodiment of their individual hopes. While these actions, like those of the followers of Anton Petrov at Bezdna, probably brought peasants more misfortune than freedom, the Soviet peasants clearly tried to use this legislation from the central government to transform local conditions while avowing their loyalty to the Soviet state. These were rebels in the name of the Stalin Constitution. While the text of the constitution did give the population real reason to challenge local officials in matters of religion, when peasants interpreted the constitution as dissolving the collective farms, they misread the document as a strategy for attaining their political goals.

The unfamiliar political language of the constitution allowed Soviet citizens to interpret other economic statutes in ways that suited their own purposes. In one village in Dagestan, Article 118, "the right to labor," which was intended by the authors of the constitution to mean a guarantee against unemployment, was interpreted as "the right to have hired workers in one's household."[81] The misinterpretation by the villagers in Dagestan suggests that these peasants wanted to return to the economic system before collectivization, when hired labor had been permitted. The villagers also believed that the new constitution would permit people who had been outcast as *kulaks* to return to their villages. These peasants interpreted the constitution as a way of turning back the clock and returning to the social and economic norms of 1928. Despite these hopes for economic relief, the collective farm order remained firmly in place after the promulgation of the constitution.

While some collective farmers inscribed the freedom that they desired into the constitution, others criticized it for giving too much freedom to other social groups. Some peasants criticized the constitution's sanction of individual farming. One collective farmer in Chernigov Region said, "In my opinion, [the individual farmer] should be either a collective farmer or a worker because in this Five Year Plan, it is expected that all classes will be liquidated."[82] This collective farmer did not want a right that he did not have to belong to others. Some peasant reactions to the constitution revealed animosity between peasants and other social groups. One collective farmer in Kirov Territory complained, "The path has been opened to the *kulak* and the priest and for us things haven't changed."[83] Throughout the discussions of the constitution, Soviet citizens in need revealed resentment against those who were more fortunate, or who they imagined to be more fortunate. They took out the frustrations of their daily lives on each other, limiting their possibilities for collective action.

The Rights of Nationalities

An important theme of the constitution celebration was that the document reflected the victory of Lenin's nationality policies. The new governmental structure elaborated in the constitution was intended to demonstrate that the eleven Soviet republics were equal members of a voluntary and harmonious federal union. The new Supreme Soviet, for example, had two equal chambers, the Soviet of the Union and the Soviet of Nationalities and Article 17 of the constitution provided for the "right of free secession" from the USSR.[84] In a number of collective farms in the Volga German Autonomous Republic, this "right of free secession" caught the attention of the population. Some peasants proposed that the Volga German Republic be turned into a Union Republic so that it could secede from the Soviet Union. Other peasants advocated a broader interpretation of this article to also include the individual right of "free departure to any country."[85] These proposed revisions to Article 17 articulated the dissatisfaction of the Volga Germans with life in the Soviet Union. These requests both fueled and reflected official paranoia about the loyalty of Volga Germans to the Soviet state, a paranoia that eventually led to the mass deportations of the Volga Germans during World War II.

The constitution could also be used by individuals of one nationality to complain to Moscow authorities about the inappropriate behavior of people of another ethnicity. After the celebration of a festival of Azeri music in Moscow in April 1938, one musician who had not been chosen to travel to Moscow wrote that if he had been excluded from the trip because he was an Italian, this would have violated "Article 123 of the constitution of the Azeri SSR," which like Article 123 of the Union constitution guaranteed equality for all citizens of the USSR "irrespective of their nationality or race."[86] In response to this and other complaints, the Committee on the Arts sent deputies to Azerbaidzhan to investigate charges of nationalism.[87] The central Soviet authorities' vigilance against any sign of "nationalism" made the anti-discrimination article of the constitution a powerful tool for some individuals, while it destroyed the lives and careers of others.

Whatever Stalin's intention was when he decided to draft a new constitution that guaranteed freedom of religion, freedom of speech, and other basic civil rights, this document was interpreted as a signal of change in the status quo at the local level. When peasants took actions based on their understandings or misunderstandings of the constitution, they took advantage of the arrival of an official document to pursue their struggles against local Soviet officials. Those who guarded the status quo in the localities had to promote the constitution and at the same time prevent the peasants from using it as a weapon against them. Local Soviet officials thus had to deal with challenges that were apparently sanctioned from the center. Some officials themselves became conscious that their actions denied Soviet citizens the rights granted by the constitution. The new discourse of democracy made contradictions in Soviet life apparent and revealed a different social and political world to cadres and citizens.

The constitution had a mixed effect on individual rights. In some cases, the rights guaranteed in the constitution caused Soviet citizens to take actions that jeopardized their safety. When citizens exercised their free speech in explicit opposition to the Soviet government, they took a tremendous risk. On the other hand, the constitution might have offered some individuals the opportunity to challenge anti-religious propagandists and justify their right to attend church. The articles of the constitution may also have given minority nationalities in the non-Russian republics a real opportunity to defend themselves against discrimination by the majority in that republic.

The Problem of Cadres

In the second half of 1936 and all throughout 1937, the Soviet government instructed propagandists and cultural workers to make the constitution and the elections a central theme in the political education of the citizenry. The promulgation of the constitution and the election laws brought questions of politics and political process to many Soviet towns and villages. Like all other Soviet propaganda campaigns, the success of the constitution and the election campaigns greatly depended on the quality of the cadres who carried them out and their willingness to do so. Central officials had very high expectations of the performance of cadres in these campaigns. A. I. Stetskii, the head of the Agitation and Propaganda Department of the Central Committee, wrote in a September 1937 directive that "preparations for the elections to the Supreme Soviet of the USSR are a testing of the practical usefulness and political maturity of the leaders of Party propaganda and agitation sections of regional committees, territorial committees and central committees of the national Communist Parties."[88] These leaders could prove their political maturity by effective organization of their subordinates at the local level.

Local and mid-level cadres had a complex array of responses to the constitution and election campaigns. Some were incapable of teaching the new language of politics, while others refused to do so. Some cadres were politically astute, able both to interpret the constitution and see the dangers created by the promotion of democratic discourse. Others were skilled enough to understand the constitution but not the pitfalls it created.

Given the variety of pressures on all Soviet officials in 1936–1937, one response to the constitution campaign was to delegate it to someone else.

In one district in Ivanovo Region, "the district committee held only a general Party meeting about the draft constitution, and the rest they entrusted to the chairmen of the village soviets; they in turn charged the collective farm chairmen with this matter . . . [and the collective farm chairmen] simply forgot about it."[89] Delegating the discussions of the constitution or preparations for the elections was simply not effective. Regional and district officials had to monitor the campaign in the localities if they wanted to prove their political maturity.

Local village cadres were usually the weakest links in the chain from Moscow to the individual collective farmers. The lowest-ranked and least-skilled cadres in charge of explaining the constitution and the elections in Soviet villages were the attendants of *izba-chital'nia* (rural reading rooms) and the directors of collective farm clubs. These poorly educated and poorly paid cadres were often only marginally more educated than the people who they served.[90] Sometimes the reading room attendant would turn out to be an untrained young relative of the collective farm chairman who collected a salary but did very little in return.[91] Some reading room attendants did not themselves know the most basic information about the Soviet government; one could not, for example, identify Molotov or Voroshilov.[92] The limited education of the reading room attendants and their lack of facility in the Soviet political language contained in the decrees and directives about the constitution created a great deal of semantic confusion at the local level.

Local cadres and the local population were both unsure about the political principles promoted in the election campaign. One Gorkii Regional Department of People's Enlightenment official complained in September 1937: "It is clear to everyone that our reading room attendants are very ignorant and do not know even the simplest political questions. When we asked one reading room attendant in Semenovskii District about how the elections to the Supreme Soviet would be conducted, he answered that the voting would be *tikhoe* (quiet) instead of saying *tainoe* (secret)."[93] One peasant woman even "thought that the secret ballot meant that the identities of the candidates were to be secret."[94] By imposing western democratic rhetoric and electoral process on the population without providing enough qualified cadres to explain them to the people, the Soviet government undermined its long-term goal of creating a politically conscious population.

In addition to the incompetence of local cadres, the constitution and election campaigns revealed conflicts and mistrust among local, regional, and central officials. The director of the House of Culture and Club Sector of the Iaroslavskii Regional Department of People's Enlightenment reported in September 1937 that at a collective farm meeting about the elections one reading room attendant was asked "Why are we having elections to the Supreme Soviet?" He answered, "Because bad people ensconced themselves in the soviets and we have to elect those positions over again."[95] In his response to this question, this Soviet official on the lowest rung of the political ladder publicly revealed both his political ignorance and his profound mistrust of those in power.

Others in the villages agreed with this local official. Some collective farmers used the constitution to underscore "the unsatisfactory work of their deputies . . . and warned them about the possibility of recalling them from the Soviet if they did not improve their work."[96] One editor of a factory newspaper extended the idea of protesting against bad officials to the factory. He believed that the constitution gave the workers the right to demonstrate against the factory committee if they were unsatisfied with its work.[97] While Soviet officials prevented these interpretations of the constitution from being put into practice, Soviet citizens embraced them as a means of putting political pressure on local officials.

Many Soviet cadres were unwilling to allow the constitution to affect their local prerogatives and perquisites. A memoirist recalled how the chairman of a local *artel* (cooperative workshop) in Tiumen greeted the constitution: "The Constitution is one thing, but local authority is something else. Everything will be at someone's discretion: who can be hired and who cannot."[98] The new constitution posed a challenge to local power structures and to the status quo at the local level and this fact conditioned the responses of cadres to the constitution.

If put into practice, the proposed change in the election laws to allow priests and other former class enemies to take part in elections could have destabilized local power relations. The sudden change in the Soviet government's policy on religion caught the people who had been directly engaged in the battle against religion unaware. The local officials and collective farmers who had most benefited by the expropriation of priests and supposed *kulaks* had reason to be apprehensive of a policy that seemed to signal the return of these elements to the political life of the village.[99]

Local officials also received contradictory signals from the central government. While guaranteeing the rights of priests and other "former people" to elect and be elected, central directives also repeatedly instructed local cadres to prevent enemies such as priests and *kulaks* from using the constitution and the elections for "their own goals."[100] Soviet officials continued to view priests as a particularly suspect category. An article in *Krest'ianka* warned, "Religious organizations are, in our country, the only legal center around which all class enemy elements group themselves and especially around which they will group themselves in the upcoming election campaign."[101] Although priests had been granted their civil rights by the constitution, Soviet educational and Party officials still viewed them as potential enemies with whom they must battle for the hearts and souls of Soviet citizens.

Either because of their personal lack of enthusiasm for the new law or because of contradictory and confusing signals from the central government, many Soviet lecturers and propagandists were not prepared to explain to their audiences why freedom of conscience and the rights of priests were now protected by the law. One propagandist speaking at a Moscow leather factory during the May Day holiday in 1937 bungled his anti-religious discussion so badly that it lowered the attendance for the May Day concert that followed. The propagandist did not know how to respond when the government's new policy was challenged by a member of the audience who asked, "Why is it forbidden to close the churches?" Nor could the propagandist respond to the question, "What do we need to do to prevent priests from getting into the soviets?"[102] Neither the factory workers who asked these questions nor the propagandist who was supposed to answer them had thoroughly understood or accepted the changes in Soviet policy. The propagandist, who was supposed to be a key player in preventing enemies from being elected to the soviets, could not even articulate what his own role in the election process would be. The provision of the constitution that enabled priests to vote complicated the political work of local officials because propagandists had to explain a public about-face in Soviet anti-religious policies at the same time that they enforced the discriminatory status quo against priests and guarded against "enemies" infiltrating the soviets.

The confusion of local propagandists about other aspects of the constitution also hindered the political education of their listeners. Aleksandr Kosarev, the head of the Komsomol, complained in early 1937 that "If a worker reading the draft constitution understood it, then after he heard a lecturer whose task it was to explain the Stalin Constitution, he stopped understanding."[103] Many propagandists were not skilled enough to make their discussions of the constitution accessible to their listeners.

Mid-level urban Party officials were more aware than local officials that making a political mistake in teaching about the constitution could be costly. The constitution and election discussions caused anxiety for these politically experienced and aware officials. Because many propagandists themselves did not have a firm grasp on the principles of the constitution they were afraid of being asked difficult or controversial questions. At a lecture on the constitution for teachers and school Party organizers, a Komsomol organizer asked, "Was there exploitation in the private-capitalist sector of the economy in 1924?" In response, the lecturer scolded him, "What, do you want to go to prison along with the Trotskyites? . . . There was no exploitation."[104] This propagandist became angry because he thought that any criticism of Soviet economic life in the early 1920s smacked of Trotskyism. The lecturer simply did not know his material well enough to answer the educated question of the Komsomol organizer. Because he felt threatened, the propagandist's immediate response was to threaten the questioner with arrest in order to silence him.

By failing to answer the question adequately and by calling the Komsomol organizer a Trotskyite, the propagandist undermined his own authority and created an opportunity for a discussion of exploitation during the Soviet period. Dubrovina, the head of the Moscow City Department of Enlightenment related in March 1937 that "as a result of this incident, a great deal of noise arose, all of the teachers leapt from their chairs, conversations began: 'How can that be? There were the holdings of *kulaks*, there were economic concessions, how can it be that there was no exploitation?'"[105] The teachers had a better grasp on the material than the lecturer, and as a group they challenged his interpretation of the Soviet economy and his unfair accusation against the Komsomol organizer. This incident revealed some of the dangers that officials propagandizing the constitution faced. Their authority as leaders was connected to their ability to explain the political, social, and economic complexities of the constitution while preventing any discussion that might reveal negative aspects of Soviet life. Yet lectures and discussions about the constitution brought audiences together explicitly to discuss the nature and history of the Soviet state. The teachers espoused a politically orthodox interpretation of the Soviet economy but at the same time focused their discussion on the failure of the Soviet leadership to root out exploitation during the early Soviet period.

Soviet secondary teachers had a particularly difficult task in explaining the constitution because their students were uninhibited in their questions. One educator warned that teachers of the constitution had to prepare themselves to answer extremely difficult questions. This teacher had had to discuss sensitive political issues with her students and believed that "if the teacher cannot answer these questions, grounds for counter-revolutionary work would be created." One child asked, for example, "How can we have freedom of the press if there is censorship?" This teacher claimed that these kinds of questions came not only from troublemakers; "good children" and "members of the Komsomol" also asked challenging questions.[106] Study of the constitution presented certain contradictions and paradoxes to Soviet schoolchildren. Some of the "good students" who were puzzled by the contradictions did not hesitate to ask about them, creating a potentially dangerous situation for the teacher who would be held responsible if politically subversive discussions were held in the classroom. These students openly discussed Soviet politics and forced their anxious teachers to address the very real contradictions in Soviet policies. If the teachers could not provide satisfactory answers that re-established political control over the conversation, political discussions about the constitution could lead to doubt about the Soviet system rather than its celebration and could threaten the teachers' livelihoods.

When the October plenum of the Central Committee decided against having contested elections, the contradictions that teachers and propagandists had to deal with became even more blatant.[107] After propagandists had expounded on the process of four-tailed suffrage for several months, voters lost their opportunity to choose among several candidates or to mark their ballots in secret. Propagandists then had to answer the charges of the very Soviet citizens to whom they had just explained how democratic elections should work. In October 1937, one bookkeeper from Moscow's October District told propagandists, "We don't have the secret ballot since only one candidate is registered."[108] The authority of the most effective Party propagandists was thus undermined.

New Visions of Government

The promulgation of the new constitution provided a model of governmental power and citizens' rights for those cadres who were in charge of organizing the population on the local level. Propagandists used their knowledge about the constitution and elections to imagine new political processes at all levels of government. Because of the myriad contradictions inherent in promoting a democratic rhetoric while maintaining a political dictatorship, local propagandists were criticized by mid-level officials when they were too successful in teaching the tenets of democratic government to the population.

Since the constitution separated the Soviet legislature into two houses for the first time, Soviet propagandists were obliged to explain why a bicameral system was created and how it would work. The very existence of a new Soviet of Nationalities implied that the interests of the national minorities were separate and distinct from all-Union interests. One propagandist, illustrating the mechanics of the new system of government, imagined a situation in which the Soviet of Nationalities would defend national interests. He explained that if the Soviet authorities in Birobidzhan (the Jewish settlement in the Far East) were to decide to teach in Russian in all their schools, the Soviet of Nationalities would intervene and prevent this from happening. A speaker at the Moscow City Soviet Plenum in honor of the draft constitution denounced this propagandist as an enemy.[109]

The propagandist's explanation of how the bicameral government would operate got him into trouble because in order to demonstrate the need for two chambers, he had to imagine how the interests of one chamber would differ from those of the other. He thus suggested that Soviet authorities might curtail the rights of the non-Russian nationalities by forcing them to study Russian.[110] The introduction of a new constitution forced Soviet propagandists to imagine and explore new political terrain. Since many of the provisions of the constitution were not consistent with Soviet practice, propagandists who properly understood the implications of the constitution but were politically unsophisticated could get into trouble simply by illustrating how the new politics described in the constitution might work.

In September 1937, the director of the House of Culture and Club Sector of the Iaroslavskii Regional Department of People's Enlightenment denounced the actions of a reading room attendant, who "explaining the 'Statute on Elections to the Supreme Soviet' began to hold a rehearsal. He pasted together envelopes out of newspaper, prepared lists of candidates and rehearsed the elections to the Supreme Soviet." The director continued, "This is undoubtedly an enemy act, for he steered the whole business toward technique, toward the vulgarization of the most important political measures. For us the technique of the elections to the Supreme Soviet proceeds from the particular politics of the secret ballot and so forth."[111]

While the focus on the mechanics of voting did draw the population away from the broader political significance of the election laws, this official's vehement reaction to the actions of the reading room attendant probably had a different cause. By practicing the elections, the reading room attendant simulated a democratic political process at the local level. In this simulation, the local population was given the right to choose freely from among the lists of candidates. By helping the local villagers to imagine how free elections would be conducted and by actually conducting free elections as a "rehearsal" for the Supreme Soviet elections, he offered the population political participation that was consistent with the letter of the election law, but not with the intentions of his superiors. Unlike the reading room attendant, the regional education official wanted to keep total control over the election process or felt compelled by pressure from above to do so. Because of the contradictory and only partially articulated nature

"Elections in the USSR are conducted by secret ballot." From *Stalinskaia Konstitutsiia sotsializma* (1938).

of the Soviet government's policies, unskilled local officials could err not only by failing to carry out official policies, but by carrying them too far.

A Moscow educational official reported in March 1937 that members of the Komsomol from an eighth-grade class in a Moscow school wrote a class constitution. These youths interpreted the Stalin Constitution as protecting the rights of Soviet citizens and affirming the Party's important leadership role. The class constitution included a "right-to-labor" clause which stated that "the teacher does not have the right to give more work than is customary." This clause, interpreting the Stalin Constitution as a contract between ruler and ruled, likewise defined the boundaries of the teacher's authority and protected the students from possible abuses of power. The class constitution also had a "single party" clause which declared that "in the class no other organizations may exist except the Komsomol and Pioneer organizations."[112] This declaration of loyalty to the Party from the leaders of the Komsomol represented their interest in maintaining their own control over class events. The school official went on to explain that there were certain elements of a "comic character" in the class constitution, for example that the "capital" of the class would be the "third desk."[113] Like the Soviet Union, the class was to have its own physical as well as moral center of power. The Komsomol leaders used the constitution to create a model for an independent local government that they would control and as a means of defending themselves against the demands of their teachers.

While this class constitution revealed the arrogance of the class Komsomol leaders, it affirmed rather than questioned the tenets of Soviet power. Yet education officials found the very idea that several youths could create their own constitution to be extremely subversive. An education official reporting on this incident declared that the creation of the class constitution was not the "conscious preparation of a document of anti-Soviet content," but that it turned out to be an "extreme, intolerable profanation of the Stalin Constitution."[114] The students' literal reading of the Stalin Constitution as a document which limited the power of the government and their creative interpretation of political power as something that could be adapted and molded by local citizens caused teachers to view their activities as profane.

Wary and experienced Soviet officials saw the Stalin Constitution as a holy document to be revered from afar rather than put into practice by Soviet citizens as they accomplished their mundane activities. The aim of the constitution was to create an awed respect for the state and its treatment of Soviet citizens. The constitution was not meant to provide a civics lesson in self-government. The fact that, entirely on their own, these Soviet students interpreted the constitution as a model for organizing their community revealed that the political lessons inherent in a constitution that guaranteed rights to its citizens reached at least some Soviet citizens. Most local officials who were in charge of propagandizing the constitution tried to channel interpretations of it away from the creation of local political processes, but as both the reading room attendant who practiced the elections and the Komsomol cell that created its own constitution show, they did not always succeed.

The celebration of the constitution and elections opened up a space for political and economic discussions in the Soviet Union both within and outside of the boundaries of Soviet orthodoxy. Unfamiliar political concepts, errors and confusion on the part of the propagandists and audience, and lack of political experience sometimes caused those discussing the constitution and elections to raise issues that regional and central officials wanted to suppress. Discussions of the constitution gave their participants insights into the nature of their leaders, the Soviet state, and local social and political relations.

The constitution campaign reached many citizens who had never been exposed to Soviet discourse. Since the constitution enumerated benefits to Soviet citizens, this new audience was quite attentive. Official rhetoric about the constitution tapped into pre-revolutionary religious discourse, depicting this document as a holy text invested with the power to transform Soviet life. Some Soviet citizens eagerly accepted the promises that the constitution made to them, becoming frustrated when obtaining the social welfare guaranteed in the constitution proved harder than they had hoped. Other citizens viewed the constitution not as a miraculous document but as a practical one that could possibly be used to achieve concrete social, economic, and political goals.

The celebration of the constitution represented an enormous change in Soviet official rhetoric. It publicized new ideas about elections, local political process, self-government, civil rights, religious freedom, and social benefits to Soviet citizens. Because this rhetoric of democracy served as an alternative to Soviet practices, this document from the center destabilized the status quo between local Soviet officials and Soviet citizens in many parts of the Soviet Union. The document raised expectations of a new social order that never came into being and, by giving rights to priests and *kulaks*, it stirred up old resentments. Some Soviet citizens embraced the constitution to simultaneously show their loyalty to Soviet power and forward their own battles with local officials, to seek privileges, and to imagine a new kind of local politics. In James Scott's terms, the constitution enumerated new promises to the dominated that they could use to resist Soviet power. Because of the constitution, local order had to be renegotiated, even if the outcome was not much different than what already existed.

The constitution campaign, like the Pushkin Centennial and the October Anniversary, was profoundly affected by the knowledge and experi-

ence of the cadres who educated the population. Confusion about the meaning of the constitution was perpetuated by ignorant or bewildered officials
who could not themselves understand its basic tenets. Other cadres found
themselves challenged by citizens who used the constitution to back up
their arguments. Still others were forced to confront the contradictions in
Soviet life when readers of the constitution asked them about glaring inconsistencies. The introduction of new democratic political rhetoric in the
constitution initiated new dialogues about Soviet life. The celebrations surrounding the Stalin Constitution of 1936 show how democratic political
concepts were recast in Soviet terms by the central government and mid-
level officials and then reinterpreted in a wide range of ways by lower-
level cadres and the Soviet people. Despite the fact that this democracy
existed only on paper, the presence of democratic ideals in Soviet political
discourse transformed the relationships of Soviet citizens to the Soviet state
and its representatives by enabling them to envision alternatives to the
Soviet political structure. The actions that Soviet citizens took based on
these new visions sometimes led to tragedy for themselves or for the local
cadres who they opposed in the name of the Stalin Constitution.

8

CELEBRATIONS AND POWER

Discourse and Soviet Identities

Soviet celebrations of the 1930s reveal the complexity of Stalinist political discourse and the myriad ways in which it could be shaped by citizens. Despite strict censorship, Soviet official discourse offered a wide variety of opportunities for Soviet citizens to think and talk about their lives in ways that did not conform to state dictates or intentions. Even without alternative discourses, Soviet citizens could articulate unofficial points of view—they could express their anxieties and hopes within the officially sanctioned discourse of celebrations. Soviet officials designed celebrations to provide a template for ideal Soviet identities and behaviors but they could not control the way that audiences actually perceived the celebrations. Celebrations thus contributed to the formation of both official Soviet identities and unofficial and individual points of view.

Virtually every aspect of Soviet celebration culture in the 1930s reflected the hierarchical nature of Soviet society and the formation of new elites. Through celebrations, elite citizens affirmed their identities as they purchased expensive food and consumer goods that few others could afford, gloried in special invitations to exclusive holiday events, watched the demonstration from the tribune, or secured an honored place in the order of the demonstration's march. These citizens embraced a Soviet identity that was built on the exclusion of others from their ranks. For less exalted Soviet citizens, the meanings of celebration were shaped, in part, by the growing distance between the rulers and the ruled. While they too usually received special food and time off from work in honor of the holiday, they also experienced their inferior status during the celebration in the symbolic hierarchies created by holiday events.

The enormous variation in the ways that celebrations took place in the center and the periphery also reveals Soviet hierarchies in the 1930s. Celebration culture was most vibrant and extensive in Moscow, where the top elite of the Soviet state symbolically demonstrated for one another the might and power at their disposal. The lion's share of celebration resources were spent in Moscow and other large urban centers. While Soviet celebration culture was enacted on a reduced scale in provincial cities and regional and district centers, central Soviet officials had little control over celebrations in the countryside and non-Russian regions. Because of a hierarchical pattern in the distribution of resources, the possibilities of creating and imposing Soviet identities through celebration decreased markedly as one moved from center to periphery and from city to countryside. Central authorities created a myth of belonging to a wonderful and united Soviet country that was most persuasive to themselves. There were far fewer opportunities for rural and non-Russian citizens to identify themselves as part of the Soviet motherland.

The differences between Soviet celebrations in the center and the periphery reveal the limits of creating a Soviet identity. While the diarist Podlubnyi and those like him may have been incapable of thinking outside of the boundaries of Soviet discourse, there were also many Frolovs who still marked time using the Orthodox rather than the Soviet calendar and remained virtually untouched by Soviet discourse. Among the urban population (particularly the population of Moscow), and among mid-level Soviet functionaries, there were many who constructed their identities mostly within Soviet discourses. The rest of the population existed on the broad continuum between Podlubnyi and Frolov.

Did people believe in the Soviet vision or "take it for granted," as Peter Kenez suggests? The answer varies tremendously depending on the social, political, economic, and geographic locations of the people in question; it even varies from day to day. The identities created by Soviet celebrations were highly variable, contingent, and constantly in the process of being reshaped. Soviet celebrations both succeeded and failed in achieving their goal of creating New Soviet Men. They most often succeeded in Russian urban areas and most often failed in the non-Russian countryside. Celebrations were more successful with youth than with the elderly, more compelling to rising elites than to workers and collective farmers. They were more likely to promote male participation and citizenship than female. Many of the loyal Soviet identities successfully created by celebrations were destabilized or destroyed, however, by the political turmoil of the purge era.

Celebrations and Stalinism

The work of Robert Thurston has suggested that the purges of the 1930s did not penetrate as deeply into Soviet society as most scholars had supposed and that normal daily life continued throughout the terror.[1] The social realities of Soviet celebrations suggest that coercion and the threat of violence were a central feature of Soviet life in the 1930s. During the purges all levels of officials and cultural workers revealed their anxieties about their work and their fear of making mistakes for which they would be held accountable. Writers refused to write, a lecturer threatened members of the audience with arrest when they challenged his interpretation of Soviet history, teachers feared that intelligent students would ask questions about the constitution for which there were no appropriate answers. Local parade organizers worried that one of the participants from their district would try to shoot Stalin. Both upper- and lower-level cultural cadres feared the consequences of political mistakes, and this fear shaped their work with the population during celebrations.

As Stephen Kotkin has argued (following Foucault), Soviet power was both repressive and productive of Soviet identities.[2] Power was exerted by and over Soviet citizens as they formed their identities through celebrations that were part of "everyday" life. Soviet celebrations were not simply "circuses" to divert the population from terror; they supplied the raw materials out of which Soviet cadres constructed their own identities and were also a crucial means of transmitting these identities to others. Celebrations, however, were far more successful in achieving the first goal than the second. Many Soviet cadres lived within the world created by celebration discourse but had difficulty extending this worldview to others. Official celebrations at the local level often turned into apolitical dances, a cover for religious practices or, worse yet, drunken brawls.

The relationship between the center and the periphery described in this work confirms the findings of J. Arch Getty and Gabor Rittersporn[3] that the purges can be explained, in part, by the Soviet government's attempts to gain more control over the countryside. The use of purges and violence to improve Soviet administration in the 1930s, however, exacerbated the inability of Soviet cadres to control celebrations and other aspects of life in the periphery. Celebrations could not be a diversion from terror in the periphery because the purges removed key social cadres and disrupted the carrying out of celebrations. Celebrations weakened as the terror increased and, as the terror progressed, cadres lost opportunities to shape worldviews in the periphery.

The relationship between terror and celebrations was much more complicated in urban centers and particularly in Moscow. The most active participants in celebrations in the cities were the elites who were also those most likely to be under pressure during the purges. The terror also weakened the impact of urban celebrations but not to the same extent that it did in the periphery. Celebrations in the center demonstrated the might of the Soviet state and affirmed the elite positions of cadres, but a close reading of celebration discourse reveals the anxieties of this elite under stress. The utopian discourse of celebration organizers also fed into the purges by allowing no explanation for social problems except sabotage. Soviet celebrations for elites in urban centers were thus profoundly multivalent. They were, in part, diversions from terror, but they were also a means of assuring the Soviet elites of the solidity of their power, opportunities for cadres to express anxieties and doubts, and mechanisms that extended the purges by promoting a rhetoric of enemies and wreckers. Celebrations thus aided terror and were weakened by it, they reflected the power of their participants and undermined that power, they provided opportunities to speak about life during the terror and masked the existence of the purges. The relationship of terror to celebration was extremely complex and varied according to social milieu, geography, and coincidence. It cannot be reduced to a simple formulation of diversion or "circus."

One of the great puzzles of the Soviet Union in the 1930s is the relationship between socialist ideology and the return of traditional values. Timasheff's classic work has called this era a "great retreat" from socialism. Recently, Stephen Kotkin has argued that there was no retreat from socialism in the 1930s. While I agree with Kotkin that Stalinist policies remained "socialist," his study fails to take into account the pervasive and multifaceted return to "traditional" values that Timasheff so ably described over fifty years ago.[4] I believe that Stalinism in the 1930s was both a retreat and an advance. Celebration discourse shows that socialist ideology interacted with traditional values in complex and diverse ways. The figure of Pushkin in the 1930s is an excellent example of this complexity. While the introduction of Pushkin can be seen as an overture to the older intelligentsia, the figure that emerged in the centennial was a new socialist and class-conscious Pushkin. Pushkin both mobilized members of the intelligentsia to work for the Soviet state and enabled them to preserve and promote pre-revolutionary intelligentsia values. The Pushkin Centennial represented a compromise designed to promote Soviet values. Ultimately however, such a compromise both forwarded and undermined official values.

While the introduction of historic images clearly enabled Soviet celebrations to appeal to a broader segment of the population and the intelligentsia than they previously had, this broader appeal came at a cost. Some Soviet cultural cadres became disenchanted when they found themselves expected to embrace what they had spent their entire lives discrediting. As drama critic V. Blium wrote to Stalin in 1938, "The most recent Soviet dramaturgy on historical themes, and I must say, Soviet defense agitation, carries all of the traits not of our Soviet defense, but the old bourgeois and racist defense of the Kadet literature of 1914 . . . We should not write in 1938 the same way we wrote 24 years ago."[5] Less sophisticated Soviet cadres also became confused and uncertain about what to promote during this period of transition when old images such as the motherland suddenly reappeared. The changes in Soviet rhetoric antagonized and puzzled some Soviet cadres but they also enabled citizens to think about their lives in a broader historical context and experience emotions that did not always affirm the success of the Soviet state.

The Soviet government's "compromises" produced a series of winners and losers. The championing of Pushkin was yet another defeat for those who had sought in the 1920s to create a distinctly proletarian culture. The return to traditional "family" values asserted the rights of men over women and the control of the state over women's bodies. The promotion of Russian cultural heroes affirmed their leadership over the "less advanced" non-Russians. Because of these compromises, the configuration of power in Soviet society changed in the 1930s, altering the relationships among citizens and between state and citizen.

The top leadership in the 1930s recognized that coercion could only go so far in creating the New Soviet Man. In the interest of increasing state power and extending socialist values, they acknowledged and accepted elements of the past that could help them to mobilize the population. While officials tried to Sovietize and maintain control over "the old," they could not always do so. The introduction of traditional culture gave Soviet citizens opportunities to think about their lives in different ways than the Soviet government intended and gave certain citizens the opportunity to exert power over others. The complexity of the 1930s cannot be reduced to a retreat or an advance. Instead, the celebrations of the 1930s reveal a complex dialogue and negotiation between citizens and the state to define a culture that could both mobilize the population and inculcate socialist values.

While one must always remember that compromise and negotiation in the Soviet Union frequently broke down and resulted in the arrests and deaths of innocent people, one cannot understand Soviet culture without taking both coercion and compromise into account. To extend Vera Dunham's analogy about the post-war period into the 1930s, Soviet celebrations in the 1930s were vehicles for the creation of a series of both big and little deals with the population. The elites benefited from the bigger deals, receiving economic and social privileges in exchange for loyalty. The rest of the population took part in smaller deals, perhaps avoiding work in honor of a holiday or using an official celebration to forward private rather than public goals. Both little and big deals were a crucial aspect of the social fabric of Stalinism. These compromises enabled violence and terror to exist by creating groups willing to carry it out and condone it.

Since the terror often upset the deals by arresting and killing some of the dealmakers, the bargains of the 1930s were constantly undone and renegotiated. The celebration culture of the 1930s was one of the channels through which state and people constructed and reconstructed the deals and identities of the 1930s. Celebrations thus reveal the complex and ever-changing relationships between terror and diversion, ideological retreat and advance, and negotiation and violence in Soviet society.

Soviet Celebrations in Historical Context

Certain holiday traditions that became fixed in the 1930s continued to dominate Soviet celebrations until the end of the Soviet era. Not only was the massive demonstration a key contemporary image of the Soviet Union in the 1930s (as shown by the fact that newsreel footage of the May Day parade was buried in the time capsule at the New York World's Fair in 1938); it also remained the signature image of the Soviet Union and a hallmark of Soviet civic life until 1991.[6]

In the post-Stalin era, Soviet officials attempted to create personally meaningful holidays and they debated how best to achieve their goals with introspection that was reminiscent of Soviet debates about holidays in the 1920s.[7] In addition to new, more personal holidays such as those in honor of the first day of work or receiving a passport, holiday organizers under Khrushchev and Brezhnev created new politically oriented celebrations. These holidays commemorated the achievements of the Soviet space program, the Centennial of Lenin's birth, the Moscow Olympics, and the Brezhnev Constitution and were the direct descendants of the Stalinist celebrations of the 1930s. The celebrations of the 1930s profoundly influenced late Soviet political discourse and practice and their legacy is still evident today in the ongoing attempts to define civic celebration in the post-Soviet era.

In the 1930s, forms of celebration discourse were important in other places besides the Soviet Union. One of the most important symbols of the supposed unity of people and state in Nazi Germany was the parade. The consumption of depoliticized mass entertainment, especially the relatively new technologies of radio and film, was an important aspect of 1930s culture in both Europe and the United States. Some historians of popular culture see the consumption of mass culture as a means to prevent political action against the repressive fascist dictatorships and the inequalities of capitalism in the United States.[8] This depoliticized culture created a fantasy world into which those who faced economic or political hardships could escape. The emphasis on celebrations in the Soviet Union and the development of Soviet popular culture thus fits into the wider trends of European and American history.

Yet the creation of a world of celebration and fantasy was profoundly different in each place where it occurred. Many analysts have noticed the similarities between Nazi and Soviet celebrations.[9] Both types of celebration took place in the context of strict censorship and political repression. Both sought to promote the political identity of "the loyal citizen" by defining categories of "enemy." Even the styles of art and culture produced in these celebrations were quite similar.[10] Yet the contexts for these celebrations were different in very significant ways. Hitler's Germany achieved major foreign policy goals and some degree of real economic recovery by the middle of the 1930s while the Soviet state had to use celebration to project a prosperity that did not yet exist in a world of "capitalist encirclement." Hitler made charismatic speeches at rallies while Stalin built his "cult" primarily from behind the walls of the Kremlin or standing silently atop Lenin's Mausoleum. Underground opponents of the Nazi state still existed after 1933, while organized resistance to the Soviet state had been wiped out in the 1920s. Each state curtailed the scope of independent groups and discourses within society, but some pre-Nazi social organizations continued to operate in Germany under Nazi supervision. Soviet citizens had little outside information while German citizens had access to foreign radio broadcasts. Because of the differences in the economic conditions of the two countries, the burden of creating representations of joy and prosperity did not fall as heavily on German celebrations as it did on Soviet festivals. While the forms of celebration and popular culture appear to be quite similar in the Soviet Union, Germany, and the United States, they were invested with a multiplicity of meanings that were specific to their social contexts.

Although Soviet rhetoric had considerable power to shape identities, it was constrained by the economic and personnel resources available to organize celebrations. The messages of the cultural media in Europe and America had many more chances to reach their populations. While citizens within reach of Soviet discourse were bombarded with carefully censored messages, they interpreted these messages in a wide variety of ways and used the discourse of the state to create alternative visions of their worlds. If the repressive dominant discourse of Stalinism was shot through with alternative and oppositional voices, and it was, then the popular culture of the United States and, to a lesser extent, Nazi Germany, must contain an even greater multiplicity of opposing voices and ideas. The discourse of these depoliticized cultures reveals not only the messages of the dominant groups, but also the many ways in which the dominated appropriated and reshaped these messages.

The images of prosperity that were transmitted by Soviet celebrations had variable effects, depending on the social locations of their participants. While aspiring elites may have viewed these images favorably as a promise of the prosperity that would soon be theirs, Soviet citizens who saw little chance of their own advancement viewed these privileges with resentment and envy and as further evidence of the unbridgeable gap between rulers and ruled. The discourse of happiness played little role in the formation of the Soviet identities of the latter group. The European and American fantasy worlds created during the Great Depression must also have played differently to people with varying amounts of economic opportunity.

The German and Soviet governments of the 1930s stood out in their endeavors to create new social identities. They were most successful among young people and where they found common ground with already existing identities. The population shaped the government's creation of identities as the government tried to mold the population. By successfully co-opting those people who most fervently embraced loyal identities, and by employing coercion, both Nazi Germany and the Soviet Union pursued their political and social goals at great human cost. The culture of the Soviet Union in the 1930s enables us to understand the variety of ways in which popular culture and cultural representations both supported and undermined dominant ideologies and shaped the formation of social identities and the nature of political action in the twentieth century.

ABBREVIATIONS

CD: Aryeh L. Unger, *Constitutional Developments in the U.S.S.R.: A Guide to the Soviet Constitutions*

ES: S. S. Bazykin and E. A. Flerina, eds., *Elka: Sbornik statei i materialov*

I: *Izvestiia*

IT: V. Garros, N. Korenevskaya, and T. Lahusen, eds., *Intimacy and Terror: Soviet Diaries of the 1930s*

Komsomol: Communist Youth League

LI: Ivan Papanin, *Life on an Ice Floe*

Narkomfin: People's Commissariat of Finance

Narkompros: People's Commissariat of Enlightenment

NKVD: People's Commissariat of Internal Affairs

OT: Lazar Brontman, *On Top of the World: The Soviet Expedition to the North Pole 1937–1938*

P: *Pravda*

Politbiuro: Political Bureau of the Central Committee of the Communist Party

RA: John McCannon, *Red Arctic: Polar Exploration and the Myth of the North in Soviet Russia, 1932–1939*

RAPP: Russian Association of Proletarian Writers

RD: Richard Stites, *Revolutionary Dreams: Utopian Visions and Experimental Life in the Russian Revolution*

RM: G. D. Kremlev, *Rabochii material dlia organizatsii Novogodnego bala-maskarada v zheleznodorozhnykh klubakh i dvortsakh kul'tury*

RR: Christel Lane, *The Rites of Rulers: Ritual in Industrial Society—The Soviet Case*

RSFSR: Russian Soviet Federated Socialist Republic

SN: Katerina Clark, *The Soviet Novel: History as Ritual*

Sovnarkom: Council of People's Commissars

VC: *Voyage of the Cheliuskin*

NOTES

1. Interpreting Soviet Celebrations

1. Christopher A. P. Binns, "The Changing Face of Power: Revolution and Accommodation in the Development of the Soviet Ceremonial System, Part I," *Man* (New Series) 14, no. 4 (December 1979): 602.

2. Robert Conquest, *The Great Terror: A Reassessment* (New York: Oxford University Press, 1990); Mikhail Heller, and Alexander Nekrich, *Utopia in Power: The History of the Soviet Union from 1917 to the Present* (New York: Summit Books, 1986).

3. This very useful concept was coined as "speaking Bolshevik" by Stephen Kotkin in *Magnetic Mountain: Stalinism as a Civilization* (Berkeley: University of California Press, 1995), 198–237.

4. See for example, V. A. Kumanev, *30-e gody v sud'bakh otechestvennoi intelligentsii* (Moscow: Nauka, 1991), 125–126.

5. Peter Kenez, *The Birth of the Propaganda State: Soviet Methods of Mass Mobilization 1917–1929* (Cambridge: Cambridge University Press, 1985), 133.

6. Ibid., 180.

7. Ibid., 253.

8. *Kulak* originally denoted a prosperous peasant; in Soviet practice, any peasant who was defined as an enemy of the state was called a *kulak*.

9. Jochen Hellbeck, "Fashioning the Stalinist Soul: The Diary of Stepan Podlubnyi (1931–1939)," *Jahrbücher für Geschichte Osteuropas* 44, no. 3 (1996): 372.

10. There is an extensive literature on the interpretation of celebrations and rituals in Russia and elsewhere. See especially *RR*; Mona Ozouf, *Festivals of the French Revolution*, translated by Alan Sheridan (Cambridge, Mass.: Harvard University Press, 1988); Richard Wortman, *Scenarios of Power: Myth and Ceremony in Russian Monarchy*, vol. 1 (Princeton, N.J.: Princeton University Press, 1995); James von Geldern, *Bolshevik Festivals 1917–1920* (Berkeley: University of California Press, 1993); Nina Tumarkin, *Lenin Lives: The Lenin Cult in Soviet Russia* (Cambridge, Mass.: Harvard University Press, 1983).

11. B. Meilakh, "Nasledie Pushkina i sotsialisticheskaia kul'tura," *Krasnaia nov'* 1 (January 1937): 112.

12. E. Cherniavskii, "Aleksandr Sergeevich Pushkin," *Krasnyi arkhiv* 1 (1937): 7.

13. Hellbeck, "Fashioning the Stalinist Soul," 372.

14. Sheila Fitzpatrick, *Stalin's Peasants: Resistance and Survival in the Russian Village after Collectivization* (New York: Oxford University Press, 1994); David L. Hoffmann, *Peasant Metropolis: Social Identities in Moscow, 1929–1941* (Ithaca, N.Y.: Cornell University Press, 1994); Kotkin, *Magnetic Mountain;* Sarah Davies, *Popular Opinion in Stalin's Russia: Terror, Propaganda and Dissent, 1934–1941* (Cambridge: Cambridge University Press, 1997).

15. See J. Arch Getty, *The Origins of the Great Purges: The Soviet Communist Party Reconsidered, 1933–37* (Cambridge: Cambridge University Press, 1985); Gabor Rittersporn, *Stalinist Simplifications and Soviet Complications: Social Tensions and Political Conflicts in the USSR, 1933–1953* (Chur, Switzerland: Hardwood Academic Press, 1991); O. V. Khlevniuk, *1937-i: Stalin, NKVD, i sovetskoe obshchestvo* (Moscow: Respublika, 1992).

16. These changes were first identified by Nicholas S. Timasheff in *The Great Retreat: The Growth and Decline of Communism in Russia* (New York: E. P. Dutton,

1946). Celebrations of the 1930s are a manifestation of what Vladimir Papernyi calls *kul'tura "dva"* in contrast to pre-1932 Soviet culture. (Vladimir Papernyi, *Kul'tura "dva"* [Ann Arbor, Mich.: Ardis, 1985].)

17. Moshe Lewin, "The Social Background of Stalinism," in *The Making of the Soviet System: Essays in the Social History of Interwar Russia* (New York: Pantheon Books, 1985), 265.

18. Vera S. Dunham, *In Stalin's Time: Middleclass Values in Soviet Fiction* (Cambridge: Cambridge University Press, 1976); Sheila Fitzpatrick, *The Cultural Front: Power and Culture in Revolutionary Russia* (Ithaca, N.Y.: Cornell University Press, 1992), see especially 149–182 and 216–237.

19. For a discussion of the status of elite consumers, see Elena Osokina, *Za fasadom "Stalinskogo izobiliia": Raspredelenie i rynok v snabzhenii naseleniia v gody industrializatsii 1927–1941* (Moscow: Rosspen, 1998), especially 99–113, 189–194.

20. I. V. Stalin, "Rech na I vsesoiuznom soveshchanii Stakhanovtsev," in *Sochineniia* 1 [XIV] 1934–40, edited by Robert H. McNeal (Stanford, Calif.: Hoover Institution, 1967), 89. Named after miner Aleksei Stakhanov, who hewed 102 tons of coal on one shift, more than fourteen times his daily quota, Stakhanovites were exemplary workers who received rewards from the state in exchange for over-fulfilling their work norms. See Lewis H. Siegelbaum, *Stakhanovism and the Politics of Productivity in the U.S.S.R, 1935–41* (Cambridge: Cambridge University Press, 1988).

21. See *SN*, 3–24.

22. See Mark Bassin, "The Greening of Utopia: Nature and Landscape Aesthetics in Stalinist Art," in James Cracraft and Daniel B. Rowland, eds., *Identities of Russian Architecture, 1500–Present*, forthcoming; Lars Erik Blomqvist, "Some Utopian Elements in Stalinist Art," *Russian History/Histoire Russe* 11, no. 2–3 (Summer–Fall 1984): 298–305.

23. RTsKhIDNI, f. 17, op. 114, d. 726, l. 17.

24. "Diary of Ignat Danilovich Frolov," in *IT*, 14, 19, 48, 153.

25. RTsKhIDNI, f. 17, op. 120, d. 236, l. 10.

26. Michel Foucault, *Discipline and Punish: The Birth of the Prison* (New York: Vintage Books, 1979); and "The Discourse on Language," in *The Archaeology of Knowledge*, translated by A. M. Sheridan Smith (New York: Pantheon Books, 1972).

27. This idea borrows from Anthony Giddens's notion of "duality of structure" in which "structure is both the medium and the outcome of the practices which constitute social systems." Anthony Giddens, *A Contemporary Critique of Historical Materialism*, vol. 1 (Berkeley: University of California Press, 1981), 27.

28. For a discussion of using Foucault in the Russian and Soviet context, see Laura Engelstein, "Combined Underdevelopment: Discipline and the Law in Imperial and Soviet Russia," *American Historical Review* 98, no. 2 (1993): 338–353.

29. Typical types of "hidden transcript" resistance are gossip, rumors, and millenarian myths. James C. Scott, *Domination and the Arts of Resistance: Hidden Transcripts* (New Haven, Conn.: Yale University Press, 1990); See also James C. Scott, *Weapons of the Weak: Everyday Forms of Peasant Resistance* (New Haven, Conn.: Yale University Press, 1985).

30. James C. Scott, *Domination*, 54.

31. Frederick Cooper and Ann Laura Stoler, introduction to *Tensions of Empire: Colonial Cultures in a Bourgeois World* (Berkeley: University of California Press, 1997), 21.

32. Resistance to extremely repressive regimes through such "weapons of the weak" has been extensively analyzed by James C. Scott in *Weapons of the Weak*. See also, Alf Lüdtke, "The Historiography of Everyday Life: The Personal and the Political," in *Culture, Ideology and Politics: Essays for Eric Hobsbawm*, History Workshop Series (London: Routledge & Kegan Paul, 1982), 38–54.

33. M. M. Bakhtin, *Rabelais and His World*, translated by Helen Iswolsky (Cambridge, Mass.: MIT Press, 1968), 9, 197–199, 271.

34. In the village of Stromyne, Moscow Region, for example, during the celebration of Harvest Day in 1935, "many collective farmers got drunk and some got into fights" (TsGAMO, f. 5849, op. 1, d. 100, l. 34).

35. See Joan Scott, *Gender and the Politics of History* (New York: Columbia University Press, 1988), for an example of this methodology.

36. For a discussion of state policies on women and the family see Wendy Z. Goldman, "Women, Abortion, and the State, 1917–36," in *Russia's Women: Accommodation, Resistance, Transformation*, edited by Barbara Evans Clements, Barbara Alpern Engel, and Christine D. Worobec (Berkeley: University of California Press, 1991), 243–266.

37. For a discussion of *korenizatsiia* and its limits, see Hélène Carrère d'Encausse, *The Great Challenge: Nationalities and the Bolshevik State 1917–1930*, translated by Nancy Festinger (New York: Holmes & Meier, 1992), 153–155 and 189–191; Gerhart Simon, *Nationalism and Policy toward the Nationalities in the Soviet Union*, translated by Karen Forster and Oswald Forster (Boulder, Colo.: Westview Press, 1991), 20–25.

38. Simon, *Nationalism and Policy*, 158.

39. Here my argument differs from that of Yuri Slezkine in "The USSR as a Communal Apartment, or How a Socialist State Promoted Ethnic Particularism," *Slavic Review* 53, no. 2 (Summer 1994): 442–444.

40. Benedict Anderson's influential argument that the concept of the modern nation was spread by the dissemination of print media across a geographic space bounded by language is relevant here. Benedict Anderson, *Imagined Communities: Reflections on the Origin and Spread of Nationalism*, rev. ed. (London: Verso, 1991).

41. RTsKhIDNI, f. 475, op. 2, d. 790, l. 6.

42. See Eric Hobsbawm, "Introduction: Inventing Traditions," in *The Invention of Tradition*, edited by Eric Hobsbawm and Terence Ranger (Cambridge: Cambridge University Press, 1983).

43. For a discussion of Soviet attempts to acquire culture, see Dunham, *In Stalin's Time*, 22–23.

44. See Hubertus F. Jahn, *Patriotic Culture in Russia during World War I* (Ithaca, N.Y.: Cornell University Press, 1995); Richard Stites, *Russian Popular Culture: Entertainment and Society since 1900* (New York: Cambridge University Press, 1992).

45. Von Geldern, *Bolshevik Festivals*, 2–3; *RR*, 154. See also I .M. Bibikova and N. I Levchenko, comps., *Agitatsionno-massovoe iskusstvo: Oformlenie prazdnestv* (Moscow: Iskusstvo, 1984); and Katerina Clark, *Petersburg: Crucible of Cultural Revolution* (Cambridge, Mass.: Harvard University Press, 1995), 100–142.

46. Von Geldern, *Bolshevik Festivals*, 12.

47. Ibid., 213–218. Many of the spectacles of the 1920s took the form of show trials. See Julie A. Cassiday, "Marble Columns and Jupiter Lights: Theatrical and Cinematic Modeling of Soviet Show Trials in the 1920s," *Slavic and East European Journal* 42, no. 4 (1998): 640–660.

48. Choitali Chatterjee, "Celebrating Women: International Women's Day in Russia and the Soviet Union, 1909–1939" (Ph.D. diss., Indiana University, 1995).

49. *RD,* 228; *RR,* 179–80. Other scholars have come to the same conclusion: See A. I. Mazaev, *Prazdnik kak sotsial'noe khudozhestvennoe iavlenie* (Moscow: Nauka, 1978), 366–370; Rosalinde Sartorti, "Stalinism and Carnival: Organization and Aesthetics of Political Holidays," in *The Culture of the Stalin Period*, edited by Hans Günther (Houndmills: Macmillan, 1990), 57–68; Alexander Zakharov, "Mass Celebrations in a Totalitarian System," in *Tekstura: Russian Essays on Visual Culture*, edited by Alla Efimova and Lev Manovich (Chicago: University of Chicago Press, 1993), 210, 214.

50. *RR,* 174.

51. These holidays replaced dates such as the anniversaries of Bloody Sunday and the February Revolution that fell out of the Soviet holiday calendar (*RR*, 154).

52. *Nashi prazdniki* (Moscow: Politizdat, 1977), 161–164; and Binns, "The Changing Face of Power," 602.

53. Following Richard Stites, I argue that the mass culture of the 1930s, "a culture constructed, promoted, and even financed by the state," resonated with the public and was appropriated by Soviet citizens despite tight political control. This culture was consumed and reinterpreted by peasants, workers, employees, and the Soviet elite, and can, therefore, be called popular (Stites, *Russian Popular Culture*, p. 5). See also Régine Robin, "Stalinism and Popular Culture," in Günther, *Culture of the Stalin Period*, 15–40.

54. For a discussion of rationing and consumption in the 1930s, see Osokina, *Za fasadom "Stalinskogo izobiliia"*; Sheila Fitzpatrick, *Everyday Stalinism: Ordinary Life in Extraordinary Times — Soviet Russia in the 1930s* (New York: Oxford University Press, 1999), especially 40–66.

55. For an overview of Russian and Soviet peasant life, see Fitzpatrick, *Stalin's Peasants*; Moshe Lewin, *Russian Peasants and Soviet Power* (New York: W. W. Norton, 1968); and "Rural Society in Twentieth Century Russia," in *The Making of the Soviet System*.

56. For a detailed discussion of peasant holidays, see Mary Matossian, "The Peasant Way of Life," in *The Peasant in Nineteenth-Century Russia*, edited by Wayne S. Vucinich (Stanford, Calif.: Stanford University Press, 1968), 31–39; Linda J. Ivanits, *Russian Folk Belief* (Armonk, N.Y.: M. E. Sharpe, 1989), 5–12, 33–35; V. Ia. Propp, *Russkie agrarnye prazdniki* (Leningrad: LGU, 1963), especially 25–26.

57. RTsKhIDNI, f. 17, op. 3, d. 994, l. 60.

58. Andrew Smith, *I Was a Soviet Worker* (New York: Dutton, 1936), 128.

59. H. G. Friese, "Student Life in a Soviet University," in *Soviet Education*, edited by George Kline (New York: Columbia University Press, 1957), 62.

60. Peter Francis, *I Worked in a Soviet Factory* (London: Jarrolds, 1939), 77.

61. See Alexander Werth, *Russia at War: 1941–45* (New York: Avon Books, 1964), 857–59; Mark von Hagen, "Soviet Soldiers and Officers on the Eve of the German Invasion: Toward a Description of Social Psychology and Political Attitudes," *Soviet Union/Union Sovietique* 18, no. 1–3 (1991): 99.

62. RTsKhIDNI, f. 17, op. 3, d. 992, ll. 103, 173. Enterprises with more than 10,000 workers, for example, were not allowed to spend more than 30,000 rubles. Enterprises with less than 1,500 workers were not allowed to spend more than 5,000 rubles. Before May 1, 1938, these admonitions were repeated, but the largest enterprises were then allowed to spend no more than 20,000 rubles. RTsKhIDNI, f. 17, op. 3, d. 998, l. 35.

63. Fitzpatrick, *Stalin's Peasants*, 7.

64. TsAODM, f. 85, op. 1, d. 1207, l. 14.

65. RTsKhIDNI, f. 17, op. 120, d. 200, l. 101. The latter song is "Marusia otravilas'."

66. TsKhDMO, f. 1, op. 3, d. 167, ll. 96–97.

67. Frolov, in *IT*, 42–3.

68. "Diary of Andrei Stepanovich Arzhilovsky," in *IT*, 120.

2. Parading the Nation

1. *P*, July 13, 1937.

2. Mazaev, *Prazdnik*, 366–370.

3. *RR*, 224, 227.

4. Shortly after the ratification of the Stalin Constitution, for example, priests organized processions and demonstrations to demand the opening of churches. RTsKhIDNI, f. 17, op. 120, d. 256, l. 37.

5. *RD*, 21–22, 247.

6. *RR*, 156. As Mona Ozouf has described in her influential work on the French Revolution, the new French ceremonies recast both time and space as a way of destroying the old order and legitimating the revolutionary order. James von Geldern argues that during the Civil War years, Soviet festivals redefined the centers of power and legitimated the Soviet foundation myth of the revolution. Ozouf, *Festivals and the French Revolution*, 126–196; von Geldern, *Bolshevik Festivals*, 175–207.

7. Quoted in *RD*, 243.

8. For a discussion of Moscow as "political center" in the pre-revolutionary period, see Richard Wortman, "Moscow and Petersburg: The Problem of Political Center in Tsarist Russia, 1881–1914," in *Rites of Power: Symbolism, Ritual, and Politics since the Middle Ages*, edited by Sean Wilentz (Philadelphia: University of Pennsylvania Press, 1985), 244–274. For a detailed discussion of the embalming of Lenin, see Tumarkin, *Lenin Lives*.

9. In the Soviet folklore of this period, Stalin's all-seeing eyes observed the entire country. See, for example, M. S. Kriukova's "Glory to Stalin Shall Be Eternal," translated in *Folklore for Stalin* by Frank Miller (Armonk, N.Y.: M. E. Sharpe, 1990), 162–163: "[Stalin] looks and looks but can't get enough. / He listens to everything with his keen ear. / He sees everything with his keen gaze. / He hears and sees how the people live, / How the people live, how they work. / He rewards everyone for good work."

10. *Fizkul'tura i sport* 15/16 (1939).

11. Physical Culture parades were usually repeated in Dinamo Stadium for a larger audience. TsAODM, f. 4, op. 7, d. 88, ll. 80–81; GARF, f. 5446, op. 20, d. 2657, l. 22a.

12. *Vsesoiuznyi parad fizkul'turnikov: Ukazaniia po stroevoi podgotovke uchastnikov vsesoiuznogo parada fizkul'turnikov 1939 g.* (Moscow, 1939), 6, located in GARF, f. 7576, op. 10, d. 1, ll. 2–2g.

13. *Fizkul'tura i sport* 15/16 (1939).

14. Ibid.

15. Z. Aleksandrova, "Na parade," *Murzilka* 1 (January 1937): 11.

16. Oleg Krasovsky, "Early Years," in *Soviet Youth*, Institute for the Study of the USSR, Series I, 51 (July 1959), 130–131.

17. Alexei Gorchakov, "The Long Road," in *Thirteen Who Fled*, edited by Louis Fischer (New York: Harper and Brothers, 1949), 63.

18. In the November 7, 1936, parade in the Electrosteel Settlement in Moscow Region, for example, the air-chemical defense brigade of the Electrosteel factory preceded the other factory workers, who marched before the local collective farmers. TsGAMO, f. 5849, op. 1, d. 489, ll. 9–10.

19. *Vsesoiuznyi parad fizkul'turnikov*, 6.

20. The parade thus continued the work of industrial efficiency experts in the 1920s who advocated both Taylorist methods of labor organization and the "cult of the machine" as an antidote to the backwardness of "peasant body culture" (*RD*, 164).

21. This phrase comes from Mary Ryan's description of American parades in the nineteenth century. Mary Ryan, "The American Parade: Representations of the Nineteenth-Century Social Order," in *The New Cultural History*, edited by Lynn Hunt (Berkeley: University of California Press, 1989), 153.

22. *Vsesoiuznyi parad fizkul'turnikov*, 6.

23. See Katerina Clark's discussion of Bolshevik discipline in *SN* and Jochen Hellbeck's discussion of purification in "Fashioning the Stalinist Soul," 361. My attention to the construction of Soviet modes of disciplining the body is, of course, inspired by Michel Foucault, whose *Discipline and Punish* discusses how modern forms of power subject individual bodies to discipline with the aim of creating "the

perfection of power" in which the subject "assumes responsibility for the constraints of power" (Foucault, *Discipline and Punish*, 201–202).

24. TsAODM, f. 432, op. 1, d. 165, l. 168; d. 178, l. 229; d. 180, ll. 115, 154–157; f. 67, op. 1, d. 1185, l. 4.

25. TsAODM, f. 432, op. 1, d. 178, l. 15.

26. TsAODM, f. 432, op. 1, d. 180, l. 155.

27. *Fizkul'tura i sport v SSSR: Materialy k vsesoiuznomu dniu fizkul'turnika 1939 god* (Moscow: Gos. izdatel'stvo fizkul'tury i sporta, 1939), 27. After 1947, the annual physical culture parade no longer took place in Red Square, but was moved to Dinamo Stadium (Robert Edelman, *Serious Fun: A History of Spectator Sport in the USSR* [New York: Oxford University Press, 1993], 122). See James Riordan, *Sport in Soviet Society* (Cambridge: Cambridge University Press, 1977), for a discussion of the changes in Soviet sports ideology from the 1920s to the 1930s. For the relationship of the parade to the physical culture movement as a whole see Edelman, *Serious Fun*, 41–44.

28. TsGAMO, f. 2180, op. 1, d. 930, l. 11.

29. There were 120,000 marchers in 1934, 80,000–100,000 in 1936, and 35,000–40,000 in 1937. Some sports clubs dealt with the excess demand to be included in the parade by sending more participants than they were allowed. *Fizkul'tura i sport v SSSR*, 27; GARF, f. 5446, op. 20, d. 2657, l. 10; TsAODM, f. 1, op. 23, d. 1435, l. 149.

30. *P*, July 13, 1937.

31. TsGAMO, f. 2180, op. 1, d. 930, l. 20.

32. Ibid., l. 11.

33. Ibid., l. 22.

34. Ibid., l. 2.

35. *Fizkul'tura i sport* 13 (1936).

36. Friedrich Jahn founded a gymnastics club to foster German national identity in 1811, in response to Napoleon's occupation of Prussia. Prussian gymnastics associations were suppressed in 1820, but after 1848 their membership grew rapidly and similar clubs were founded all over Europe, including in Bohemia and Russia. The similarity in the development of gymnastics in the two countries was also fostered by the many cultural ties between German Communist sports clubs and the Soviet physical culture movement during the 1920s. George L. Mosse, *The Nationalization of the Masses* (Ithaca, N.Y.: Cornell University Press, 1991), 28, 129–130; *Fizkul'tura i sport* 34 (1930).

37. Hans Günther, "Geroi v totalitarnoi kul'ture," in *Agitatsiia za schast'e: Sovetskoe iskusstvo stalinskoi epokhi*, Gosudarstvennyi Russkii Muzei, Sankt-Peterburg (Dusseldorf-Bremen: Interarteks-Temmen Edition, 1994), 74–75.

38. Lane claims that sexual symbolism was absent from body movement displays, and Edelman argues that "descriptions of parades avoided making naked bodies an expression of otherwise repressed eroticism." *RR*, 224; Edelman, *Serious Fun*, 43.

39. The absence of sexuality in 1930s public discourse stands in marked contrast to the 1920s, when, as Eric Naiman has shown, debates over sexuality were used to attract youth to the Komsomol and Party. Eric Naiman, *Sex in Public: The Incarnation of Early Soviet Ideology* (Princeton, N.J.: Princeton University Press, 1997), 101–103.

40. Hubertus Gassner and Eckhart Gillen, "Ot sozdaniia utopicheskogo poriadka k ideologii umirotvoreniia v svete esteticheskoi deistvitel'nosti," in *Agitatsiia za schast'e*, 42.

41. Gassner and Gillen, "Ot sozdaniia utopicheskogo poriadka k ideologii umirotvoreniia," 37; Victoria Bonnell, *Iconography of Power: Soviet Political Posters under Lenin and Stalin* (Berkeley: University of California Press, 1997), 122.

42. Naiman, *Sex in Public*, 208–249.

43. One physical culture participant, for example, mentioned that he enjoyed watching "our contemporary, healthy, blossoming girls dancing" in the 1934 parade. RGALI, f. 2451, op. 1, d. 9a, ll. 33–34.

44. George L. Mosse, *Nationalism and Sexuality* (New York: Howard Fertig, 1985), 80.

45. Quoted in Naiman, *Sex in Public*, 142.

46. Dorinda Outram argues that the charismatic mass politics and physical violence against opponents characteristic of the 1930s originated in the transfer of sovereignty from the "King's Body" to masculinized and self-controlled individual bodies during the French Revolution. While the Soviet case suggests that violence can occur even when the symbolic public sphere explicitly includes female bodies, her argument that "the body is the only space in which intentionality can be restored to the historical subject," is pertinent to my discussion of the individual meanings generated in the parade (Dorinda Outram, *The Body and the French Revolution* [New Haven, Conn.: Yale University Press, 1989], 5). For an example of how the experience of the body can generate transformations in political discourse, see Kathleen Canning, "Feminist History after the Linguistic Turn: Historicizing Discourse and Experience," *Signs* 19, no. 2 (Winter 1994): 368–404.

47. When groups of Russian nudists marched naked after the revolution, carrying signs that read "Down with shame," the outraged population threw rotten eggs, tomatoes, and garbage at them, and the police arrested them. Valentina Bogdan, *Mimikriia v SSSR* (Frankfurt a.M.: Polyglott-Druck GmbH, n.d.), 76; *RD*, 133.

48. At least one Soviet etymologist has suggested that the Russian word for tank top, *maika*, might derive from the word *mai* (May) and, therefore, might be connected to May Day celebrations. O. N. Trubachev, "Ob etimologicheskom slovare russkogo iazyka," *Voprosy iazykoznaniia* 3 (1960): 64.

49. GARF, f. 2306, op. 70, d. 512a, l. 70 (1937).

50. The responses of Muslim males to unveiling campaigns in the late 1920s included beatings, rape, and even murder of the unveiled women. See Gregory Massell, *The Surrogate Proletariat: Moslem Women and Revolutionary Strategies in Soviet Central Asia, 1919–1929* (Princeton, N.J.: Princeton University Press, 1974), 265–266, 281, 354.

51. David Welch, *The Third Reich: Politics and Propaganda* (London: Routledge, 1993), 67–68.

52. Central Asian women wore their hair in dozens of small braids. *Fizkul'tura i sport* 15 (1937).

53. TsKhDMO, f. 1, op. 23, d. 1435, l. 129.

54. On the other hand, one participant in physical culture parades who I interviewed suggested that in the selection of athletes in the Russian republic, Slavs were privileged over Jews. Interview with R. Sh. Ganelin, St. Petersburg, Russia (November 1991).

55. *P*, July 13, 1937.

56. *CD*, 141.

57. The price of this trip to the capital was paid out of the individual republican budgets rather than the Soviet budget. GARF, f. 5446, op. 20, d. 2657, l. 25.

58. *Komsomol'skaia pravda—na stroitel'stve VSKhV*, July 18, 1939.

59. TsKhDMO, f. 1, op. 23, d. 1435, ll. 28, 45–46.

60. GARF, f. 7576, op. 10, d. 1, l. 100.

61. *P*, July 19, 1939.

62. In 1937, for example, Moscow composers were commissioned to write "national" music for various republics. RGALI, f. 962, op. 5, d. 74, ll. 22–37.

63. *Tsvetuiushchaia iunost'*, documentary film (1939).

64. Simon, *Nationalism and Policy,* 104–106.

65. GARF, f. 7576, op. 10, d. 1, l. 65 ob.

66. This theme coincided with the 1939 celebration of the thousandth anniversary of the epic poem *David of Sasun,* even though this date was only an approximate one. *David of Sassoun,* translated by Artin K. Shalian (Athens: Ohio University Press, 1964), xx. Interestingly, one of the major themes of this epic was the heroic refusal of the Armenian people to pay tribute to their Arab rulers. This theme might well have provided an opportunity for Aesopian commentary on Armenia's relationship with the Soviet government.

67. GARF, f. 7576, op. 10, d. 1, l. 69.

68. TsKhDMO, f. 1, op. 23, d. 1364, ll. 20–22.

69. In 1940, the column of the Russian delegation included representatives from the autonomous republics of the R.S.F.S.R. for the first time. TsKhDMO, f. 1, op. 23, d. 1435, l. 26.

70. Recent work by architectural historian Greg Castillo suggests that the construction of national images in physical culture parades paralleled the architectural definitions of nationality being created at the same time at the All-Union Agricultural Exhibition (VSKhV) in Moscow. The exhibition had pavilions for the ten non-Russian republics but not for Russia; the interior of the Uzbek Pavilion was decorated with cotton plants and grapevines; the Bashkir Pavilion had a mural depicting a harvest festival. Greg Castillo, "Peoples at an Exhibition: Soviet Architecture and the National Question," *The South Atlantic Quarterly* 94, no. 3 (Summer 1995): 728, 731, 733. See also Jamey Gambrell, "The Wonder of the Soviet World," *New York Review of Books* (December 22, 1994): 30–35.

71. *P,* July 19, 1939.

72. GARF, f. 7576, op. 10, d. 3, l. 232 ob.

73. In 1937, while Narkomfin tried to limit the amount of time delegations spent in Moscow for budgetary reasons, officials from the Committee on Physical Culture and Sport pressed for longer stays for republican delegations. GARF, f. 5446, op. 20, d. 2657, ll. 22a–b.

74. The documentary film *Tsvetuiushaia iunost'* and the album of photographs *A Pageant of Youth* (Moscow and Leningrad: State Art Publishers, 1939) are the best examples of this phenomenon.

75. GARF, f. 7576, op. 10, d. 3, ll. 196–200.

76. TsAODM, f. 69, op. 1, d. 1160, l. 16.

77. TsAODM, f. 69, op. 1, d. 1063, l. 8.

78. Ibid., l. 8.

79. Ibid., l. 5.

80. See Hoffmann, *Peasant Metropolis,* for a discussion of the ways in which peasant culture influenced Soviet policies in the city of Moscow.

81. TsKhDMO, f. 1, op. 23, d. 1363, l. 1.

82. Bogdan, *Mimikriia v SSSR,* 179–80.

83. TsAODM, f. 85, op. 1, d. 1207, l. 17 (1937).

84. TsAODM, f. 369, op. 1, d. 174, l. 167 (1937).

85. TsAODM, f. 74, op. 1, d. 1, l. 17 (1936).

86. TsAODM, f. 432, op. 1, d. 178, l. 86 (1937).

87. GARF, f. 5451, op. 20, d. 191, ll. 155–57 (1936).

88. TsAODM, f. 432, op. 1, d. 165, l. 49 (1936); d. 179, l. 108 (1937); d. 191a, l. 91(1938); d. 178, ll. 75–6 (1937).

89. TsAODM, f. 85, op. 1, d. 1207, l. 14.

90. TsKhDMO, f. 1, op. 23, d. 1435, l. 144.

91. Ibid.

92. TsAODM, f. 432, op. 1, d. 180, l. 171(1937).

93. TsAODM, f. 73, op. 1, d. 17, l. 19 (1936).

94. For a discussion of subversive wordplay, see Fitzpatrick, *Everyday Stalinism,* 184.

95. GARF, f. 5451, op. 18, d. 554, l. 10.

96. Other officials defended the announcer, claiming that his remarks were taken out of context. RTsKhIDNI, f. 17, op. 114, d. 761, l. 27.

97. TsAODM, f. 67, op. 1, d. 1338, l. 9.

98. TsAODM, f. 73, op. 1, d. 17, l. 19.

99. Ibid., l. 20.

100. Friese, "Student Life in a Soviet University," 61– 62.

3. Imagining the Motherland

1. See Georgii Baidukov, *Russian Lindbergh: The Life of Valery Chkalov* (Washington, D.C.: Smithsonian Institution Press, 1991).

2. See, for example, Peter Fritzsche, *A Nation of Fliers: German Aviation and the Popular Imagination* (Cambridge, Mass.: Harvard University Press, 1992), 3–4, 30–35; Scott W. Palmer, "On Wings of Courage: Public 'Air-Mindedness' and National Identity in Late Imperial Russia," *The Russian Review* 54 (April 1995): 219–221.

3. See *RA* for an account of the political struggles for control of the Arctic and the men behind the polar and aviation myths; Kendall Bailes argues that the Soviet Union's use of aviation exploits to foster legitimacy hampered the development of air defenses and ultimately weakened the Soviet war effort. Kendall E. Bailes, *Technology and Society under Lenin and Stalin* (Princeton, N.J.: Princeton University Press, 1978), 381.

4. Anderson, *Imagined Communities.*

5. In the 1930s, the Soviet government used aviation and polar achievements to define the Soviet Union's place in the world and increase its international prestige as well as to promote legitimacy at home. My work focuses, however, only on the ways in which aviation and polar celebration defined the Soviet Union for a domestic audience. The decision of the Council of People's Commissars to send hero pilots Chkalov, Baidukov, Beliakov, the documentary films *The Mastery of the Arctic* and *The Conquest of the Pole,* and a copy of polar explorer Papanin's tent to the Paris International Exhibition of 1937 indicated the centrality of polar and aviation feats to the image that the Soviet Union wanted to project abroad. Promoters of Soviet aviation claimed that the Soviet Union was different from capitalist countries because of its superior scientific abilities and its desire to use aviation only for peaceful purposes. GARF, f. 9499, op. 1, d. 1, ll. 1–7; RTsKhIDNI, f. 17, op. 3, d. 989, l. 26.

6. See Joan Scott, "Gender: A Useful Category of Historical Analysis," in *Gender and Politics,* 28–50.

7. See, for example, Robert Conquest, *The Great Terror,* 236, 238; GARF, f. 9499, op. 1, d. 5, ll. 13–14.

8. See *RA,* 59–80.

9. For pre-revolutionary versions of this myth during the reigns of Catherine II and Alexander II, see Wortman, *Scenarios of Power,* 139–142, 364–367.

10. Kuibyshev, the head of the government commission to save the Cheliuskinians, became furious with Bukharin when *Izvestiia* published the dispatches of a reporter who had flown to the Arctic without Kuibyshev's permission. The Politbiuro issued explicit instructions about the publication of books relating to the Cheliuskin expedition, detailing whose stories and which episodes should be included. RTsKhIDNI, f. 79, op. 1, d. 725, ll. 3–7; f. 17, op. 3, d. 947, ll. 31–32.

11. Ivan Papanin, *Zhizn' na l'dine: Dnevnik* (Moscow: Pravda, 1938). All page numbers refer to the English edition, *LI,* 165.

12. Dziga Vertov, *Tri geroiny,* RGAKFD, 1-4188, 1938.

13. RGALI, f. 617, op. 1, d. 10, l. 14.

14. See Jeffrey Brooks, *When Russia Learned to Read: Literacy and Popular Literature, 1861–1917* (Princeton, N.J.: Princeton University Press, 1985), 130–153, for a discussion of installment novels. One might also note the extreme popularity of western television soap operas in contemporary Russia and the Commonwealth of Independent States.

15. RTsKhIDNI, f. 475, op. 2, d. 764, l. 9.

16. M. Troianovskii and A. Shafran filmed the sinking of the *Cheliuskin* and life on "Camp Shmidt." Troianovskii documented the North Pole expedition in 1937. See also *Radostnaia vstrecha*, RGAKFD, 1–4187, 1937.

17. For the scenarios of Vertov's newsreels about the heroine pilots see RGALI, f. 2091, op. 2, d. 70, 71, 72, 73; See also Vertov, *Tri geroiny.*

18. *Soiuzkinozhurnal* 11 (April 1935), RGAKFD, 1-2525.

19. *LI*, 171–172, 219.

20. The relationships between the explorers and their wives were thus defined as public rather than private.

21. *I*, October 28, 1938.

22. As of September 22, 1937, 90 percent of all village projectors were not equipped to show sound films. During the summer of 1937, not a single mobile film projection unit in the Republic of Belorussia was in operation because of a shortage of fuel. GARF, f. 5446, op. 20, d. 2567, ll. 42, 120.

23. The figure of forty to fifty radios in Russian cities is my estimate, based on the figures for urban and rural radios in the Second Five Year Plan. In 1937, the United States had 177 radio sets per thousand inhabitants. GARF, f. 5446, op. 20, d. 2638, ll. 125–126.

24. RTsKhIDNI, f. 17, op. 3, d. 755, l. 59.

25. *Everyday Life in Russia*, compiled by Bertha Malnick (London: George G. Harrap, 1938), 77.

26. Mikhail Alekseev, *Kariukha; Drachuny; Dilogiia* (Moscow, 1985), 282–283.

27. RGALI, f. 617, op. 1, d. 10, l. 1.

28. Ibid., ll. 5–6.

29. Arzhilovsky, in *IT*, 161–162. These words were underlined by NKVD agents when the diary was confiscated. For other negative responses to the Arctic myth, see *RA*, 140–143.

Heroic aviators did receive substantial rewards from the Party and the state: In November 1936, for example, the Moscow Party Committee gave pilots Chkalov and Levanevskii four-room apartments in Moscow and Beliakov a three-room apartment. TsAODM, f. 4, op. 7, d. 14, ll. 309–311.

30. Although the word "fatherland" (*otechestvo*) was also commonly used to describe the Soviet Union throughout this period, it was never symbolically depicted or embodied in the way that motherland was.

31. James von Geldern, "The Centre and the Periphery: Cultural and Social Geography in the Mass Culture of the 1930s," in *New Directions in Soviet History*, edited by Stephen White (Cambridge: Cambridge University Press, 1992), 77.

32. See *SN*, 114–134.

33. *P*, July 13, 1937.

34. *I*, October 27, 1938.

35. Isaac Dunaevskii and V. Lebedev-Kumach, "Pesnia o rodine," in *Pesni Krasnoi Armii* (Moscow, 1937), 13. First stanza translated by von Geldern, "The Centre and the Periphery," 65.

36. Von Geldern, "The Centre and the Periphery," 65–66.

37. In the climactic scene in *Circus*, a multi-ethnic circus audience sings a lullaby in the many languages of the Soviet Union, representing the unity of the motherland.

38. Sergei Semenov, "What the Communists Did," in *Pokhod Cheliuskina* (Moscow, 1934). All page numbers refer to the English edition, *VC*, 170.

39. Lazar Brontman and L. Khvat, *Geroicheskii perelet "Rodiny"* (Moscow, 1938). Published in English as *The Heroic Flight of the "Rodina"* (Moscow: Foreign Languages Publishing House, 1938), 78. All page numbers refer to the English edition.

40. Lazar Brontman, *Na vershine mira* (Moscow: Khudozhestvennaia literatura, 1938). All page numbers refer to the English edition, *OT*, 91.

41. This struggle to control the elements was a cornerstone of Soviet mythology. See *SN*, 100–106.

42. A. Ivanov, *Taezhnye druz'ia* (1939). Summary taken from *Sovetskie khudozhestvennye filmy: Annotirovannyi katalog* II (Moscow: Iskusstvo, 1961), 222. See also *Soviet Films 1938–1939* (Moscow: State Publishing House for Cinema Literature, 1939).

43. Victoria E. Bonnell, "The Peasant Woman in Stalinist Political Art of the 1930s," *American Historical Review* 98, no. 1 (February 1993): 58–68, 78–82.

44. Von Geldern, "The Centre and the Periphery," 77.

45. Ivan Doronin, "Ivan Doronin's Story," in *VC*, 325.

46. A. Tvardovskii, "Muzhestvo," *P*, October 28, 1938.

47. *P*, October 28, 1938.

48. On November 7, 1938, the heroine pilots were designated "Heroes of the Soviet Union."

49. Alexei Bobrov, "How Shmidt Camp Was Closed Down," in *VC*, 238.

50. TsGAMO, f. 2180, op. 1, d. 883, l. 23.

51. Vassili Molokov, "Vassili Molokov's Story," in *VC*, 282.

52. Doronin, "Ivan Doronin's Story," in *VC*, 325.

53. Letters to aviation heroes often described how the writers were "moved to tears." See RGALI, f. 617, op. 1, d. 10, ll. 9, 11, 16, 30, 32. This tendency toward weeping also existed in the tsarist ceremonial of Nicholas I, where "individual feelings [were] politicized and generalized to express adoration and worship of the emperor and his family" (Wortman, *Scenarios of Power*, 285).

54. TsGAMO, f. 2180, op. 1, d. 883, l. 1.

55. *I*, October 27, 1938.

56. Poster RU/SU-1816, Hoover Institution Archives, Stanford University, celebrates the achievements of the three heroine pilots but is dominated by a silhouette of Stalin and the Kremlin.

57. Peter Buiko, "Hail, Solid Land," in *VC*, 227–228.

58. Brontman and Khvat, *The Heroic Flight of the "Rodina*," 54.

59. *P*, October 28, 1938.

60. These images were radically different than those of female pilots in the United States. According to historian Joseph Corn, American female pilots "sold" flying to the public by "purging it of associations with death and terror." Joseph J. Corn, *The Winged Gospel* (New York: Oxford University Press, 1983), 88.

61. *P*, October 28, 1938. Official rhetoric forecasted a future war in which the Soviets would swiftly repel the attacking enemies and pursue them beyond the borders of the Soviet Union.

62. Ibid.

63. See Wendy Z. Goldman, *Women and the Soviet State: Soviet Family Policy and Social Life, 1917–1936* (Cambridge: Cambridge University Press, 1993), 331–336.

64. *P*, October 28, 1938.

65. *SN*, 3–24.

66. Ibid., 125–128. A particularly good example of this tension is a scene in the 1941 film *Valerii Chkalov*, directed by Mikhail Kalatozov, in which Chkalov recklessly pilots his plane under a Leningrad bridge.

67. *P*, August 11, 1936. The editors of *Pravda* constructed a family hierarchy by

including a picture of Chkalov and Stalin embracing on page one, and a picture of Chkalov being given a bouquet of flowers by his wife on page four.

68. *OT*, 232. This event was also captured on film in the documentary film *Bogatyry rodiny*, RGAKFD, 1-4034, 1937.

69. *OT*, 233.

70. *P*, October 28, 1938.

71. Ibid.

72. Ibid.

73. The other female heroes were noted Stakhanovites such as tractor driver Pasha Angelina and collective farm worker Maria Demchenko.

74. See Siegelbaum, *Stakhanovism*, for a discussion of the creation of other elites at this time.

75. *I*, October 27, 1938.

76. *Geroicheskaia epopeia: Al'bom foto-dokumentov* (Moscow: Pravda, Partizdat, 1935), insert after 62.

77. Otto Shmidt, "The 'Cheliuskin' Expedition," in *VC*, 9.

78. TsGAMO, f. 2180, op. 1, d. 883, l. 22.

79. Kotkin, *Magnetic Mountain*, 217–221.

80. *OT*, 133.

81. Ibid., 63–64.

82. Ibid., 126.

83. Ibid., 241. Their emotional farewell was captured on film by cameraman Troianovskii, and was shown to Soviet audiences in the documentary film *Papanintsy*. RGAKFD, 1-4145, 1938.

84. Alexander Mironov, "Arctic Winter in Arctic Ice," in *VC*, 70.

85. Semenov, "What the Communists Did," in *VC*, 178.

86. Bobrov, "How Shmidt Camp Was Closed Down," in *VC*, 231.

87. *LI*, 79, 169.

88. Ibid., 94, 119.

89. Ibid., 50.

90. Ibid., 252.

91. *OT*, 309.

92. *LI*, 257.

93. *OT*, 191.

94. Ivan Papanin, et al., *Deviat' mesiatsev na dreifuiushchei stantsii "Severnyi Polius"* (Moscow: OGIZ, Gos. izdatel'stvo politicheskoi literatury, 1938), 11.

95. While *Deviat' mesiatsev na dreifuiushchei stantsii "Severnyi Polius,"* (published by the State Publishing House of Political Literature in 5,000 copies) eliminated complexities from Papanin's character and exaggerated his heroism, *Zhizn' na l'dine* (published by *Pravda* in 100,000 copies) contained remarkably frank reflections on the daily life and personal struggles of an Arctic explorer. The edition of Papanin's memoirs that was meant for the political elite was more ideological and less oriented toward private life and entertainment than the edition meant for the general public.

96. *LI*, 205.

97. *RA*, 133.

98. Shmidt, "The 'Cheliuskin' Expedition," in *VC*, 8.

99. Ibid., 9.

100. *Geroicheskaia epopeia*, 57.

101. Leonid Martisov, "Inventors by Compulsion," in *VC*, 158.

102. Sushkin, "The Flight of March the Fifth," in *VC*, 212.

103. Ibid., 216.

104. Sigismund Levanevskii, "Sigismund Levanevskii's Story," in *VC*, 255.

105. Georgii Baidukov, *Over the North Pole,* translated by Jessica Smith (New York: Harcourt, Brace and Company, 1938), translation of *Iz dnevniki pilota* (Moscow, 1937), 5. All page numbers refer to the English edition.

106. The exclusion of females from heroic narratives and perceptions of women as a threat to the heroism of males were characteristic of European and American adventure discourses as well. Anxieties about women were also prevalent in Soviet discourses of the 1920s. See Robert Wohl, *A Passion for Wings: Aviation and the Western Imagination, 1908–1918* (New Haven, Conn., and London: Yale University Press, 1994), 280–282; Lisa Bloom, *Gender on Ice: American Ideologies of Polar Expeditions* (Minneapolis: University of Minnesota Press, 1993), 6–7; Naiman, *Sex in Public,* 193, 205.

107. Chapaev was a famous Civil War partisan who was immortalized in one of the most popular films of the 1930s. *Everyday Life in Russia,* 62–63.

108. TsKhDMO, f. 1 op. 3, d. 170, l. 82.

109. RGALI, f. 2091, op. 2, d. 72, ll. 33–42.

110. Brontman and Khvat, *The Heroic Flight of the "Rodina,"* 66–67, 88.

111. "Pis'mo Marii Semenovny Babushkinoi," *Krestian'ka* 16–17 (1937): 4.

112. For a discussion of barriers women faced in the Komsomol in the 1920s, see Anne E. Gorsuch, "A Woman Is Not a Man: The Culture of Gender and Generation in Soviet Russia, 1921–1928," *Slavic Review* 55, no. 3 (Fall 1996): 636–660.

113. *P,* October 28, 1938.

114. For a discussion of Northern peoples becoming Soviet, see Yuri Slezkine, *Arctic Mirrors: Russia and the Small Peoples of the North* (Ithaca, N.Y.: Cornell University Press, 1994), 283–286.

115. He made this pronouncement in 1937. RTsKhIDNI, f. 475, op. 2, d. 164, l. 27 ob.; d. 394, l. 10.

116. Yuri Slezkine, "From Savages to Citizens: The Cultural Revolution in the Soviet Far North," *Slavic Review* 51, no. 1 (Spring 1992): 76.

117. John M. MacKenzie, *Propaganda and Empire: The Manipulation of British Public Opinion, 1880–1960* (Manchester: Manchester University Press, 1984), 254.

118. Anatolii Liapidevskii, "Anatolii Liapidevskii's Story," in *VC,* 243.

119. Ibid., 251.

120. Bassin, "The Greening of Utopia."

121. Liapidevskii, "Anatolii Liapidevskii's Story," in *VC,* 252–253.

122. Buiko, "Hail, Solid Land," in *VC,* 230.

123. Nikolai Kamanin, "Nikolai Kamanin's Story," in *VC,* 291–292.

124. Bloom's discussion of the denial of Inuit and African-American accomplishments in American exploration of the North Pole served as a model here. *RA,* 51; Bloom, *Gender on Ice,* 101–107.

125. Bassin, "The Greening of Utopia"; Blomqvist, "Some Utopian Elements in Stalinist Art."

126. *OT,* xi.

127. See A. Garri and L. Kassil', *Potolok mira* (Moscow: Sovetskaia literatura, 1934), 42–46, for a discussion of risk-taking.

128. Baidukov, *Over the North Pole,* 13.

129. *P,* October 28, 1938.

130. The Politbiuro set the expedition's arrival time in Moscow on June 21, 1937. See RTsKhIDNI, f. 17, op. 3, d. 989, l. 3.

131. *OT,* 230.

132. Shmidt, "The 'Cheliuskin' Expedition," in *VC,* 6.

133. GARF, f. 5446, op. 15, d. 2322, l. 2.

134. The Soviet government was worse than careless in its treatment of prisoners. One reason the Soviet government supposedly rejected foreign participation in

the *Cheliuskin* rescue was that a prison ship called the *Dzhurma*, with 12,000 prisoners on board, was stranded near the *Cheliuskin*. All of these prisoners were said to have perished. *RA*, 65.

135. "Nikolai Kamanin's Story," in *VC*, 284–285.

136. Kuibyshev and the Soviet government wanted to organize an aviation rescue. When the prominent Arctic expert V. Vize wrote a letter to *Izvestiia* suggesting an overland rescue, Kuibyshev did not allow the letter to appear in print. RTsKhIDNI, f. 79, op. 1, d. 726, l. 2.

137. *OT*, 122.

138. Ibid., 306.

139. *RA*, 77.

140. *LI*, 233.

141. Ibid., 148, 265.

142. Ibid., 82–83.

143. TsKhDMO, f. 1, op. 23, d. 1137, l. 23.

144. Ibid., l. 31.

145. TsKhDMO, f. 1, op. 23, d. 1197, l. 25.

146. Ibid., l. 18.

147. RTsKhIDNI, f. 17, op. 3, d. 976, l. 33; d. 980, l. 56.

148. Bailes, *Technology and Society*, 387.

149. Wohl, *A Passion for Wings*, 206.

4. Fir Trees and Carnivals

1. *Komsomol'skaia pravda*, December 28, 1935.

2. *Nashi prazdniki*, 149.

3. *Bezbozhnik* 24 (December 1928): 9; *Bezbozhnik* 3 (February 1929): 19. The class nature of the fir tree had been criticized in pre-revolutionary Russia as well; Fedor Dostoevsky's short story "The Heavenly Christmas Tree" depicted a starving, freezing, little boy who watched through a window as happy rich children celebrated around the tree. When he tried to join them, he was cast out and froze to death. Fyodor Dostoevsky, "The Heavenly Christmas Tree," in *An Honest Thief and Other Stories*, translated by Constance Garnett (New York: Macmillan, 1923), 248–251.

4. Nina M. Sorochenko, "Pre-school Education in the U.S.S.R.," in *Soviet Education*, edited by George L. Kline (New York: Columbia University Press, 1957), 18.

5. *RD*, 230.

6. RGALI, f. 963, op. 1, d. 1234, ll. 1–2, 32–34.

7. Frederick S. Starr, *Red and Hot: The Fate of Jazz in the Soviet Union, 1917–1980* (New York: Oxford University Press, 1983), 92.

8. L. P. Postyshev, "Ob ottse," in *Pavel Postyshev: Vospominaniia, vystupleniia, pis'ma*, edited by K. N. Atarov (Moscow: Politizdat, 1987), 302–303.

9. According to V. Ia. Propp, the fir tree tradition was imported from Germany to Russian cities and never had any ritual significance in the Russian countryside. Propp, *Russkie agrarnye prazdniki*, 56.

10. GARF, f. 5451, op. 19, d. 485, l. 71.

11. Siegelbaum, *Stakhanovism*, 246.

12. *Soiuzkinozhurnal* 1 (1937), RGAKFD, 1-2911.

13. Fitzpatrick, *Cultural Front*, 112–114.

14. See Hayden White, *The Content of the Form: Narrative Discourse and Historical Representation* (Baltimore: Johns Hopkins University Press, 1987); Mabel Berezin, "Cultural Form and Political Meaning: State-Subsidized Theater, Ideology, and the Language of Style in Fascist Italy," *American Journal of Sociology* 99, no. 5 (March 1994): 1237–1286.

15. TsKhDMO, f. 1, op. 3, d. 124, l. 103.

16. TsKhDMO, f. 1, op. 3, d. 123, l. 54; d. 152, l. 117.

17. TsKhDMO, f. 1, op. 3, d. 152, ll. 12, 15.

18. *Detiam novogodniuiu elku* (Novosibirsk: Zapadno-Sibirskogo Kraikom VLKSM, 1936), 1–4.

19. Byleeva i dr., *Novogodniaia elka: Sbornik dlia uchashchikhsia nachal'noi shkoly* (Moscow: MGK VLKSM, 1936), 5–6, 11, 16–18, 21.

20. E. Flerina, "Elka v detskom sadu," in *ES*, 3–4, 7. This volume was published primarily for teachers, to give them detailed instructions on how to create a fir tree celebration in school.

21. Flerina, "Elka v detskom sadu," 8.

22. Ibid., 4.

23. Sorochenko, "Pre-school Education in the U.S.S.R.," 17.

24. Ibid. The fox trot had been called "a form of human degradation" during the Cultural Revolution. Larry Holmes, *The Kremlin and the Schoolhouse* (Bloomington: Indiana University Press, 1991), 118.

25. Sorochenko, "Pre-school Education in the U.S.S.R.," 16–17.

26. Ibid., 17.

27. E. Bykovskaia, "Elochnye igrushki i ikh izgotovlenie," in *ES*, 42.

28. Flerina, "Elka v detskom sadu," 6.

29. TsKhDMO, f. 1, op. 23, d. 1180, l. 125.

30. One memoirist reported that her grandmother continued to have a Christmas tree each year despite the ban, while her mother, a teacher, did not, because she was afraid of losing her job. Tatyana Senkevich, "A Soviet Girl's Diary," in *Thirteen Who Fled*, edited by Louis Fischer (New York: Harper and Brothers, 1949), 116.

31. Bogdan, *Mimikriia v SSSR*, 52–53.

32. Ibid., 53.

33. Galina Vladimirovna Shtange, "Diary of Galina Vladimirovna Shtange," in *IT*, 211.

34. S. Bazykin, "Ukrasheniia i igrushki dlia elki," in *ES*, 39–40.

35. *RM*, 10.

36. TsKhDMO, f. 1, op. 3, d. 170, l. 152.

37. TsGAMO, f. 2180, op. 1, d. 972, l. 1.

38. E. Ovchinnikova, "Elka v dome soiuzov," in *ES*, 16.

39. This fir tree celebration coincided with the commemoration of the centennial of Aleksandr Pushkin's death. See Chapter 4.

40. TsGAMO, f. 2180, op. 1, d. 972, ll. 3–7.

41. Ibid., ll. 6–7.

42. B. Grinberg, "Pesni, muzyka na prazdnike elki," in *ES*, 21–23.

43. TsGAMO, f. 2180, op. 1, d. 972, ll. 7–8.

44. Ibid., ll. 9–10: "My ne znaem zabot i pechali. / Genii liubit detei. / Zhit' velit veselei. / Genii smel nam s puti vse pechali. / My rezvimsia poem, / Ego imia zovem, / Eto genii liubimyi nash Stalin."

45. Ibid., l. 3.

46. TsKhDMO, f. 1, op. 3, d. 161, l. 25 (1936).

47. Svetlana Gouzenko, *Before Igor: Memories of My Soviet Youth* (New York: W. W. Norton, 1960), 147.

48. Shtange, in *IT*, 167, 210.

49. Bogdan, *Mimikriia v SSSR*, 52.

50. This novella was written in 1939–1940. Lydia Chukovskaya, *Sofia Petrovna*, translated by Aline Werth (Evanston, Ill.: Northwestern University Press, 1988), 29–30.

51. The Christmas tree also reinforced hierarchy in pre-revolutionary Russia. In Dostoevsky's short story "A Christmas Tree and a Wedding," he described how

at a tree-trimming celebration, the hosts distributed the gifts to children according to rank, with the richest and most important little girl receiving the "costliest doll" and the poor son of the governess getting a book without "pictures or even wood-cuts." Fyodor Dostoevsky, "A Christmas Tree and a Wedding," in *White Nights and Other Stories,* translated by Constance Garnett (Melbourne: William Heinemann, 1950), 202.

52. These oranges turned out to be from Republican Spain. Bogdan, *Mimikriia v SSSR,* 52.

53. *P,* January 1, 1937.

54. The plan had called for 50–55 million rubles' worth of decorations to be produced for the 1937 holiday. TsKhDMO, f. 1, op. 3, d. 165, ll. 150, 158. Elena Osokina's work has shown that Moscow and Leningrad alone consumed about half of the goods marketed by the Soviet state. Osokina, *Za fasadom "Stalinskogo izobiliia,"* 192.

55. *S novom godom,* RGAKFD, 1-13366, 1936; *Soiuzkinozhurnal* 1 (1937), RGAKFD, 1-2911; *Zdrastvui novyi god,* RGAKFD, 1-4923, 1937.

56. *S novom godom;* Isaac Dunaevskii and V. Lebedev-Kumach, "Nu, kak ne zapet," in *Pesni Krasnoi Armii,* 20.

57. Iu. Gol'dberg, "Kak organizovat' vstrechu novogo goda," *Klub* 23 (December 1937): 51.

58. Sartorti, "Stalinism and Carnival," 70, 72.

59. Bakhtin, *Rabelais and His World,* 9.

60. RTsKhIDNI, f. 475, op. 2, d. 164, l. 7.

61. *RM,* I.

62. "Vsem prikazyvalo strogo grust' ostavit' u doroga." *Soiuzkinozhurnal* 1 (1937).

63. *RM,* 17–18.

64. Ibid., 18.

65. Ibid.

66. V. Ia Propp, "The Russian Folk Lyric," in *Down along the Mother Volga,* translated and edited by Roberta Reeder (Philadelphia: University of Pennsylvania Press, 1975), 5; Lidia Zinovieva-Annibal, "Thirty-three Abominations," translated by Samuel Cioran, *Russian Literature Triquarterly* 9 (Spring 1974): 103–104.

67. Arzhilovsky, in *IT,* 138.

68. Gol'dberg, "Kak organizovat' vstrechu novogo goda," 52.

69. *RM,* 20.

70. Robert A. Rothstein, "Homeland, Home Town, and Battlefield: The Popular Song," in *Culture and Entertainment in Wartime Russia,* edited by Richard Stites (Bloomington: Indiana University Press, 1995), 90–91; Dunham, *In Stalin's Time.*

71. For an example of Soviet satire about the loss of a receipt, see Mikhail Zoshchenko's 1924 short story "Bania" in *Sobranye sochineniia* 1 (Leningrad, 1986), 278–280.

72. "chas likvidatsii tantseval'noi negramotnosti" (*RM,* 6).

73. Ibid., 25–27.

74. Ibid., 37.

75. *Nashi prazdniki,* 163.

76. The elite Hall of Columns fir tree in Moscow was, of course, lit with electric lights. Gouzenko, *Before Igor,* 147.

77. *P,* January 2, 1937.

78. Ibid.

79. TsKhDMO, f. 1, op. 3, d. 170, ll. 156–158.

80. TsKhDMO, f. 1, op. 3, d. 165, ll. 158–160.

81. TsKhDMO, f. 1, op. 3, d. 170, l. 152.

82. Ibid., l. 166.

83. Gabor Rittersporn emphasizes the "inefficiency and petty tyranny" of a large number of people in the economic and political apparatus. Rittersporn, *Stalinist Simplifications and Soviet Complications*, 41.

84. *ES*, 92.

85. TsKhDMO, f. 1, op. 3, d. 170, ll. 151–152.

86. Almost no men mention fir tree celebrations in their memoirs; Leonid Postyshev is an exception. See, for example, Markoosha Fischer, *My Lives in Russia* (New York: Harper and Brothers, 1944), 128–131; Gouzenko, *Before Igor*, 163; Shtange, in *IT*, 210; Vera Ivanovna Malakhova, "Four Years as a Frontline Physician," in *A Revolution of Their Own: Voices of Women in Soviet History*, edited by Barbara Alpern Engel and Anastasia Posadskaya-Vanderbeck (Boulder, Colo.: Westview Press, 1998), 205–206.

During the Arctic expedition of the icebreaker *Sedov*, it was two female scientists who contrived to make a New Year's tree out of, "an old oar, broom twigs, marine biological specimens, and other unlikely objects." Terence Armstrong, *The Russians in the Arctic: Aspects of Soviet Exploration and Exploitation of the Far North, 1937–57* (London: Methuen and Co., 1958), 25.

87. Chukovskaya, *Sofia Petrovna*, 29–30.

5. A Double-Edged Discourse on Freedom

1. Resolution of the Central Executive Committee of the USSR about the Formation of an All-Union Pushkin Committee in Connection with the Hundredth Anniversary of the Death of A. S. Pushkin, *Izvestiia TsIK Soiuza SSR i VTsIK*, 292, December 17, 1935.

2. Pushkin Committee members included Narkompros officials, prominent Pushkin scholars, and the heads of many important Soviet cultural institutions.

3. Nina Kosterina, *Diary of Nina Kosterina*, translated by Mirra Ginsberg (New York: Avon Books, 1968), 32–35; and *Literaturnyi sovremennik* (April 1936): inside covers.

4. RGALI, f. 2196, op. 1, d. 30, l. 5.

5. The commercialization of Pushkin was a hallmark of the 1899 Pushkin Celebrations. See Marcus Levitt, "Pushkin in 1899," in *Cultural Myths of Russian Modernism: From the Golden Age to the Silver Age*, edited by Boris Gasparov, Robert P. Hughes, and Irina Paperno (Berkeley: University of California Press, 1992), 192–193.

6. *Materialy k zasedaniiu vsesoiuznogo pushkinskogo komiteta, 29 ianvaria 1937 goda* (Moscow: Vsesoiuznyi pushkinskii komitet, 1937), 1. Also located in GARF, f. 305, op. 1, d. 3, l. 61. Marcus Levitt estimates the number of Pushkin publications in 1937 at 19 million (Levitt, "Pushkin in 1899," 184).

7. *P*, December 17, 1935.

8. Fitzpatrick, *The Cultural Front*, 248–250.

9. *P*, February 10, 1937.

10. See Katerina Clark, "Little Heroes and Big Deeds: Literature Responds to the First Five-Year Plan," in *Cultural Revolution in Russia, 1928–1931*, edited by Sheila Fitzpatrick (Bloomington: Indiana University Press, 1978), 204–206.

11. This was the title of an article by V. Kirpotin in *Komsomol'skaia pravda* 130, June 6, 1936.

12. The 1937 official version of Pushkin's biography was the mirror image of the 1899 government version, which suppressed the ties between Pushkin and the Decembrists by "pruning the poet's life story to fit a narrow ideological mold." Levitt, "Pushkin in 1899," 188.

13. David Magarshack, *Pushkin: A Biography* (London: Chapman and Hall, 1967), 279–280, 305–306. For an excellent discussion of the development of Pushkin's im-

age as a martyr, see Paul Debreczeny, *"Zhitie Aleksandra Boldinskogo:* Pushkin's Elevation to Sainthood in Soviet Culture," *South Atlantic Quarterly* 90, no. 2 (Spring
1991): 269–292. Sam Driver argues that Pushkin's political thinking actually cham-
pioned the old aristocracy who had been displaced by the reforms of Peter the
Great. Sam Driver, *Pushkin: Literature and Social Ideas* (New York: Columbia University Press, 1989), 10–14.

14. B. Kazanskii, "Gibel' poeta," *Literaturnyi sovremennik* 3 (1937): 243.

15. For a survey of the development of the Pushkin myth in the nineteenth and
twentieth centuries, see Catharine Theimer Nepomnyashchy, introduction to *Strolls
with Pushkin,* by Abram Tertz, translated by Catharine Theimer Nepomnyashchy
and Slava I. Yastremski (New Haven, Conn.: Yale University Press, 1993), 25–41.

16. Marcus Levitt, *Russian Literary Politics and the Pushkin Celebration of 1880*
(Ithaca, N.Y.: Cornell University Press, 1989), 9.

17. For a discussion of *perekovka* (reforging), see Cynthia Ruder, *Making History
for Stalin: The Story of the Belomor Canal* (Gainesville: University Press of Florida,
1998), 2–3.

18. In January 1937, for example, members of the Pushkin Committee expressed
a desire that Pushkin literary circles not be "mechanically stopped" after the Pushkin
Days were over (GARF, f. 305, op. 1, d. 14, l. 136). It is likely that they hoped in vain.
In a 1938 meeting with educational officials, Nadezhda Krupskaia lamented that
"after the Pushkin jubilee passed, all [of the book exhibits] were taken down." She
charged that there was no depth to the cultural work currently being done
(RTsKhIDNI, f. 12, op. 1, d. 574, l. 27). Even the prestigious *Collected Works* of Pushkin
of the Academy of Sciences suffered from the transitory nature of Soviet campaigns.
In late 1937, publishing houses prioritized materials for the twentieth anniversary
of the October Revolution and the progress of the edition was slowed (Ludwig L.
Domherr, *The Pushkin Edition of the U.S.S.R. Academy of Sciences,* East European Research Fund, Mimeographed Series No. 45 [New York: Research Program of the
U.S.S.R., 1953], 59).

19. *P,* February 2, 1937.

20. *Vecherniaia Moskva,* February 7, 1937.

21. RGALI, f. 384, op. 1, d. 121, l. 20.

22. Ibid., ll. 41–2.

23. *Vecherniaia Moskva,* February 9, 1937.

24. Meilakh, "Nasledie Pushkina i sotsialisticheskaia kul'tura," 111.

25. RGALI, f. 384, op. 1, d. 121, l. 16.

26. Quoted in A. S. Tolstov, "Pushkin v shkole," *Krasnaia nov'* 1 (January 1937):
227.

27. *Vecherniaia Moskva,* February 9, 1937.

28. Kenez, *Birth of the Propaganda State,* 180.

29. RGALI, f. 384, op. 1, d. 121, l. 40.

30. *P,* February 8, 1937.

31. Nadezhda Mandelshtam, *Hope against Hope,* translated by Max Hayward
(New York: Atheneum, 1979), 30.

32. A. A. Akhmatova, "'Adol'f' Benzhamena Konstana v tvorchestve Pushkina,"
in *Vremennik* 1 (Leningrad and Moscow: Akademiia Nauk, 1936), 91–114.

33. While the Politbiuro approved the plenum, they did not respond to Stavskii
until nearly two months had gone by. RTsKhIDNI, f. 17, op. 114, d. 794, ll. 204–205.

34. GARF, f. 305, op. 1, d. 1, l. 75 (1936).

35. See Siegelbaum, *Stakhanovism.*

36. *Krokodil* 3 (January 1937): 4–5; *Krokodil* 5 (February 1937): 8–9.

37. Mikhail Zoshchenko, "V Pushkinskie dni," in *Sobrannye sochineniia* II
(Leningrad, 1986), 416–418.

38. Zoshchenko, "V Pushkinskie dni," 418–421.

39. GARF, f. 305, op. 1, d. 15, l. 31 (1936).

40. GARF, f. 305, op. 1, d. 3, l. 7. Sovnarkom seems only to have provided 250,000 rubles for this purpose, however. *Materialy k zasedaniiu vsesoiuznogo push-kinskogo komiteta, 29. ianvaria 1937 goda,* 2. For a discussion of earlier Soviet attempts to preserve Mikhailovskoe, see Stephanie Sandler, "Remembrance in Mikhailov-skoe," in *Cultural Myths of Russian Modernism: From the Golden Age to the Silver Age,* edited by Boris Gasparov, Robert P. Hughes, and Irina Paperno (Berkeley: University of California Press, 1992), 231–250.

41. GARF, f. 305, op. 1, d. 3, ll. 17–20; d. 6, ll. 135–136. The archives contain two different sets of budget figures for these events, one allocating approximately 15 percent less money than the other. The figures in the text refer to the lower set of figures where they were available. It is likely that Sovnarkom did not fulfill these requests in full.

42. GARF, f. 305, op. 1, d. 1. l. 57.

43. GARF, f. 305, op. 1, d. 15, ll. 3, 7.

44. Ibid., l. 18.

45. One Pushkin Committee official projected that materials needed to be sent out at the end of September 1936 for them to reach their intended audience in time for the centennial. GARF, f. 305, op. 1, d. 10, l. 13 ob.

46. RGALI, f. 384, op. 1, d. 121, l. 8.

47. GARF, f. 305, op. 1, d. 1, l. 12.

48. *Vecherniaia Moskva,* February 11, 1937.

49. GARF, f. 305, op. 1, d. 10, ll. 6, 8.

50. GARF, f. 305, op. 1, d. 9, ll. 7–9.

51. GARF, f. 305, op. 1, d. 1, l. 77 (1936).

52. TsMAM, f. 2007, op. 1, d. 61, l. 31.

53. RTsKhIDNI, f. 17, op. 3, d. 983, l. 93.

54. GARF, f. 305, op. 1, d, 15, l. 2. The article is taken from the journal *Plamia* (Ivanovo).

55. GARF, f. 305, op. 1, d. 14, ll. 69–70. Letters with similar requests for materi-als are located on ll. 71–73.

56. Ibid., l. 108.

57. TsKhDMO, f. 1, op. 3, d. 167, ll. 7–8.

58. GARF, f. 305, op. 1, d. 7, ll. 70–83; d. 14, ll. 22–32.

59. GARF, f. 305, op. 1, d. 14, ll. 16–21.

60. GARF, f. 305, op. 1, d. 1, ll. 74–75.

61. Ibid., ll. 55–56.

62. GARF, f. 305, op. 1, d. 14, l. 147.

63. Levitt, "Pushkin in 1899," 159.

64. "Vstupitel'naia rech' Prezidenta Akademii Nauk SSSR, Akad. V. L. Koma-rova," in *Sto let so dnia smerti A.S. Pushkina,* Akademiia Nauk SSSR (Moscow-Len-ingrad, 1938), 8.

65. *P,* February 1, 1937.

66. *Vecherniaia Moskva,* February 4, 1937; February 2, 1937.

67. GARF, f. 305, op. 1, d. 5, l. 6.

68. GARF, f. 305, op. 1, d. 8, ll. 1–2.

69. In their comments on the film *Iunost' poeta* in late 1936, Soviet cultural au-thorities objected to the portrayal of Pushkin's "stormy African temperament." RGALI, f. 2450, op. 2, d. 1636, ll. 9–10.

70. Simon, *Nationalism and Policy,* 88.

71. *RR,* 177.

72. RGALI, f. 384, op. 1, d. 121, l. 22 (1937).

73. *P,* February 2, 1937.

74. Willard Sunderland, "Russians into Iakuts? 'Going Native' and Problems

of Russian National Identity in the Siberian North, 1870s–1914," *Slavic Review* 55, no. 4 (Winter 1996): 816.

75. I. Luppol, "Velichie Pushkina," *Oktiabr'* 4 (April 1937): 155.

76. GARF, f. 305, op. 1, d. 14, ll. 51–52, 57.

77. *P,* September 21, 1936.

78. S. Reiser, "Nenuzhnoe izdanie," *Literaturnoe obozrenie* 13 (1937): 40–41.

79. Levitt, *Russian Literary Politics,* 7.

80. TsMAM, f. 528, op. 1, d. 519, ll. 5–7; *Murzilka* 2 (February 1937): 12–13.

81. See A. Naroditskii, *Iunost' poeta* (Leningrad: Lenfilm, 1937). The screenplay was written by A. Slonimskii; Moisei Levin, *Puteshestvie v Arzrum* (Leningrad: Lenfilm, 1937). The screenplay was written by Mikhail Bleiman.

82. RGALI, f. 2450, op. 2, d. 1635, l. 101. Unfortunately, since I did not have access to the film, I do not know whether this dialogue was preserved in the film itself.

83. GARF, f. 305, op. 1, d. 1, ll. 78–79.

84. Ibid., l. 79.

85. *Letopisi Gosudarstvennogo Literaturnogo Muzeia, kniga pervaia: Pushkin,* edited by M. Tsiavlovskii (Moscow, 1936). See pp. 96–98 for commentary about Ol'ga and Mikhail Kalashnikov. It is not possible to establish, however, how and to whom the 10,000 copies were distributed.

86. GARF, f. 305, op. 1, d. 6, l. 100.

87. RGALI, f. 384, op. 1, d. 121, l. 15.

88. Ibid.

89. *Puteshestvie v Arzrum,* 16.

90. RGALI, f. 2450, op. 2, d. 1636, ll. 54–57, 66.

91. GARF, f. 305, op. 1, d. 1, l. 79.

92. Gorbov was probably arrested, since he was accused of being a member of the "Trotskyite group Pereval." "O Trotskistskoi gruppe Pereval," *Literaturnoe obozrenie* 15 (1937): 22.

93. G. S. Smith, "Introduction," in *D. S. Mirsky: Uncollected Writings on Russian Literature* (Berkeley: Berkeley Slavic Specialties, 1989), 26.

94. Ibid., 27–28.

95. D. S. Mirsky, *Pushkin* (London: G. Routledge, 1926).

96. D. Mirskii, "Problema Pushkina," *Literaturnoe nasledstvo* 16–18 (1934): 101, 103, 110.

97. D. Zaslavskii, "Rekord kritika Mirskogo," *P,* August 28, 1936.

98. D. Mirskii, "Moim kritikam," *Vremennik* 1, 262–264.

99. I. Sergievskii, review of *Vremennik* in *Literaturnaia gazeta* 42 (1936): 4.

100. *Literaturnaia gazeta* 50 (1936): 6; "Formalism" and "vulgar sociologism" were criticisms used to define enemies in the literary and scholarly world in the same way that *"kulak"* described an enemy in the village during collectivization. The antagonists of formalism rejected the idea of art for art's sake and argued that all art had to be politically engaged.

101. Smith, "Introduction," 28; Conquest, *The Great Terror,* 298.

102. Although Kirpotin continued to publish literary criticism throughout the Stalin period, his biography in the 1976 edition of the *Great Soviet Encyclopedia* omits all of his scholarly activities between 1936 and 1956. His own autobiographical writing is similarly silent about the years between 1937 and 1965. "Kirpotin, Valerii Iakovlevich," *Great Soviet Encyclopedia* 12 (New York: Macmillan, 1976, 517–518; V. Ia. Kirpotin, *Nachalo: Avtobiograficheskie stranitsy* (Moscow: 1986), 245–246.

103. The book was serialized in numbers 9, 10, and 11 of the journal *Oktiabr'* in 1936. Kirpotin also published several articles about Pushkin's opposition to Nicholas I. See, for example, "Pushkinskii ideal politicheskoi svobody," *Literaturnaia gazeta* 56 (1936); "Pevets svobodoliubiia," *Komsomol'skaia pravda* 130 (1936).

104. V. Kirpotin, *Nasledie Pushkina k kommunizmu* (Moscow, 1936), 57.

105. Ibid., 89–90.

106. Ibid., 85.

107. *P,* September 21, 1936.

108. GARF, f. 305, op. 1, d. 1, l. 73.

109. Quoted in Domherr, *The Pushkin Edition,* 43.

110. RTsKhIDNI, f. 17, op. 3, d. 983, l. 94. The lack of commentary was also due to time pressure.

111. Domherr, *The Pushkin Edition,* 45.

112. Domherr argues that under the leadership of M. Tsiavlovskii, the editors were able to include additional commentary by disguising it as an index. He also records that only one Pushkinist Iu. Oksman was arrested during the purges. Oksman was later released and continued his work as a Pushkin scholar. Domherr, *The Pushkin Edition,* 57–58, 62.

113. *Vecherniaia Moskva,* February 11, 1937.

114. *P,* September 21, 1936.

115. According to one theoretician, Aesopian language has as its subject "that which products of the opposite, propagandistic, genre take as their theme: the power of the State in all its manifestations." Lev Loseff, *On the Beneficence of Censorship* (Munich: Verlag Otto Sagner in Kommission, 1984), 221.

116. Kirpotin, *Nasledie,* 82.

117. Roy Medvedev, *Let History Judge: The Origins and Consequences of Stalinism,* revised and expanded edition (New York: Columbia University Press, 1989), 832; Aleksandr Gladkov, "Piat' let s Meierkhol'dom," in *Meierkhol'd* 2 (Moscow: Soiuz Teatr. Deiatelei RSFSR, 1990), 180.

118. See Fitzpatrick, *Everyday Stalinism,* 184, for a discussion of subversive messages conveyed through typographical errors.

119. Nicholas V. Riasanovsky, *The Image of Peter the Great in Russian History and Thought* (Oxford: Oxford University Press, 1985), 256.

120. See Robert C. Tucker, *Stalin in Power: The Revolution from Above, 1928–1941* (New York: W. W. Norton and Company, 1990), 114–118, for a discussion of Stalin's direct involvement with the transformation of the image of Peter the Great from villain to hero. See also Juri Jelagin, *Taming of the Arts,* translated by Nicholas Wreden (New York: E. P. Dutton & Co., 1951), 112.

121. *Literaturnyi sovremennik* (March 1936): 208–209.

122. Although I have not been able to uncover any specific information about Cherniavskii, most contributors to the journal *Krasnyi arkhiv* were historians, literary scholars, and archivists. It was rare that the journal devoted an entire volume to one subject (it only happened on four occasions in twenty years.) On two of these four occasions the introductory articles were written by M. N. Pokrovskii, the noted Soviet historian who directed the journal. That Cherniavskii wrote the introduction to the Pushkin volume thus suggests that he may have played a significant leadership role in the journal. After early 1938, I found no further publications by Cherniavskii or any other mention of him in Soviet sources. *Krasnyi arkhiv: Istoricheskii zhurnal 1922–1941, annotirovannyi ukazatel' soderzhaniia,* compiled by R. I. Zverev (Moscow, 1960), 3–4; 202–203; 211.

123. Cherniavskii, "Aleksandr Sergeevich Pushkin," 5–12.

124. Ibid., 8.

125. Loseff, *On the Beneficence of Censorship,* 109.

126. Cherniavskii, "Aleksandr Sergeevich Pushkin," 8. Here Cherniavskii quotes the title of Pushkin's poem to the Decembrists, "Vo glubine sibirskikh rud."

127. See Raisa Orlova, *Memoirs* (New York: Random House, 1983), 81; see also Mikhail Gol'dshtein, *Zapiski muzykanta* (Frankfurt / Main: Possev-verlag, 1970), 33,

for an example of how the author was obliged to insert this cliché into his newspaper articles about music.

128. Cherniavskii, "Aleksandr Sergeevich Pushkin," 7.

129. Luppol, "Velichie Pushkina," 155–156.

130. Discussion with Boris N. Mironov, Institute of History, St. Petersburg, July 1989.

131. Mandelshtam, *Hope against Hope*, 281; Aleksandr Afinogenov, "Dnevnik 1937 goda," *Sovremennaia dramaturgiia* 2 (1993): 227; In her memoirs, Raisa Orlova described Luppol as belonging "to the first generation of intellectuals. The organic and ongoing connections with pre-revolutionary culture had not entirely been broken" (Orlova, *Memoirs*, 71).

132. Mandelshtam, *Hope against Hope*, 408.

133. Iu. U. Babushkin, introduction to *V. V. Veresaev* (Moscow, 1966), 26–27.

134. V. M. Nol'de, *Veresaev: Zhizn' i tvorchestvo* (Tula, 1986), 150–151, 164.

135. GARF, f. 305, op. 1, d. 1, l. 59.

136. V. V. Veresaev, *Zhizn' Pushkina* (Moscow, 1936), 151–152. English translation taken from *A. S. Pushkin: A Biographical Sketch*, translated by H. G. Scott (Moscow, 1937), 47–48; I am indebted to Monika Greenleaf of Stanford University for help concerning this play.

137. A. S. Pushkin, *Stseny iz rytsarskikh vremen*, in *Sobranie sochinenii* VII (Moscow, 1937), 346.

138. The proofs for this manuscript located in the Russian State Archive for Literature and Art show that the second paragraph about the destruction of the old order was written at a later date than the first paragraph summarizing the play. In his unpublished draft, Veresaev wrote "routes leading to a completely new, open road are needed." RGALI, f. 1041, op. 1, d. 29, l. 212.

6. Anniversary of Turmoil

1. In 1936, the *Komitet po delam iskusstvo*, under the auspices of Sovnarkom, took over the general supervision of theater and the arts that had previously been the purview of the People's Commissariat of Enlightenment. The Committee on the Arts supervised the work of republican, regional and city administrations of the arts and coordinated the work of Soviet cultural institutions such as the Union of Soviet Writers, the Union of Soviet Composers and the Central Administration of the Cinema and Photo Industry. T. P. Korzhikina, *Istoriia gosudarstvennykh uchrezhdenii SSSR* (Moscow, 1986), 119.

2. RGALI, f. 962, op. 3, d. 326, l. 43.

3. In the early years of the revolution, some members of the proletarian culture organization, Proletkul't, sought to create a distinctly proletarian art, while others worked to bring Chaikovskii and Chekhov to the masses. Lynn Mally, *The Culture of the Future: The Proletkult Movement in Revolutionary Russia* (Berkeley: University of California Press, 1990), xxvi–xxvii.

4. Clark, "Little Heroes and Big Deeds," 195; Lynn Mally, "The Problem of the Amateur: Defining *Samodeiatel'nyi teatr*," (paper presented at the conference "Inventing the Soviet Union: Language, Power and Representation, 1917–1945," Indiana University, November 7–9, 1997), 13–17. For a discussion of Soviet literature in the 1920s, see Robert A. Maguire, *Red Virgin Soil: Soviet Literature in the 1920's* (Princeton, N.J.: Princeton University Press, 1968); Edward J. Brown, *The Proletarian Episode in Russian Literature* (New York: Columbia University Press, 1953).

5. Kerzhentsev, who had played a major role in the proletarian culture movement, was now in charge of promoting cultural forms that he had previously rejected.

6. Tucker, *Stalin in Power,* 279–280.

7. TsGAMO, f. 4341, op. 4, d. 80, l. 95; GARF, f. 2306, op. 70, d. 1090, l. 36. See I. V. Stalin, "Ob uchebnike istorii VKP(b)," *Sochineniia* 1 [XIV]: 250–252, for Stalin's periodization of Party history. See also David Brandenberger, "The 'Short Course to Modernity': Stalinist History Textbooks, Mass Culture and the Formation of Popular Russian National Identity, 1934–1956" (Ph.D. diss., Harvard University, 1999).

8. Lowell Tillett, *The Great Friendship: Soviet Historians on the Non-Russian Nationalities* (Chapel Hill: University of North Carolina Press, 1969), 51.

9. The Dramatists' Section of the Union of Soviet Writers, for example, held a meeting on June 19, 1935, to discuss the preparation of jubilee plays. RGALI, f. 631, op. 2, d. 91, ll. 2–21.

10. RGALI, f. 962, op. 3, d. 288, l. 7.

11. RGALI, f. 962, op. 3, d. 287, l. 30.

12. RGALI, f. 631, op. 2, d. 171, ll. 57–58 (1936).

13. RGALI, f. 962, op. 3, d. 288, l. 7 (1937).

14. For a discussion of how the amateur movement itself became more and more professionalized during these years, see Mally, "The Problem of the Amateur," 22–24.

15. RGALI, f. 962, op. 3, d. 287, l. 103 (1937); f. 631, op. 2, d. 177, l. 57 (1936). Both of these men lost their jobs before the anniversary. Kirshon was arrested and killed in July 1937.

16. The Malyi Theater's plans for this show fell through, and for the jubilee the theater produced the Soviet opera *Virgin Soil Upturned.* RGALI, f. 631, op. 2, d. 98, ll. 2–3; f. 962, op. 3, d. 330, l. 7.

17. RGALI, f. 962, op. 3, d. 287, ll. 124-125.

18. Ibid., l. 127.

19. TsMAM, f. 2007, op. 1, d. 61, l. 89.

20. Ibid., l. 85.

21. Ibid., l. 91.

22. GARF, f. 5446, op. 20, d. 2571a, l. 15.

23. *O podgotovke i provedenii prazdnovaniia 20-letiia Velikoi Sotsialisticheskoi Oktiabr'skoi Revoliutsii v shkolakh i detsadakh Voronezhskoi oblasti,* edited by V. K. Nechapaev (Voronezh: Voronezhskoi Oblastnoi Otdel Narodnogo Obrazovaniia, 1937), 3, 4.

24. Semioticians Lotman and Uspenskij have argued that the use of sharply divided binary oppositions with no middle ground is a particularly Russian cultural model. Ju. M. Lotman and B. A. Uspenskij, "The Role of Dual Models in the Dynamics of Russian Culture," in *The Semiotics of Russian Culture,* Michigan Slavic Contributions 11 (Ann Arbor: Department of Slavic Languages and Literatures, University of Michigan, 1984), 4–5.

25. K. G. Granich, et al., *Metodicheskoe pis'mo po podgotovke k XX-god. Oktiabr'skoi Revoliutsii* (Sverdlovsk: Sverdlovskii Oblastnoi Dom Narodnogo Tvorchestva, 1937), 6.

26. TsGAMO, f. 4341, op. 4, d. 80, l. 6.

27. *Dvadtsat' let sovetskoi vlasti: Statisticheskii sbornik. Tsifrovoi material dlia propagandistov* (Moscow: Partizdat, 1937).

28. *O podgotovke i provedenii prazdnovaniia 20-letiia,* 11–15.

29. TsGAMO, f. 4341, op. 4, d. 80, l. 74.

30. TsMAM, f. 2007, op. 1, d. 60, l. 12 (1937).

31. As Lars Erik Blomqvist has pointed out, because of the increasing tendency in the 1930s toward representing the Soviet Union as an ideal society, the only possible conflict was that between "good and better." Blomqvist, "Some Utopian Elements," 300.

32. TsMAM, f. 2007, op. 1, d. 60, l. 75.

33. Ibid., l. 87.

34. K. P. Chudinova, "V te trudnye gody . . . ," *Voprosy istorii KPSS* 12 (1989): 123–124. My thanks to Kathleen E. Smith of Hamilton College for helping me to identify Chudinova.

35. TsMAM, f. 2007, op. 1, d. 60, l. 101.

36. Ibid., l. 19.

37. The other important film *Lenin in October* will be discussed below.

38. Although the film was not actually shown during the anniversary, its design reveals the attempts of cultural authorities to reshape the tsarist past in 1937, and therefore is pertinent here.

39. RGALI, f. 962, op. 3, d. 287, l. 59.

40. Ibid.

41. Ibid., l. 34.

42. Ibid.

43. A. Tolstoi and V. Petrov, *Petr I* (Series 1 and 2), in *Izbrannye stsenarii sovetskogo kino* 1 (Moscow, 1951), 543–544, 576, 602–605.

44. Tucker, *Stalin in Power*, 63, 116.

45. RGALI, f. 962, op. 3, d. 288, l. 6 (1937).

46. Stalin, "Ob uchebnike istorii VKP(b)," 248–250.

47. *Dvadtsat' let Velikoi Oktiabr'skoi Sotsialisticheskoi Revoliutsii v SSSR: Tezisy dlia propagandistov* (Moscow: Partizdat, 1937).

48. Tumarkin, *Lenin Lives*, 252.

49. Bonnell, *Iconography of Power*, 160.

50. See Miller, *Folklore for Stalin*.

51. Dzhambul Dzhabaev, "Pesnia o Staline," *Krest'ianka* 2 (1937): overleaf.

52. RGALI, f. 631, op. 15, d. 223, l. 36.

53. RTsKhIDNI, f. 17, op. 3, d. 976, ll. 24–25. Screenwriters received less: 5,000 for a submission; 30,000 for first place; and 20,000 for second and third places.

54. RGALI, f. 962, op. 3, d. 293, l. 11.

55. Ibid.

56. *Literaturnaia gazeta,* December 12, 1937.

57. *P,* December 14, 1937.

58. Peter Kenez, *Cinema and Soviet Society, 1917–1953* (Cambridge: Cambridge University Press, 1992), 230. In November 1937, Kerzhentsev was severely criticized for including the role of Stalin in *Man with a Rifle* without his permission. RTsKhIDNI, f. 17, op. 120, d. 256, ll. 162–163.

59. A. Kapler, *Lenin v oktiabr',* in *Izbrannye stsenarii sovetskogo kino* 2 (Moscow, 1951), 9, 12.

60. Robert M. Slusser, *Stalin in October: The Man Who Missed the Revolution* (Baltimore: Johns Hopkins University Press, 1990), 229, 249.

61. RTsKhIDNI, f. 12, op. 2, d. 177, l. 1–2.

62. Ibid., ll. 4–5.

63. Ibid., l. 7.

64. For a discussion of Krupskaia's relationship with Stalin in the 1930s, see V. A. Kumanev and I. S. Kulikova, *Protivostoianie: Krupskaia—Stalin* (Moscow: Nauka, 1994).

65. RGALI, f. 962, op. 3, d. 293, l. 4.

66. The ending to the first part of the film showed Peter celebrating the birth of a son and presumably heir by his new wife Catherine. The second part of the film dealt with the treachery of Peter's eldest son, Alexei, and depicted the Senate sentencing Alexei to death. Tolstoi and Petrov, *Petr I,* 607–608.

67. This male heir did not, however, survive into adulthood.

68. RGALI, f. 962, op. 3, d. 287, l. 3; d. 288, l. 8.

69. Five out of ten playwrights did not submit plays for various reasons. A. Afinogenov, for example, could not submit his jubilee play *Velikii Vybor* because he had been excluded from the Party. Afinogenov, "Dnevnik 1937 goda," *Sovremennaia dramaturgiia* 3 (1993): 220, note 13; RGALI, f. 962, op. 3, d. 293, l. 1.

70. RGALI, f. 962, op. 3, d. 293, l. 12.

71. RGALI, f. 962, op. 3, d. 327, l. 4.

72. RGALI, f. 962, op. 3, d. 293, l. 21.

73. RGALI, f. 962, op. 3, d. 327, l. 4.

74. Tumarkin, *Lenin Lives*, 198–199; "Ilich Will Wake Up Soon: A Fairy Tale from Viatka," in *Mass Culture in Soviet Russia: Tales, Poems, Movies, Plays and Folklore, 1917–53*, edited by James von Geldern and Richard Stites (Bloomington: Indiana University Press, 1995), 125–127.

75. TsMAM, f. 2007, op. 1, d. 60, l. 7.

76. TsMAM, f. 2007, op. 1, d. 61, l. 115.

77. Ibid., l. 116.

78. RGALI, f. 962, op. 3, d. 330, l. 8.

79. RTsKhIDNI, f. 17, op. 120, d. 256, ll. 161–163.

80. RGALI, f. 631, op. 2, d. 177, ll. 32–33.

81. Pseudonym of A. Gol'denberg.

82. RGALI, f. 631, op. 2, d. 177, l. 37.

83. Ibid.

84. RGALI, f. 631, op. 2, d. 155, ll. 3–5.

85. Susan Amert, "Bill'-Belotserkovskii, V. M.," in *Modern Encyclopedia of Russian and Soviet Literature*, 3, edited by Harry Weber (Gulf Breeze, Fla.: Academic International Press, 1977), 23–27.

86. RGALI, f. 631, op. 2, d. 155, ll. 46–56; f. 962, op. 3, d. 330, ll. 7–8.

87. RGALI, f. 631, op. 15, d. 223, l. 7.

88. RGALI, f. 962, op. 3, d. 287, l. 1.

89. RGALI, f. 631, op. 15, d. 237, l. 20.

90. RGALI, f. 631, op. 15, d. 223, l. 9.

91. Nakoriakov himself was purged in 1937 and rehabilitated in 1957.

92. RGALI, f. 962, op. 3, d. 293, l. 4.

93. TsMAM, f. 2007, op. 1, d. 61, l. 107.

94. RGALI, f. 962, op. 3, d. 293, l. 67.

95. Jay Leyda, *Kino: A History of the Russian and Soviet Film*, 3rd ed. (Princeton, N.J.: Princeton University Press, 1983), 339–340.

96. RGALI, f. 962, op. 3, d. 288, l. 3.

97. Ibid., l. 40.

98. GARF, f. 2306, op. 70, d. 515, l. 67.

99. RGALI, f. 962, op. 3, d. 288, l. 3.

100. With the help of a friend, she then found a position as a director of a small sewing collective. She was arrested in 1938. Chudinova, "V te trudnye gody," 123–124.

101. For a discussion of the effect of the purges on Soviet administration, see Moshe Lewin, "Stability, Society and Ideology," in *The Making of the Soviet System*, 221–222.

102. RGALI, f. 962, op. 3, d. 288, l. 59–60.

103. RGALI, f. 962, op. 3, d. 317, ll. 87, 82, 86, 88.

104. Ibid., ll. 22, 25.

105. Ibid., ll. 18–19.

106. Ibid., l. 39.

107. Ibid., l. 73.

108. RGALI, f. 962, op. 3, d. 293, l. 57.

109. Ibid., l. 64.

110. Ibid., l. 68.

7. Celebrating Civic Participation

1. RTsKhIDNI, f. 17, op. 114, d. 726, l. 17.

2. See Ellen Wimberg, "Socialism, Democratism and Criticism: The Soviet Press and the National Discussion of the 1936 Draft Constitution," *Soviet Studies* 44, no. 2 (1992): 323–324, for an analysis of the different stages of the draft discussion.

3. *CD*, 80.

4. In October 1937, the Central Committee approved a budget of over 885 million rubles for the elections and even discussed whether citizens on long distance trains and in leper hospitals would vote. RTsKhIDNI, f. 17, op. 3, d. 992, l. 79; d. 993, ll. 9–10.

5. J. Arch Getty, "State and Society under Stalin: Constitutions and Elections in the 1930s," *Slavic Review* 50, no. 1 (Spring 1991): 18–35.

6. Sarah Davies arrives at a similar conclusion using NKVD reports that corroborate the institutional sources used here. See Davies, *Popular Opinion*, 102–112.

7. Getty, "State and Society under Stalin," 25–27.

8. Fitzpatrick, *Everyday Stalinism*, 178.

9. Quoted in Daniel Field, *Rebels in the Name of the Tsar* (Boston: Unwin Hyman, 1989), 33.

10. Ibid., 42.

11. Maurice Hindus, *Red Bread: Collectivization in a Russian Village* (Bloomington: Indiana University Press, 1988), 149.

12. RTsKhIDNI, f. 17, op. 114, d. 761, l. 102.

13. GARF, f. 2306, op. 70, d. 512a, l. 124 (February 1937).

14. *CD*, 133.

15. Ibid., 113.

16. Davies, *Popular Opinion*, 112.

17. Wimberg, "Socialism, Democratism and Criticism," 318–324.

18. GARF, f. 3316, op. 41, d. 105, l. 83.

19. RTsKhIDNI, f. 17, op. 120, d. 232, ll. 40, 44.

20. *SSSR na ekrane*, 10 (1936), RGAKFD, 1–3470; RGALI, f. 962, op. 3, d. 293, l. 35.

21. TsAODM, f. 432, op. 1, d. 179, ll. 32–33, 69.

22. Although they are not a focus of this work, elections to the republic-level soviets and local soviets took place in 1938 and 1939.

23. TsGAMO, f. 5832, op. 1, d. 136, l. 15.

24. *CD*, 157.

25. I. V. Stalin, "O proekte konstitutsii soiuza SSR," in *Sochineniia* 1 [XIV] 1934–40 (Stanford, Calif.: Hoover Institution, 1967), 180.

26. Ibid., 179.

27. RTsKhIDNI, f. 17, op. 120, d. 232, l. 76.

28. RTsKhIDNI, f. 78, op. 1, d. 605, l. 11; TsAODM, f. 63, op. 1, d. 716, l. 18 (1937). See Terence Emmons, "The Peasant and the Emancipation," in *The Peasant in Nineteenth-Century Russia*, edited by Wayne S. Vucinich (Stanford, Calif.: Stanford University Press, 1968), 59–61; Lynne Viola, *Peasant Rebels under Stalin: Collectivization and the Culture of Peasant Resistance* (New York: Oxford University Press, 1996), 63.

29. Arzhilovsky, in *IT*, 127.

30. TsMAM, f. 528, op. 1, d. 409, l. 7.

31. TsAODM, f. 63, op. 1, d. 716, l. 4.

32. These representations of Stalin's holy power were similar to Muscovite depictions of the role of the tsar. See Daniel B. Rowland, "Did Muscovite Literary Ideology Place Any Limits on the Power of the Tsar (1540's–1660's)?" *Russian Review* 49 (1990): 125–155.

33. TsMAM, f. 150, op. 5, d. 26, l. 163.

34. RTsKhIDNI, f. 17, op. 114, d. 800, l. 30.

35. TsMAM, f. 528, op. 1, d. 517, ll. 16–17.

36. TsGAMO, f. 5849, op. 1, d. 1053, l. 10.

37. TsMAM, f. 528, op. 1, d. 409, l. 7.

38. In Noginskii District, Moscow Region.

39. TsGAMO, f. 5849, op. 1, d. 1001, l. 2.

40. RTsKhIDNI, f. 475, op. 2, d. 164, l. 7.

41. TsGAMO, f. 5849, op. 1, d. 1001, l. 7.

42. RTsKhIDNI, f. 17, op. 120, d. 232, l. 45.

43. Stalin, "O proekte konstitutsii," 156–166.

44. Ibid., 157, 162.

45. Ibid., 157.

46. Ibid., 161.

47. Ibid., 162–64.

48. See *CD*, 156 (Articles 124, 125, 127); 141, 155 (Articles 7–10, 118–120); 156 (Article 123).

49. *CD*, 156.

50. GARF, f. 3316, op. 41, d. 105, l. 23.

51. GARF, f. 2306, op. 70, d. 512a, ll. 165–66.

52. GARF, f. 3316, op. 41, d. 105, l. 51.

53. RTsKhIDNI, f. 17, op. 120, d. 256, l. 42.

54. GARF, f. 2306, op. 70, d. 512a, ll. 110, 125.

55. GARF, f. 3316, op. 41, d. 105, l. 23.

56. TsKhDMO, f. 1, op. 23, d. 1180, l. 122.

57. RTsKhIDNI, f. 17, op. 120, d. 232, l. 52.

58. GARF, f. 2306, op. 70, d. 512a, l. 126 (1937).

59. TsAODM, f. 432, op. 1, d. 180, l. 120.

60. GARF, f. 3316, op. 41, d. 105, l. 24.

61. Ibid., l. 126.

62. For a discussion of rumors in the Soviet countryside as a form of resistance, see Viola, *Peasant Rebels under Stalin*, 46–66.

63. GARF, f. 2306, op. 70, d. 512a, l. 124.

64. RTsKhIDNI, f. 17, op. 120, d. 232, l. 71.

65. GARF, f. 3316, op. 41, d. 105, l. 105.

66. RTsKhIDNI, f. 17, op. 120, d. 232, l. 82.

67. RTsKhIDNI, f. 17, op. 114, d. 761, ll. 105–106.

68. *CD*, 155.

69. See Chatterjee, "Celebrating Women," for a discussion of the Soviet population's adoption of the state's language of welfare.

70. TsAODM, f. 432, op. 1, d. 179, l. 33.

71. TsAODM, f. 432, op. 1, d. 165, l. 146.

72. Getty, "State and Society under Stalin," 26.

73. RTsKhIDNI, f. 17, op. 120, d. 232, l. 50.

74. *CD*, 141.

75. RTsKhIDNI, f. 12, op. 1, d. 647, ll. 13–14.

76. Ibid., l. 8. Many workers confused the constitution with the 1936 abortion law that the Soviet government also circulated for public discussion in June 1936.

77. *CD*, 141.

78. GARF, f. 3316, op. 41, d. 105, l. 52.
79. RTsKhIDNI, f. 17, op. 120, d. 232, l. 49.
80. GARF, f. 3316, op. 41, d. 105, ll. 24, 51–52, 80.
81. Ibid., l. 80.
82. RTsKhIDNI, f. 17, op. 120, d. 232, l. 50.
83. Ibid., l. 86.
84. *CD*, 143.
85. GARF, f. 3316, op. 41, d. 105, l. 157.
86. *CD*, 156.
87. RGALI, f. 962, op. 21, d. 16, ll. 37, 92.
88. TsKhDMO, f. 1, op. 23, d. 1251, l. 18.
89. RTsKhIDNI, f. 17, op. 114, d. 761, l. 96.
90. In 1937, out of 38,000 reading room attendants in the RSFSR, only 1,379 had a secondary education; 54 percent of reading room attendants had only four years of education. Because these jobs paid very little, people did not remain in them for long. In order to work effectively, the reading room attendant or club director had to have the financial and moral support of the chairman of the village soviet; this support was often not forthcoming. GARF, f. 2306, op. 70, d. 515, ll. 3, 48.
91. RTsKhIDNI, f. 12, op. 1, d. 574, l. 21.
92. GARF, f. 2306, op. 70, d. 515, l. 8 (1937).
93. Ibid., l. 49.
94. Getty, "State and Society under Stalin," 25.
95. GARF, f. 2306, op. 70, d. 515, l. 33.
96. RTsKhIDNI, f. 17, op. 120, d. 232, l. 48.
97. RTsKhIDNI, f. 17, op. 114, d. 761, l. 97.
98. Arzhilovsky, in *IT*, 127.
99. For the objections of local activists see Fitzpatrick, *Everyday Stalinism*, 131.
100. RTsKhIDNI, f. 17, op. 114, d. 761, l. 87.
101. *Krest'ianka* 12 (1937): back cover.
102. TsAODM, f. 85, op. 1, d. 1207, ll. 13–14.
103. TsKhDMO, f. 1, op. 3, d. 170, l. 60.
104. TsMAM, f. 528, op. 1, d. 517, l. 4.
105. Ibid.
106. Ibid., ll. 82–3.
107. Getty, "State and Society under Stalin," 31.
108. TsAODM, f. 78, op. 1, d. 203, l. 121.
109. TsMAM, f. 150, op. 5, d. 26, l. 75.
110. By the end of the 1930s, Russian classes did become mandatory in all Soviet schools.
111. GARF, f. 2306, op. 70, d. 515, l. 33.
112. TsMAM, f. 528, op. 1, d. 517, l. 75. For a similar episode in a different school, see Davies, *Popular Opinion*, 107.
113. TsMAM, f. 528, op. 1, d. 517, l. 75.
114. Ibid.

8. Celebrations and Power

1. Robert W. Thurston, *Life and Terror in Stalin's Russia* (New Haven, Conn.: Yale University Press, 1996).
2. Kotkin, *Magnetic Mountain*, 22–23.
3. See Getty, *Origins of the Great Purges;* Rittersporn, *Stalinist Simplifications*.
4. Kotkin, *Magnetic Mountain*, 3–6.

5. RTsKhIDNI, f. 17, op. 120, d. 348, l. 74 ob.

6. Alice G. Marquis, *Hopes and Ashes: The Birth of Modern Times, 1929–1939* (New York: Free Press, 1986).

7. For a detailed analysis of these celebrations, see *RR*.

8. For a discussion of the use of depoliticized culture to promote consent, see Victoria de Grazia, *The Culture of Consent: Mass Organization of Leisure in Fascist Italy* (Cambridge: Cambridge University Press, 1981); Detlev J. K. Peukert, *Inside Nazi Germany: Conformity, Opposition, and Racism in Everyday Life,* translated by Richard Deveson (New Haven, Conn.: Yale University Press, 1987); Terry A. Cooney, *Balancing Acts: American Thought and Culture in the 1930s* (New York: Twayne Publishers, 1995), 99–103.

9. For a discussion of the everyday life, culture and mythology of Nazism, see Peukert, *Inside Nazi Germany;* George L. Mosse, *Nazi Culture* (New York: Grosset and Dunlap, 1966). Ian Kershaw, *The Hitler Myth: Image and Reality in the Third Reich* (New York: Oxford University Press, 1987).

10. See Igor Golomstock, *Totalitarian Art In the Soviet Union, the Third Reich, Fascist Italy, and the People's Republic of China* (London: Collins Harvill, 1990).

BIBLIOGRAPHY

Archival Materials

GARF (Gosudarstvennyi arkhiv Rossiiskoi Federatsii)
From the former TsGA RSFSR
    f. 305—Vsesoiuznyi pushkinskii komitet
    f. 2306—Narkompros RSFSR
From the former TsGAOR
    f. 3316—Tsentral'nyi ispolnitel'nyi komitet SSSR
    f. 5451—Vsesoiuznyi tsentral'nyi sovet professional'nykh soiuzov
    f. 5446—Sovet narodnykh komissarov
    f. 6887—Redaktsiia zhurnala *Krasnyi arkhiv*
    f. 7576—Komitet po fizicheskoi kul'ture i sportu pri sovete ministrov SSSR
    f. 9499—Sovetskaia sektsiia mezhdunarodnoi vystavki v Parizhe v 1937g.
Hoover Institution Archives, Stanford University, Poster Collection
RGALI (Rossiiskii gosudarstvennyi arkhiv literatury i iskusstva) (formerly TsGALI)
    f. 384—Pushkinskii komitet
    f. 617—Pis'ma izdateliam *Pravdy*
    f. 631—Soiuz sovetskikh pisatelei
    f. 962—Komitet po delam iskusstva pri Sovnarkom SSSR
    f. 963—Gosudarstvennyi teatr im. Meierkhol'da
    f. 1041—Veresaev, V. V. (Lichnyi fond)
    f. 2091—Vertov, Dziga (Lichnyi fond)
    f. 2196—Kirpotin, V. (Lichnyi fond)
    f. 2450—Ministerstvo kinematografii SSSR
    f. 2451—Glavnoe upravlenie po proizvodstvu khronikal'no-dokumental'nykh fil'mov
    f. 2591—Popov, Petr (Lichnyi fond)
    f. 2652—Romas, Iakov (Lichnyi fond)
    f. 2778—Frolov, Andrei (Lichnyi fond)
    f. 2932—Tsentral'nyi dom rabotnikov iskusstva SSSR
RTsKhIDNI (Rossiiskii tsentr khraneniia i izucheniia dokumentov noveishei istorii) (formerly TsPA IML pri TsK KPSS)
    f. 12—Krupskaia, Nadezhda (Lichnyi fond)
    f. 17—Tsentral'nyi komitet VKP(b)
    f. 78—Kalinin, Mikhail (Lichnyi fond)
    f. 79—Kuibyshev, Valerian (Lichnyi fond)
    f. 475—Glavsevmorput'
TsAODM (Tsentral'nyi arkhiv obshchestvennykh dvizhenii Moskvy) (formerly Partiinyi arkhiv Instituta istorii partii MGK I MK KPSS)
    f. 4—Moskovskii gorodskoi komitet VKP (b)
    f. 63—Raionnyi komitet VKP (b) Baumanskogo raiona
    f. 67—Raionnyi komitet VKP (b) Kirovskogo raiona
    f. 69—Raionnyi komitet VKP (b) Krasnopresnenskogo raiona
    f. 73—Raionnyi komitet VKP (b) Krasnogvardeiskogo raiona
    f. 74—Raionnyi komitet VKP (b) Leningradskogo raiona
    f. 78—Raionnyi komitet VKP (b) Oktiabr'skogo raiona
    f. 85—Raionnyi komitet VKP (b) Sokol'nicheskogo raiona

f. 369—VKP (b) Trekhgornoi manufaktury im. Dzerzhinskogo
f. 432—VKP (b) zavoda Dinamo im. Kirova
TsGAMO (Tsentral'nyi gosudarstvennyi arkhiv Moskovskoi oblasti)
    f. 2180—Moskovskii oblastnoi sovet professional'nykh soiuzov
    f. 4341—Moskovskii oblastnoi otdel narodnogo obrazovaniia
    f. 5832—Ispolkom Pushkinskogo gorodskogo soveta
    f. 5849—Raionnyi sovet Noginskogo raiona
TsKhDMO (Tsentr khraneniia dokumentov molodezhnykh organizatsii) (formerly
    TsA VLKSM)
    f. 1—Tsentral'nyi komitet Komsomola
TsMAM (Tsentral'nyi Munitsipal'nyi arkhiv Moskvy) (formerly TsGA g. Moskvy)
    f. 12—Moskovskaia tsentral'naia gorodskaia biblioteka
    f. 150—Moskovskii gorodskoi sovet
    f. 415—Gosudarstvennyi avtozavod im. Stalina
    f. 528—Moskovskii gorodskoi otdel narodnogo obrazovaniia
    f. 718—Moskovskii gorodskoi sovet professional'nykh soiuzov
    f. 2007—Upravlenie po delam iskusstva Mosgorispolkoma
    f. 2411—Moskovskii kommunal'nyi musei

Journals and Newspapers

Bezbozhnik
Fizkul'tura i sport
Izvestiia
Klub
Kolkhoznik
Komsomol'skaia pravda
Komsomol'skaia pravda—na stroitel'stve V.S.Kh.V.
Krasnaia nov'
Krasnyi arkhiv
Krest'ianka
Krokodil
Literaturnaia gazeta
Literaturnoe nasledstvo
Literaturnoe obozrenie
Literaturnyi sovremennik
Murzilka
Nashi dostizheniia
Novaia Sibir' (Irkutsk)
Oktiabr'
Plamia (Ivanovo)
Pravda
Prokatka (Goskozhzavod im. L. M. Kaganovicha)
Sovetskoe studenchestvo
Vecherniaia Moskva

Films

Alexandrov, G. *Tsirk*, 1936.
Bogatyry rodiny. Rossiiskii gosudarstvennyi arkhiv kinofoto dokumentov (RGAKFD)
    (formerly TsGAKFD) 1-4034, 1937.
Ivanov, A. *Taezhnye druz'ia.* Animated film, 1939.

Kalatozov, Mikhail. *Valerii Chkalov,* 1941.
Levin Moisei. *Puteshestvie v Arzrum.* Written by Mikhail Bleiman, 1937.
Naroditskii, A. *Iunost' poeta.* Written by A. Slonimskii, 1937.
Papanintsy. RGAKFD 1-4145, 1938.
Petrov, V. *Petr I.* Written by A. Tolstoi and V. Petrov. Series 1, 1937; Series 2, 1939.
Radostnaia vstrecha. RGAKFD 1-4187, 1937.
Romm, Mikhail. *Lenin v Oktiabr'.* Written by A. Kapler, 1937.
S novom godom. RGAKFD 1–13366, 1936.
Soiuzkinozhurnal 11 (1935). RGAKFD 1-2525.
Soiuzkinozhurnal 1 (1937). RGAKFD 1-2911.
SSSR na ekrane 10 (1936). RGAKFD 1-3470.
Tsvetuiushchaia iunost'. Documentary film, 1939.
Vertov, Dziga. *Tri geroiny.* RGAKFD 1-4188, 1938.
Zdrastvui novyi god. RGAKFD 1-4923, 1937.

Other Primary Sources

Afinogenov, Aleksandr. "Dnevnik 1937 goda." *Sovremennaia dramaturgiia* 1 (1993); 2 (1993): 223–241; 3 (1993): 217–230.
Agitatsiia za schast'e: Sovetskoe iskusstvo stalinskoi epokhi. Gosudarstvennyi Russkii Muzei, Sankt-Peterburg. Dusseldorf-Bremen: Interarteks-Temmen Edition, 1994.
Akhmatova, A. A. "'Adol'f' Benzhamena Konstana v tvorchestve Pushkina." In *Vremennik* 1. Leningrad and Moscow: Akademiia Nauk, 1936.
Aleksandrova, Z. "Na parade." *Murzilka* 1 (January 1937): 11.
Alekseev, Mikhail. *Kariukha; Drachuny; Dilogiia.* Moscow, 1985.
Aptekar', M. *Russkaia istoricheskaia zhivopis'.* Moscow and Leningrad: State Art Publishers, 1939.
Arzhilovsky, Andrei Stepanovich. "Diary of Andrei Stepanovich Arzhilovsky." In *Intimacy and Terror: Soviet Diaries of the 1930's,* edited by Veronique Garros, Natalia Korenevskaya, and Thomas Lahusen. Translated by Carol A. Flath. New York: New Press, 1995.
Baidukov, Georgii. *Iz dnevnika pilota.* Moscow, 1937.
———. *Over the North Pole.* Translation of *Iz dnevnika pilota,* by Jessica Smith. New York: Harcourt, Brace and Company, 1938.
———. *Russian Lindbergh: The Life of Valery Chkalov.* Washington, D.C.: Smithsonian Institution Press, 1991.
Bazykin, S. S. "Ukrasheniia i igrushki dlia elki." In *Elka: Sbornik statei i materialov,* edited by S. S. Bazykin and E. A. Flerina. Moscow: Uchpedgiz, 1937.
Bazykin, S. S., and E. A. Flerina, eds. *Elka: Sbornik statei i materialov.* Moscow: Uchpedgiz, 1937.
Bogdan, Valentina. *Mimikriia v SSSR.* Frankfurt a. M.: Polyglott-Druck GmbH, n.d.
Brontman, Lazar. *Na vershine mira.* Moscow, 1938.
———. *On Top of the World: The Soviet Expedition to the North Pole, 1937–38.* Translation of *Na vershine mira.* New York: Covici Friede, 1938.
Brontman, Lazar, and L. Khvat. *Geroicheskii perelet "Rodiny."* Moscow, 1938.
———. *The Heroic Flight of the "Rodina."* Translation of *Geroicheskii perelet "Rodiny."* Moscow: Foreign Languages Publishing House, 1938.
Bykovskaia, E. "Elochnye igrushki i ikh izgotovlenie." In *Elka: Sbornik statei i materialov,* edited by S. S. Bazykin and E. A. Flerina. Moscow: Uchpedgiz, 1937.
Byleeva, et al. *Novogodniaia elka: Sbornik dlia uchashchikhsia nachal'noi shkoly.* Moscow: MGK VLKSM, 1936.
Cherniavskii, E. "Aleksandr Sergeevich Pushkin." *Krasnyi arkhiv* 1 (1937): 5–12.

Chudinova, K. P. "V te trudnye gody. . . . " *Voprosy istorii KPSS* 12 (1989): 116–124; 1 (1990): 131–142.
Chukovskaya, Lydia. *Sofia Petrovna*. Translated by Aline Werth. Evanston, Ill.: Northwestern University Press, 1988.
David of Sassoun. Translated by Artin K. Shalian. Athens: Ohio University Press, 1964.
Detiam novogodniuiu elku. Novosibirsk: Zapadno-Sibirskogo Kraikom VLKSM, 1936.
Deviat' mesiatsev na dreifuiushchei stantsii "Severnyi Polius." Moscow, 1938.
Dostoevsky, Fyodor. "A Christmas Tree and a Wedding." In *White Nights and Other Stories*, translated by Constance Garnett. Melbourne: William Heinemann, 1950.
———. "The Heavenly Christmas Tree." In *An Honest Thief and Other Stories*, translated by Constance Garnett. New York: Macmillan, 1923.
Dunaevskii, Isaac, and V. Lebedev-Kumach. "Nu, kak ne zapet." In *Pesni Krasnoi Armii*. Moscow, 1937.
———. "Pesnia o rodine." In *Pesni Krasnoi Armii*. Moscow, 1937.
Dvadtsat' let Sovetskoi vlasti: Statisticheskii sbornik. Tsifrovoi material dlia propagandistov. Moscow: Partizdat, 1937.
Dvadtsat' let Velikoi Oktiabr'skoi Sotsialisticheskoi Revoliutsii v SSSR. Tezisy dlia propagandistov. Moscow: Partizdat, 1937.
Dzhabaev, Dzhambul. "Pesnia o Staline." *Krest'ianka* 2 (1937): overleaf.
Elizarov, I. Ia. *Prazdniki nastoiashchego i prazdniki proshlogo*. Leningrad, 1926.
Everyday Life in Russia. Compiled by Bertha Malnick. London: George G. Harrap, 1938.
Fischer, Louis, ed. *Thirteen Who Fled*. New York: Harper and Brothers, 1949.
Fischer, Markoosha. *My Lives in Russia*. New York: Harper and Brothers, 1944.
Fizkul'tura i sport v SSSR: Materialy k vsesoiuznomy dniu fizkul'turnika 1939 god. Moscow: Gos. izdatel'stvo fizkul'tury i sporta, 1939.
Flerina, E. "Elka v detskom sadu." In *Elka: Sbornik statei i materialov*, edited by S. S. Bazykin and E. A. Flerina. Moscow: Uchpedgiz, 1937.
Francis, Peter. *I Worked in a Soviet Factory*. London: Jarrolds, 1939.
Friese, H. G. "Student Life in a Soviet University." In *Soviet Education*, edited by George L. Kline. New York: Columbia University Press, 1957.
Frolov, Ignat Danilovich. "Diary of Ignat Danilovich Frolov." In *Intimacy and Terror: Soviet Diaries of the 1930's*, edited by Veronique Garros, Natalia Korenevskaya, and Thomas Lahusen. Translated by Carol A. Flath. New York: New Press, 1995.
Ganelin, R. Sh. Interview by author. St. Petersburg, Russia, November 1991.
Garri, A., and L. Kassil'. *Potolok Mira*. Moscow: Sovetskaia Literatura, 1934.
Garros, Veronique, Natalia Korenevskaya, and Thomas Lahusen, eds. *Intimacy and Terror: Soviet Diaries of the 1930's*. Translated by Carol A. Flath. New York: New Press, 1995.
Geroicheskaia epopeia: Al'bom foto-dokumentov. Moscow: Pravda, Partizdat, 1935.
Gide, Andre. *Afterthoughts: A Sequel to "Back from the USSR."* London: Martin Secker and Warburg, n.d.
———. *Back from the USSR*. London: Martin Secker and Warburg, 1937.
Ginzburg, Evgeniia Semenovna. *Journey into the Whirlwind*. New York: Harcourt, Brace and World, 1967.
Gladkov, Aleksandr. "Piat' let s Meierkhol'dom." In *Meierkhol'd* 2. Moscow: Soiuz Teatr. Deiatelei RSFSR, 1990.
Glan, Betti. *Prazdnik vsegda s nami*. Moscow, 1988.
———. *Udarno rabotat'—kul'turno otdykhat'*. Moscow, 1933.
Gol'dberg, Iu. "Kak organizovat' vstrechu novogo goda." *Klub* 23 (December 1937): 51–53.
Gol'dshtein, Mikhail. *Zapiski muzykanta*. Frankfurt/Main: Possev-Verlag, 1970.

Gorchakov, Alexei. "The Long Road." In *Thirteen Who Fled*, edited by Louis Fischer. New York: Harper and Brothers, 1949.

Gorkii, A. M. "Soviet Intellectuals." In *Culture and the People*. New York: Books for Libraries Press, 1970.

Gornev, Peter. "The Life of a Soviet Soldier." In *Thirteen Who Fled*, edited by Louis Fischer. New York: Harper and Brothers, 1949.

Gouzenko, Svetlana. *Before Igor: Memories of My Soviet Youth*. New York: Norton, 1960.

Granich, K. G., et al. *Metodicheskoe pis'mo po podgotovke k XX-god Oktiabr'skoi Revoliutsii*. Sverdlovsk: Sverdlovskii Oblastnoi Dom Narodnogo Tvorchestva, 1937.

Grinberg, B. "Pesni, muzyka na prazdnike elki." In *Elka: Sbornik statei i materialov*, edited by S. S. Bazykin and E. A. Flerina. Moscow: Uchpedgiz, 1937.

Hindus, Maurice. *Red Bread: Collectivization in a Russian Village*. 1931. Reprint, Bloomington: Indiana University Press, 1988.

"Ilich Will Wake Up Soon: A Fairy Tale from Viatka." In *Mass Culture in Soviet Russia: Tales, Poems, Movies, Plays and Folklore, 1917–53*, edited by James von Geldern and Richard Stites. Bloomington: Indiana University Press, 1995, 125–127.

Iunost' poeta. Leningrad: Lenfilm, 1937.

Jelagin, Juri. *Taming of the Arts*. Translated by Nicholas Wreden. New York: E. P. Dutton & Company, 1951.

Kak chitat' Pushkina. Ordzhonikidzegrad, 1937.

Kapler, A. *Lenin v oktiabr'*. In *Izbrannye stsenarii sovetskogo kino* 2. Moscow, 1951.

Kazanskii, B. "Gibel' poeta." *Literaturnyi sovremennik* 3 (1937): 219–243.

Kirpotin, V. *Aleksandr Sergeevich Pushkin*. Moscow, 1937.

———. *Nachalo: Avtobiograficheskie stranitsy*. Moscow, 1986.

———. *Nasledie Pushkina k kommunizmu*. Moscow, 1936.

———. "Pevets svobodoliubiia." *Komsomol'skaia pravda* 130 (June 6, 1936).

———. "Pushkinskii ideal politicheskoi svobody." *Literaturnaia gazeta* 56 (1936).

Kosterina, Nina. *Diary of Nina Kosterina*. Translated by Mirra Ginsberg. New York: Avon Books, 1968.

Koval, Nikolai. "One of the Many Millions." In *Thirteen Who Fled*, edited by Louis Fischer. New York: Harper and Brothers, 1949.

Krasovsky, Oleg. "Early Years." In *Soviet Youth*. Institute for the Study of the USSR, Series I, 51 (July 1959).

Krazhin, Petr. "False Dawn." In *Soviet Youth*. Institute for the Study of the USSR, Series I, 51 (July 1959).

Kremlev, G. D. *Rabochii material dlia organizatsii Novogodnego bala-maskarada v zheleznodorozhnykh klubakh i dvortsakh kul'tury*. Moscow, 1938.

Kriukova, M. S. "Glory to Stalin Shall Be Eternal." In *Folklore for Stalin*, by Frank Miller. New York: M. E. Sharpe, 1990.

Letopisi Gosudarstvennogo Literaturnogo Muzeia, kniga pervaia: Pushkin. Edited by M. Tsiavlovskii. Moscow, 1936.

Luppol, I. "Velichie Pushkina." *Oktiabr'* 4 (April 1937): 155–170.

Malakhova, Vera Ivanovna. "Four Years as a Frontline Physician." In *A Revolution of Their Own: Voices of Women in Soviet History*, edited by Barbara Alpern Engel and Anastasia Posadskaya-Vanderbeck. Boulder, Colo.: Westview Press, 1998.

Mandelshtam, Nadezhda. *Hope against Hope*. Translated by Max Hayward. New York: Atheneum, 1979.

Materialy k zasedaniiu vsesoiuznogo pushkinskogo komiteta, 29 ianvaria 1937 goda. Moscow: Vsesoiuznyi pushkinskii komitet, 1937.

Meilakh, B. "Nasledie Pushkina i sotsialisticheskaia kul'tura." *Krasnaia nov'* 1 (January 1937): 111–117.

Melikadze, E. S., and P. Sysoev. *Sovetskaia zhivopis'*. Moscow: Iskusstvo, 1939.

Metody obsluzhivaniia chitatelei v massovoi biblioteke: Uchebnoe posobie dlia bibliotechnykh tekhnikumov. Edited by E. V. Seglin. Moscow, 1938.

Mirskii, D. S. "Moim kritikam." In *Vremennik*, vol. 1. Leningrad and Moscow: Akademiia Nauk, 1936.

———. "Problema Pushkina." *Literaturnoe nasledstvo* 16–18 (1934): 91–112.

———. *Pushkin*. London: G. Routledge, 1926.

Moskva rekonstruiruetsia: Al'bom diagramm, toposkhem i fotografii po rekonstruktsii gor. Moskvy. Moscow, 1938.

Nash prazdnik: Sbornik proizvedenii dlia estrady. Moscow-Leningrad: Iskusstvo, 1938.

O podgotovke i provedenii prazdnovaniia 20-letiia Velikoi Sotsialisticheskoi Oktiabr'skoi Revoliutsii v shkolakh i detsadakh Voronezhskoi oblasti. Edited by V. K. Nechapaev. Voronezh: Voronezhskii Oblastnoi Otdel Narodnogo Obrazovaniia, 1937.

Orlova, Raisa. *Memoirs*. New York: Random House, 1983.

"O Trotskistskoi gruppe *Pereval*." *Literaturnoe obozrenie* 15 (1937): 20–24.

Ovchinnikova, E. "Elka v dome soiuzov." In *Elka: Sbornik statei i materialov*, edited by S. S. Bazykin and E. A. Flerina. Moscow: Uchpedgiz, 1937.

A Pageant of Youth. Moscow and Leningrad: State Art Publishers, 1939.

Papanin, Ivan. *Life on an Ice Floe: The Diary of Ivan Papanin*. Translation of *Zhizn' na l'dine: Dnevnik*. New York: Julian Messner, 1939.

———. *Zhizn' na l'dine: Dnevnik*. Moscow: Pravda, 1938.

Papanin, Ivan, et al. *Deviat' mesiatsev na dreifuiushchei stantsii "Severnyi Polius"*. Moscow: OGIZ, Gos. izdatel'stvo politicheskoi literatury, 1938.

Pesni Krasnoi Armii. Moscow, 1937.

Pisarevskii, D. *Organizatsiia narodnykh prazdnestv i gulianii: V pomoshch' sel'skomu politprosvetrabotniku*. Moscow: Narkompros RSFSR, 1939.

"Pis'mo Marii Semenovny Babushkinoi." *Krest'ianka* 16–17 (1937): 4–5.

Pokhod Cheliuskina. Moscow, 1934.

Postanovlenie biuro Kirovskogo RK VKP(b) o provedenii raionogo detskogo prazdnika posviashchennogo okonchaniiu 1935–36 uchebnogo goda. June 14, 1936.

Postyshev, L. P. "Ob ottse." In *Pavel Postyshev: Vospominaniia, vystupleniia, pis'ma*, edited by K. N. Atarov. Moscow: Politizdat, 1987.

Pushkin, A. S. *Stseny iz rytsarskikh vremen*. In *Sobranie sochinenii*, VII. Moscow, 1937.

Puteshestvie v Arzrum. Leningrad: Lenfilm, 1937.

Reiser, S. "Nenuzhnoe izdanie." *Literaturnoe obozrenie* 13 (1937): 40–41.

Report of Court Proceedings in the Case of the Anti-Soviet "Bloc of Rights and Trotskyites." Moscow: People's Commissariat of Justice of the USSR, 1938. Reprint, New York: Howard Fertig, 1988.

Rozanov, Sergei. *Spasibo: Stsenarii teatralizovannogo detskogo prazdnika posviashchennogo 20-letiiu Velikoi Oktiabr'skoi Revoliutsii*. Moscow: Tsentral'nyi Dom Vospitaniia Detei RSFSR, 1937.

Senkevich, Tatyana. "A Soviet Girl's Diary." In *Thirteen Who Fled*, edited by Louis Fischer. New York: Harper and Brothers, 1949.

Sergievskii, I. "Review of *Vremennik*." *Literaturnaia gazeta* 42 (1936).

Shtange, Galina. "Diary of Galina Vladimirovna Shtange." In *Intimacy And Terror: Soviet Diaries of the 1930's*, edited by Veronique Garros, Natalia Korenevskaya, and Thomas Lahusen. Translated by Carol A. Flath. New York: New Press, 1995.

Smith, Andrew. *I Was a Soviet Worker*. New York: Dutton, 1936.

Sorochenko, Nina. "Pre-school Education in the U.S.S.R." In *Soviet Education*, edited by George L. Kline. New York: Columbia University Press, 1957, 1–24.

Sovetskoe kino. Moscow: Iskusstvo, 1937.

Soviet Aviation. Moscow and Leningrad: State Art Publishers, 1939.

Soviet Films, 1938–1939. Moscow: State Publishing House for Cinema Literature, 1939.

Soviet Youth. Institute for the Study of the USSR, Series I, 51 (July 1959).

Stalin, I. V. "O proekte Konstitutsii Soiuza SSR." In *Sochineniia* 1 [XIV] 1934–40, edited by Robert H. McNeal. Stanford, Calif.: Hoover Institution, 1967.

———. "Ob uchebnike istorii VKP(b)." In *Sochineniia* 1 [XIV] 1934–40, edited by Robert H. McNeal. Stanford, Calif.: Hoover Institution, 1967.

Stalinskaia Konstitutsiia sotsializma. 2nd ed. Moscow, 1938.

Sto let so dnia smerti A. S. Pushkina. Akademiia Nauk SSSR. Moscow-Leningrad, 1938.

Tolstoi, A., and V. Petrov. *Petr I* (Series 1 and 2.) In *Izbrannye stsenarii sovetskogo kino*, 1. Moscow, 1951.

Tolstov, A. S. "Pushkin v shkole." *Krasnaia nov'* 1 (January 1937): 223–229.

Tvardovskii, A. "Muzhestvo." *Pravda* (October 28, 1938).

Tvorchestvo Narodov SSSR. Edited by A. M. Gorkii and L. Z. Mekhlis. Moscow, 1937.

Veresaev, V. V. *Zhizn' Pushkina.* Moscow, 1936.

Voyage of the Cheliuskin. By Members of the Expedition. Translation of *Pokhod Cheliuskina.* Translated by Alec Brown. New York: Macmillan, 1935.

Vsesoiuznyi parad fizkul'turnikov: Ukazaniia po stroevoi podgotovke uchastnikov vsesoiuznogo parada fizkul'turnikov 1939 g. Moscow, 1939.

Zaslavskii, D. "Rekord kritika Mirskogo." *Pravda* (August 28, 1936).

Zelnik, Reginald, ed. *A Radical Worker in Tsarist Russia: The Autobiography of Semen Ivanovich Kanatchikov.* Stanford, Calif.: Stanford University Press, 1986.

Zinovieva-Annibal, Lidia. "Thirty-three Abominations." Translated by Samuel Cioran. *Russian Literature Triquarterly* 9 (Spring 1974): 94–116.

Zoshchenko, Mikhail. "Bania." In *Sobranie sochinenii* I. Leningrad, 1986.

———. "V Pushkinskie dni." In *Sobranie sochinenii* II. Leningrad, 1986.

Secondary Sources

Anderson, Benedict. *Imagined Communities: Reflections on the Origins and Spread of Nationalism.* Rev. ed. London: Verso, 1991.

Armstrong, Terence. *The Russians in the Arctic: Aspects of Soviet Exploration and Exploitation of the Far North, 1937–57.* London: Methuen and Company, 1958.

Babushkin, Iu. U. Introduction to *V. V. Veresaev.* Edited by Iu. U. Babushkin. Moscow, 1966.

Bailes, Kendall. *Technology and Society under Lenin and Stalin.* Princeton, N.J.: Princeton University Press, 1978.

Bakhtin, M. *Rabelais and His World.* Translated by Helen Iswolsky. Cambridge, Mass.: M.I.T. Press, 1968.

Bank, B. V. "Iz istorii izucheniia chitatelei v SSSR." In *Sovetskii chitatel': Opyt konkretnosotsiologicheskogo issledovaniia.* Moscow: Kniga, 1968.

Bassin, Mark. "The Greening of Utopia: Nature and Landscape Aesthetics in Stalinist Art." In *Identities of Russian Architecture, 1500–Present*, edited by James Cracraft and Daniel B. Rowland. Forthcoming.

Berezin, Mabel. "Cultural Form and Political Meaning: State-Subsidized Theater, Ideology, and the Language of Style in Fascist Italy." *American Journal of Sociology* 99, no. 5 (March 1994): 1237–1286.

Bibikova, I. M., and N. I Levchenko, comps. *Agitatsionno-massovoe iskusstvo: Oformlenie prazdnestv.* Moscow: Iskusstvo, 1984.

Binns, Christopher A. P. "The Changing Face of Power: Revolution and Accommodation in the Development of the Soviet Ceremonial System." Part I: *Man* (New Series) 14, no. 4 (1979): 585–606. Part II: *Man* (New Series) 15, no. 1 (1980): 170–187.

Blomqvist, Lars Erik. "Some Utopian Elements in Stalinist Art." *Russian History/ History Russe* 11, no. 2–3 (Summer–Fall, 1984): 298–305.

Bloom, Lisa. *Gender on Ice: American Ideologies of Polar Expeditions.* Minneapolis: University of Minnesota Press, 1993.

Bonnell, Victoria E. *Iconography of Power: Soviet Political Posters under Lenin and Stalin.* Berkeley: University of California Press, 1997.

———. "The Peasant Woman in Stalinist Political Art of the 1930s." *American Historical Review* 98, no. 1 (February 1993): 55–82.

Bourdieu, Pierre. *Outline of a Theory of Practice.* Translated by Richard Nice. Cambridge: Cambridge University Press, 1977.

Brandenberger, David. "The 'Short Course to Modernity': Stalinist History Textbooks, Mass Culture and the Formation of Popular Russian National Identity, 1934–1956." Ph.D. diss., Harvard University, 1999.

Brooks, Jeffrey. *When Russia Learned to Read: Literacy and Popular Literature, 1861–1917.* Princeton, N.J.: Princeton University Press, 1985.

Brown, Edward J. *The Proletarian Episode in Russian Literature.* New York: Columbia University Press, 1953.

———. *Russian Literature since the Revolution.* Cambridge, Mass.: Harvard University Press, 1982.

Burbank, Jane. "Controversies over Stalinism: Searching for a Soviet Society." *Politics & Society* 19, no. 3 (1991): 325–340.

Canning, Kathleen. "Feminist History after the Linguistic Turn: Historicizing Discourse and Experience. *Signs* 19, no. 2 (Winter 1994): 368–404.

Cassiday, Julie A. "Marble Columns and Jupiter Lights: Theatrical and Cinematic Modeling of Soviet Show Trials in the 1920s." *Slavic and East European Journal* 42, no. 4 (1998): 640–660.

Castillo, Greg. "Peoples at an Exhibition: Soviet Architecture and the National Question." *South Atlantic Quarterly* 94, no. 3 (Summer 1995): 715–746.

Chartier, Roger. "Texts, Printing, Reading." In *The New Cultural History,* edited by Lynn Hunt. Berkeley: University of California Press, 1989.

Chatterjee, Choitali. "Celebrating Women: International Women's Day in Russia and the Soviet Union, 1909–1939." Ph.D. diss., Indiana University, 1995.

Clark, Katerina. "Little Heroes and Big Deeds: Literature Responds to the First Five-Year Plan." In *Cultural Revolution in Russia, 1928–1931,* edited by Sheila Fitzpatrick. Bloomington: Indiana University Press, 1978.

———. *Petersburg: Crucible of Cultural Revolution.* Cambridge, Mass.: Harvard University Press, 1995.

———. *The Soviet Novel: History as Ritual.* Chicago: University of Chicago Press, 1985.

Conquest, Robert. *The Great Terror: A Reassessment.* New York: Oxford University Press, 1990.

Cooney, Terry A. *Balancing Acts: American Thought and Culture in the 1930s.* New York: Twayne Publishers, 1995.

Cooper, Frederick, and Ann Laura Stoler, eds. *Tensions of Empire: Colonial Cultures in a Bourgeois World.* Berkeley: University of California Press, 1997.

Corn, Joseph J. *The Winged Gospel.* New York: Oxford University Press, 1983.

Curtiss, John. *The Russian Church and the Soviet State, 1917–50.* Boston: Little, Brown and Company, 1953.

Davies, Sarah. *Popular Opinion in Stalin's Russia: Terror, Propaganda and Dissent, 1934–1941* Cambridge: Cambridge University Press, 1997.

———. "'Us Against Them': Social Identity in Soviet Russia, 1934–41." *Russian Review* 56, no. 1 (January 1997): 70–89.

Davis, Susan G. *Parades and Power: Street Theater in Nineteenth Century Philadelphia.* Philadelphia: Temple University Press, 1986.

Debreczeny, Paul. "*Zhitie Aleksandra Boldinskogo:* Pushkin's Elevation to Sainthood in Soviet Culture." *South Atlantic Quarterly* 90, no. 2 (Spring 1991): 269–292.

de Grazia, Victoria. *The Culture of Consent: Mass Organization of Leisure in Fascist Italy.* Cambridge: Cambridge University Press, 1981.

Domherr, Ludwig L. *The Pushkin Edition of the U.S.S.R. Academy of Sciences.* East European Research Fund, Mimeographed Series No. 45. New York: Research Program of the U.S.S.R., 1953.

Driver, Sam. *Pushkin: Literature and Social Ideas.* New York: Columbia University Press, 1989.

Dunham, Vera S. *In Stalin's Time: Middleclass Values in Soviet Fiction.* Cambridge: Cambridge University Press, 1976.

d'Encausse, Hélène Carrère. *The Great Challenge: Nationalities and the Bolshevik State 1917–1930.* Translated by Nancy Festinger. New York: Holmes & Meier, 1992.

Edelman, Robert. *Serious Fun: A History of Spectator Sport in the USSR.* New York: Oxford University Press, 1993.

Emmons, Terence. "The Peasant and the Emancipation." In *The Peasant in Nineteenth Century Russia,* edited by Wayne S. Vucinich. Stanford, Calif.: Stanford University Press, 1968.

Engelstein, Laura. "Combined Underdevelopment: Discipline and the Law in Imperial and Soviet Russia." *American Historical Review* 98, no. 2 (April 1993): 338–353.

Field, Daniel. *Rebels in the Name of the Tsar.* Boston: Unwin Hyman, 1989.

Fitzpatrick, Sheila. *The Cultural Front: Power and Culture in Revolutionary Russia.* Ithaca, N.Y.: Cornell University Press, 1992.

———. "Cultural Revolution as Class War." In *Cultural Revolution in Russia, 1928–1931.* Bloomington: Indiana University Press, 1978.

———. *Everyday Stalinism: Ordinary Life in Extraordinary Times—Soviet Russia in the 1930s.* New York: Oxford University Press, 1999.

———."'Middle Class Values' and Soviet Life in the 1930s." In *Soviet Society and Culture: Essays in Honor of Vera S. Dunham,* edited by Terry L. Thompson and Richard Sheldon. Boulder, Colo.: Westview Press, 1988.

———. "Stalin and the Making of a New Elite, 1928–1939." *Slavic Review* 38, no. 2 (September 1979): 377–402.

———. *Stalin's Peasants: Resistance and Survival in the Russian Village after Collectivization.* New York: Oxford University Press, 1994.

Foucault, Michel. *Discipline and Punish: The Birth of the Prison.* Vintage Books, 1979.

———. "The Discourse on Language." In *The Archaeology of Knowledge,* translated by A. M. Sheridan Smith. New York: Pantheon Books, 1972.

Fritzsche, Peter. *A Nation of Fliers: German Aviation and the Popular Imagination.* Cambridge, Mass.: Harvard University Press, 1992.

Gambrell, Jamey. "The Wonder of the Soviet World." *New York Review of Books* (December 22, 1994): 30–35.

Gasparov, Boris, Robert P. Hughes, and Irina Paperno, eds. *Cultural Myths of Russian Modernism: From the Golden Age to the Silver Age.* Berkeley: University of California Press, 1992.

Gassner, Hubertus, and Eckhart Gillen. "Ot sozdaniia utopicheskogo poriadka k ideologii umirotvoreniia v svete esteticheskoi deistvitel'nosti." In *Agitatsiia za schast'e: Sovetskoe iskusstvo stalinskoi epokhi.* Gosudarstvennyi Russkii Muzei, Sankt-Peterburg. Dusseldorf-Bremen: Interarteks-Temmen Edition, 1994.

Geertz, Clifford. "Deep Play: Notes on the Balinese Cockfight." In *Interpretation of Cultures.* New York: Basic Books, 1973.

Getty, J. Arch. *The Origins of the Great Purges: The Soviet Communist Party Reconsidered, 1933–1938.* Cambridge: Cambridge University Press, 1985.

———. "State and Society under Stalin: Constitutions and Elections in the 1930s." *Slavic Review* 50, no. 1 (1991): 18–35.

Giddens, Anthony. *A Contemporary Critique of Historical Materialism.* Berkeley: University of California Press, 1981.

Goldman, Wendy Z. "Women, Abortion, and the State, 1917–36." In *Russia's Women: Accommodation, Resistance, Transformation*, edited by Barbara Evans Clements, Barbara Alpern Engel, and Christine D. Worobec. Berkeley: University of California Press, 1991.

———. *Women and the Soviet State: Soviet Family Policy and Social Life, 1917–1936.* Cambridge: Cambridge University Press, 1993.

Golomstock, Igor. *Totalitarian Art: In the Soviet Union, the Third Reich, Fascist Italy and the People's Republic of China.* London: Collins Harvill, 1990.

Gorsuch, Anne E. "A Woman Is Not a Man: The Culture of Gender and Generation in Soviet Russia, 1921–1928." *Slavic Review* 55, no. 3 (Fall 1996): 636–660.

Great Soviet Encyclopedia. 3rd ed. New York: Macmillan, 1973–1983.

Günther, Hans, ed. *The Culture of the Stalin Period.* Houndmills: Macmillan, 1990.

———."Geroi v totalitarnoi kul'ture." In *Agitatsiia za schast'e: Sovetskoe iskusstvo stalinskoi epokhi.* Gosudarstvennyi Russkii Muzei, Sankt-Peterburg. Dusseldorf-Bremen: Interarteks-Temmen Edition, 1994.

Habermas, Jürgen. *The Structural Transformation of the Public Sphere.* Cambridge, Mass.: MIT Press, 1989.

Hellbeck, Jochen. "Fashioning the Stalinist Soul: The Diary of Stepan Podlubnyi (1931–1939)." *Jahrbücher für Geschichte Osteuropas* 44, no. 3 (1996): 344–373.

Heller, Mikhail, and Alexander Nekrich. *Utopia in Power: The History of the Soviet Union from 1917 to the Present.* New York: Summit Books, 1986.

Hobsbawm, Eric. "Introduction: Inventing Traditions." In *The Invention of Tradition*, edited by Eric Hobsbawm and Terence Ranger. Cambridge: Cambridge University Press, 1983.

Hoffmann, David L. *Peasant Metropolis: Social Identities in Moscow, 1929–1941.* Ithaca, N.Y.: Cornell University Press, 1994.

Holmes, Larry. *The Kremlin and the Schoolhouse.* Bloomington: Indiana University Press, 1991.

Honneth, Axel. *The Critique of Power: Reflective Stages in a Critical Social Thought.* Cambridge, Mass.: The MIT Press, 1991.

Iskusstvo millionov: Sovetskoe kino, 1917–1957. Moscow, 1958.

Ivanits, Linda J. *Russian Folk Belief.* Armonk, N.Y.: M. E. Sharpe, 1989.

Jahn, Hubertus F. *Patriotic Culture in Russia during World War I.* Ithaca, N.Y.: Cornell University Press, 1995.

Kenez, Peter. *The Birth of the Propaganda State: Soviet Methods of Mass Mobilization, 1917–29.* Cambridge: Cambridge University Press, 1985.

———. *Cinema and Soviet Society, 1917–1953.* Cambridge: Cambridge University Press, 1992.

Kershaw, Ian. *The Hitler Myth: Image and Reality in the Third Reich.* New York: Oxford University Press, 1987.

Khlevniuk, O. V. *1937-i: Stalin, NKVD i sovetskoe obshchestvo.* Moscow: Izdatel'stvo "Respublika," 1992.

Khrenov, N. A. "Kul'tura i vlast': Sotsial'no-psikhologicheskie aspekty razvitiia khudozhestvennoi kul'tury 30–40-kh godov." Unpublished manuscript.

Korzhikina, T. P. *Istoriia gosudarstvennykh uchrezhdenii SSSR.* Moscow, 1986.

Kotkin, Stephen. *Magnetic Mountain: Stalinism as a Civilization.* Berkeley: University of California Press, 1995.

Krasnyi arkhiv: Istoricheskii zhurnal 1922–1941, Annotirovannyi ukazatel' soderzhaniia. Compiled by R. I. Zverev. Moscow, 1960.

Kumanev, V. A. *30-e gody v sud'bakh otechestvennoi intelligentsii.* Moscow: Nauka, 1991.

Kumanev, V. A., and I. S. Kulikova. *Protivostoianie: Krupskaia — Stalin.* Moscow: Nauka, 1994.

Lane, Christel. *The Rites of Rulers: Ritual in Industrial Society—The Soviet Case*. Cambridge: Cambridge University Press, 1981.

Lebovics, Herman. *True France; The Wars over Cultural Identity, 1900–1945*. Ithaca, N.Y.: Cornell University Press, 1992.

Levitt, Marcus. "Pushkin in 1899." In *Cultural Myths of Russian Modernism: From the Golden Age to the Silver Age*, edited by Boris Gasparov, Robert P. Hughes, and Irina Paperno. Berkeley: University of California Press, 1992.

———. *Russian Literary Politics and the Pushkin Celebration of 1880*. Ithaca, N.Y.: Cornell University Press, 1989.

Lewin, Moshe. *The Making of the Soviet System: Essays in the Social History of Interwar Russia*. New York: Pantheon Books, 1985.

———. *Russian Peasants and Soviet Power*. New York: W. W. Norton and Company, 1968.

Leyda, Jay. *Kino: A History of the Russian and Soviet Film*. 3rd ed. Princeton, N.J.: Princeton University Press, 1983.

Loseff, Lev. *On the Beneficence of Censorship*. Munich: Verlag Otto Sagner in Kommission, 1984.

Lotman, Ju. M., and B. A. Uspenskij. "The Role of Dual Models in the Dynamics of Russian Culture." In *The Semiotics of Russian Culture*, Michigan Slavic Contributions, 11. Ann Arbor: Department of Slavic Languages and Literatures, University of Michigan, 1984.

Lüdtke, Alf. "The Historiography of Everyday Life: The Personal and the Political." In *Culture, Ideology and Politics: Essays for Eric Hobsbawm*, History Workshop Series. London: Routledge & Kegan Paul, 1982, 38–54.

MacKenzie, John M. *Propaganda and Empire: The Manipulation of British Public Opinion, 1880–1960*. Manchester: Manchester University Press, 1984.

Magarshack, David. *Pushkin: A Biography*. London: Chapman and Hall, 1967.

Maguire, Robert A. *Red Virgin Soil: Soviet Literature in the 1920's*. Princeton, N.J.: Princeton University Press, 1968.

Mally, Lynn. *The Culture of the Future: The Proletkult Movement in Revolutionary Russia*. Berkeley: University of California Press, 1990.

———. "The Problem of the Amateur: Defining *Samodeiatel'nyi teatr*." Conference paper presented at "Inventing the Soviet Union: Language, Power and Representation, 1917–1945." Indiana University, November 7–9, 1997.

Mandell, Richard D. *The Nazi Olympics*. New York: Macmillan, 1971.

Marquis, Alice G. *Hopes and Ashes: The Birth of Modern Times, 1929–1939*. New York: Free Press, 1986.

Martin, D. W. "The Pushkin Celebrations of 1880: The Conflict of Ideals and Ideologies." *Slavonic and East European Review* 66, no. 4 (October 1988): 505–525.

Massell, Gregory. *The Surrogate Proletariat: Moslem Women and Revolutionary Strategies in Soviet Central Asia, 1919–1929*. Princeton, N.J.: Princeton University Press, 1974.

Massovye prazdniki i zrelishcha. Compiled by B. N. Glan. Moscow, 1961.

Matossian, Mary. "The Peasant Way of Life." In *The Peasant in Nineteenth Century Russia*, edited by Wayne S. Vucinich. Stanford, Calif.: Stanford University Press, 1968.

Mazaev, A. I. *Prazdnik kak sotsial'noe-khudozhestvennoe iavlenie*. Moscow: Nauka, 1978.

McCannon, John. *Red Arctic: Polar Exploration and the Myth of the North in Soviet Russia, 1932–1939*. New York: Oxford University Press, 1998.

Medvedev, Roy. *Let History Judge: The Origins and Consequences of Stalinism*. Rev. and expanded ed. New York: Columbia University Press, 1989.

Millar, James. "Mass Collectivization and the Contribution of Soviet Agriculture to the First-Five Year Plan: A Review Article." *Slavic Review* 33, no. 4 (December 1974): 750–766.

Miller, Frank. *Folklore for Stalin*. Armonk, N.Y.: M. E. Sharpe, 1990.

Modern Encyclopedia of Russian and Soviet History. Edited by Joseph L. Wieczynski. Gulf Breeze, Fla.: Academic International Press, 1976–1993.

Modern Encyclopedia of Russian and Soviet Literature. Edited by Harry Weber. Gulf Breeze, Fla.: Academic International Press, 1977–1996.

Morton, Henry W. *Soviet Sport: Mirror of Soviet Society*. New York: Collier Books, 1963.

Mosse, George L. *Nationalism and Sexuality*. New York: Howard Fertig, 1985.

———. *The Nationalization of the Masses*. Ithaca, N.Y.: Cornell University Press, 1991.

———. *Nazi Culture*. New York: Grosset and Dunlap, 1966.

Naiman, Eric. *Sex in Public: The Incarnation of Early Soviet Ideology*. Princeton, N.J.: Princeton University Press, 1997.

Nashi prazdniki. Moscow: Politizdat, 1977.

Nemiro, O. *V gorod prishel prazdnik*. Leningrad, 1973.

Nepomnyashchy, Catherine T. Introduction to *Strolls with Pushkin*, by Abram Tertz. Translated by Catherine Theimer Nepomnyashchy and Slava I. Yastremski. New Haven, Conn.: Yale University Press, 1993.

Nol'de, V. M. *Veresaev: Zhizn' i tvorchestvo*. Tula, 1986.

Nove, Alec. *An Economic History of the U.S.S.R*. Reprint with revisions. Harmondsworth: Penguin Books, 1982.

O'Dell, Felicity Ann. *Socialisation through Children's Literature: The Soviet Example*. Cambridge: Cambridge University Press, 1978.

Osokina, Elena. *Za fasadom "Stalinskogo izobiliia": Raspredelenie i rynok v snabzhenii naseleniia v gody industrializatsii 1927–1941*. Moscow: Rosspen, 1998.

Outram, Dorinda. *The Body and the French Revolution*. New Haven, Conn.: Yale University Press, 1989.

Ozouf, Mona. *Festivals and the French Revolution*. Translated by Alan Sheridan. Cambridge, Mass.: Harvard University Press, 1988.

Palmer, Scott W. "On Wings of Courage: Public 'Air-Mindedness' and National Identity in Late Imperial Russia." *Russian Review* 54 (April 1995): 209–226.

Papernyi, Vladimir. *Kul'tura "dva."* Ann Arbor, Mich.: Ardis, 1985.

Parsons, Talcott. "Democracy and Social Structure in Pre-Nazi Germany." In *Essays in Sociological Theory*, rev. ed. Glencoe, Ill.: Free Press, 1954.

Peukert, Detlev J. K. *Inside Nazi Germany: Conformity, Opposition, and Racism in Everyday Life*. Translated by Richard Deveson. New Haven, Conn.: Yale University Press, 1987.

Pipes, Richard. *The Formation of the Soviet Union: Communism and Nationalism, 1917–1923*. Rev. ed. New York: Atheneum, 1968.

Poovey, Mary. *Uneven Developments*. Chicago: University of Chicago Press, 1988.

Propp, V. Ia. "The Russian Folk Lyric." In *Down along the Mother Volga*, translated and edited by Roberta Reeder. Philadelphia: University of Pennsylvania Press, 1975.

———. *Russkie agrarnye prazdniki*. Leningrad: LGU, 1963.

Riasanovsky, Nicholas V. *The Image of Peter the Great in Russian History and Thought*. Oxford: Oxford University Press, 1985.

Riordan, James. *Sport in Soviet Society*. Cambridge: Cambridge University Press, 1977.

Rittersporn, Gabor. *Stalinist Simplifications and Soviet Complications: Social Tensions and Political Conflicts in the USSR, 1933–1953*. Chur, Switzerland: Hardwood Academic Press, 1991.

Robin, Régine. "Stalinism and Popular Culture." In *The Culture of the Stalin Period*, edited by Hans Günther. Houndmills: Macmillan, 1990.

Rothstein, Robert A. "Homeland, Home Town, and Battlefield: The Popular Song." In *Culture and Entertainment in Wartime Russia*, edited by Richard Stites. Bloomington: Indiana University Press, 1995.

Rowland, Daniel B. "Did Muscovite Literary Ideology Place Any Limits on the Power of the Tsar (1540's–1660's)?" *Russian Review* 49 (1990): 125–155.

Ruder, Cynthia. *Making History for Stalin: The Story of the Belomor Canal.* Gainesville: University Press of Florida, 1998.

Ryan, Mary. "The American Parade: Representations of the Nineteenth-Century Social Order." In *The New Cultural History*, edited by Lynn Hunt. Berkeley: University of California Press, 1989.

Sandler, Stephanie. "Remembrance in Mikhailovskoe." In *Cultural Myths of Russian Modernism: From the Golden Age to the Silver Age*, edited by Boris Gasparov, Robert P. Hughes, and Irina Paperno. Berkeley: University of California Press, 1992.

Sartorti, Rosalinde. "Stalinism and Carnival: Organization and Aesthetics of Political Holidays." In *The Culture of the Stalin Period*, edited by Hans Günther. Houndmills: Macmillan, 1990.

Scobey, David. "Anatomy of the Promenade: The Politics of Bourgeois Sociability in Nineteenth Century New York." *Social History* 17 (May 1992): 203–227.

Scott, James C. *Domination and the Arts of Resistance: Hidden Transcripts.* New Haven, Conn.: Yale University Press, 1990.

———. *Weapons of the Weak: Everyday Forms of Peasant Resistance.* New Haven, Conn.: Yale University Press, 1985.

Scott, Joan. *Gender and the Politics of History.* New York: Columbia University Press, 1988.

Siegelbaum, Lewis H. *Stakhanovism and the Politics of Productivity in the U.S.S.R., 1935–41.* Cambridge: Cambridge University Press, 1988.

Simon, Gerhart. *Nationalism and Policy toward the Nationalities in the Soviet Union.* Translated by Karen Forster and Oswald Forster. Boulder, Colo.: Westview Press, 1991.

Slezkine, Yuri. *Arctic Mirrors: Russia and the Small Peoples of the North.* Ithaca, N.Y.: Cornell University Press, 1994.

———. "From Savages to Citizens: The Cultural Revolution in the Soviet Far North." *Slavic Review* 51, no. 1 (Spring 1992): 52–76.

———. "The USSR as a Communal Apartment, or How a Socialist State Promoted Ethnic Particularism." *Slavic Review* 53, no. 2 (Summer 1994): 414–452.

Slusser, Robert M. *Stalin in October: The Man Who Missed the Revolution.* Baltimore: Johns Hopkins University Press, 1990.

Smith, G. S. Introduction to *D. S. Mirsky: Uncollected Writings on Russian Literature.* Berkeley, Calif.: Berkeley Slavic Specialties, 1989.

Sovetskaia istoricheskaia entsiklopediia. Moscow, 1961–1976.

Sovetskaia kul'tura v rekonstruktivnyi period, 1928–41. Moscow, 1988.

Sovetskie khudozhestvennye filmy: Annotirovannyi katalog. 4 vols. Moscow: Iskusstvo. 1961.

Starr, S. Frederick. *Red and Hot: The Fate of Jazz in the Soviet Union, 1917–1980.* New York: Oxford University Press, 1983.

Stites, Richard. *Revolutionary Dreams: Utopian Visions and Experimental Life in the Russian Revolution.* New York: Oxford University Press, 1989.

———. *Russian Popular Culture: Entertainment and Society since 1900.* Cambridge: Cambridge University Press, 1992.

———, ed. *Culture and Entertainment in Wartime Russia.* Bloomington: Indiana University Press, 1995.

Sunderland, Willard. "Russians into Iakuts? 'Going Native' and Problems of Russian National Identity in the Siberian North, 1870s–1914." *Slavic Review* 55, no. 4 (Winter 1996): 806–825.

Suny, Ronald Grigor. *The Revenge of the Past: Nationalism, Revolution and the Collapse of the Soviet Union.* Stanford, Calif.: Stanford University Press, 1993.

Thurston, Robert. "Fear and Belief in the USSR's 'Great Terror': Response to Arrest, 1935–39." *Slavic Review* 45, no. 2 (1986): 213–234.

———. *Life and Terror in Stalin's Russia, 1934–1941.* New Haven, Conn.: Yale University Press, 1996.

———. "Social Dimensions of Stalinist Rule: Humor and Terror in the USSR, 1935–41." *Journal of Social History* 24 (Spring 1991): 541–562.

———. "The Soviet Family during the Great Terror." *Soviet Studies* 43, no. 3 (1991): 553–574.

Tillett, Lowell. *The Great Friendship: Soviet Historians on the Non-Russian Nationalities.* Chapel Hill: University of North Carolina Press, 1969.

Timasheff, Nicholas S. *The Great Retreat: The Growth and Decline of Communism in Russia.* New York: E. P. Dutton & Company, 1946.

Trubachev, O. N. "Ob etimologicheskom slovare russkogo iazyka." *Voprosy iazykoznaniia* 3 (1960).

Tucker, Robert C. *Stalin in Power: The Revolution from Above, 1928–1941.* New York: W. W. Norton and Company, 1990.

Tumarkin, Nina. *Lenin Lives: The Lenin Cult in Soviet Russia.* Cambridge, Mass.: Harvard University Press, 1983.

Unger, Aryeh L. *Constitutional Developments in the U.S.S.R.: A Guide to the Soviet Constitutions.* London: Methuen, 1981.

Varfolomeeva, M. V. *Rol' massovykh bibliotek v kul'turnoi revoliutsii v SSSR, 1928–1941gg.* Moscow: Nauka, 1974.

Viola, Lynne. *The Best Sons of the Fatherland: Workers in the Vanguard of Soviet Collectivization.* New York: Oxford University Press, 1987.

———. "The Peasant Nightmare: Visions of Apocalypse in the Soviet Countryside." *Journal of Modern History* 62 (December 1990): 747–770.

———. *Peasant Rebels under Stalin: Collectivization and the Culture of Peasant Resistance.* New York: Oxford University Press, 1996.

von Geldern, James. *Bolshevik Festivals, 1917–1920.* Berkeley: University of California Press, 1993.

———. "The Centre and the Periphery: Cultural and Social Geography in the Mass Culture of the 1930s." In *New Directions in Soviet History,* edited by Stephen White. Cambridge: Cambridge University Press, 1992.

von Hagen, Mark. "Soviet Soldiers and Officers on the Eve of the German Invasion: Toward a Description of Social Psychology and Political Attitudes." *Soviet Union/Union Sovietique* 18, no. 1–3 (1991): 79–101.

Welch, David. *The Third Reich: Politics and Propaganda.* London: Routledge, 1993.

Werth, Alexander. *Russia at War: 1941–1945.* New York: Avon Books, 1964.

White, Hayden. *The Content of the Form: Narrative Discourse and Historical Representation.* Baltimore: Johns Hopkins University Press, 1987.

Williams, Raymond. *Culture and Society, 1780–1850.* New York: Columbia University Press, 1958.

Wimberg, Ellen. "Socialism, Democratism and Criticism: The Soviet Press and the National Discussion of the 1936 Draft Constitution." *Soviet Studies* 44, no. 2 (1992): 313–332.

Wohl, Robert. *A Passion for Wings: Aviation and the Western Imagination, 1908–1918.* New Haven, Conn., and London: Yale University Press, 1994.

Wortman, Richard. "Moscow and Petersburg: The Problem of Political Center in

Tsarist Russia, 1881–1914." In *Rites of Power: Symbolism, Ritual and Politics since the Middle Ages,* edited by Sean Wilentz. Philadelphia: University of Pennsylvania Press, 1985.

———. *Scenarios of Power: Myth and Ceremony in Russian Monarchy.* Vol. I. Princeton, N.J.: Princeton University Press, 1995.

Zakharov, A. V. "Karnaval v dve sherengi." *Chelovek* 1 (1990).

———. "Mass Celebrations in a Totalitarian System." In *Tekstura: Russian Essays on Visual Culture,* edited by Alla Efimova and Lev Manovich. Chicago: University of Chicago Press, 1993.

INDEX

abortion, 10, 190
absenteeism, 8
Academy of Sciences of the USSR, 140
accidents, 4, 9, 47–48, 82–83, 105–107
Aesopian language, 8, 142–47, 220n66,
  233n115
Afinogenov, A., 237n69
Africa, 128
agriculture: state control of, 9; subordina-
  tion of, in demonstration, 28
Air Force Day, 15
Akhmatova, Anna, 119
alcohol, 19, 43, 94, 99
Alekseev, Mikhail, 52
All-Union Agricultural Exhibition, 220n70
All-Union Radio Committee, 44
Anderson, Benedict, 46
"André Chénier" (Pushkin), 142
*Annals of the State Literature Museum; Book
  One: Pushkin*, 134–35
ANT-25, 52
Anti-Soviet Trotskyite Center, 114
Arctic, 49, 50, 51, 58; conquest of, 55, 59, 63,
  65, 66, 69; myth of, 53; under tsarism, 76;
  as untamed nature, 77, 78, 80–81
Arctic Museum, 11
Argo (playwright), 168–69
Armenia, 36, 37, 38–39
arson, 19
art, 3, 87, 155; mass vs. elite, 149–54, 173
athletes, 26, 30–33
audience, 5; of Constitution campaign, 177–
  79; of demonstrations, 25–26, 39, 41
authority, 2; limits of, 40, 43, 200; representations of, 46–47, 66–69, 80, 164, 173
Aviation Day, 82–83, 85
aviators, 48, 59, 61–62, 64–65, 80, 90; female,
  56–59, 64, 71, 74–75, 77, 80, 83, 223n60.
  See also individual pilots' names
Azerbaidzhan, 37, 192

Babushkin, Mikhail, 75
Babushkina, Maria, 75
Babushkina, Nata, 82
Baidukov, G., 52, 64, 73
Bakhtin, Mikhail, 9, 100
balls. *See* masquerade
Bazykin, S., 93–94
bedniak, 188
Beethoven, L., 150
Beliakov, A. V., 52–53, 64, 222n29

Belorussia, 37–39
Benkendorf, A., 118–19, 137
Berezyn (Cheliuskinian), 66
Berlin, 86
"best people," 64, 65, 75
Bezbozhnik, 86
Bezdna (Kazan Province), 176
Bezymianskii, A., 162
Bill'-Belotserkovskii, V., 169
Birobidzhan, 198
Blium, V., 206
Bloody Sunday, anniversary of, 216n51
body, 34, 219n46; discipline of, 24, 217nn20,
  23; symbolism of, 31–33
Bogdan, Valentina, 42, 93, 98–99
Bolshoi Theater, 145, 153, 163, 171
Bonch-Bruevich, V., 123, 128
Bonnell, Victoria, 56, 162, 168
Border Guard Day, 15
borders of Soviet Union, 11, 35, 51;
  representations of, 47, 54–56
Boris Godunov (Pushkin), 142
Brezhnev, L., 208
Brontman, Lazar, 63–64, 66–67, 74, 80
"Bronze Horseman" (Pushkin), 143–44
Bubnov, Andrei, 113, 123, 146
Buiko, Peter, 59, 77–78
Bukharin, Nikolai, 161, 221n10
bureaucracy, Soviet, 4–5, 103
Busygin (Stakhanovite), 87
Bykovskaia, E., 92

Cadres: and new political discourse, 198–
  202; and organization of celebrations,
  4–5, 9, 15, 20, 31, 42–43, 83, 193–97;
  problems with, 6, 12, 18–19, 44, 105–107,
  122, 171, 197–98, 205–206
calendars, Soviet and religious, 16
capitalism, 86
carnival, 18, 86, 89, 100–105, 109; defined, 9;
  and limited social critique, 100, 103–105;
  suppressed, 23, 87
Caucasus, 36, 39
celebrations: failure of, 9; and political
  ideology, 5–7, 15; private, 92–94; and
  social practices, 7, 13–16; and terror, 1,
  206
censorship, 1, 3, 70, 134–37, 142, 168–70,
  197, 203, 208
center vs. periphery, 47, 54, 65, 75, 130, 178,
  203–205

Karen Petrone is Associate Professor
of History at the University of Kentucky.